James Manning

First President of Brown University — From a Portrait painted in 1770.

LIFE,

TIMES, AND CORRESPONDENCE

OF

JAMES MANNING,

AND THE

Early History

OF

BROWN UNIVERSITY.

BY

REUBEN ALDRIDGE GUILD.

"People will not look forward to posterity, who never look backward to their ancestors."
BURKE.

BOSTON:
GOULD AND LINCOLN,
59 WASHINGTON STREET.
NEW YORK: SHELDON AND COMPANY.
CINCINNATI: GEORGE S. BLANCHARD.
1864.

To

THE MEMORY

OF

MY MOTHER,

This Volume

IS

INSCRIBED.

List of Illustrations.

PREFACE.

A CENTURY has elapsed since BROWN UNIVERSITY was founded, and nearly three quarters of a century have passed away since the death of DR. MANNING; yet no extended history of the one or life of the other has been published. This neglect to record the honors, the struggles, and triumphs of the founder, so to speak, of the venerable seat of learning, with the early history of which his own history is so thoroughly identified, must be ascribed, in part, to the almost habitual indifference which Baptists have thus far manifested to the characters and the fame of their fathers and departed worthies.

"It is mortifying," says a writer in one of the earlier numbers of the *Christian Review*, "that we have allowed men like Clarke and Callender, Backus and Manning, — each of them an honored and true-hearted advocate of the faith which we profess, at a time when this faith was despised and derided over the greater part of New England, — to pass away so nearly from the memory of men. They were all scholars, who compared well with the foremost of their time. Some of them, also, have linked their names with the history of the country, by the services they rendered in the days of her early settlements, and her subsequent struggles for national independence. But no one of them has found among their own brethren a biographer to set forth their labors and sacrifices, and to delineate their characters in connection with the peculiar faith which they professed. Their lives, in some instances, at least, were filled with important events, which illustrated the civil and religious character of the age to which they belong. They were made beautiful, too, by their simple manners, their all-enduring faith, their deep devotion to truth. It is sad to think that their memory has so nearly perished, and it is humiliating to think that this would have been permitted in no other denomination than our own."

In 1815, twenty-four years after Dr. Manning's death, a brief sketch of his character and life, by the late John Howland, Esq., was published in the *Rhode Island Literary Repository*. It comprises sixteen pages, and consists chiefly of personal recollections. Mr. Howland, although his calling was humble, possessed original and vigorous powers of mind, which he had cultivated by extensive reading, and a close observation of men and manners. He was a warm admirer of President Manning, who, with the leading men of the town, used to frequent his shop. Although differing from him in his religious sentiments, he has furnished a sketch of Manning which the Rev. Dr. Hague, in his "Historical Discourse," pronounces "an elegant tribute to his memory."

Nearly a quarter of a century later, a memoir of President Manning, from the pen of William Giles Goddard, LL.D., at that time the accomplished Professor of Belles-letters in Brown University, was published in the *American Quarterly Register*. This memoir is necessarily brief, and although an admirable specimen of the author's skill in literary writing, furnishes but little additional information respecting Manning, his materials having been limited mainly to the College records, and the traditions that had come down to his time. As an illustration of this dearth of material, the Rev. Dr. Elton, a few years later, in his "Literary Remains of Jonathan Maxcy," D.D., thus remarks: "President Manning embodied in an enduring form few of the productions of his noble mind. Of his writings, after diligent inquiry for several years, we have been able to obtain only two of his familiar letters, and an address delivered to the graduating class in 1789."

The present work owes its origin to a train of circumstances, by which the author came into the possession of new and original sources of information in regard to Manning and his associates. In the year 1848, soon after he entered upon his duties as librarian of Brown University, a handsome morocco portfolio, lettered on the back "MANNING PAPERS," was placed in his hands, as the custodian of the Library. These papers, containing thirteen packages carefully arranged by Manning himself, were found on examination to be his correspondence with friends in England, he having preserved copies of his own letters to them. They came from the late Mrs. Ludlow, wife of the Rev. Peter Ludlow, and daughter of the Rev. Stephen Gano. Mr. Gano, upon the death of Mrs. Manning, who was his aunt, took possession of Mr. Manning's papers, as administrator of the estate. Upon his own death, in 1828, the portfolio containing Manning's foreign correspondence, as above described, fell into the hands of his daughter, Mrs. Ludlow, who finally presented it to the Library. The greater portion, however, of Dr. Manning's papers, being loosely kept in barrels, were, through a sad mistake which good housewives sometimes make, unfortunately destroyed. These papers comprised without doubt private diaries, important narratives, records pertaining to the Church, the College, the Association, — in short, ample materials for his own personal history, and the history of his times. An instance like this illustrates the folly of making the garrets and storehouses of private dwellings places of deposit for valuable manuscript papers, for the care and preservation of which historical societies are instituted.

The acquisition of the "MANNING PAPERS" awakened on the part of the author a desire to obtain further information in regard to the early history of the College, and the life of its first President. By means of letters and circulars, and by persistent effort, a large number of manuscript documents, printed pamphlets, sermons, addresses, catalogues, theses, programmes, minutes of the Warren Association, etc., have been collected and carefully arranged for preservation in the College Library. The titles of most of these are given in Bartlett's Bibliography of Rhode Island (see under BROWN UNIVERSITY, pp. 45-66). From these varied materials the present work has been mainly compiled.

In preparing a history of this kind, a large number of books and pamphlets have of necessity been consulted and used, many of which are referred to, both in the text and in foot-notes. The "MANNING PAPERS," the papers and correspondence of Hezekiah

Smith, D.D., the papers of the Hon. David Howell, and the early College records, together with files of the *Providence Gazette*, constitute, it may be added, the basis of the book.

The author takes great pleasure in acknowledging herewith his obligations to David Benedict, D.D., the veteran historian, from whom he obtained Manning's diary and the correspondence of Hezekiah Smith, together with other valuable letters and documents, including a set of the printed Minutes of the Warren Association, from the year 1771; William B. Sprague, D.D., of Albany, who kindly furnished copies of Manning's letters to General Miller, and who also presented to the Library the original draft of the College Charter, of which an account is given in the first chapter, and in the Appendix; Horatio Gates Jones, Esq., of Philadelphia, from whom he obtained copies of Manning's letters to the Rev. Thomas Ustick, and also much information essential to his work; the Rev. Silas Hall, of Raynham, Mass., to whom he is indebted for a copy of Backus's manuscript minutes of the first four meetings of the Warren Association; Capt. G. L. Dwight, for papers belonging to his great-grandfather, the Hon. David Howell, including letters to him from Manning; the Rev. Thomas S. Drowne, of Brooklyn, N. Y., for many rare documents and pamphlets pertaining to the early history of the College; the Rhode Island Historical Society, for the free use of their accumulated treasures; and, in fine, to all the numerous friends who have in any manner aided him in his work.

Justice to his feelings requires the author to express his special gratitude to Barnas Sears, D.D., President of Brown University, for valuable suggestions and counsels, and for friendly encouragement, given him from time to time while engaged in the prosecution of his labors. The publishers also, Messrs. Gould and Lincoln, deserve grateful mention for the interest which they have taken in the publication of the book, the good taste which they have displayed in its mechanical execution, and for the liberality and promptness with which all their arrangements have been made and completed.

The undertaking was entered upon with great diffidence. It has been continued from year to year, under all the disadvantages of accumulated public and professional duties, and amidst frequent interruptions. Historical accuracy, and not literary excellence, is all, therefore, to which the author has been able to aspire. Sincerely wishing that he had possessed greater skill and more ample leisure for the performance of the task to which his position as librarian seems naturally to have assigned him, the work, with all its imperfections, is herewith submitted to the public, in the hope that it may be acceptable to the general reader, and especially useful to the College, and to the religious denomination under whose auspices the College was founded.

R. A. G.

BROWN UNIVERSITY, SEPTEMBER 1, 1864.

CONTENTS.

CHAPTER I.

1738–1764.

CHAPTER II.

1764-1769.

CHAPTER III.

1769-1770.

CHAPTER IV.

1770–1773.

CHAPTER V.

1774-1779.

CHAPTER VI.

1779.

CHAPTER VII.

1780-1783.

CHAPTER VIII.

1784-1785.

CHAPTER IX.

1786–1788.

CHAPTER X.

1789-1791.

MANNING AND BROWN UNIVERSITY.

CHAPTER I.

1738-1764.

Manning's Birth and Parentage — Home Influence — Early Education — Sent to the Hopewell Academy — Isaac Eaton — Conversion and Baptism — Benjamin Miller — Admitted into the College of New Jersey at Princeton — His Instructors, Davies, Finley, and Blair — Extracts from the College Laws — Student Life — Letter from the Rev. Oliver Hart — Manning's Classmates — Graduates with Salutatory Honors — Marriage — Ordination — Sketch of his Brother-in-law, John Gano — Isaac Stelle — Travels through the Colonies — Receives a Call from the Baptist Church in Charleston, S. C., which he declines — Plan for establishing a Baptist College for the Education more especially of Young Men for the Ministry — Colleges in Existence at this time — Formation of the Philadelphia Association — Early Efforts of the Association in behalf of Education — Hollis and the Hollis Scholarships at Harvard University — Hopewell Academy — Annual Meeting of the Philadelphia Association in 1762 — Rhode Island College projected — Morgan Edwards — Enterprise specially intrusted to Manning — His first Appearance in Rhode Island — Movements at Newport in Relation to the College, as narrated by Manning — Ezra Stiles — Thomas Eyres — Daniel Jenckes — Jenckes's History of the Charter — Analysis of the Statements of Manning and Jenckes — Extracts from the early Minutes of the Philadelphia and Warren Associations pertaining to the College — Liberal Spirit of the Charter — Extract from Backus's Church History of New England pertaining to the early History of the College.

"It is a homage due to departed worth, whenever it rises to such a height as to render its possessor an object of general attention, to endeavor to rescue it from oblivion; that, when it is removed from the observation of men, it may still live in their memory, and transmit, through the shades of the sepulchre, some reflection, however faint, of its living lustre." This language of Robert Hall, on the death of Dr. Ryland, is especially applicable to the subject of the present memoir. Nearly three quarters of a century have elapsed since he passed from earth. "His own times," says the Hon. William Hunter, our late Ambassador to Brazil, "he inspired with a deep sense of his qualities as a scholar, an orator, a statesman, a theologian, and an educationist." A general impression of his remarkable talent and influence still remains, but what composed them has become a matter of tradition. Of all Dr. Manning's intimate associates, and of his numerous pupils, not one is now living to aid by personal recollections any endeavor to embody, in a suitable form, memorials of his character and deeds. To perpetuate, therefore, his memory through his life and correspondence, and to exhibit the origin and early progress of the institution of learning whose infancy he fostered, and whose resources he nurtured and developed, will be the object of our present work.

The Reverend James Manning, D.D., was born in Elizabethtown, New Jersey, on the 22d of October, 1738. Concerning his remote ancestors we have no authentic information. His father, Isaac Manning, was one of the original thirteen members of the Scotch Plains Baptist Church, which, as appears from the records, was constituted on the 7th of August, 1747. Being a proprietor and cultivator of the soil, his children were trained to agricultural pursuits, and thus James acquired that skill in husbandry for which he was ever distinguished. His mother, Catharine, was also a member of the church. So far as we may judge from the character and disposition of her son, she was a woman of superior mental and physical endowments, — one who exemplified in her daily life the happy and sanctifying influences of the Christian religion. James thus enjoyed all those advantages which are derived from the watchful care of sensible and religious parents. To their counsel and example he was indebted for those principles of right conduct, and those cultivated moral sensibilities, which saved his youth from frivolity and vice, and to which, ere he had attained to manhood, God was pleased to add the regenerating influences of his Holy Spirit.

Concerning his schoolboy days we can ascertain but little. It is a matter of regret that no memorials of his early life have been transmitted to his descendants. He probably enjoyed better advantages for education than most lads of that early colonial period. Elizabethtown was then the chief city of New Jersey, and the centre of comparative wealth and refinement. Whatever was the character of its schools, it is certain that he was thoroughly instructed in the elementary branches of learning. He was an accomplished reader, an excellent penman, and a good speller. His manuscript writings furnish abundant evidence of his thorough proficiency in this latter useful though too often neglected "rudiment." These may be regarded as matters of trivial importance, yet they show that he did not neglect his early opportunities, whatever they were, for mental culture.

At the age of eighteen he left the parental roof to prepare for college, under the instruction of the Rev. Isaac Eaton.[1] This gentleman had recently opened an academy at Hopewell, New Jersey, "for the education of youth for the ministry." To him, therefore, says a distinguished

[1] Mr. Eaton was a son of Joseph Eaton of Montgomery. At an early age, having made a profession of religion, he commenced his career as a public speaker. In April, 1748, he came to Hopewell, and on the 29th of November following was ordained pastor of the Baptist Church. In this relation he continued until July 4, 1772, when he died, in the forty-seventh year of his age. His funeral sermon was preached by the Rev. Dr. Samuel Jones, one of his

writer, belongs the high honor of being the first American Baptist to establish a seminary for the literary and theological training of young men. For this work his natural endowments of mind, his varied attainments in knowledge, and his genuine piety happily qualified him. Here, under the guidance of his faithful and beloved teacher, Manning became the subject of renewing grace. Of the exercises of his mind at this interesting period of his life, he has left no record. How much the prayers of pious loved ones at home contributed towards his conversion, and how great an influence was thus to be exerted over the destiny of multitudes in his after career, eternity alone will reveal. A striking instance of the importance of prayer in behalf of colleges and seminaries of learning is here presented. Little did the Principal of the Hopewell Academy realize how greatly the interests of learning and religion were to be affected by the conversion to God of this promising youth.

Having finished his preparatory studies, Manning returned to Elizabethtown, where he made a public profession of religion. He was baptized by the Rev. Benjamin Miller,[1] who for many years had been the pastor of the Scotch Plains Baptist Church. Soon afterwards, being now twenty years of age, he was admitted into the College

earliest pupils, who thus briefly portrays his character: "The natural endowments of his mind, the improvement of these by the accomplishments of literature, his early and genuine piety, his abilities as a divine and a preacher, his extensive knowledge of men and books, his catholicism, etc., would afford ample scope to flourish in a funeral oration; but it is needless." He received the degree of Master of Arts from three colleges, — the College of New Jersey, in 1756; the College of Philadelphia, in 1761; and Rhode Island College, in 1770.

"In him, with grace and eminence, did shine
The man, the Christian, scholar, and divine."

[1] Benjamin Miller, a native of Scotch Plains, was a wild and reckless youth,

of New Jersey as a member of the Freshman Class. This flourishing institution had been founded by the Presbyterian Synod of New York, in the year 1746. Its first location was Elizabethtown, whence it was removed to Newark, where it remained eight years. In 1756 it was again removed to Princeton, its present location, where Nassau Hall, one of the largest and finest buildings in the colonies, had been erected for its use. Here he enjoyed the instruction of the Rev. Dr. Davies, a man distinguished for his wisdom, piety, and eloquence,[1] and whose varied gifts and talents gave lustre and efficiency to the college over which he presided. During his Senior year he was taught Latin, Greek, and Hebrew by President Finley, Mr. Davies' successor. Mr. Finley possessed extensive learning, and was especially remarkable for sweetness of disposition and politeness of behavior. He was also instructed by tutors Halsey, Treat, Ker, and Blair, all of whom afterwards became eminent clergymen. The last named, Dr. Samuel Blair, was in 1767 elected to the presidency of the college, Dr. Witherspoon having declined this honor.

but was converted in consequence of a sermon preached by the celebrated Gilbert Tennent, who encouraged him to enter the ministry. He was ordained on the 13th of February, 1748, as pastor of the church in his native place. Here he continued until November 14, 1780, or about thirty-four years, when he died, in the sixty-sixth year of his age. He was a good, laborious, and successful minister. "Never," said the Rev. John Gano, who preached his funeral sermon, "did I esteem a ministering brother so much as I did Mr. Miller, nor feel so sensibly a like bereavement as that which I sustained by his death."

[1] Dr. Davies spent the early part of his professional life in Virginia. It is well known, says one, that from the eleventh to the twenty-second year of his age, Patrick Henry heard the patriotic sermons which Mr. Davies was accustomed to deliver, and which were said to have produced effects as powerful as those ascribed to the orations of Demosthenes; that he was an enthusiastic admirer of Mr. Davies and his opinions; and that it was Mr. Davies who first kindled the fire and afforded the model of Henry's elocution. (See History of the College of New Jersey, 1746-1783, in the "Princeton Whig" for February, 1844.)

Blair did not accept the appointment, and Witherspoon was afterwards reëlected by the Trustees. Such were Manning's instructors. That the teachings of these excellent men, and the associations of his academic and collegiate life, had a most important influence in developing his character, and in determining his subsequent career, no one will deny.

Among the requirements for admission to the College of New Jersey, was one obliging every student to transcribe the laws and customs thereof, which copy, being signed by the President, was to be in testimony of his admission, and to be kept by him while in college as a rule of his good behavior. From a manuscript copy of these laws, made by the Rev. Dr. Hezekiah Smith in the summer of 1758, we make a few extracts, illustrating as they do the character and spirit of the institution where Manning, and Howell, who was afterwards associated with him, received their education. These laws, somewhat modified, became, it may be added, a basis for the government and discipline of Rhode Island College: —

1. No students may expect to be admitted into the college but such as have been examined by the President and tutors, and shall be found able to render Virgil and Tully's Orations into English, to turn English into true and grammatical Latin, and to be so well acquainted with Greek as to render any part of the four Evangelists in that language into Latin or English, and give the grammatical construction of the words.

2. Those who have prosecuted their studies for the space of three years after obtaining their first degree, if they have not been scandalous in their lives and conversation, shall be admitted to the degree of Master of Arts.

3. The students, on every Lord's Day, shall attend divine service in some place of public worship; which, if they without sufficient excuse omit, they shall be punished in a fine of fourpence; and they shall also pay a religious regard to the Lord's Day, by keeping in their rooms, and not visiting, or admitting others into their company. And it is judged

expedient, and hereby ordered, that no student be out of his room, on the evening next after Saturday, or next after Lord's Day, except for religious purposes, or some necessary occasion, under penalty of fourpence for every said offence.

4. If any student shall be convicted of drunkenness, fornication, lying, theft, or any other scandalous crime, he shall be admonished, make a public confession, or be expelled, according to the aggravation of the crime; provided, always, that no member be expelled the college without the consent of at least six of the Trustees, — the President, in the interim, having power to suspend such offenders.

5. None of the students shall frequent taverns or places of public entertainment, or keep company with persons of known scandalous lives, who will be likely to vitiate their morals. Those that practise contrary to this law, shall first be admonished, and if they still persist in such dangerous courses, they shall be expelled the college.

6. None of the students shall play at cards, or dice, or any other unlawful game, upon the penalty of a fine not exceeding five shillings for the first offence; for the second, public admonition; and for the third, expulsion.

7. Those students who bring into their chambers, without a permit from the President or some of the tutors, wine, metheglin, or any kind of distilled spirituous liquors, shall be punished in a fine not exceeding five shillings for each offence.

8. None of the students shall be absent from their chambers, without leave first obtained from the President or one of the tutors, unless half an hour after morning prayers and recitation, an hour and a half after dinner, and from evening prayers till seven o'clock, on the penalty of fourpence for each offence.

9. If any scholar shall persist in the careless neglect of his studies, and shall not make suitable preparation for the stated recitations, and other scholastic exercises appointed for his instruction, he shall, after due admonition, be expelled.

10. Scholars shall not go out of town, except by the President's or tutor's license, unless it be in the stated vacation, on penalty of such fine as the President shall think proper, not exceeding five shillings for the first offence; and if, after admonition, they continually repeat the offence, they shall be expelled.

11. The tutors shall frequently visit their pupils in their chambers, to

direct and encourage them in their studies, and see that they are diligently employed about their proper business.

12. No jumping, hollaring, or boisterous noise shall be suffered in the college at any time, or walking in the gallery in the time of study.

13. Whoever shall do any damage, designedly, by writing, marking, etc., in any part of the college, shall pay fourfold the real damage ; if accidentally, shall make it good ; and what damage is done, and the authors thereof cannot be detected, shall be levied equally on them that live in the room or in the gallery where it is done ; if in the library or hall, or any part of the college unoccupied, to be levied equally on all.

14. If any scholar refuses to open his door to the President or tutors, who may signify their presence by a stamp, they may break it down ; and the scholar so refusing shall be punished as in a case of contempt of authority.

15. The students of the college shall be obliged to appear in such habits as the President, tutors, and any of the Trustees shall fix upon.

16. Every member of the college shall treat the authority of the same, and all superiors, in a becoming manner, paying that respect to every one considered in his proper place.

17. Every scholar in college shall keep his hat off about ten rods to the President, and five to the tutors.

18. Every Freshman sent of an errand shall go and do it faithfully, and make quick return.

19. Every scholar shall rise up and make obeisance when the President goes in or out of the hall, or enters the pulpit on days of religious worship.

20. If walking with a superior, he shall give him the highest place.

21. If called upon or spoken to by a superior, he shall, if within hearing, give a direct and pertinent answer, with the word Sir at the end thereof.

22. If overtaking a superior, or if met by him going up or down stairs, he shall stop, giving him the banister side.

23. No Freshman shall wear a gown.

24. No member of the college shall wear his hat in the college at any time, or appear in the dining-room at meal-time, or in the hall at any public exercise, or knowingly in the presence of the superiority of the college, without an upper garment, and having shoes and stockings tight.

While a member of college, Manning occasionally returned to Hopewell, and assisted Mr. Eaton in the instruction of the pupils under his care. Concerning his student-life our information is very limited. He was remarkable for diligence and attention to his studies, — habits which soon gained for him a reputation for superior scholarship. In rhetoric, eloquence, moral philosophy, and the classics, he especially excelled. He was fond of athletic exercise, and devoted many of his hours for recreation to manly and invigorating sports. "*Sana mens in sano corpore*" was his motto. In his conduct he was uniformly regular, and he thus maintained a good standing with the officers of the college, without losing thereby the friendship and esteem of his fellow-students.

While a student at the academy, Manning had formed an acquaintance with the Rev. Oliver Hart, pastor of the Baptist Church in Charleston, S. C. This proved to him a source of great pleasure and profit. Mr. Hart was his senior by about fifteen years, and was eminently a religious man. He was the main founder of the "Charleston Baptist Association," that venerable and useful body, through the medium of which he continued to shed upon the denomination at the South the benign influences of his well-balanced mind, for thirty years. He also, in connection with the Rev. Francis Pelot and others, founded, in 1755, "The Religious Society," to aid pious young men in obtaining an education for the public services of the church. One of the earliest beneficiaries of this society was the Rev. Dr. Stillman, whose name occurs so frequently throughout these pages. During the latter part of Manning's Junior year in college, and shortly after the death of President Davies, Mr. Hart addressed to him a letter, which we here introduce, although it interrupts for a moment the narrative : —

CHARLESTON, April 27, 1761.

MY DEAR FRIEND:

I received your kind letter of the 1st of March, ult., together with President Davies' sermon on the death of his late Majesty, — for which favors I return my most unfeigned thanks. You intimate that you have written me several letters heretofore. I have received only one of them, — as near as I can remember, above two years ago, — and to which I returned an answer by the first opportunity. I lament with you (and surely all the friends of Zion must mourn) the loss of the justly celebrated President Davies. Oh, what floods of sorrow must have overwhelmed the minds of many, when it was echoed from house to house and from village to village, as in the dismal sound of hoarse thunder, *President Davies is no more!* Oh, sad and melancholy dispensation! Arise, all ye sons of pity, and mourn with those that mourn. And thou, my soul, let drop the flowing tear while commiserating the bereaved and distressed. Alas for the dear woman, whose beloved is taken away with a stroke! May Jesus be her husband, her strength, and her stay. Alas for the bereaved children! May their father's God be their God in covenant. Alas for the church of Christ! Deprived of one of the principal pillars, how grievous the stroke to thee! But Jesus, thy head and foundation, ever lives.

And thou, Nassau Hall, lately so flourishing, so promising, under the auspicious management of so worthy a President — what might we not have expected from thee! But alas! How is the mighty fallen in thee! How doth the large and beautiful house appear as a widow in sable weeds! And thy sons, lately so gay and pleasant, as well as promising and contented — how do they retire into their apartments, and there with bitter sighs, heavy groans, and broken accents, languish out, My Father, my Father! — the chariot of Israel, and the horsemen thereof! But I can write no more.

Yours, affectionately,

OLIVER HART.

Manning graduated on the 29th of September, 1762, with the second honors of his class. This class consisted of twenty-one, and included some excellent scholars, who afterwards distinguished themselves in their several professions and walks of life. Among them may be mentioned his most intimate friend and companion, the Rev. Dr. Hezekiah Smith, of Haverhill, Mass.; Ebenezer Hazard, who was the first Postmaster General of the United States after the adoption of the Federal Constitution, and who afterwards published in two quarto volumes a valuable collection of documents relating to American history; Jonathan Dickinson Sergeant, a member of Congress and the first Attorney General of Pennsylvania; Joseph Periam, for several years a tutor in the college; Hugh Alison, a Presbyterian clergyman; and the Hon. Isaac Allen, who was the valedictorian of the class. The distinction conferred upon Manning by the college authorities, in awarding to him the salutatory addresses, provoked, it is said, some discontent among his ambitious compeers. This, however, is by no means an unusual thing in the annals of our literary institutions. His Latin oration, with which the exercises of Commencement were introduced, is spoken of in the *Pennsylvania Gazette* as "an elegant salutatory."

Soon after his graduation, he made arrangements to enter upon the duties of the profession to which he had already consecrated his life. By a vote of the church, taken, as appears from the records, on the 30th of November, 1762, he was called to engage in the work of the Christian ministry. On the 23d of March following, he was united in marriage to Miss Margaret Stites, daughter of John Stites, Esq., of Elizabethtown. Mr. Stites was a "ruling elder" in the Scotch Plains Church, to the usefulness and respectability of which his judicious counsels and large liberality greatly contributed. He was in affluent circumstances,[1] and for several years was the mayor

[1] Mr. Stites lost the greater part of his property during the revolutionary war. This will in part account for various allusions to Dr. Manning's straitened circumstances towards the close of his life.

or chief magistrate of the place. His home at Connecticut Farms, in the immediate neighborhood of the city, was the centre of an abundant hospitality, where Manning and his wife were ever welcome guests. This marriage proved a source of great domestic felicity. Mrs. Manning possessed those elegant accomplishments and superior qualities which well accorded with her husband's character, and happily fitted her for the discharge of duties inseparable from public positions of honor and usefulness. She was also lovely and attractive in person, if we may judge from her portrait in the possession of a branch of the family. The blessings of offspring were, however, denied them. She survived her beloved companion many years, and, after a long and retired widowhood, died in Providence, Nov. 9, 1815, at the advanced age of seventy-five. At the time of their marriage, she was not a professor of religion. During a revival under her husband's preaching, in 1775, she became a hopeful convert, and was received into the fellowship of the Baptist Church. The joys and consolations of a well-grounded hope in Christ thus comforted her in her bereavement, soothed her declining years, and cheered her dying hours.

On the 19th of April, a few weeks after his marriage, he was publicly ordained, and set apart for his chosen work. The sermon on the occasion was preached by his brother-in-law, the Rev. John Gano,[1] who had but recently been

[1] Mr. Gano, whose name frequently occurs throughout these pages, was regarded by the early Baptists as a "star of the first magnitude," a "prince among the hosts of Israel." Possessed of superior natural talents and a great knowledge of human nature, he adapted himself with singular readiness to the varied circumstances of his eventful life. His ancestors were Huguenots. Francis Gerneaux, his great-grandfather, escaped from the island of Guernsey during the bloody persecution that arose in consequence of the revocation of the Edict of Nantes, and, arriving in this country, settled at New Rochelle, where he died

settled over the newly-constituted Baptist church in New York. His teacher and spiritual guide at the academy, the Rev. Isaac Eaton, gave the charge, and his beloved

at the extraordinary age of one hundred and three years. John was born at Hopewell, N. J., July 22, 1727. His parents were eminently pious, and from his earliest years he was faithfully instructed in the great principles of religion. At the close of 1754, or early in 1755, he was united in marriage to Miss Sarah Stites, who proved to be a most agreeable companion, and an efficient auxiliary to his usefulness. Eleven children — seven sons and four daughters — were the fruits of this union; one of whom, Dr. Stephen Gano, was for a period of thirty-six years (1792-1828) the honored pastor of the First Baptist Church in Providence. In June, 1762, the First Baptist Church in New York, consisting of twenty-seven members dismissed for this purpose from the Scotch Plains Church, was organized, and Mr. Gano became its pastor. Here he continued for a quarter of a century, excepting the time he was absent from the city in consequence of the war. During his ministry the church was greatly prospered, receiving by baptism about three hundred members.

Mr. Gano early espoused the cause of his country in the contest with Great Britain. At the commencement of the war he joined the standard of freedom in the capacity of chaplain, and by his preaching contributed not a little to impart a determined spirit to the soldiers. He continued in the army till the conclusion of the war. Many anecdotes are told of him illustrative of his skill in administering reproof. A lieutenant, after uttering some profane expressions, accosted him, saying, "Good-morning, Doctor."—"Good-morning, sir," replied the chaplain. "You pray early this morning."— "I beg your pardon, sir," said the lieutenant. "Oh, I cannot pardon you; carry your case to God." Standing near some soldiers who were disputing whose turn it was to cut wood for the fire, one of them said he would be d——d if he would cut it. Mr. Gano immediately stepped up, saying, "Give me the axe." "Oh no," replied the soldier; "the chaplain sha'n't cut wood." "Yes," said he, "I must. I just heard you say you would be d——d if you would cut it; and I should rather take the labor off your hands than to have you made miserable forever."

In 1788, Mr. Gano left his society in New York, and removed to Kentucky. He died at Frankfort, in 1804, in the seventy-eighth year of his age. "He was in person," says Dr. Furman, "below the middle stature, and when young of a slender form; but of a firm, vigorous constitution, well fitted for performing active services with ease, and for suffering labors and privations with constancy. In the more advanced stages of life, his body tended to corpulency. His presence was manly, open, and engaging, and his voice strong and commanding. Like John, the harbinger of our Redeemer, 'he was a burning and a shining light, and many rejoiced in his light.' Resembling the sun, he arose in the church with morning brightness, advanced regularly to his station of meridian splendor, and then gently declined, with mild effulgence, till he disappeared, without a cloud to intercept his rays or obscure his glory."

friend, the Rev. Isaac Stelle,[1] of Piscataway, made the ordaining prayer. For about a year after this event, Manning travelled through the colonies, to ascertain the actual state of religion, and to prepare himself for more widely-extended usefulness, by a thorough acquaintance with men and manners, and an accurate knowledge of the condition and wants of the denomination to which he was attached. No record is left to indicate the extent, or to exhibit the incidents, of his journeyings. He preached during this period to various destitute churches, and everywhere his labors appear to have been highly acceptable.

By the following letter from the Rev. Oliver Hart, it appears that Manning was invited to assist him in his

Memoirs of Mr. Gano's life, written principally by himself, were published, in a small duodecimo, in 1806. He was one of the first trustees of Rhode Island College, and, until his removal to Kentucky, coöperated most efficiently with President Manning in his efforts to promote the cause of sound learning and ministerial education.

[1] Mr. Stelle was the son of Benjamin Stelle, a worthy magistrate, who for many years was pastor of the Piscataway Church. Upon the death of Benjamin, in 1759, he was succeeded by his son Isaac, who continued in this pastoral office until Oct. 9, 1781, when he died, in the sixty-third year of his age. He possessed a temperament exceedingly active, and a disposition uncommonly amiable. Fired by ardent piety, he longed for usefulness, and, under the guidance of Mr. Miller, to whom we have already referred as Manning's early pastor, he engaged in itinerating labors remarkable even for that age. Between these brethren there existed the strongest ties of personal friendship and esteem. "Lovely and pleasant," says one, "were they in their lives, and in death they were not much divided, — the one having survived the other only about thirty-five days."

"If one was grieved, it did them both annoy;
If one rejoiced, the other felt the joy;
When one was gone, the other could not stay,
But quickly hastened to eternal day."

Benjamin, a son of the Rev. Isaac Stelle, graduated at the College of New Jersey in the year 1766. He came to Providence and established a Latin school, as we learn from a letter of President Manning to David Howell, dated July 14, 1766. The late Hon. Nicholas Brown married a daughter of this Mr. Stelle for his second wife.

labors as pastor of the Baptist church in Charleston. This invitation, or, strictly speaking, call from the church, fortunately for the interests of learning and religion in New England, he declined, having already entered upon the great educational work to which his future life was to be consecrated. The Rev. Nicholas Bedgegood, it may be added, was afterwards employed as an assistant to Mr. Hart; and, by his popular talents and pleasing address, gained so much upon the admiration of many, that an attempt, although unsuccessful, was made to supplant Mr. Hart, and to place the assistant in the pastoral office.

CHARLESTON, June 20, 1763.

DEAR MR. MANNING:

A few days ago I had the pleasure to forward a call to you, from this church, to come over and assist me in breaking the bread of life to the dear people of my charge. I hope enough has been said to induce you to come over to this "delightful region," if I may use your own words. Since I wrote to you last, I have received letters from Mr. Gano, who informs me that you are married, ordained, and not settled; or that you intend a journey to the eastward before you settle anywhere. I assure you that this gives me hope that you will settle to the southward, seeing you are not yet engaged.

I congratulate you on your having entered into a new state of life, and hope you will enjoy all the comforts which the married state can afford. I welcome you into the vineyard of the Lord as one of his laborers. You are now an ambassador for the King of kings. I doubt not but that a sense of the importance of the work lies with weight upon your mind. Well, he who is the Lord our righteousness is also the Lord our strength. I have only to say, I hope God will send you upon an embassy to this place, where you will be welcomed to my heart, to my house, and to my people, and where you will have a hopeful prospect of doing much good.

Remember me in kind love to your other self. Tell her I wish her joy in her new state, and hope for the pleasure of saluting her in Charleston, where many whose ambition will be to make her happy will rejoice to see her. If the call should happen, by any means, to miscarry, pray look upon this as one, and do not engage till you receive a duplicate of that already sent. I wish you great grace, and am

Yours, in Jesus,

OLIVER HART.

It was about the time of Manning's graduation that the plan of establishing a Baptist college or university for the education, more especially, of young men for the ministry, was freely discussed by many prominent men in the denomination. There were important reasons for a movement of this kind. The only colleges in New England were Harvard[1] and Yale,[1] both under the control of Congregationalists. The College of New Jersey[1] had been established by the Presbyterians. The remaining colleges, Columbia[1] in New York, William and Mary[1] in Virginia, and the University of Pennsylvania,[1] had been established by Episcopalians, and were under their control. Those who consult the pages of our early historians, and, indeed, the correspondence of Manning in future chapters of this work, will readily perceive that towards the Baptists, as a people, the Congregationalists of New England entertained unfriendly feelings, — taxing them unjustly, and oppressing them in various ways, in accordance with the narrow and illiberal policy of a past age. In regard to Episcopalians, the opinion was entertained, "whether correctly or not," says Prof. Kingsley in his Life of Dr. Stiles, "it is unimportant here to determine, that the Episcopal clergy generally, and the leading individuals among the laity in the same communion, especially in New England,

[1] Harvard College was founded in 1638; William and Mary, in 1692; Yale, in 1701; College of New Jersey, in 1746; University of Pennsylvania, in 1753; and Columbia College, in 1754. Of the two hundred and thirty-six colleges mentioned in the National Almanac for 1864, Brown University, therefore, which was founded in 1764, is the seventh in the order of date.

were hostile to the privileges granted in several of the royal charters, and were endeavoring to undermine them." Hence from political considerations, aside from all others, the majority of religious people throughout the colonies found themselves opposed to the interests of the Episcopal church. In this feeling the Baptists, who from their earliest history have always advocated religious freedom, and equality among men, very naturally shared. The fact that the English Government, in its appointments to office, restricted its selection to members of the Episcopal church, contributed not a little to this feeling. It is not, therefore, unreasonable to infer that they regarded with no favorable eye institutions of learning where sectarian and restrictive influences prevailed. In order, however, to a proper understanding of the origin of Brown University, it may be well at this point to go back half a century, and consider briefly the first distinct organization on this continent of the Baptists as a religious society.

In the year 1707, on the 27th of July, a meeting of delegates from Baptist churches in Pennsylvania, New Jersey, and Delaware was held at Philadelphia. The object of this meeting, as appears from the records, was "to consult about such things as were wanting in the churches, and set them in order," and in general to promote the welfare of the denomination. Hence the origin of the Philadelphia Association. The brethren who assembled on this occasion represented the churches at Lower Dublin, Middletown, Piscataqua, Cohansie, and Welsh Tract. The General Meeting, so called, which had been held at Philadelphia from 1689, was thus transformed into an *Association of Messengers*, authorized by their respective churches to devise and execute designs of public good. From its beginning, it has been a flourishing body. According to the statistics of its 156th anniversary, held on the 6th, 7th, and 8th of October, 1863, it now comprises sixty churches, with a membership, if we may so speak, of 12,862. At a comparatively early period, the churches thus associated projected plans to secure an educated ministry. In looking over the records, we find in 1722 a proposition "for the churches to make inquiry among themselves, if they have any young persons hopeful for the ministry, and inclinable for learning; and if they have, to give notice of it to Mr. Abel Morgan, before the first of November, that he might recommend such to the academy, on Mr. Hollis, his account." Reference is here had to Thomas Hollis, Esq., of London, the distinguished benefactor of Harvard University.[1] He had recently founded ten scholarships, directing that the incumbents should be poor students, who were intended for the "ministry of the gospel of Jesus Christ;" "and that none," to use his own language, "be refused on account of his belief and practice of adult baptism, if he be sober and religiously inclined." In a letter to the Rev. Ephraim Wheaton, of Swanzey, Massachusetts, which we find published in the first volume of the *Massachusetts Missionary Magazine*, Mr. Hollis, in reference to

[1] Mr. Hollis commenced his donations to Harvard in 1719. Besides making valuable additions to the library and philosophical apparatus, he established a fund for the support of ten poor scholars, a Professor of Divinity, and a Professor of Mathematics and Natural Philosophy; the scholars to receive each £10 currency per annum, and the professors each a salary of £80 currency, or £26 sterling. "The aggregate of his donations," says Peirce in his history of the University, "was not much, if at all, short of £2000 sterling. So large an amount was never given to the college before by any one individual; and when it is considered that all this came from a stranger in a distant land, from one of the then *poor*, *despised Baptists*, during the lifetime of the donor, and at a time when the value of money was vastly greater than it is now, what breast does not glow with grateful admiration! Some idea may be formed of the difference in the value of money then and now, by considering that the salary of a professor was at first only £26 sterling, and that this was then called an honorable stipend."

these scholarships, speaks of having made provision for "*Baptist* youth to be educated for the ministry, and equally regarded with Pædobaptists," and requests Mr. Wheaton to inform him of any duly qualified, that he may recommend them for the first vacancy. He also corresponded with the Philadelphia Association on the subject. Hence the churches were fully authorized to avail themselves of his generosity. This provision, however, of Mr. Hollis, proved of little avail to the Baptists, in consequence of the growing unfriendliness exhibited towards them throughout most of the New England States. Meanwhile, churches of their faith and order were rapidly multiplying; and as educated ministers could not be had in numbers sufficient to supply the demand, they were compelled to accept the services of men, who, though destitute of the aids of literary and scientific culture, were nevertheless taught by the Holy Spirit; and who, with hearts overflowing with love and zeal, proclaimed the precious truths of the gospel with a power, unction, and success which have not always been the accompaniments of a learned ministry.

In the year 1756, the academy at Hopewell was established, as we have already stated, by the Rev. Isaac Eaton, a name dear to the Baptist society in America, and to all true friends of learning and religion. In the welfare and progress of this academy, the Philadelphia and Charleston Associations ever manifested a lively interest. They appointed certain trustees to have a general oversight of its affairs, and generously contributed towards its support a fund, of which the parent association furnished about four hundred pounds. Under the wise supervision of its founder and principal, it was continued eleven years, during which time, many, who afterwards became eminent in the ministry, received thereat the rudiments of an education. Among them may be mentioned, besides Manning, Dr. Samuel Jones, Dr. Hezekiah Smith, Dr. Isaac Skillman, David Thomas, John Davis, William Williams, Robert Keith, Charles Thompson, David Jones, John Sutton, David Sutton, James Talbot, John Blackwell, Joseph Powell, William Worth, and Levi Bonnel. Not a few of Mr. Eaton's students distinguished themselves in the professions of medicine and law. Of this latter class was the Hon. Judge Howell, of whom we shall have occasion hereafter to make frequent mention.

This attempt to introduce learning in the Baptist society having succeeded beyond the most sanguine expectations of its friends, the churches were encouraged to extend their designs for the promotion of letters, by the establishment, in some part of the colonies, of a college or university. Many of them had been supplied with able pastors from the academy, and had thus become convinced from experience of the great usefulness of a classical and scientific education, in more thoroughly furnishing the man of God for the work of the gospel ministry. At first it seemed most fitting to commence the undertaking in some one of the southern colonies; but several members of the Association having visited the New England States, and seen the great increase of Baptist churches there, and having ascertained the fact that the government of Rhode Island[1] was chiefly in the hands of those who would be likely to favor

[1] Mr. Edwards, in his "Materials," etc., says, "The Province of Rhode Island and Providence may on some accounts be styled the Land of Baptists;" first, because "they who settled the country were chiefly of that denomination;" secondly, because "they have always been more numerous than any other sect of Christians which dwell therein, two fifths of the inhabitants, at least, being reputed Baptists;" thirdly, because "the Baptists in this Government have always had much power in their hands, both legislative and executive. Their governors, deputy governors, judges, assembly men, justices, and officers (military and

the design, it was determined to make the effort in that colony, which originally had been settled by persons of the Baptist persuasion.

On the 12th of October, 1762, the Association, now comprising twenty-nine churches, met at the Lutheran Church, in Fifth Street, Philadelphia. The Rev. Morgan Edwards was chosen moderator, and the Rev. Abel Morgan, clerk. At this meeting, says Backus, "the Association obtained such an acquaintance with the affairs of Rhode Island, as to bring themselves to an apprehension that it was practicable and expedient to erect a college in the colony of Rhode Island, under the chief direction of the Baptists, in which education might be promoted, and superior learning obtained, free from any sectarian tests." The principal mover in this matter was Morgan Edwards, to whom, with the Rev. Samuel Jones, the business in general appears to have been intrusted. This gentleman, who had but recently been settled in Philadelphia, was a native of Wales, having come to this country upon the recommendation of Dr. Gill and other prominent ministers in London. He had been bred an Episcopalian, but in 1738 he embraced the sentiments of the Baptists. He received his academical education in Bristol, under Dr. Foskett, and in his sixteenth year entered upon the work of the Christian ministry. Possessing superior abilities, united with great perseverance and zeal, he became the leader in various denominational enterprises, devoting to them his time and talents, and thereby rendering essential service to the cause. Many of his sermons, treatises, and historical

civil) have been chiefly of that denomination. The last reason I shall mention is, that their college is a Baptist college; the Baptists only made the motion for it; the Baptists only gathered money to endow it; the head of it, and about two thirds of the Fellows and Trustees, must ever be of that denomination."

works have been published. In one of them, entitled "Materials towards a History of the Baptists in Pennsylvania," he speaks of himself as having "labored hard to settle a Baptist college in Rhode Island Government, and to raise money to endow it; which he deems the greatest service he has done or hopes to do for the Baptist interest." This was in 1770. Mr. Edwards died on the 28th of January, 1795, in the seventy-third year of his age. His funeral sermon, preached by the Rev. Dr. William Rogers, was published in Dr. Rippon's *Annual Register*, a work printed in London. This sermon gives an analysis of his character,[1] and an enumeration of his published writings.

[1] Dr. Rogers' friendly estimate of Mr. Edwards's character and influence, as recorded in this sermon, was that of his brethren and associates generally. It is understood, however, that Mr. Edwards's relations with the church in Philadelphia during the latter part of his ministry were not entirely harmonious. In 1770, he preached a New Year's sermon from the text, "This year thou shalt die." He had, from some unaccountable impulse, been led to believe that he should die on a particular day, and this sermon was supposed by some to have been intended as his own funeral sermon. This circumstance could not but effect his reputation injuriously. In addition to this, he is said to have indulged, occasionally, in the excessive use of intoxicating drinks. Under these circumstances, he voluntarily resigned his charge, preaching occasionally until the settlement of his successor, Dr. Rogers, in 1772. The following extract from letters addressed to the Rev. Hezekiah Smith, by the Rev. Francis Pelot, of Eutaw, South Carolina, shows Mr. Edwards's position at this time in a friendly light. The letter is dated Oct. 28, 1771. "I then wish" (referring to the Philadelphia church) "they would agree with their Mr. Edwards again. Thus I argue to myself: 'If he may preach occasionally, why not steadily?' 'Oh! but he has not behaved as well as he should.' I reply, 'There cannot be anything immoral, or he would not be allowed to preach occasionally, and the mantle CHARITY, would easily cover small imperfections. Besides, the present dissatisfaction, no doubt, would make him more cautious for the future, and might be a means of preserving the usefulness of a talented man, — a man who has scarce his fellow in a warm attachment to the Baptist interest.'" In a letter dated April 8, 1772, Mr. Pelot adds, "We were favored with the company of Rev. Morgan Edwards at my house for about a week in last January. We also had his company at our Association. We all esteem him as a sensible, good man, and he left us all full of love to him."

Rev. Oliver Hart, of Charleston, South Carolina, in a letter also to Mr. Smith,

It was while on his tour through the colonies, after his ordination, that Manning, to whom this enterprise had been specially intrusted, first made his appearance in Rhode Island, accompanied by the Rev. John Sutton, of Elizabethtown. Both were members, at this time, of the Philadelphia Association. He was now twenty-five years of age, of a fine, commanding appearance, pleasing manner, and polished address. His person, says a writer, was graceful, and his countenance handsome and remarkably expressive of sensibility, dignity, and cheerfulness. He possessed a voice of extraordinary compass and harmony, to which, in no small degree, may be ascribed the vivid impression which he made upon other minds. In his manners, which seemed to be the natural expression of dignity and grace, he combined ease without negligence, and politeness without affectation. Blest with an amiable disposition, and possessing versatile colloquial powers, he was most engaging and instructive as a companion. He possessed, moreover, genuine piety, and a benevolence which beamed in every feature. And when to all these

dated Feb. 27, 1772, thus writes: "Rev. Mr. Edwards from Philadelphia has been here, and tarried with us about three weeks. He is a great good man, but some say he preaches too slow." And in a second letter, written the next month, he further adds, "In my last I informed you that we had the pleasure of Mr. Edwards's company at our Association. He is a great good man; firmly attached to the Baptist interest, to promote which he cheerfully encounters all difficulties." These testimonials, coming voluntarily from two of the most prominent Baptist ministers of the South, show that Mr. Edwards, even at a time when his sun appeared to be obscured, was a man highly esteemed, and that he was worthy of the honor, which is accorded to him, of having been the prime mover in originating and founding Brown University.

Mr. Edwards was twice married. His first wife was Mary Nunn, originally of Cork, Ireland, by whom he had several children. His second wife was Mrs. Sinclair, of Delaware, whose decease occurred previous to his own. One of his sons was a military officer in the British service. During the war he himself adhered to the cause of Great Britian, and was justly ranked with the Tories; although his Toryism seemed rather a matter of principle than of action.

gifts and accomplishments we add sterling good sense, for which he was preëminently distinguished, and superior learning, it will readily be perceived that he was well fitted to act as a pioneer in the great educational work before him. The history of the enterprise from this point may best be given in Manning's own language, which we find in a work among the manuscript writings of the Rev. Morgan Edwards, entitled "Materials towards a History of the Baptists in Rhode Island."

MANNING'S NARRATIVE.

"In the month of July, 1763, we arrived at Newport, and made a motion to several gentlemen of the Baptist denomination — whereof Col. Gardner, the Deputy Governor, was one — relative to a seminary of polite literature, subject to the government of the Baptists. The motion was properly attended to, which brought together about fifteen gentlemen of the same denomination at the deputy's house, who requested that I would draw a sketch of the design, against the day following. That day came; and the said gentlemen, with other Baptists, met in the same place, when a rough draught was produced and read, — the tenor of which was, that the institution was to be a Baptist one, but that as many of other denominations should be taken in as was consistent with the said design.[1] Ac-

[1] "Never," says the Rev. Dr. Cutting, in an article in the *New York Recorder*, published Sept. 20, 1854, which we here quote, "were men more decided in religious faith than the settlers of Rhode Island. It was their positive and zealous traits which from the four quarters of the earth sent them thither for shelter, and there they contended with each other like earnest men. And yet they practised mutual tolerance, because the rights of conscience were inviolable, and charity was a duty and a grace.

"We suppose this to be the true spirit of Brown University in its relations to religion. Providing in its charter for a majority of Baptists in its corporation, it embraces in certain proportions, likewise, Episcopalians, Quakers, and Congregationalists; not because the differences between Baptists, Episcopalians, Quakers, and Congregationalists are not of importance, but because the things which they hold in common, and the spirit of their common faith, furnish ample ground for coöperation in the cause of 'polite literature.' It is the honor of the Baptists that, when, by the intolerance of other colonies, they were driven to

cordingly, the Hon. Josias Lyndon and Col. Job Bennet were appointed to draw a charter to be laid before the next General Assembly, with a petition that they would pass it into a law. But the said gentlemen pleading unskilfulness touching an affair of the kind, requested that their trusty friend, the Rev. Ezra, now Dr. Stiles, might be solicited to assist them. This was opposed by me as unwilling to give the Doctor trouble about an affair of other people; but they urged that his love of learning and catholicism would induce him readily to give his assistance. Accordingly their proposition was consented to, and his assistance obtained; or, rather, the draughting of the charter was left entirely to him,[1] after being told that the Baptists were to have the lead in the institution, and

Rhode Island to establish their college, they proceeded at once, and of their own motion, to call in the counsels of gentlemen of other denominations, and to admit them to a share in the government, though their catholicity had well-nigh cost them the total loss of all which they had undertaken. They did this, not to merge their faith in a common indifferentism, but to illustrate a comprehensive charity. They had a 'main design,' and a subordinate and collateral one. The 'main design' was a Baptist college, especially for the education of their ministry; subordinate to this, and consistent with it, was the design of an institution which, enlisting a common interest, should confer common blessings upon other denominations and upon the State. Such a scheme was at the time utterly without a parallel, and must have been regarded in the other colonies with something of the amazement with which the inhabitants of Massachusetts Bay had looked, at an earlier day, upon the broad religious liberty of Rhode Island and the Providence Plantations. In this original spirit, as we believe, should the University be administered forever; men of diverse faiths working together, not because of indifferentism, but of charity, — not as the less Baptists, Episcopalians, Quakers, and Congregationalists, but as men of common interests in a work which honors and blesses all. It would be a shame if such an institution should not be, as always it has been, in the highest and best sense catholic. In our view, if its catholicity degenerated to indifferentism, it would cease to represent both the spirit and the designs of its founders."

[1] Prof. Kingsley, in his Life of Dr. Stiles, states that "a committee of Baptists and Congregationalists was appointed to draft a charter of a college; and of this body, Mr. Stiles and Mr. William Ellery were designated to prepare such an instrument for their consideration." "It is highly probable," he further adds, "from internal evidence, that the charter was drawn principally by Mr. Stiles; Mr. Ellery having little concern in preparing it, except to see to the correctness of the legal language. Whoever drew it, he had obviously before him the charters of Yale College, and was familiar with the questions which had arisen with respect to them. The privileges secured to the University by this charter are very ample; and the language of the several provisions is remarkably full,

the government thereof, forever; and that no more of other denominations were to be admitted than would be consistent with that. The charter was drawn, and a time and place were appointed for the parties concerned to meet and hear it read. But the vessel in which I was to sail for Halifax going off that day, prevented my being present with them long enough to see whether the original design was secured; and as the corporation was made to consist of two branches, Trustees and Fellows, and these branches to sit and act by distinct and separate powers, it was not easy to determine, by a transient hearing, what those powers might be. The Trustees were presumed to be the principal branch of authority; and as nineteen out of thirty-five were to be Baptists, the Baptists were satisfied, without sufficient examination into the authority vested in the fellowship, which afterwards appeared to be the soul of the institution, while the trusteeship was only the body. Placing, therefore, an entire confidence in Dr. Stiles, they agreed to join in a petition to the Assembly to have the charter confirmed by authority. The petition was preferred, and cheerfully received, and the charter read; after which a vote was called for, and urged by some to pass into a law. But this was opposed by others, particularly by Daniel Jenckes, Esq., member for Providence, who contended that the Assembly required more time to examine whether it was agreeable to the design of the first movers for it, and therefore prayed the house to have the perusal of it, while they adjourned for dinner. This was granted, with some opposition. Then he asked the Governor, who was a Baptist, whom they intended to invest with the governing power in said institution? The Governor answered, "The Baptists, by all means." Then Mr. Jenckes showed him that the charter was so artfully constructed as to throw the power into the Fellows' hands, whereof eight out

precise, and explicit. It is, undoubtedly, in many respects, one of the best college charters in New England." (See Appendix.)

From Prof. Kingsley's statements, it would appear that Baptists and Congregationalists were alike interested in the movement, and that a joint committee representing the two denominations was appointed to draft the charter. From the statements, however, of Backus, Edwards, Manning, and Jenckes, it is evident that Baptists alone were the originators of the undertaking; that Baptists alone met at the Deputy Governor's house in Newport, in July, 1763; that, of their number, Lyndon and Bennet were appointed to draft a charter in accordance with a plan sketched by Manning; that these gentlemen, "pleading unskilfulness," requested that Dr. Stiles "might be solicited to assist them;" and that this was at first opposed by Manning, who was "unwilling to give the Doctor trouble about an affair of other people."

of twelve were Presbyterians, usually called Congregationalists, and that the other four might be of the same denomination, for aught that appeared in the charter to the contrary. Convinced of this, Governor Lyndon immediately had an interview with Dr. Stiles, the Presbyterian minister of Newport, and demanded why he had perverted the design of the charter. The answer was, "I gave you timely warning to take care of yourselves, for that we had done so with regard to our society;"[1] and finally observed, that "he was not the rogue." When the Assembly was convened again, the said Jenckes moved that the affair might be put off to the next ses-

[1] In Prof. Kingsley's Life of Dr. Stiles, to which we have already alluded, we find it stated that the project of a college in Rhode Island had been the subject of serious deliberation a considerable time before the charter was actually granted by the Legislature, and that in this matter Dr. Stiles had taken a prominent part, collecting statistics, etc. His plan was, to unite several denominations of Christians in the enterprise, both in America and in Great Britain, and thus, by proper care, make the dissenting interest eventually exceed the Episcopal establishment. The whole number of churches of the Congregational, Presbyterian, and Baptist denominations, not only in the colonies, but in Great Britain and Ireland, he ascertained to be three thousand six hundred and thirty-eight. "He supposed that all these churches might be induced to contribute to the establishment and support of an institution which would so greatly subserve their interests." The arrival at Newport of Mr. Manning, and the proposition made by him for the establishment of a Baptist college, interfered, of course, with his cherished views and plans. It is therefore not surprising that he should have been unwilling to see them defeated, without a struggle on his part to carry them into effect. We can understand how an attempt should have been made, either by Dr. Stiles or his associates, in drafting an act of incoporation for a college in Rhode Island, to pay special "regard" to the interests of their own "society." That there was disappointment on both sides, and at the time mutual recriminations, is evident from the narrative. Under similar circumstances there doubtless would be again, human nature being very much the same now as in the days of our ancestors. It is due to Dr. Stiles, to state that he afterwards cherished friendly feelings towards the institution. Having been elected to a fellowship in the college, and solicited by repeated deputations from the corporation to accept the trust, he thus writes to the chancellor and Trustees. "I was too sincere a friend to literature not to have taken part in the institution at first, upon my nomination in the charter, had I not been prevented by reasons which a subsequent immediate election could not remove." One of the reasons assigned in this letter, as stated by Dr. Manning, in a letter to the Rev. John Ryland, dated May 20, 1773, was "the offence he should give his brethren should he accept it." Whatever the reasons were, they still influenced him to decline the office to which he was invited, with suitable acknowledgments of the politeness and respect with which he was treated on this occasion. His letter

sion; adding, that the motion for a college originated with the Baptists, and was intended for their use, but that the charter in question was not at all calculated to answer their purpose; and since the committee intrusted with this matter by the Baptists professed they had been misled, not to say imposed upon, it was necessary that the Baptists in other parts of the colony should be consulted previous to its passing into a law, especially as few, if any of them except himself, had seen it; and he prayed that he might have a copy for the said purpose, which he promised to return. All which was granted. When the charter came to be narrowly inspected, it was found to be by no means answerable to the design of the agitators and the instructions given the committee. Consequently, application was made to the Philadelphia Association, where the thing took its rise, to have their mind on the subject, who immediately sent two gentlemen[1] hither to join with the Baptists of this colony in making such alterations and amendments as were to them specified before their departure. When they arrived, Dr. Eyres[2] of Newport was added to the committee, and they

concludes with the catholic and pious wish that "the Father of lights, from whom comes down every good and perfect gift, may excite the public munificence, and raise up benefactors, through whose liberalities this institution shall be completed with an ample endowment." (Holmes's Life of President Stiles, page 117.)

[1] On the margin of the manuscript, in the handwriting of the Rev. Dr. Jones, who was Morgan Edwards's intimate friend, is the following, namely, "Why their names are not mentioned, I cannot say. However, there was no one sent but myself, although Mr. Robert Strettle Jones was so kind as to bear me company to Rhode Island on the occasion. — SAMUEL JONES." Mr. Jones, it will be remembered, in connection with Mr. Edwards, had been intrusted by the Association with the business in general of founding a Baptist college or university. He had, at this date, but recently been ordained in Philadelphia. He was a young man of liberal education, and a ready and skilful writer; hence his special fitness for the duty assigned him in this emergency. The following extract from notes to a century sermon delivered by him before the Philadelphia Baptist Association, Oct. 6, 1807, nearly fifty years afterwards, shows the manner in which he performed his mission: "In the fall of 1763, the writer of these sheets, on request, repaired to Newport in Rhode Island, and new-modelled a rough draught they had of a charter of incorporation for a college, which soon after obtained legislative sanction."

[2] Thomas Eyres, a physician, the first secretary of the corporation, and a Fellow of the college from 1764 until his death in 1788. He was graduated at Yale College, in the Class of 1754. His father, Elder Nicholas Eyres, was pastor of the Second Baptist Church in Newport from 1731 until his death, Feb. 13, 1759. (See Backus.)

happily draughted the present charter, and lodged it, with a new petition, in proper hands. The most material alterations were, appointing the same number of Baptists in the fellowship that had been appointed of the Presbyterians, by Dr. Stiles; settling the presidency in the Baptist society; adding five Baptists to the Trustees, and putting more Episcopalians than Presbyterians in the corporation."

Among the alterations not here enumerated by Manning, were, electing the President by the corporation instead of exclusively by the Trustees; providing for convoking an assembly of the corporation on twenty days' notice instead of six; making five a quorum of the Board of Fellows instead of eight; and striking out the clause making the places of Trustees or Fellows who should remove out of the State, vacant. By confining membership in the corporation to persons residing within the limits of the colony, the original charter excluded the originators and founders of the college. Hence, in the list of names proposed by Dr. Stiles to be incorporated, the following, which we find in the printed charter, as suggested by the committee, are omitted; namely, Rev. Morgan Edwards, Rev. Samuel Jones, Rev. James Manning, Rev. Isaac Eaton, Rev. John Gano, Rev. Samuel Stillman, Rev. Jeremiah Condy, and Robert Strettle Jones, Esq. The names of Hezekiah Smith, Isaac Backus, William Williams, and others from out of the State, who rendered such signal service in the early history of the college, would also have been excluded from membership in the corporation by the charter as originally drafted. (See Appendix.)

Mr. Jenckes, to whom Manning refers in his Narrative, was a wealthy merchant of Providence, and an active member of the Baptist church. He died July 7, 1774, in the seventy-third year of his age, having continued, says the record, a church-member forty-eight years " without censure." He was for forty years a member of the General Assembly, and for nearly thirty years Chief Justice of the Providence County Court. His daughter Rhoda was the mother of the Hon. Nicholas Brown, from whom the University derives it name, and also of the late Mrs. Hope Ives, after whom Hope College was named. Among the manuscript writings of Morgan Edwards, we also find, in the same volume from which Manning's Narrative is taken, a history of the college charter, by Judge Jenckes, which we here give, as follows: —

JENKES'S HISTORY OF THE CHARTER.

"While I attended the business of the Assembly, held August, 1763, Capt. William Rogers came to the Council Chamber and presented me with a paper, with a design I should sign it; adding, that, as it was a petition for a Baptist college, he knew I would not refuse. Business not permitting me to attend to it immediately, I requested he would leave with me the petition and charter. Meanwhile, the sergeant made proclamation requiring the members to take their seats. In my seat I began to read the papers, but had not done before the petition and charter were called for, which I gave to the sergeant, and he to the speaker at the board. The petition being read, a motion was made to receive it, and grant the charter. After some time I stood up to oppose, proceeding immediately on the petition, giving my reason in words to this effect. 'I understood that the college in question was sought for by the Baptists; and that it was to be under their government and direction, with the admission only of a few of other religious denominations to share with them therein, that they might appear as catholic as could be, consistent with their main design; but, on the contrary, I perceived by glancing over the charter, while I sat in my place just now, that the main power and direction is vested in twelve Fellows, and that eight out of the twelve are to be Presbyterians; and that the others may or may not be of the same denomination; but of necessity, none of them are to be Baptists. If so, there is treachery somewhere, and a design of gossly imposing on the honest people who first moved for the institution. I desire, therefore, that the matter may lie by till the afternoon.' This was granted. In the afternoon the matter was resumed, with a seeming resolution in some to push it through at all events ; but I had influence enough to stop proceedings then also. That evening and the next morning, I made it my business to see Governor Lyndon and Col. Bennet, and to inform them of the construction of the charter. They could not believe me, for the confidence they had in Dr. Stiles's honor and integrity, until seeing convinced them; what reflections followed may be better concealed than published. However, we all agreed to postpone passing the charter into a law, and did effect our purpose for that session, notwithstanding the attempts of Mr. Ellery and others of the Presbyterians to the contrary. Before the breaking up of the Assembly, the house, at my request, directed the speaker to deliver the charter to me, after I had made a promise it should be forthcoming at the next meeting of the Assembly.

I took the charter to Providence, and showed it to many who came to my house; others borrowed it to peruse at home. Meanwhile, the messengers from the Philadelphia Association arrived in Newport, which occasioned the committee of Newport to send to me for the charter. I asked for it of Dr. Ephraim Bowen, who had borrowed it last. The Doctor said he lent it to Samuel Nightingale, Esq. Search was made for it there, but it could not be found; neither do I know to this day what became of it.[1] When the next General Assembly met (last Wednesday in October, 1763), the second charter was presented; which was much faulted, and opposed by the gentry who concerned themselves so warmly about the other. And one in particular demanded that the first charter, which had been intrusted to me, might be produced. Then I related, as above, that it was lost, and the manner how it was lost; but the party, instead of believing this, very rudely suggested that I had secreted the charter, and in the

[1] This important document, which was lost for nearly a century, has recently been placed among the archives of the University. It was found, some twenty years since, among the files and papers of the church over which Dr. Stiles presided. It is in the handwriting of the author, and was evidently copied from the "rough draft" with great care. A careful comparison of this document with the charter which was finally granted by the General Assembly, fully confirms all the statements in reference thereto made by Manning and Jenckes. It shows also how much the University is indebted to Dr. Stiles for the phraseology of the instrument that gave it an existence, and for the fulness and precision with which all its privileges are granted and its provisions stated. The document is published in the Appendix, with the changes made by the committee or "messengers."

face of the court charged me with a breach of trust; which brought on very disagreeable altercations and bickerings, until, at last, I was necessitated to say, that 'if there had been any foul doings, it was amongst them of their own denomination at Providence.' Their clamors continued; and we gave way to them that session for peace sake. Meanwhile, Dr. Bowen, who is a man of strict honor and integrity, used all means to recover the former charter, posting an advertisement in the most public places in town, and making diligent inquiry; but to no purpose. At the next Assembly, which met in February, 1764, the new charter was again brought on the carpet; and the same clamor against it, and unjust reproaches against me, were repeated. It was said that the new charter was not like the old, and was constructed to deprive the Presbyterians of the benefit of the institution. To which it was replied, 'that it was agreeable to the designs of the first undertakers, and if calculated to deprive the Presbyterians of the power they wanted, it was no more than what they themselves had attempted to do to the Baptists.' After much and warm debate, the question was put and carried in favor of the new charter, by a great majority."

From the foregoing accounts, or narratives, it appears, (1) That President Manning drew up a plan of the college, and presented it to a company of Baptist gentlemen, at Newport, in the month of July, 1763. (2) That the Hon. Josias Lyndon and Colonel Job Bennet were appointed to draw a charter, in accordance with said plan, to be laid before the next General Assembly, with a petition that it might be made a law. (3) That the assistance of the Rev. Dr. Stiles, afterwards President of Yale College, was solicited and obtained. (4) That the drafting of the charter was left entirely to Dr. Stiles; and that he, in turn, was assisted by the Hon. William Ellery. (5) That the charter was accordingly drawn, and a time and place were appointed for the parties concerned to meet and hear it read. (6) That Manning, being obliged to leave on that day for Halifax, was unable to be with the committee long enough to see whether the original design was secured, and that the Baptists, being satisfied, without sufficient examination into the authority vested in the fellowship, and reposing entire confidence in Dr. Stiles, agreed to join in a petition to the General Assembly to have the charter confirmed by authority. (7) That the petition and charter were accordingly presented to the General Assembly in August, 1763, but that action thereon was postponed until the next session, through the influence of the Hon. Daniel Jenckes, the attempts of Mr. Ellery and others of the Presbyterians to the contrary notwithstanding. (8) That the charter was found on inspection to be so drawn as to vest the main power and direction of the institution in a board of twelve Fellows, eight of whom were to be Presbyterians, and the other four of the same denomination, for aught that appeared to the contrary; and that in general it did not answer to the original design. (9) That in this emergency application was made to the Philadelphia Association, "where the thing took its rise," to have their mind on the subject. (10) That they immediately sent to Newport the Rev. Samuel Jones, who was accompanied by Robert Strettle Jones, and that when they arrived, Dr. Eyres, of Newport, was added to the committee. (11) That, meanwhile, the original copy of the charter, presented to the General Assembly in August, which had been intrusted by that body to Mr. Jenckes, had been lost. (12) That the committee found at Newport a rough draft of a charter, which they happily remodelled, and that the most material alterations were, appointing the same number of Baptists in the fellowship that had been appointed of the Presbyterians by Dr. Stiles; settling the presidency in the Baptist society; adding five Baptists to the Trustees; putting more Episcopalians than Presbyterians in the corporation; and extending the membership of the corporation to persons residing out of the colony or state. From all this it is evident that the "rough draft" which the last committee remodelled was the one originally drawn by Dr. Stiles, and presented to the first committee in July, and from which a copy was undoubtedly made for the General Assembly. This copy, as we have already remarked, has recently been found among the archives of Dr. Stiles's church, and is now in the possession of the University.

That the college owes its origin to the efforts of men who were members of the Philadelphia Association, is evident from its history thus far. The following extracts from the minutes of this venerable body show the interest which it continued to manifest in the welfare and progress of an institution which it had aided in bringing into being: —

1764. "Agreed, to inform the churches to which we respectively belong, that, inasmuch as a charter is obtained in Rhode Island Government towards erecting a Baptist college, the churches should be liberal in contributing towards carrying the same into execution." 1766. "Agreed, to recommend warmly to our churches the interest of the college, for which a subscription is opened all over the continent. This college hath been set on foot upwards of a year, and has now in it three promising youths under the tuition of President Manning." 1767. "Agreed, that Rev. Isaac Eaton, and John Hart, Esq., executors of Mrs. Hubs's will, be allowed to pay £14 towards the education of Charles Thompson (student in Rhode Island College) out of the interest of the legacy left by said Mrs. Hubs for the use of the Association in Philadelphia." "Agreed, that the churches be requested to forward the subscription for Rhode Island College." 1769. "We received pleasing accounts from Rhode Island College. Seven commenced this fall. The colony has raised £1200 towards the building, which will be begun early in the spring. About £1000, lawful currency of New England, have been sent us from home (Great Britain) towards making up a salary for the President; and all the ministers of this Association have explicitly engaged to exert themselves in endeavoring to raise money for the same purpose." "Resolved, That the moneys which may be raised in the provinces of New York, New Jersey, and Pennsylvania, shall be put to interest, in those provinces, and not be taken out of either; except the interest which shall be subject to the order of the college to pay the President's salary, and for no other use. The persons appointed for receiving the donations are: In New York, the Rev. John Gano; in the Jerseys, John Stites, Esq.; in Pennsylvania, the Rev. Morgan Edwards. They are to see that the securities be sufficient, and that the bonds, mortgages, etc., be deposited with the treasurer of the college." "Voted, That £14, Jersey currency, be given Mr. Thomas Eustick, towards defraying his expenses at the college," etc.

1774. "The minutes and letters from Charleston Association, South Carolina, were read. The plan adopted by them respecting Rhode Island College, recommended to us." "Agreed, to recommend the same to the churches we stand respectively related unto; and that our brethren John Gano and William Rogers receive the moneys so raised, and remit the same to Colonel Job Bennet, treasurer." "The money raised for increasing the fund of Rhode Island College is as follows: The church at New York raised above what was proposed by the plan adopted; church of Cohansie, 15s.; church at Salem, 4s. 6d.; Hugh Glassford, 7s.; Andrew Bray, 5s. The last four sums above mentioned were received by Brother William Rogers."

1782. "Voted, That the seventh article of the Warren Association Minutes be adopted by us, which is as follows: "The Association, from a representation made to them by the corporation of the college in Providence of the low state of the funds of said college, and the urgent necessity of increasing them, in order to support suitable instructors therein, and from an idea of the great importance of good education, have taken into consideration, as the most probable method to accomplish this valuable end, the recommendation of a subscription throughout all the Baptist societies on this continent, as well as to all the friends of literature of every denomination, on the following conditions: —

"We, the subscribers, promise and engage to pay the several sums affixed to our names, to ——, to be by him paid to John Brown, Esq., of Providence, treasurer of the corporation, or his successor in said office, or order, to be placed at interest, and the interest only to be applied for the above purpose.

"N. B. The several churches are desired to insert in the above blank the name of the most suitable person in the society for this service."

The plan proposed by the Association in Charleston, S. C., for raising a fund for Rhode Island College, and adopted by the Philadelphia Association in 1774, as we learn from the foregoing extracts, and also during the same year by the Warren Association, was, in the language of the record, the "recommending to every member to pay *sixpence* sterling, annually, for three years successively, to their elder, or some suitable person: this money to be paid to the treasurer of the college." At the same time, the Rev. Messrs. John Gano, Oliver Hart, and Francis Pelot were appointed, says Benedict, to address the Baptist associations throughout America, and urge their co-operation in these efforts to raise funds for the college. In reading this record, we are amused at the gravity with which a body of men recommended the payment of so small a sum as sixpence, or twelve and one half cents, towards endowing an institution of learning, especially when we contrast this with the princely benefactions of later days. But further reflection soon changes any disposition of this kind into a feeling of respect, and even of admiration. The Baptists of that early period were, as a people, poor, and, as Dr. Manning in one of his letters adds, "despised and oppressed." The gifts and offerings which they thus contributed for the college were from the "*res angusta domi*," from "pious enlightened penury," to the noblest of all causes, the advancement of human learning. All honor for the zeal and perseverance, the sacrifices and the prayers, of these early friends of the college! Were their spirit emulated by their descendants, how soon would the resources of our public institutions be augmented, and their means of influence largely increased!

But to return. The charter finally granted by the General Assembly, out of which, says Mr. Edwards, "the

Baptists narrowly escaped being jockied by a set of men in whom they reposed full confidence," is now, and must forever continue to be, the unalterable constitution of the college or university. By it the corporation is made to consist of two branches; namely, that of the Trustees and that of the Fellows, with distinct, separate, and respective powers. The Trustees are thirty-six in number, of whom twenty-two are forever to be elected of the denomination called Baptists or Antipædobaptists, five of the denomination called Friends or Quakers, five of the denomination called Episcopalians, and four of the denomination called Congregationalists. These were the denominations of New England a century ago. The number of the Fellows, including the President, who must always be a Fellow, is twelve, of whom eight are forever to be elected of the denomination called Baptists, and the rest indifferently of any or all denominations. The President must forever be a Baptist. Once in three years the corporation, at its annual meetings, must choose from among the Trustees a chancellor of the university, and a treasurer; and from among the Fellows, a secretary. The office of the chancellor is merely to preside as moderator of the Trustees; the President, or, in his absence, the senior Fellow, being the moderator of the Fellows. The instruction and immediate government of the college is, and must forever continue to rest in the President and Fellows, or fellowship, to whom, as a "learned faculty," belongs exclusively the privilege of adjudging and conferring the academical degrees.

This charter, although it secures to the Baptists, as already stated, the control of the college, recognizes repeatedly, and in most unequivocal terms, the grand principles of religious freedom, for which the descendants of Roger Williams, and all true Baptists of every age, have always resolutely contended. Some of its provisions are as follows: —

And, furthermore, it is hereby enacted and declared, That into this liberal and catholic institution shall never be admitted any religious tests; but, on the contrary, all the members hereof shall forever enjoy full, free, absolute, and uninterrupted liberty of conscience: And that the places of professors, tutors, and all other officers, the President alone excepted, shall be free and open for all denominations of Protestants: And that youth of all religious denominations shall and may be freely admitted to the equal advantages, emoluments, and honor of the college or university, and shall receive a like fair, generous, and equal treatment during their residence therein — they conducting themselves peaceably, and conforming to the laws and statutes thereof: And that the public teaching shall, in general, respect the sciences: And that the sectarian differences of opinions shall not make any part of the public and classical instruction; although all religious controversies may be studied freely, examined, and explained by the President, professors, and tutors, in a personal, separate, and distinct manner, to the youth of any or each denomination: And, above all, a constant regard shall be paid to, and effectual care taken of, the morals of the college.

The statutes of the college have been framed from time to time in accordance with the spirit of this charter. So long ago as 1783, those students who regularly observed the *seventh* day as the Sabbath, were exempted from the operation of the law which required every student, as a moral duty, to attend public worship on the *first* day of the week. Those who statedly attended the *Friends'* meeting were expressly "permitted to wear their hats within the college walls," etc., and "young gentlemen of the Hebrew persuasion" were formally exempted from the operation of the law which commanded, on penalty of expulsion, that no student should deny the divine authority of the Old and New Testaments. And yet more, — in

1770, the corporation of the college declared, as appears from the records, that "the children of Jews may be admitted into this institution, and entirely enjoy the freedom of their own religion, without any constraint or imposition whatever." These provisions of the charter, and of the statutes of the college, manifest, says a distinguished writer, a "delicate regard for the rights of conscience, for which, it is believed, hardly a parallel can be found in the history of similar institutions."

And to "this liberal and catholic institution" the youth of all religious denominations have freely resorted, during the first century of its existence, for their education. Not a few of the prominent religious teachers and theologians connected with our various Christian sects or societies, throughout the land, received their permanent serious impressions during the revivals with which the college or university has, from its beginning, been graciously visited.

We close this chapter with the following extract from Backus's Church History of New England. Were the work generally accessible to the reading public, a mere reference might answer our purpose; which is, to remove, as far as possible, all doubts in regard to the origin of this venerable seat of learning. It is, as will be seen, a brief recapitulation of the leading facts in the early history of the college, and serves to establish and confirm the statements already presented. The accuracy of Backus as an historian has never, we believe, been questioned. Bancroft awards to him the highest praise. Being in the prime and vigor of life when the college was established, and one of the first Trustees, he was, of course, familiar with all the facts pertaining to its origin and early progress.

EXTRACT FROM BACKUS.

"The uppermost party among Christians have ever had the command of all colleges, to educate religious teachers, as well as other men of superior learning, until very lately. Even in 1780, no ministers but *Congregational* ministers were allowed to be Overseers of the University at Cambridge, by the Massachusetts constitution of government. And great sums have been given to that University by the government, from time to time, ever since it began in 1638. But as Providence and Rhode Island Colony was planted by men who were banished from the Massachusetts, because they conscientiously dissented from the use of force in religious affairs, and that colony suffered amazingly from neighbor colonies for more than an hundred years, the people have grown up with great prejudices against colleges, and against obeying the laws of Christ for the support of his ministers. But as a minister hath died this year (Dr. Manning) who has done much towards removing those prejudices, I shall give a concise account of the affair. Mr. Isaac Eaton, who was pastor of the Baptist Church at Hopewell in New Jersey from 1748 to 1772, set up a school for the education of youth for the ministry, as well as for other callings, in 1756, and kept it for eleven years. One of his scholars was Mr. James Manning, who went from his school to the college at Princeton, where he took his first degree in September, 1762. And as the Philadelphia Association were for erecting a college in Rhode Island Government, they fixed their eyes upon him as a proper leader in the affair. He therefore called in at Newport, on his voyage to Halifax, in July, 1763, and proposed the matter to a number of Baptist gentlemen, who readily concurred therewith; and as they had a high opinion of a learned Congregational minister among them, they desired him to make a draught of a charter for a college in that Government. It was proposed to take in some members of the several denominations among them, but that the Baptists should always be the majority of the corporation. He drew a charter, which appeared to be upon this plan, and it was introduced into their legislature; but a Baptist gentleman discerned that there was a door left open for the Congregational denomination to become the majority hereafter. Therefore the charter was not then passed into a law; and when their legislature met again, the charter was not to be found. When this was heard of at Philadelphia, two gentlemen were sent from thence, who assisted in drawing a new charter, which was established by the legislature of Rhode Island, in February, 1764."

CHAPTER II.

1764-1769.

First Meeting of the Corporation, at Newport — Character of the twenty-four members present, representing the four religious denominations recognized in the Charter — Manning removes with his family to Warren — Begins a Latin School, now the "University Grammar School" — Employs a part of his time in preaching — Formation of the Warren Baptist Church — Appointed President of the College — Extract from a Letter of Rev. Isaac Backus to Dr. Gill of London — Suggests the formation of the Warren Association — Difficulties to be overcome — First Meeting of the Association, in 1767 — Letter from the Philadelphia Association — Second and third Meetings — Sentiments and Plan of the Warren Association as drawn up by Manning — Plan to collect grievances — Character and influence of the Association — Manning's prominence and usefulness as a member of the two Associations — Circular Letter by Manning — Letter to Hon. David Howell — Howell appointed Tutor of the College — Sketch of his Character — First Commencement of the College — Account from the *Providence Gazette* — Rev. Morgan Edwards's efforts in England and Ireland to secure funds for the College — Biographical Sketches of members of the first Graduating Class: Rev. Dr. William Rogers, Hon. James Mitchell Varnum, Rev. Charles Thompson, Rev. William Williams.

THE first meeting of the "Corporation for founding and endowing a College or University within the Colony of Rhode Island and Providence Plantations in New England in America," was held at Newport, on the first Wednesday in September, 1764. From this point, therefore, the commencement of the college properly dates. At this meeting the following gentlemen, twenty-four in number, as appears from the records, were present, and qualified themselves by taking the oath prescribed by the charter; namely, Hon. Stephen Hopkins, Hon. Joseph Wanton, Hon. Samuel Ward, John Tillinghast, Simon Pease, James

Honeyman, Nicholas Easton, Nicholas Tillinghast, Daniel Jenckes, Nicholas Brown, Joshua Babcock, John G. Wanton, Rev. Edward Upham, Rev. Jeremiah Condy, Rev. Gardner Thurston, Rev. John Maxson, Rev. Samuel Winsor, Rev. James Manning, Josias Lyndon, Job Bennet, Jr., Ephraim Bowen, Edward Thurston, Jr., Thomas Eyres, and Peleg Barker. The Hon. Stephen Hopkins, Esq., was chosen chancellor, John Tillinghast, Esq., treasurer, and Dr. Thomas Eyres, secretary. The form of a certificate, authorizing persons to receive donations for the college, was adopted, and also the form of a receipt therefor. A " Preamble " was adopted, setting forth the nature and design of the institution, and its need of funds. Committees to receive subscriptions for the college were appointed throughout Rhode Island, in the southern and western parts of the continent, and in the States of Massachusetts and Connecticut. Committees were also appointed to provide a seal for the use of the corporation, and to assist in digesting and recording the proceedings of the meeting.

It is interesting, in this connection, to observe the character of the men, who, a century ago, met for the first time, as a corporate body, to transact business for the college. Of the four religious denominations recognized in the charter, the Congregationalists were represented by Dr. Ephraim Bowen, one of the most distinguished physicians in Providence previous to the Revolutionary War. To him, Lieut. Gov. Arnold, in his History of Rhode Island, ascribes the peculiar honor of originating a patriotic order, composed of the gentler sex, known as the "Daughters of Liberty." The Episcopalians were represented by Governor Joseph Wanton and Hon. James Honeyman, both residents of Newport, and gentlemen of culture, wealth, and high social position. The former was first elected

Governor in the year 1769. He continued to fill the office from year to year, with great acceptance, until 1775, when he was suspended by the General Assembly for disloyalty. Mr. Honeyman was the son of the Rev. James Honeyman, Rector of Trinity Church, Newport. He was an able lawyer and a prominent politician, filling many high offices in the State. For many years he was Advocate General of the Court of Vice Admiralty for the colony, having been appointed to this office by the British Government. The Quakers or Friends were represented by the Hon. Stephen Hopkins, John G. Wanton, Edward Thurston, and Nicholas Easton. No name is more prominent in the history of this period than that of Hopkins, and few men of any period have exerted so wide an influence upon the destinies of the country. For nearly forty-five years, as chief justice, governor, member of Congress, legislator, or representative, he was engaged in some kind of official duty connected with the town, the State, or the national Congress. His name appears among the signers of the Declaration of Independence. The office of chancellor of the corporation, to which he was elected at this first meeting, he held until his death, in 1785, a period of twenty-one years. He was a warm personal friend of President Manning, and, by his extensive learning and genuine love of literature, proved a most efficient coadjutor in all the plans and efforts of the latter for the efficiency and usefulness of the college. Mr. Wanton was an opulent merchant of Newport, and was allied by blood and affinity with the wealthiest and most popular families in the colony. The name of Nicholas Easton appears in Arnold's History of Rhode Island, as a member of the General Assembly from Middletown, in the year 1776. He was probably a descendant of Governors Nicholas and John Easton. Of

Thurston we have been unable to ascertain anything definite. He was a trustee, as appears from the Triennial Catalogue, until the year 1782. The remaining seventeen members of the corporation were Baptists, or, as they are also designated in the charter, Antipædobaptists. They were mostly from the towns of Providence, Newport, Warren, Westerly, and Boston. Among them we notice Samuel Ward, the popular Governor of Rhode Island during the years 1762, 1765, and 1766, a Justice also of the Supreme Court, and one of the most influential members of the First Congress, in 1774 (his Life, written by Prof. Gammell, is published in Spark's American Biography); Judge Daniel Jenckes, a brief sketch of whom has already been given in connection with the history of the college charter; Josias Lyndon, who, in 1768, was elected Governor, by an overwhelming majority of nearly fifteen hundred; Nicholas Brown, the distinguished merchant and liberal benefactor of the college, and also father of the Hon. Nicholas Brown, after whom the institution was finally named; Rev. Edward Upham, pastor of the First Church at Newport, and a graduate of Harvard College, in the class of 1734; Rev. Gardner Thurston, an intimate friend and associate of Dr. Stiles; Rev. Jeremiah Condy, of Boston, also a graduate of Harvard College, in the class of 1721; Dr. Joshua Babcock, of Westerly, who, in 1775, was appointed a major-general of the Rhode Island militia, and who also held various public offices of responsibility and trust; and Dr. Thomas Eyres, of Newport, who held the office of secretary of the corporation until the breaking out of the Revolutionary War.

In the records of subsequent meetings of the corporation, previous to the removal of the college to Providence, we find among the Baptist members the names also of Rev.

Morgan Edwards of Philadelphia, Rev. Hezekiah Smith of Haverhill, Rev. Samuel Stillman of Boston, Rev. John Gano of New York, Rev. Isaac Backus of Middleborough, Rev. John Davis of Boston, Rev. Russell Mason of Swanzey, Nathan Spear of Boston, Sylvester Child of Warren, and Joseph, brother of Nicholas Brown, of Providence. Among the Episcopal members we find the names of Rev. George Bisset of Newport, Joseph Russell and George Hazard Esquires. The last named was mayor of Newport, and for upwards of thirty years was a member of the State Legislature. Among the Quakers, Jonathan Easton, a physician. Among the Congregationalists, Nicholas Cook, for several years Governor of the colony, and Jabez Bowen, LL.D., Deputy Governor. The latter succeeded Gov. Hopkins as chancellor of the college.

During the spring previous to this first meeting of the corporation, Manning had removed with his family to Warren, a pleasant town in Bristol County, R. I., about ten miles from Providence. Here he at once opened a Latin school, with an ultimate view to the commencement of college instruction. This school, which soon became flourishing, he continued to teach or superintend for many years, in connection with his professional duties and calling. It was removed to Providence in 1770, and, upon the completion of "University Hall," to rooms in that building. In 1810, a brick house for its accommodation was erected by the friends of the college, under the direction of a committee of the corporation, consisting of Thomas P. Ives, Moses Lippitt, and Thomas Lloyd Halsey. It is now called the "University Grammar School," and is taught by Messrs. Merrick and Emory Lyon, they having the entire responsibility of its management. This school has ever been an efficient auxiliary to the college or university.

At the time of Manning's arrival in Warren, there were nearly sixty Baptist communicants residing in that town, the majority of whom were members of the venerable church in Swanzey. The population of the village was then rapidly increasing, and the time seemed to have arrived when they could best secure their religious interests by forming themselves into a separate and independent body, instead of being considered as a branch of the mother church. It was this fact, perhaps, which determined the first location of the college. Without funds it could not, of course, in its feeble beginning, support itself. It seemed therefore desirable to connect it with some church, over which its President should be pastor, that he might thereby derive an income sufficient for the maintenance of his family. The time and circumstances pointed to Warren as the place for this design, and accordingly Manning settled himself here,[1] and, while engaged in teaching, employed also a portion of his time in preaching to the people the gospel. His zeal and eloquence soon attracted a numerous congregation. The fruits of his ministry were apparent, and not a few persons became believers in Christ and were baptized. On the 15th day of November, 1764, a church of fifty-eight members was duly organized and constituted. By previous appointment, they had engaged the Rev. John Gano of New York, the Rev. Gardner Thurston of Newport, and the Rev. Ebenezer Hinds of Middleborough, Mass., to assist in the proposed undertaking. The day

[1] In an early diary of the Rev. Dr. Hezekiah Smith, we find the following: "*Saturday*, April 21, 1764. I went to Warren (from Newport) with Mrs. Manning, Esq. Coles, Capt. Wheaton, and Mr. Lillibridge. *Sabbath*, 22. Preached in Littletown in Warren, from John iii. 4, two sermons. Staid in Warren till Wednesday, 25th, at Esq. Coles's."

Mr. Smith, it appears, with Mr. and Mrs. Manning, left New York for Newport, Wednesday, April 11. They reached Newport on the 13th, when Mr. Manning proceeded at once to Warren.

being kept in the solemn exercise of fasting and prayer, "in the forenoon," says the record, "Mr. Thurston preached a sermon, and after a short intermission of service, the people returned, and Messrs. Gano, Manning, and Hinds each made a prayer suitable to the occasion, after which the church covenant, previously prepared by Mr. Manning, was presented and read."

This covenant, the original of which, in Manning's handwriting, is still in existence, we here present, as follows: —

COVENANT OF THE BAPTIST CHURCH, WARREN, R. I.

Whereas we, unworthy sinners, through the infinite riches of free grace, as we trust, brought out of darkness into the marvellous light of the gospel, and the grace of it, transformed into the kingdom of God's dear Son Jesus Christ our only Lord and Saviour, and made partakers of all those privileges which Christ purchased with his precious blood, think it our duty, and the greatest privilege we can enjoy here on earth, to walk in all the commandments and ordinances, not only for our own comfort and peace, but for the manifestation of the glory of God and for the mutual help and society of each other; and as it hath pleased God to appoint a visible church relation, to be the way and manner whereby he is pleased to communicate to his people the blessings of his presence, a growth in grace, and furtherance in the knowledge of our Lord God —

We, therefore, this day, after solemn fasting and prayer for help and direction, in the fear of His holy name, and with hearts lifted up to the most high God, humbly and freely offer up ourselves a living sacrifice unto him who is our God, in covenant, through Jesus Christ, to walk together according to his revealed word, in visible gospel relation, both to Christ our only head and to each other as fellow-members and brethren of the same household of faith.

And we do humbly engage, that, through His strength, we will endeavor to perform all our respective duties towards God and each other, and to practise all the ordinances of Christ, according to what is and shall be made known to us in our respective places; to exercise, practise, and submit to the government of Christ in this church.

And we declare that it is our mind that none are properly qualified members of this Christ's visible church but such as have been wrought upon by the grace of God, delivered from their sins by the justifying righteousness of Christ, have the evidence of it in their souls, have made profession thereof, — that is, of a living faith in Christ, — and have been baptized, by immersion, in the name of the Holy Trinity.

Further, it is our mind that the imposition or non-imposition of hands upon believers, after baptism, is not essential to church communion, and that where the image of Christ is discerned, according to the rules of God's word, and those previous duties but now mentioned are submitted to according to gospel rules, we are ready to hold communion with all such walking orderly in the church of Christ.

And now we humbly hope, that, although of ourselves we are altogether unworthy and unfit thus to offer up ourselves to God, or to do him any service, or to expect any favor or mercy from him, yet that he will graciously accept of this our freewill offering, in and through the merits and mediation of our dear Redeemer, and that he will employ and improve us in his service to his own praise, — to whom be all the glory, both now and forever.

After the members had signed the foregoing covenant, "they were asked," continues the record, "by the Rev. Mr. Manning, whether they, in the presence of that assembly, viewed that as their covenant and plan of union in a church relation, which question was answered by them all in the affirmative, standing up; after which, three of the brethren, Samuel Hix, Amos Haile, and John Coomer, in behalf of the church, presented a call, previously prepared by the brethren, to the Rev. James Manning to become their pastor. The call was read publicly by the Rev. Mr. Gano, after which, he asked the Rev. James Manning if he accepted it, which was answered in the affirmative.

"Then Mr. Gano preached a sermon, suitable to the occasion, in which he reminded both pastor and people of their respective duties, and urged the mutual performance of both, from those important motives which the nature of the relation requires. Thus ended the solemnities of the day."

The relations which Manning now assumed proved alike pleasant and profitable to pastor and flock. During the six years of his ministry in Warren, the church greatly increased in numbers and strength, while the college flourished under its fostering care.

At the second meeting of the corporation, held in Newport, on the first Wednesday in September, 1765, he was formally appointed "President of the College, Professor of Languages, and other branches of learning, with full power to act in these capacities at Warren, or elsewhere." This is the language of the record, which, as has been playfully remarked, "though not obnoxious to the charge of legal precision, seems to imply, on the part of the corporation, no want of confidence in the variety of the President's attainments." A letter addressed by Backus to the Rev. Dr. Gill, of London, an extract from which we here present, illustrates Manning's position at this time, as a pioneer in introducing polite literature or learning among the Baptists of New England: —

One grand objection made use of against believers' baptism, has been that none but ignorant and illiterate men have embraced the Baptist sentiments. And there was so much color for it as this, namely, that ten years ago there were but two Baptist ministers (Jeremiah Condy of Boston, and Edward Upham of Newport) in all New England who had what is called a liberal education; and they were not clear in the doctrines of grace. But three others have lately come from the Southern governments; namely, Mr. Samuel Stillman, who is settled in Boston; Mr. Hezekiah Smith, who has had remarkable success at Haverhill, where he has gathered a large society; and Mr. James Manning, who is settled at Warren, R. I. And as the Baptists have met with a great deal of abuse from those who are called learned men in our land, they have been not a little prejudiced against learning itself; but, latterly, there has been considerable alteration in this respect. A charter was obtained from the General Assembly of Rhode Island in February, 1764, incorporating a number of Trustees and Fellows, for founding and endowing a college for the education of youth (of which you will be likely to hear more in due time); and this corporation, at their annual meeting, last September, chose the aforesaid Mr. Manning President. He has commenced a school, which appears in a likely way to increase fast. But as there are scarce any books suitable for such business to be sold in that colony, he has thought of sending to London for a quantity; and as he is unknown there, he requested that I would write a few lines in his favor. Therefore, my dear sir, if my poor testimony may be thought worthy of any notice, I desire that you would mention to Mr. Keith, to whom he has thoughts of sending, that, from near two years' acquaintance with him, I am well satisfied that he is a man of piety, integrity, and ability, who will make conscience of fulfilling his engagements.

I remain, sir, your humble servant,

ISAAC BACKUS.

It was about this time that Manning conceived the plan of uniting the churches of New England on some common basis, in order to promote their harmony and growth, to resist more successfully acts of oppression on the part of the "Standing Order" in Massachusetts and Connecticut, and especially to disarm his brethren of all existing prejudices against human learning, and thereby effectually advance the interests of the college. The undertaking was one of no ordinary magnitude. The government of Baptist churches had been from time immemorial, as now, of the independent form, each particular church having an exclusive right of jurisdiction over its own members, electing and dismissing its own officers, and transacting all its business by final issue within itself, without appeal to any power on earth, either civil or ecclesiastical. With the Baptist churches of New England, especially, it had long been an article of belief, that civil government, although desirable and necessary for civil purposes, has nothing to do with Christ's kingdom, which is spiritual and not of this world, and has nothing to do with the visible church, which is subject to Jesus Christ alone as the head thereof. Hence they regarded all synods, conventions, associations, and councils to decide religious controversies, revoke acts of particular churches, inflict censure, form platforms, and prepare articles of faith, as useless and unfriendly to the independency of the churches; as having more or less respect to the civil state, and therefore partaking too much of the carnal wisdom of this world. They had suffered too much from measures adopted at these meetings among the Congregational ministers of Massachusetts and Connecticut to be easily persuaded to meet in any association, even though it were upon a plan altogether different from the associations and conventions in New England. It is true that at a former period the Baptists had been united in some kind of an organization. Knight, in his History of the Six-Principle Baptists, whose sentiments generally prevailed in the early history of Rhode Island, says, "The churches of Providence, Newport, Swanzey, and North Kingston, about the close of the seventeenth century, united in a *yearly meeting* composed of elders, messengers," etc. Comer, who was a decided advocate for the doctrine of "laying on of hands," in his manuscript diary gives an account of this meeting in 1729. Callender, also, in his Historical Discourse, alludes to the same meeting or association. We have before us now a letter printed in 1741, from sundry persons in Newport, addressed to the "several Baptist churches in New England, that are, or have been, united in the general meetings usually held at Providence, Swanzey," etc. In the progress of time, however, some of the Six-Principle churches which organized this meeting became extinct, others ceased to maintain their peculiar sentiments, and it was gradually, by most of the regular Baptist churches, at the period of which we are now speaking, abandoned.

It was Manning's wish to unite all the churches of his faith and order in New England in an association similar to the one formed in Philadelphia, which was simply advisory in its character, having respect to the advancement of the Redeemer's kingdom by spreading through the churches an account of the welfare and prosperity of each. He submitted his plan to the members of his own church, who cordially seconded his views, as appears from a formal vote on the subject, which we find recorded under date of August 28, 1766. He also conferred with his brethren in the ministry, who were occasionally at his house.[1] Letters of invitation were accordingly sent out, and on the 8th of September, 1767, a meeting of pastors and delegates from the principal Baptist churches in Massachusetts and Rhode Island met at Warren. Hence the origin of the Warren Association, the first organization of the kind in New England, and, according to Benedict, the sixth in America. The Rev. Isaac Backus, of Middleborough, who was chosen clerk of this meeting, thus commences the minutes: —

"Whereas there hath of late been a great increase of Baptist churches in New England, which yet have not such an acquaintance with each other and orderly union together as ought to be, it has been thought by many that a general meeting or association might be a likely means to remove this evil, and to promote the general good of the churches. There-

[1] Mr. Manning, it seems, also visited the pastors and churches in person, and conferred with them on the subject. From the diary to which we have already referred, we learn, for instance, that he visited the Rev. Hezekiah Smith, Tuesday, April 15, 1766, and stopped until Thursday, preaching both days in his meeting-house. On Monday, April 21, Mr. Smith set out for Rhode Island, joining Mr.

fore a number of elders, being occasionally together last year, did appoint a meeting at Warren, in Rhode Island Colony, on Sept. 8, 1767; and sent an invitation to others of their brethren to meet them there, to confer upon these affairs. Accordingly a considerable number of elders and brethren met at the time and place appointed; and Elder John Gano, from New York, opened the meeting with a suitable sermon, from Acts xv. 9."

Eleven churches were represented at this meeting by pastor and delegates, as follows; namely, Warren — Rev. James Manning, and brethren Benjamin Cole and Daniel Brown; Second, Rehoboth — Rev. Richard Round, and brethren Samuel Bullock and Daniel Bullock; Haverhill — Rev. Hezekiah Smith, and brethren Jacob Whittier and Jonathan Shepard; Norton — Rev. William Carpenter; Bellingham — Rev. Noah Alden; First, Middleborough — Rev. Isaac Backus; Second, Middleborough — Rev. Ebenezer Hinds; Cumberland — Rev. Daniel Miller; First, Boston — Dea. Josiah Colburn; Second, Boston — Brother Philip Freeman; Attleborough — brethren Abraham Bloss and Joseph Guild. There were also present from the Philadelphia Association, Rev. Messrs. John Gano, Abel Griffith, and Noah Hammond. Mr. Gano was chosen moderator, and, after looking to Heaven for guidance and direction, they proceeded to the business before them. The occasion, as we may well suppose, was one of unusual interest. The Philadelphia Association, having been informed of the proposed meeting by President Manning, sent them the following timely letter, written by the Rev. Dr. Samuel Jones: —

Manning at Boston. Mr. Smith remained in Warren and Newport until Saturday, May 8th, a little more than two weeks, spending most of his time with Manning. On Monday, Aug. 4, of this same year, Mr. Smith again visited Warren, stopping until Friday with his friend and classmate. On Wednesday, Nov. 12th, Mr. Manning was in Haverhill, and gave the charge at Mr. Smith's ordination.

LETTER TO THE WARREN ASSOCIATION.

The Elders and Messengers of the several Baptist churches met in Association at Philadelphia, the 14th, 5th, and 16th days of October, 1766. To the Elders and Messengers of the several Baptist Churches of the same faith and order, to meet in Association at Warren, in the Colony of Rhode Island, the 8th day of September, 1767, send greeting.

DEARLY BELOVED BRETHREN : — When we understood that you had concluded to meet at the time and place above mentioned, with a view to lay the foundation-stone of an associational building, it gave us peculiar joy, in that it opened to our view a prospect of much good being done. You will perhaps judge this our address to you premature, because as yet you have only an *ideal* being, as a body by appointment. But if you should call this our forwardness blind zeal, we are still in hopes you will not forget that our embracing the first opportunity of commencing Christian fellowship and acquaintance with you, affords the strongest evidence of our approbation of your present meeting, and how fond we should be of mutual correspondence between us in this way.

A long course of experience and observation has taught us to have the highest sense of the advantages which accrue from associations; nor indeed does the nature or thing speak any other language. For, as particular members are collected together and united in one body, which we call a particular church, to answer those ends and purposes which could not be accomplished by any single member, so a collection and union of churches into one associational body may easily be conceived capable of answering those still greater purposes which any particular church could not be equal to. And by the same reason, a union of associations will still increase the body in weight and strength, and make it good that a threefold cord is not easily broken.

Great, dear brethren, is the design of your meeting; great is the work which lies before you. You will need the guidance and influence of the Divine Spirit, as well as the exertion of all prudence and wisdom. It is therefore our most ardent prayer that you may meet in love, that peace and unanimity may subsist among you during your consultations, that you may be animated with zeal for the glory of God, and directed to advise and determine what may most conduce to promote the Redeemer's kingdom.

From considering the divided state of our Baptist churches in your quarter, we foresee that difficulties may arise, such as may call for the exercise of the greatest tenderness and moderation, that if haply, through the blessing of God on your endeavors, those lesser differences may subside, and a more general union commence.

As touching our consultations at this our meeting, the minutes of our proceedings (a printed copy whereof we shall herewith enclose) will inform you; and if in anything further you should be desirous of information with regard to us, we refer you to our reverend and beloved brethren Morgan Edwards, John Gano, and Samuel Jones, who, as our representative delegates, will present you with this our letter, and whom we recommend to Christian fellowship with you.

And now, dear brethren, farewell. May the Lord bless and direct you in all things, and grant that we may all hereafter form one general assembly at his right hand, through infinite riches of free grace in Christ Jesus our Lord.

Signed by order and in behalf of the Association, by

BENJAMIN MILLER, *Moderator.*
SAMUEL JONES, *Clerk.*

Neither Edwards nor Jones was present at this meeting, but, in their stead, Messrs. Griffith and Hammond, as has already been stated. Although the delegates in attendance "generally manifested," says Backus, "a good will toward this attempt for promoting the union and welfare of the churches, most of them thought they were not prepared to join in an association." The pastors and messengers of but four were ready at this time to unite; namely, Warren, Haverhill, Bellingham, and Second Middleborough. The other delegates present seem to have hesitated, through fear of some usurpation of authority by the associated body over the particular churches composing it; an evil which they were determined, if possible, to avoid. Besides, they were not altogether satisfied with the plan of organization and action now adopted. This plan was substantially that of the Philadelphia Association, and was thought to give undue authority to the united body. It was, however, soon after so explained and amended as to be less objectionable. At the second meeting, also held in Warren, the churches of Sutton, Leicester, and Ware, and the First Church in Boston, over which the Rev. Dr. Stillman had recently been settled, joined the Association, thus swelling the number to eight. The Rev. Benjamin Miller and the Rev. Isaac Stelle, of New Jersey, both warm personal friends of Manning, were present upon this occasion, as delegates from the parent body at Philadelphia. In 1769, the churches of Sturbridge, Enfield, Wilbraham, and Montague joined the Association. At this meeting the following sentiments and plan, drawn up by President Manning, were adopted as a final basis for organization and action.

SENTIMENTS TOUCHING AN ASSOCIATION.

1. That such a combination of churches is not only prudent, but useful, as has appeared even in America by the experience of upwards of sixty years. Some of the uses of it are, union and communion among themselves; maintaining more effectually the order and faith once delivered to the saints; having advice in cases of doubt, and help in distress; being more able to promote the good of the cause, and becoming important in the eye of the civil powers, as has already appeared in many instances on this continent. 2. That such an association is consistent with the independency and power of particular churches, because it pretends to be no other than an *advisory council*, utterly disclaiming superiority, jurisdiction, coercive right, and infallibility. 3. That an association should consist of men knowing and judicious, particularly in the Scriptures. The reasons are obvious: such men are the fittest to represent communities who profess the Scriptures to be the only rule of faith and practice in religious matters, and who expect that every advice, opinion, or direction they receive from an association be Scriptural. They should be skilled and expert in the laws of their God, as counsellors are in the laws of the land; for that is the ground of the church's application to them.

PLAN OF THE ASSOCIATION.

1. The Association to consist only of messengers chosen and sent by the churches. These messengers to be their ministers (for a reason given in sentiment 3), together with some judicious brethren. Their expenses to be borne by the churches which send them.

2. With the messengers the churches send letters addressed to the Association. In these letters mention is made of the messengers, and their authority to act for their churches; also of the state of the churches touching their peace; their increase by baptism, and by letters dismissive and commendatory from other churches; touching their diminution by death, excommunication, and dismission to other churches, and the present number of members. If any questions are to be put to the Association, any advice to ask, or business to propose, these are to be expressed in said letters.

3. All matters to be determined in this Association by the suffrage of the messengers, except what are determinable by Scripture: such matters are never put to the decision of votes. All that speak are to address the moderator, who is to take care that none be interrupted while speaking, and that no other indecorum take place.

4. Churches are to be received into this Association by petitions setting forth their desire to be admitted, their faith, order, and willingness to be conformable to the rules of the associated body. When a petition is read, and the matter ripened for a vote, the moderator states the question. Suffrage being given in favor of the petition, the said moderator declares that such a church is received into the Association, in token of which he gives the messengers the *right hand of fellowship*, and bids them take their seats.

5. The Association to meet annually, at Warren, on Tuesday next after the first Wednesday in September,[1] at two o'clock in the afternoon, and to continue till business be finished. It is to be opened with divine service: after which a moderator and clerk are chosen; the letters from the churches are read; the names of the messengers are written, that they may

[1] "And as the annual Commencement at our college is on the first Wednesday in September, and some who come to it from a distance would desire to attend the Association also, it was appointed to be on the Tuesday after the Commencement." (Backus's Church History, Vol. III., p. 113.)

be called over at after meetings; then business is attended to, and minutes thereof made; a circular letter to the churches is prepared and signed, and a copy of it sent to every church, containing the minutes of the Association, the state of the churches, when and by whom vacancies are to be supplied, who is to preach the next Association sermon, and whatever else is needful for the churches to know.

6. A connection to be formed and maintained between this Association and that of Philadelphia, by annual letter and messengers from us to them and from them to us.

7. The faith and order of this Association are expressed in a confession put forth by upwards of a hundred congregations in Great Britain, in the year 1689, and adopted by the Association of Philadelphia in 1742. Some of the principles in said confession are: The imputation of Adam's sin to his posterity; the inability of man to recover himself; effectual calling by sovereign grace; justification by imputed righteousness; immersion for baptism, and that on profession of faith and repentance; congregational churches and their independency; reception into them upon evidence of sound conversion, etc.

The meeting this year (1769) was rendered unusually interesting by the presence, as messengers from the Philadelphia Association, of Rev. Messrs. Morgan Edwards (who had but recently returned from England and Ireland on his mission in behalf of the college), Samuel Jones, and John Davis. "Many of the letters from the churches," says Backus, "mentioned grievous oppressions and persecutions from the 'standing order,' especially the one from Ashfield, where religious tyranny had been carried to great lengths." Whereupon petitions to the General Courts of Massachusetts and Connecticut for redress were prepared, by a committee of seven, of which the Rev. John Davis acted as chairman. The same having been read and approved, Messrs. Samuel Stillman, Philip Freeman, Philip Freeman Jr., John Proctor, and Nathan S. Spear, all of Boston, were chosen a committee to present them.

The following proposal and plan to collect grievances,

which we copy from the manuscript minutes of Backus, was also read at this meeting and approved: —

"Whereas, complaints of oppressions occasioned by a non-conformity to the religious establishment in New England have been brought to this Association; and whereas the laws obtained for preventing and redressing such oppressions have, upon trial, been found insufficient (either through defect in the laws themselves or iniquity in the execution thereof); and whereas humble remonstrances and petitions have not been duly regarded, but the same oppressive measures continue; This is to inform all the oppressed Baptists in New England that the Association of Warren (in conjunction with the Western or Philadelphia Association) is determined to seek remedy for their brethren where a speedy and effectual one may be had. In order to pursue this resolution by petition and memorial, the following gentlemen are appointed to receive well-attested grievances, to be by them transmitted to the Rev. Samuel Stillman of Boston; namely, Rev. Hezekiah Smith of Haverhill, Rev. Isaac Backus of Middleborough, Mr. Richard Montague of Sunderland, Rev. Joseph Meacham of Enfield, and Rev. Thomas Whitman of Groton in Connecticut."

The efforts put forth by the Baptists in behalf of civil and religious freedom, through the agency of the Warren Association, will be further illustrated in successive chapters of our present work. Those who may wish to consult fuller and more detailed accounts, are referred to Backus's Church History of New England, and especially to Prof. Hovey's Memoir of the Life and Times of Backus.

Gradually the Association won the confidence of the denomination, until in a few years it had extended over New England. By its means mutual acquaintance and harmony were promoted; the weak and the oppressed were relieved; errors in doctrine and in practice were exposed and guarded against; warnings against false teachers in religion were published; feeble and destitute flocks were provided with preachers; the college was materially aided and strengthened; students were encouraged to study for the ministry, and the gospel was preached in the wilderness. During the period of the Revolution it presented able addresses in behalf of civil and religious freedom to the Governments of Massachusetts and Connecticut, and to the Continental Congress. Although, says Arnold, in his History of Rhode Island, it no longer has that intimate connection with the University which at first existed, and the growth of Baptist churches in New England has given rise to numerous other associations of a similar character, the parent body still continues to exert a widespread and beneficent influence over the objects of its charge.

The Minutes[1] of the Association show that Manning, during the whole period of his connection with it, was one of its most prominent and useful members. By his counsels and personal influence he first called it into being. As has already been stated, he drew up the plan of its organization. In the years 1776, 1781, 1784, and 1787, he presided over its deliberations as moderator. In 1778 and in 1787 he preached the introductory sermon. In 1785 he made the opening prayer. From year to year we find his name on various important committees. He was likewise prominent as a member of the Philadelphia Association, rarely failing, especially during the latter part of his life, to attend its sessions, although thereby subjected to great

[1] The manuscript minutes of the first four meetings of the Warren Association are among the Backus papers, from which they have been carefully copied by the Rev. Silas Hall, a graduate of the college in the class of 1809. To his kindness in placing them at our disposal we are greatly indebted. The Minutes were first printed in the year 1771, since which time they have been published without interruption down to the present date. A set, including the aforesaid manuscript minutes, from the meeting of the Association in 1767 down to the present time, is in our possession. The years 1773, 1780, and 1783 are copied from a set in the possession of Mr. John Carter Brown; otherwise it is complete.

trouble, expense, and loss of time. He was once clerk, twice moderator, and three times the preacher at its annual meetings. We close this portion of our narrative with the following circular letter, presented by him to the Warren Association, and by them adopted, at its third meeting in 1769. It affords a happy illustration of the author's temper and spirit, and of his peculiar fitness to guide and instruct his brethren.

CIRCULAR LETTER BY MANNING.

The Elders and Messengers of several churches belonging to the Association, met in Warren, in the Colony of Rhode Island, etc. To the several churches they represent, greeting.

Dear Brethren : — We have had the pleasure of meeting your representatives at the Association, who in general have brought us good news from the churches. We rejoice to see that the Son of man is pleased to walk in the midst of his golden candlesticks, the churches, to dispense his blessings to his people, and to attend the word of the kingdom with divine power to the salvation of sinners. Come! help us to magnify the Lord for his unspeakable mercy and goodness! Yet we find that the enemies of truth are busily employed in endeavoring to subvert it, and in vexing and oppressing those who stand up for the cause of God. Brethren, we sympathize with you under your afflictions, while we call to mind the declaration of your ascended Head to his beloved flock whom he left behind, — *In the world ye shall have tribulation.* Yet how refreshing is what follows, — *But be of good cheer, I have overcome the world.* Those who live godly in Christ Jesus shall suffer persecution. Let not the powers of the world, who set themselves to oppose, discourage you. Search for the mind of Christ in his word; which being discovered, pay a sacred regard thereto. Call no man master on earth; and remember that the followers of Christ carry their cross in imitation of their Divine Master. Brethren, suffer us, however, to beseech you to use all proper means to obtain relief from the burdens imposed upon you, by taking heed to the general plan which we as a body propose to pursue. But while you attend to human means, let your cries be incessant to Him who hears and who will redress the cries of the oppressed. Pray for those who despitefully use you. Remember that love enters deeply into the spirit of our holy religion; and that the glorious Founder thereof has given us the most striking example of it in living and dying for his enemies. Walk soberly and inoffensively toward those without; and let your conduct prove that it is the power of truth, the force of conscience, that makes you Baptists, and not an affectation of singularity. And as you are persuaded that you have been taught by the Spirit of God, so let your light shine before others that you may win them to the truth. In the meantime, carefully guard against any designs to ensnare you, or to engage you in any combination with them that may eventually prove to the detriment of the cause.

Finally, may the Lord Jesus afford you his presence, and bless you with abundant increase in all grace, to the glory of his great name.

Signed by order and in behalf of the Association.

HEZEKIAH SMITH, *Moderator.*
SAMUEL STILLMAN, *Clerk.*

The first letter from Manning, of which we have any knowledge, is the following, addressed to David Howell, a student about to graduate from the College of New Jersey: —

SIR: — I some time ago received a line from you by Mr. Stelle, in which you requested my advice relative to your destination when you have done with college. I was glad to find that you had not yet determined upon any place or employment, because I was desirous that you should make a visit to these parts before your settlement. But to give advice, without having some prospect of advantage, I should think imprudent; and indeed the matter is important, for if it should not succeed according to your wishes, you might entertain hard thoughts of me. However, at present it appears to me that you cannot do better than to visit Rhode Island. The success Mr. Stelle has met with encourages me. He has a Latin school in the town of Providence of nearly twenty scholars, and may have more if he finds himself able to manage them. I believe he gives good satisfaction, and is much esteemed by the gentlemen of the town. I thought when he came here that he would much more readily have found employ in Newport; and although the people there were for making the attempt, yet he chose first to see Providence, whither I accompanied him. They would not, however, consent that he should go back, but immediately employed him; so that if you are disposed to keep a school, I imagine one may easily be obtained in Newport. I would gladly invite you to come and live in my family, if the infant state of our college could promise you proper encouragement; but at present it is hardly to be expected, although in the revolution of a year it will doubtless need more help. Upon the whole, I think if I were in your circumstances, as near as I can judge, I should come; and I would advise you to see me before you engage anywhere. A taste for learning is greatly upon the increase in this colony. Mr. Stelle can give you a more particular account of matters in these parts, as he will be with you at Commencement; and if you can get your affairs in readiness, he will be your company over. After telling you my family is well, as also your friend Stites, etc., I bid you farewell, wishing you the best blessings of heaven, and that I may have the pleasure of waiting upon Mr. Howell at the house of

Sir, your humble servant,

JAMES MANNING.

WARREN, July 14, 1766.

Agreeably to President Manning's advice, Mr. Howell came to Warren, and was at once associated with him as tutor in the college. In 1769 he was appointed Professor of Mathematics and Natural Philosophy, which position he occupied until the breaking up of the college in consequence of the Revolutionary War. In addition to the regular studies of his professorship, he taught the French, German, and Hebrew languages. For thirty-four years he was Professor of Law, although he never delivered any lectures in connection with this department of instruction. He was fifty-two years a member of the Board of Fellows, and for many years was secretary of the corporation. He was thus intimately connected with the college during a large portion of his protracted life. On several occasions, after President Manning's decease, he presided at the college Commencements, and delivered to the graduating classes Baccalaureate addresses, which were greatly admired. He practised law in Providence for many years, and was regarded as the leading member of the Rhode Island bar. Under the Confederation, he was a member of Congress, and he subsequently filled, with great ability, several high offices, civil and judicial. In 1812, he was appointed United States Judge for the District of Rhode Island, and this office he sustained until his death, in 1824. "Judge Howell," says Prof. Goddard, "was endowed with extraordinary talents, and he superadded to his endowments extensive and accurate learning. As an able jurist, he established for himself a solid reputation. He was, however, yet more distinguished as a keen and brilliant wit, and as a scholar extensively acquainted not only with the ancient, but with several of the modern languages. As a pungent and effective political writer, he was almost unrivalled; and in conversation, whatever chanced to be the theme, whether politics or law, literature or theology, grammar or criticism, a Greek tragedy or a difficult problem in mathematics, he was never found wanting. Upon all occasions which made any demands upon him, he gave the most convincing evidence of the vigor of his powers, and of the variety and extent of his erudition." To all this may be added extraordinary physical powers, and a majestic, dignified presence. Such was the intimate friend and early academical associate of Manning.

The first Commencement of the college was held in the meeting-house at Warren, on the 7th of September, 1769. Four years had elapsed since the President, with a solitary pupil,[1] commenced his collegiate duties as an instructor.

[1] It is stated that the Rev. Dr. William Rogers, of Philadelphia, was the first, and for several days the only student of Rhode Island College. He was then a mere lad of fourteen. Indeed, the entire Freshman Class of 1765-6 consisted of but three students.

Through toils, and difficulties, and opposition, he had quietly persevered in his work, until the seminary under his care had won its way to public favor. And now his first pupils were about to take their Bachelor's degree in the Arts, and to go forth to the duties of life. They were young men of promise. Some of them were destined to fill conspicuous places in the approaching struggle for independence; others were to be leaders in the church, and distinguished educators of youth. Probably no class that has gone forth from the University, in her palmiest days of prosperity, has exerted so widely extended and beneficial an influence, the times and circumstances taken into consideration, as this first class of seven that graduated at Warren. The occasion drew together a large concourse of people from all parts of the colony, inaugurating the earliest State holiday in the history of Rhode Island. "And as each recurring anniversary of this time-honored institution of learning calls together from distant places the widely-scattered alumni of Brown University, we do but renew, on a more extended scale, the congratulations that crowned this earliest festival."[1] The performances of the day excited universal admiration. "We can readily imagine," says a writer,[2] "how the beautiful and benevolent face of President Manning was radiant with smiles on this occasion; with what joy he beheld the first fruits of his anxieties, and labors, and prayers; with what glowing eloquence he poured forth, at the throne of grace, the pious effusions of a grateful heart, invoking the blessing of God upon the future efforts of the friends of the infant

[1] Arnold's History of Rhode Island, Vol. II. p. 299.

[2] Hon. John Pitman, LL. D. See Address to the Alumni Association of Brown University, delivered at Providence at their first Anniversary, Sept. 5, 1843.

institution, and filling every heart with emotion, if not every eye with tears, as, with the affection of a friend and the solicitude of a father, he commended to the care of Heaven those who were about to depart from him, and, at a period of no ordinary moment, to enter a world of temptation and trial."

The following account of this "first Commencement," taken from *The Providence Gazette and Country Journal*, needs no apology for its insertion here. It will be read with special interest by those who have attended the commencements of a later day.

FIRST COMMENCEMENT. 1769.

On Thursday, the seventh of this instant, was celebrated at Warren the first Commencement in the college of this colony; when the following young gentlemen commenced Bachelors of Arts; namely, Joseph Belton, Joseph Eaton, William Rogers, Richard Stites, Charles Thompson, James Mitchel Varnum, and William Williams.

About ten o'clock, A. M., the gentlemen concerned in conducting the affairs of the college, together with the candidates, went in procession to the meeting-house.

After they had taken their seats respectively, and the audience were composed, the President introduced the business of the day with prayer; then followed a salutatory oration in Latin, pronounced with much spirit, by Mr. Stites, which procured him great applause from the learned part of the assembly. He spoke upon the advantages of liberty and learning, and their mutual dependence upon each other; concluding with proper salutations to the Chancellor of the college, Governor of the colony, etc., particularly expressing the gratitude of all the friends of the college to the Rev. Morgan Edwards, who has encountered many difficulties in going to Europe to collect donations for the institution, and has lately returned.

To which succeeded a forensic dispute, in English, on the following thesis; namely, "The Americans, in their present circumstances, cannot, consistent with good policy, affect to become an Independent State." Mr. Varnum ingeniously defended it, by cogent arguments handsomely dressed;

though he was subtly but delicately opposed by Mr. Williams; both of whom spoke with emphasis and propriety.

As a conclusion to the exercises of the forenoon, the audience were agreeably entertained with an oration on benevolence, by Mr. Rogers; in which, among many other pertinent observations, he particularly noticed the necessity which that infant seminary stands in of the salutary effects of that truly Christian virtue.

At three o'clock, P. M., the audience being convened, a syllogistic dispute was introduced on this thesis: "*Materia cogitare non potest,*"—Mr. Williams the respondent; Messieurs Belton, Eaton, Rogers, and Varnum the opponents, — in the course of which dispute, the principal arguments on both sides were produced towards settling that critical point.

The degree of Bachelor of Arts was then conferred on the candidates. Then the following gentlemen (graduated in other colleges) at their own request received the honorary degree of Master in the Arts; namely, Rev. Edward Upham, Rev. Morgan Edwards, Rev. Samuel Stillman, Rev. Hezekiah Smith, Hon. Joseph Wanton Jun. Esq., Mr. Jabez Bowen, and Mr. David Howell, Professor of Philosophy in said college.

The following gentlemen, being well recommended by the Faculty for literary merit, had conferred on them the honorary degree of Master in the Arts; namely, Rev. Abel Morgan, Rev. Oliver Hart, Rev. David Thomas, Rev. Samuel Jones, Mr. John Davis, Mr. Robert Strettle Jones, Mr. John Stites, Rev. James Bryson, Rev. James Edwards, Rev. William Boulton, Rev. John Ryland, Rev. William Clark, Rev. Joshua Toulmin, and Rev. Caleb Evans.

A concise, pertinent, and solemn charge was then given to the Bachelors by the President, concluding with his last paternal benediction, which naturally introduced the valedictory orator, Mr. Thompson, who, after some remarks upon the excellences of the oratorial art, and expressions of gratitude to the patrons and officers of the college, together with a valediction to them, and all present, took a most affectionate leave of his classmates. The scene was tender, the subject felt, and the audience affected.

The President concluded the exercises with prayer. The whole was conducted with a propriety and solemnity suitable to the occasion. The audience (consisting of the principal gentlemen and ladies of this colony, and many from the neighboring governments), though large and crowded, behaved with the utmost decorum.

In the evening, the Rev. Morgan Edwards, by particular request, preached a sermon,[1] especially addressed to the graduates and students, from Phil. iii. 8: "Yea, doubtless, and I count all things but loss for the excellency of the knowledge of Christ Jesus my Lord;" in which (after high encomiums on the liberal arts and sciences) the superior knowledge of the knowledge of Christ, or the Christian science, was clearly and fully illustrated in several striking examples and similes; one of which follows: "When the sun is below the horizon, the stars excel in glory; but when his orb irradiates our hemisphere, their glory dwindles, fades away, and disappears."

Not only the candidates, but even the President, were dressed in American manufactures. Finally, be it observed, that this class are the first sons of that college which has existed for more than four years; during all which time it has labored under great disadvantages, notwithstanding the warm patronage and encouragement of many worthy men of fortune and benevolence; and it is hoped, from the disposition which many discovered on that day, and other favorable circumstances, that these disadvantages will soon, in part, be happily removed.

Mr. Edwards, to whose labors in behalf of the college we have already referred, set out for Europe in February, 1767, and returned in 1769, having been absent about two years. The amount which he obtained, and which was afterwards invested in a permanent fund for the payment of the President's salary, was £888 10s. 2d. sterling. This was truly a noble benefaction, considering the value of money at that period, and greatly encouraged the friends of the institution. The original subscription-book, containing the names of the subscribers in their own hand-writing, was presented to the Library in the year 1849, by Mr. Joshua Edwards, a son of the Rev. Morgan Edwards. He was then living, being at the time upwards of eighty years of

[1] The custom, thus inaugurated by Morgan Edwards, of having a sermon preached on Commencement occasions, was continued down to the beginning of Dr. Wayland's administration in 1828, when the "President's Levee" took the place of the "Commencement Sermon." The usual preachers on these occasions, were Drs. Stillman and Smith, and, in later years, Dr. Baldwin.

age. Among the subscribers thus obtained to the first funds of the college, we notice the names of our own countrymen, Benjamin Franklin and Benjamin West, both residing in London at this time; Thomas Llewelyn, LL.D., the distinguished Cambro-British scholar; Samuel Roffey, Esq., whose name appears upon the earliest records of the corporation as a benefactor of the college; Rev. Dr. Samuel Stennett; Thomas Penn; Rev. Dr. A. Gifford, for many years sub-librarian at the British Museum; Thomas Hollis and Timothy Hollis, the well-known benefactors of Harvard College; and Rev. Dr. Gill, author of "Exposition of the Old and New Testaments," a work published in nine folio volumes.

Mr. Edwards, speaking a few years afterwards of these his efforts to collect funds for the college, says that he "succeeded pretty well, considering how angry the mother country then was with the colonies for opposing the Stamp Act."

The following brief biographies of several members of the class, who more particularly distinguished themselves in public life, may very appropriately close this chapter.

WILLIAM ROGERS.

If, among her "first fruits," Trinity College of Dublin may boast of her Archbishop Usher, and Harvard University of her Dr. Woodbridge, Brown University may, with equal reason and propriety, boast of her Dr. Rogers, as the first student who enrolled his name upon her records, and as one whose character and life reflect the highest honor alike upon his revered instructor and the institution over which he presided.

William, the second son of Capt. William and Sarah

Rogers, was born in Newport, R. I., on the 22d of July, 1751. Having finished a preparatory course of study under the care of the Rev. Aaron Hutchinson, a Congregational minister of Grafton, Mass., he, at the early age of fourteen, entered Rhode Island College, over which Dr. Manning had just been appointed President. In the year 1770, while engaged in teaching in his native city, he became personally interested in religion, and was baptized by the Rev. Gardner Thurston, and received as a member of the Second Baptist Church, by prayer and the imposition of hands. This latter fact is mentioned, as an illustration of the views that prevailed in many of the Rhode Island churches in reference to this point. Soon afterwards, he removed from his native city to Philadelphia, where, on the 31st of May, 1772, he was ordained pastor of the Baptist church. The sermon on the occasion was preached by the Rev. Isaac Eaton, from the words, "And who is sufficient for these things?" It proved to be the last sermon that Mr. Eaton ever preached, while the text was the basis of Mr. Rogers' first discourse. During the three years that Mr. Rogers continued his pastoral relations, the church appears to have been greatly prospered, and the congregation largely increased. Among his hearers, whom his eloquence attracted, was the celebrated Dr. Rush, who afterwards, it is stated, became an adherent of the Rev. Elhanan Winchester.

During the war of the Revolution, Dr. Rogers held important offices, as chaplain of the forces appointed by Pennsylvania for the defence of the State, and also as chaplain of a brigade in the Continental army. His relations with the prominent actors of the Revolution were intimate, and he enjoyed in a high degree the confidence and esteem of the commanding general. He was an honored member of the Masonic fraternity, and frequently addressed them on public occasions. In the year 1789, he was appointed Professor of Oratory and Belles-lettres in the College and Academy of Philadelphia, and in 1792 he was elected to the same office in the University of Pennsylvania. His last years were spent in dignified retirement, and in the cultivation of pious and devout feelings. He died in Philadelphia, April 7, 1824, universally beloved and lamented. As an instance of the general estimation in which he was held as a preacher, it may be stated, that, at one time, during the year 1782, he received invitations from three very important churches, and of as many different denominations, in the States of Rhode Island, Connecticut, and Maryland, either to supply the pulpit steadily, or to settle as pastor. One of these invitations was from the Episcopal church of St. John's in Providence. The invitation was given, of course, with a proviso, as will be seen by a reference to Updike's History of the Narraganset Church.

A fine picture of Dr. Rogers, executed by his only surviving daughter, Miss Eliza J. Rogers, has recently been added to the collection of portraits in Rhode Island Hall. It is copied from an original portrait by Rembrandt Peale, taken in the year 1795, when the subject was in the prime and vigor of life.

In Evans's Life of Richards occurs the following pleasant account of Dr. Rogers, as given by an English gentleman, in a letter dated New York, June 25, 1793. The writer was travelling through the country with a view to final settlement. The extract serves to illustrate Rogers's social character, and also gives an agreeable view of Gen. Washington in his private relations.

"After travelling through an extreme pleasant country, we arrived at Philadelphia, and waited on Dr. Rogers. Dr. Rogers is a most entertaining and agreeable man, and received your letter with much pleasure. We were with him a great part of the time we remained in the city, and were introduced by him to Gen. Washington. The *General* was not at home when we called, but, while we were talking with his private secretary in the hall, he came in, and spoke to Dr. Rogers with the greatest ease and familiarity. He immediately asked us up into the drawing-room, where was *Lady Washington and his two nieces.* When we were seated, *the General* called for wine and cake, of which we partook, he drinking our 'health, and wishing us success in all our undertakings.' *The General* asked us a number of questions respecting the situation of things in Europe, to all which we answered, you may be sure, in our best manner. It is his general custom to say little; but on this occasion we understood he was more than usually talkative. He made one remark, which, under the circumstances in which it was delivered, has a peculiar energy, —'that we had chosen a *happy country,* and *one large* enough!' After sitting about half an hour, we retired, highly gratified with having conversed with the *first* character of *the age.*"

Dr. Rogers was of the middle size, and in his habits and manners was more than ordinarily refined. In seasons of relaxation, he was agreeably facetious. He was very active, and walked with the agility of youth, until within a few weeks of his decease. The light and beauty of his character were especially manifest in the circle of his family, by the members of whom he was almost worshipped. He was twice married. His first wife, a daughter of William Gardner, of Philadelphia, died Oct. 10, 1793, of the yellow fever, at that time prevalent. The following extract from a letter dated Philadelphia, Dec. 9, 1793, and addressed to the Rev. William Button, of London, is in reference to this event. The letter, with an engraved likeness of the author, was first published in London, in the *New Baptist Magazine* for 1825.

Before this reaches you, you will probably have heard of the irreparable loss I have met with in the death of my dear and lovely Mrs. Rogers. She died during the prevalence of the awful epidemic with which our city was lately visited. I enclose you a paper which contains a short account of her exit. It is needless for me to enlarge on this mournful visitation, having by the William Penn, which sailed ten or twelve days ago, forwarded for Dr. Rippon's *Register* a concise narrative of her life and bodily dissolution. Suffice it to say, that as she lived, so she died, a uniform and sincere Christian. But oh! my rebellious heart cannot yet submit. Dear brother, pray for me, that while I mourn, I may not murmur. Had you known her worth, you would not blame me. She was — I must desist; my swelling breast forbids my proceeding. I am a poor lonely creature! The week following her decease, I was taken down with the fever myself, and anticipated a speedy and eternal union with my dear departed wife, and other saints in glory. The dark valley began to assume the appearance of a flowered path; but, contrary to my own and the expectations of all my neighbors and attendants, I was summoned back into life; being snatched, as it were, from the very brink of the grave. Jehovah grant that my future days may be more zealously devoted to the service of our Redeemer Jesus than my past has ever been. My only son, who was my constant nurse by day and night, providentially escaped the dire contagion; so that your afflicted brother can and ought to sing of mercy as well as of judgment.

Wishing you, Mrs. Button, and the whole family, health and happiness,

I subscribe myself, reverend and dear sir,

Your afflicted brother,

WILLIAM ROGERS.

On the 15th of Jan., 1795, he was married to Susannah Marsh, daughter of Joseph Marsh, of Philadelphia. The following letter to his friend, the Rev. Dr. Hezekiah Smith, refers to his second marriage, and also to the death of the Rev. Morgan Edwards, whose funeral sermon he published by special request: —

PHILADELPHIA, April 14, 1795.

REVEREND AND DEAR SIR:

A combination of causes has prevented my addressing you for some time past. It is with pleasure that I once more resume my pen to inform you of my welfare, etc.

Your favors of April 13 and Aug. 22 last were duly received, for both of which accept my thanks. You complain of my not writing to you. On this head I have only to say, that, previous to your two last, you were in my debt; and as you do not mention a small packet I sent you, I am very fearful that it miscarried. Before this, I dare say, you have heard of my having once more formed a matrimonial connection. My present wife, like my former one, is a good religious Baptist. She is a worthy member of our church, and peculiarly well calculated, should God spare her life, of rendering me much assistance, both in my temporal and spiritual progress. You see by this that I have married in the Lord. Our union took place on the 15th of January; and we join in soliciting an interest in your prayers. She is at present confined with an intermitting fever, though much better to-day than she was yesterday. You must also have heard of the death of the Rev. Morgan Edwards. He died Jan. 28. At his own request I preached his funeral sermon, from 2 Cor. vi. 8. The congregation was numerous and attentive.

We are at peace in our church and congregation, but there is nothing remarkable among us of a religious kind. Yet we are not without encouragement. There is considerable solemnity in our place of public worship, and a few instances of serious inquirers. The French go on gloriously. Surely the Lord will in his own appointed time shower grace upon his people universally, and build up the walls of his Jerusalem.

I must conclude, but not without assuring you that my most fervent supplications shall not cease for the preservation and long continuance of your valuable life. My son, through mercy, is well. Mrs. Rogers joins in affectionate regards to self and dear Mrs. Smith.

Yours, in a precious Saviour,

WILLIAM ROGERS.

JAMES MITCHELL VARNUM.

Hon. James Mitchell Varnum was born in Dracut, Mass., in the year 1749. At the time of his graduation he was twenty years of age. While a student he developed a remarkable capacity for learning, and, although somewhat dissipated in his habits, made liberal acquisitions in general knowledge and literature. He was especially attached to mathematical science, and delighted in its pursuit. After leaving college he taught a classical school, and to this period of his life he ever afterwards referred as a season of special benefit. In the year 1771 he was admitted to the bar, having studied law in the office of Oliver Arnold, Esq., then the Attorney General of the colony. Soon afterwards he established himself in the town of East Greenwich, where he rapidly rose to distinction in his profession ; his great talents securing for him an extensive practice. The following extract from the "Memoirs of Elkanah Watson, or Men and Times of the Revolution," presents a pleasing description of his powers of eloquence at this period: —

"Mr. Varnum was one of the most eminent lawyers and distinguished orators in the colonies. I first saw this learned and amiable man in 1774, when I heard him deliver a Masonic oration. Until that moment I had formed no conception of the power and charms of oratory. I was so deeply impressed, that the effect of his splendid exhibition has remained for forty-eight years indelibly fixed upon my mind. I then compared his mind to a beautiful parterre, from which he was enabled to pluck the most gorgeous and fanciful flowers, in his progress, to enrich and embellish his subject. Lavater would have pronounced him an orator, from the vivid flashing of his eye and the delicate beauty of his classic mouth."

Mr. Varnum had a decided taste for military life, and in 1774 was appointed commander of the "Kentish Guards," a company which, from their acquirements in military tactics, became the nursery of many distinguished officers during the Revolutionary War. Among them may be mentioned Major Whitmarsh, Col. Christopher Greene, and Rhode Island's greatest general, Nathanael Greene, who was second only to Washington. The prominent part which Varnum had taken in the colonial controversy induced him, upon the breaking out of hostilities, to offer his services to the Government. He was at first a colonel in the American army, but in Feb., 1777, Congress promoted him to the rank of brigadier-general. He continued in the army several years, and saw some service, commanding a brigade in Sullivan's expedition on Rhode Island. He was a good disciplinarian, and invaluable in council. He wielded a vigorous pen, commanding a rich flow of eloquence, embellished by the ornaments and graces of rhetoric.

While in command at Taunton, he addressed an admirable letter to the chief officer of the Hessians in Rhode Island, and sent it in by a flag. The letter was a transcript of his views on the great controversy with England, and was considered an able argument on the subject. It was subsequently published in England, and reflected much credit on the author. In 1779 he resigned his commission, and returned to his former profession. The Legislature, in consideration of his national services, and the more effectually to secure them in defence of the State, elected him Major-General of the Militia of Rhode Island, an office to which he was annually reëlected during the remainder of his life. In 1780 he was appointed a delegate to the Congress of the Confederation, and again in 1786. As that body sat with closed doors, his voice could not be heard by the public; but his name often appears in the published journals of the proceedings.

The great forensic effort of Gen. Varnum was in the celebrated case of Trevett against Weeden, in the fall of the year 1786. The General Assembly, at its May session, with a wilful blindness unparalleled in the annals of civilization, had emitted the enormous sum of £100.000 in paper bills, making them "a good and lawful tender for the complete payment and final discharge of all fines, forfeitures, judgments, and executions of every kind and nature whatsoever." They also passed acts making it criminal to refuse said bills in exchange for articles of merchandise, and depriving their opponents of the sacred palladium of Britons, the trial by jury, and furthermore rendering them, even though freemen, ineligible to any office. In the case referred to, John Trevett, of Newport, had purchased meat of John Weeden, a butcher, and tendered to him bills of the emission of the May session of the Legislature in payment; which bills Weeden refused. Whereupon a complaint was made and filed, in accordance with the acts of the General Assembly, before Paul Mumford, Chief Justice of the Supreme Court. The court consisted of Paul Mumford, Chief Justice, and Joseph Hazard, Thomas Tillinghast, and David Howell, associates. When the case came up for trial, the whole public was in a state of feverish excitement. The merchant closed his store, the farmers left their fields, the mechanic his workship, and all congregated in and around the courthouse to await the final issue. If the complaint was sustained, then would they be prostrated in utter ruin, and the commerce and business of the State be effectually destroyed. Varnum proved himself equal to this emergency. By his resistless eloquence he stemmed the tide of power and misrule, and successfully vindicated the claims of equity and justice. The court adjudged that the amended acts of the Legislature were unconstitutional, and so void. The tyranny of the demagogues was thus overthrown, and the State was saved.

In the year 1787, Gen. Varnum was appointed by Congress one of the judges of the Northwestern Territory, and in the following spring entered upon his duties. But disease had enfeebled his body, and his race was nearly run.

He died at Marietta, Ohio, on the 10th of January, 1789, at the early age of forty. His funeral was conducted with great solemnity and respect. A long procession of mourners — private citizens, civil and military officers, gentlemen of the Order of Cincinnati, and Free Masons — followed his remains to the grave.

Early in life Gen. Varnum married Martha, the eldest daughter of Cromel Child, of Warren, a most estimable lady, whose acquaintance he had formed while prosecuting his college studies. She survived her husband forty-eight years, dying at Bristol, without issue, Oct. 10, 1837, at the advanced age of eighty-eight. The following affectionate and interesting letter, addressed to Mrs. Varnum in the autumn of 1788, shows the religious views and feelings of the writer in a pleasing light, and affords good evidence that he died in the full assurance of a blessed immortality, notwithstanding the sceptical and philosophical opinions in which he had previously indulged. The letter was first published in the *Massachusetts Magazine* for November, 1790, with the following note from the author's friend and early instructor prefixed: —

TO THE EDITORS, etc.:

GENTLEMEN: — From a full conviction that the enclosed letter from the late Gen. Varnum to his most amiable lady (written a few days before his departure from this distempered state of being) will give pleasure to every feeling heart, I have obtained leave to present it to your numerous readers.

I am, with respectful esteem, yours, etc.,

JAMES MANNING.

MY DEAREST AND MOST ESTIMABLE FRIEND:

I now write from my sick-chamber; and perhaps it will be the last letter that you will receive from me. My lungs are so far affected that it is impossible for me to recover but by exchange of air and a warmer climate. I expect to leave this place on Sunday or Monday next for the Falls of the Ohio. If I feel myself mend by the tour, I shall go no further; but if not, and if my health should continue, I expect to proceed to New Orleans, and from thence by the West Indies to Rhode Island. My physicians, most of them, think the chances of recovery in my favor. However, I am neither elevated nor depressed by the force of opinion, but shall meet my fate with humility and fortitude.

I cannot but indulge the hope that I shall again embrace my lovely friend in this world, and that we may glide smoothly down the tide of time for a few years, and enjoy together the more substantial happiness and satisfaction, as we have had already the desirable pleasures, of life.

It is now almost nineteen years since Heaven connected us by the tenderest and the most sacred ties, and it is the same length of time that our friendship hath been increased by every rational and endearing motive; it is now stronger than death, and I am firmly persuaded will follow us into an existence of never-ending felicity. But, my lovely friend, the gloomy moment will arrive when we must part; and should it arrive during our present separation, my last and only reluctant thoughts will be employed about my dearest Martha. Life, my dearest friend, is but a bubble: it soon bursts, and is remitted to eternity. When we look back to the earliest recollections of our youthful hours, it seems but the last period of our rest, and we appear to emerge from a night of slumbers to look forward to real existence. When we look forward, time appears as indeterminate as eternity, and we have no idea of its termination but by the period of our dissolution. What particular relation it bears to a future state, our general notions of religion cannot point. We feel something constantly active within us, that is evidently beyond the reach of mortality; but whether it is a part of ourselves, or an emanation from the pure Source of existence, or reabsorbed when death shall have finished his work, human wisdom cannot determine; whether the demolition of the body introduces only a change in the manner of our being, or leaves it to progress infinitely, alternatively elevated and depressed according to the propriety of our conduct, or whether we return to the common mass of unthinking matter, philosophy hesitates to decide.

I know, therefore, but one source from whence can be derived complete consolation in a dying hour, and that is the divine system contained in the gospel of Jesus Christ. There life and immortality are brought to light, — there we are taught our existence is to be eternal; and, secure in an interest in the atoning merits of a bleeding Saviour, that we shall be inconceivably happy. A firm and unshaken faith in this doctrine must raise us above the doubts and fears that hang upon every other system, and enable us to view with a calm serenity the approach of the king of terrors, and to behold him as a kind and indulgent friend, spending his shafts only to carry us the sooner to our everlasting home. But should there be a more extensive religion beyond the veil, and without the reach of mortal observation, the Christian religion is by no means shaken thereby, as it is not opposed to any principle that admits of the perfect benevolence of Deity. My only doubt is, whether the punishment threatened in the New Testament is annexed to a state of unbelief which may be removed hereafter, and so restoration take place, or whether the state of the mind at death irretrievably fixes its doom forever. I hope and pray that the Divine Spirit will give me such assurances of an acceptance with God, through the merits and sufferings of his Son, as to brighten the way to immediate happiness.

Dry up your tears, my charming mourner, nor suffer this letter to give too much inquietude. Consider the facts at present as in theory, but the sentiments such as will apply whenever the change shall come.

I know that humanity must and will be indulged in its keenest grief; but there is no advantage in too deeply anticipating our inevitable sorrows. If I did not persuade myself that you would conduct with becoming prudence and fortitude upon this occasion, my own unhappiness would be greatly increased, and perhaps my disorder too; but I have so much confidence in your discretion as to unbosom my inmost soul.

You must not expect to hear from me again until the coming spring, as the river will soon be shut with ice, and there will be no communication from below; if in a situation for the purpose, I will return as soon as practicable.

Give my sincerest love to those you hold dear. I hope to see them again, and love them more than ever. Adieu, my dearest friend. And while I fervently devote in one undivided prayer our immortal souls to the care, forgiveness, mercy, and all-prevailing grace of Heaven, in time and through eternity, I must bid you a long, long, long farewell.

JAMES M. VARNUM.

CHARLES THOMPSON.

The Rev. Charles Thompson, valedictorian of the class, was born at Amwell, N. J., on the 14th of April, 1748. Before graduating he had already commenced preaching. Upon the removal of President Manning to Providence, the church at Warren were left without a minister, and Thompson was accordingly invited to preach to them with a view to settlement. The following year he was ordained as pastor of the church, being at this time twenty-three years of age. His labors in the ministry were attended with a rich blessing; so that during the four years of his continuance at Warren, the membership of the church was nearly doubled. But when the war of the Revolution broke out, its sad effects were specially visible among his people. He was at once appointed a chaplain in the American army, which office he held till 1778, a period of three years. While at home on a visit, the English troops came up to Warren, and on the morning of May 25, 1778, burned the meeting-house, parsonage, arsenal, and several private dwellings, and carried away Mr. Thompson as a prisoner. He was confined at Newport; but in about a month he was released, by what means he never knew. He afterwards preached at Ashford, Ct., until 1779, when he became pastor of the church in Swanzey. During his ministry of twenty-three years at this latter place, there were several extensive revivals of religion: one immediately after his settlement, when seventy-five persons were baptized and added to the church; one in 1789, when fifty persons were baptized; and a third in 1800, of still greater extent, which resulted in the admission to the church of a hundred new members. He died in Charlton, Worcester County, Mass., on the 4th of May 1803, at the age of fifty-five. Mr. Thompson, says his biographer, was tall, spare, and of a fine figure. The expression of his countenance was indicative both of a vigorous intellect and an amiable disposition. He placed a high value upon time, and improved all his hours to good purpose. In his family and in the church he was a model of kindness combined with firmness. As a preacher he held a very high rank. He had a voice of great compass, and its tones were at once sweet and commanding. His sermons were carefully studied, and were sometimes written; but his manuscript was never seen in the pulpit, and his language was generally such as was supplied to him at the moment. He was very successful in the instruction of youth, and for several years received young men under his care, with a view to direct their education. He was fully master of whatever he attempted to teach. In a word, he may be regarded as an accomplished scholar, a devout Christian, and a successful preacher. From the year 1795 until his death he was a Trustee of the college. The original manuscript of his valedictory oration is still carefully preserved among the archives of the college library.[1]

WILLIAM WILLIAMS.

The Rev. William Williams was born in Hilltown, Bucks County, Pa., in the year 1752. His father emigrated from Wales, and settled in this country as a farmer, accumulating a handsome property. The son was fitted for college at the Hopewell Academy, taught by the Rev. Isaac Eaton. He came to Warren in 1766, and entered the Sophomore Class. In the autumn following his graduation, he was married to Patience, daughter of Col. Nathan

[1] Sprague's Annals of the American Pulpit.

Miller, of Warren. In September, 1771, he was baptized by his classmate, Mr. Thompson, and received as a member of the church under his care. For several years after leaving college he engaged in teaching, — an employment for which his talents and inclinations especially qualified him. In 1773, he removed with his family to Wrentham, Mass., where he opened an academy, which soon attained to high distinction among the literary institutions of that day. He is supposed to have had under his care nearly two hundred youth, about eighty of whom he fitted for his Alma Mater. Not a few of these became distinguished in professional and political life; among whom may be mentioned the Rev. Dr. Maxcy, successor to Manning; the Hon. David R. Williams, Governor of South Carolina; and the Hon. Tristam Burgess, LL. D., Professor of Oratory and Belles-lettres in Brown University, and for many years a distinguished Representative in Congress. Mr. Williams also conducted the theological studies of young men with a view to their entering the ministry.[1] On the 3d of July, 1776, he was publicly ordained as pastor of the Baptist church in Wrentham, — an office which he held for nearly half a century. Though strictly evangelical in his doctrines, he was not regarded as a popular preacher. Quite a number of his early manuscript sermons are among the archives of the college library. They are written in a plain, legible hand, and exhibit marks of careful preparation. Mr. Williams, says his biographer, certainly had the ability to keep his church in a quiet, orderly state, and, by a steady course of enlightened Christian activity, to accomplish a great amount of good among his people. Few men have contributed more than he to the social and

[1] One of his pupils in theology was the lamented William Gammell of Newport, father of Professor William Gammell.

intellectual improvement of the Baptist denomination in New England. He died on the 22d of September, 1823, aged seventy-one. He was a Fellow of the college from 1789 to 1818. In 1777, when the college building was occupied by the army, the library was removed to Wrentham, and intrusted to his care and keeping. Mr. Williams was twice married. His first wife, as already stated, was a daughter of Col. Miller, Dr. Manning's colleague in Congress. In 1804 he was married to Mrs. Dolly Hancock, of Wrentham, daughter of a Mr. Titus. He was the father of seven children, several of whom still survive him.[1]

We append to the foregoing sketch a copy of Mr. Williams's "parchment," which the curious may wish to compare with the diplomas of the present day :—

Omnibus ad quos praesentes Literae pervenerint salutem. Notum sit quod Collegii in Anglicana Rhodiorum Providentiatiumque Colonia inter Nov. Anglos in America Sociorum Ordo Gulielmo Williams juveni probo et ingenuo, in omnibus Humanitatis Literarumque Studiis in nostra Academia instituto, et Examine sufficiente previo approbato Baccalaurei Gradum decrevit, publicis in Comitiis apud Warren in Colonia supradicta habitis Die Septimo Septembris Annoque Domini Millesimo Septingentessimo Sexagessimo Nono. In Cujus Rei Testimonium Sigillum Collegii huic Membranae affixum Nominaque nostra subscripta sunt.

JACOBUS MANNING, *Praeses.*
DAVID HOELL, *Phil. Professor.*
THOMAS EYRES, *Secretary.*

[1] Sprague's Annals of the American Pulpit.

HOPE COLLEGE, ERECTED 1822. MANNING HALL, ERECTED 1834. UNIVERSITY HALL, ERECTED 1770.

BROWN UNIVERSITY.

CHAPTER III.

1769–1770.

Erection of a College edifice, and place of location — Warren, East Greenwich, Newport, and Providence contend for the honor — Meeting of the Corporation at Newport in reference thereto — Final contest between Newport and Providence — Subscriptions in Newport — Final meeting of the Corporation on the question of location— Names of the thirty-five members present — Decision in favor of Providence — Letter to Rev. Hezekiah Smith giving a detailed account of this meeting — Proceedings of the Corporation with reference to Manning's removal to Providence — Comparison between Providence and Newport at this time — Attempt to establish another college, at Newport — Home-lot of Chad Brown selected for the location of the College — Plans of Nassau Hall, Princeton, adopted for the building — Corner-stone laid by John Brown — Manning sunders his connection with the church at Warren — His struggles of mind in regard to duty — Removes to Providence — Remarks of Prof. Goddard respecting his position at this time — Letter to Rev. Dr. Stennett, of London — Stennett's reply — Efforts of Rev. Hezekiah Smith to secure funds for the College, in South Carolina and Georgia — Letter from Rev. Oliver Hart in reference thereto — Account of the first Commencement in Providence — Letter to Thomas Lapham, of Smithfield, illustrating the early discipline of the College — Biographical Sketch of Rev. Isaac Backus — Sketch of Rev. Dr. Samuel Stillman —Sketch of Rev. Dr. Hezekiah Smith — Extracts from Smith's correspondence while in the Army — Influence of the Brown family upon the College — Biographical sketches of their Ancestors: I. Chad Brown; II. John Brown; III. James Brown; IV. James Brown — Biographical sketches of the "Four Brothers," Nicholas, Joseph, John, and Moses Brown — Transit of Venus — Destruction of the schooner Gaspee.

At the time of the Commencement at Warren, the college, says Edwards, "was for the most part friendless and moneyless, and therefore forlorn, insomuch that an edifice was hardly thought of. But frequent remittances being made from England, some began to hope, and many to fear that the institution would come to something, and stand.

Then a building and the place of it were talked of, which opened a new scene of troubles and contentions, that had well-nigh ruined all."

Warren was at first selected as a suitable place for the final location of the college, and a committee was appointed to purchase materials for an edifice, secure a lot, and solicit subscriptions. The church in Warren anticipating, perhaps, the action of the corporation, voted that "the meeting-house in this town be and is for the use of the corporation and President at Commencement times, and oftener, if wanted by either, only so as not to interfere with divine worship; provided, that the college edifice be founded and built in the county of Bristol; and that the parsonage-house in said Warren be for the use of the President, so long as the President be our minister."

But soon afterwards, continues Edwards, "some, who were unwilling it should be anywhere, did so far agree as to lay aside the said location, and propose that the county which should raise the most money should have the college."

Application having been made to the corporation by gentlemen from East Greenwich and vicinity, setting forth that they had opened a subscription for the college, on condition that the edifice be erected in the county of Kent, and requesting an opportunity for assigning their reasons why the vote of Sept. 7th, fixing the location at Warren should be reconsidered, a special meeting of the corporation was held at Newport, on the 14th of November, 1769.[1]

[1] Although no formal action in reference to a building and location was taken by the corporation until about this time, it appears from the following extract from Hezekiah Smith's Diary, that subscriptions were secured at an earlier period: —

"*Tuesday*, Sept. 3, 1765. Went to Newport, and stayed at Col. Bennet's till Saturday. Wednesday and Thursday I was with the corporation, which sat upon

At this meeting, which was adjourned from day to day, after a protracted discussion it was voted that the edifice be at Providence, unless within six weeks a larger subscription should be raised in Newport County, "superior to any now offered." The main contest was from this time between Providence and Newport. The friends of the college who desired its location in the latter place soon succeeded in obtaining a subscription amounting to about four thousand pounds, lawful money, being a larger subscription than any that had yet been obtained.[1] Accordingly a final meeting on the subject was held at Warren, on Wednesday, Feb. 7th, 1770.

the college business, and was elected one of the Fellows of the college. On Thursday, 5th, Mr. Manning was chosen President. We, although but part of the corporation, subscribed for the building and endowing the college nineteen hundred and ninety-two dollars."

[1] The following is the heading and preamble to this subscription, which we copy from an original paper. Among the largest subscribers on this occasion was Abraham Redwood, Esq., founder of the "Redwood Library." He afterwards subscribed, says the *Providence Gazette*, five hundred pounds sterling towards a second college or university, which it was proposed to erect in Newport.

SUBSCRIPTIONS FOR THE RHODE ISLAND COLLEGE.

Whereas the Governor and Company of the English Colony of Rhode Island and Providence Plantations, in New England in America, by an act passed at their session in Feb., 1764, incorporated certain persons, therein mentioned, into a body politic, and granted them full power and ample authority to found and endow a college or university in said colony: And whereas a sufficient number of the persons so appointed have qualified themselves agreeable to said act, and are taking the most probable measures for forming so useful and honorable an institution, which will necessarily be attended with considerable expense: We, therefore, the subscribers, sensible that nothing hath a greater tendency to adorn human nature and to promote the true interest and happiness of mankind than useful literature, and that the fixing the college in the town of Newport will be attended with the greatest advantages to the said institution, do, in consideration thereof, each one for himself, promise and engage to give, and accordingly to pay, unto Job Bennet, Esq., treasurer of the said corporation, or his successor in said office, or order, the several sums affixed to our names, respectively, to be applied primarily to the building a suitable college edifice, and the surplus in such a manner as the said corporation shall think most conducive to answer

10

Thirty-five members of the corporation were present; namely, *Trustees* (giving their names as they stand upon the records) — The Chancellor, Hon. Samuel Ward Esq., George Hazard Esq., Mr. Peleg Barker, Rev. Russell Mason, Mr. John Warner, Nicholas Brown Esq., Mr. Nathan Spear, Nicholas Cook Esq., Mr. Sylvester Childs, Hon. Josias Lyndon, Mr. John Tanner, Hon. Joseph Wanton Jr., Mr. Thomas Greene, Mr. Joseph Brown, Joseph Russell Esq., Ephraim Bowen Esq., Mr. Edward Thurston Jr., Mr. John G. Wanton, Rev. Gardner Thurston, Rev. Samuel Winsor, Rev. Isaac Backus, Daniel Jenckes Esq., Job Bennet Esq., James Helme Esq., Mr. William Brown, Rev. John Maxson, Darius Sessions Esq. — 28.

Fellows — The President, Rev. Edward Upham, Mr. Thomas Eyres, Joshua Babcock Esq., Rev. Samuel Stillman, Henry Ward Esq., Jabez Bowen Jr. Esq. — 7.

At this meeting subscriptions and securities were finally offered to the corporation, from the town and county of Newport, to the amount of £4558 14s., lawful money, the greater part being expressly conditioned that the college be placed in said town. From the town and county of Providence were offered subscriptions and securities amounting to £4399 13s. The final vote, as appears from the records, was as follows: —

" Whereas the corporation have fully heard committees from the counties of Newport, Kent, and Bristol, upon their application for a repeal of the vote of this corporation, on the 16th day of November last, for locating the college edifice in the town of Providence, and maturely considered the several sums offered, and all the arguments used by all the parties concerned, and thereupon the vote being put, Recede or Not, it passed in the negative — twenty-one votes to fourteen. It is therefore *Resolved,*

the ends of their institution. Provided, nevertheless, and this subscription is made upon express condition, that the college edifice be erected in the said town of Newport; otherwise the same shall be void.

That the said edifice be built in the town of Providence, and there be continued forever."

We have thus given a brief account of the location of the college, compiled mainly from the original records. The following letter from the President to the Rev. Hezekiah Smith, who was now collecting funds for the institution, in South Carolina and Georgia, gives a very animated account of this memorable meeting of the corporation: —

WARREN, Feb. 12, 1770.

REVEREND SIR: — Last week I received a letter from you of the 2d ult., in which you inform me of your success at Georgia, and your expectations from the South province. All your friends here rejoice that you succeed so well in getting the needful for the college. "Great luck to you," as said Mr. Francis in his prayer. I thought it strange that I had no letter by Capt. Durphee from you or Mr. Hart, as I wrote by him to you both. Last week I received a letter from Nelson, at Haverill, and he gives me a pleasing account of matters there. Had not his modesty forbid, I imagine he would have told me that the people were well suited with him. We had another meeting of the corporation last Wednesday, when there were thirty-five members present. They were called to consider proposals from Newport in favor of setting the edifice in that town, as they had raised by subscription £4000, lawful money,[1] taking in their unconditional subscription. But Providence presented £4280, lawful,[1] and advantages superior to Newport in other respects. The dispute lasted from Wednesday last, ten o'clock, A. M., until the same hour on Thursday, P. M. The matter was debated with great spirit, and before a crowded audience. The vote was put, Recede or Not? It went Not, by 21 against 14. You asked me in your last whether it had not raised a party in the government. I answer no; but it has warmed up the old one something considerable. I was greatly censured by people in Newport for not joining to call a meet-

[1] The reader will observe here a discrepancy between Manning's statement and the records. This we can only account for on the supposition that Manning presents, in a familiar way, the general aspect of the question at the commencement of the dispute, whereas the records give the final result. It is evident that other considerations besides those of a pecuniary character determined the location of the college.

ing about the first of January, and a great noise was made because I would not act contrary to an express vote of the corporation at the meeting on the 10th of November. But at our last meeting the house gave me liberty to attempt a vindication of my conduct, and after hearing me through in the matter, they came to a vote, *nemine contradicente*, that they saw no reason why I should be blamed in this matter, and that they approved of my conduct. In the course of the debates there was sometimes undue warmth, but, upon the whole, it subsided, and all parties seemed much more unanimous than I expected, in after business. Many of the gentlemen of Newport said they had had a fair hearing, and had lost it; but their friendship to the college remained, and they would keep their places, pay their money, and forward to their utmost the design. The college edifice is to be on the same plan as that of Princeton, built of brick, four stories high, and one hundred and fifty feet long. I wish I had a draught to send you, but it is not in my power. They determine to have the roof on next fall, and to cover it with slate, as they are now able. Now if we can get it endowed, we shall be *compos voti*. This I hope you will in part accomplish. I have thought of going to the Jerseys in the spring. If I should, I cannot go to Haverill the first of May; for I must consult my westward friends in a matter of so much consequence as moving or not moving with the college. If I go to the Jerseys, it will probably be about the middle of April. Religion is upon the revival in these parts. Messrs. Stillman and Spear were up from Boston, and Backus from Middleborough. It is said that the eight ministers at the corporation meeting were all for Providence. This I shall not assert, however. But I believe the Baptist society in general are not dissatisfied at the determination. I could tell you a long tale if I had time, but can only tell you that we have twenty-three scholars, eighteen of whom are matriculated. Mrs. Manning joins in love to you, Mr. and Mrs. Hart, etc., with, sir,

Your unworthy brother, and servant in the gospel,

JAMES MANNING.

At this meeting of the corporation it was also resolved:—

"That the Rev. Messrs. Edward Upham, Isaac Backus, Samuel Stillman, Gardner Thurston, John Maxson, Russell Mason, and Samuel Winsor, or any three of them, be a committee to wait upon Mr. President Manning, and inform him of the hearty approbation we have of his conduct, care, and government of the college, and request him still to sustain the office he hath discharged with so much honor, and to go with the college to

Providence when it shall be removed; and that they treat with the congregation of which the President is pastor, and inform them of this request, and endeavor to procure their consent to his removal; and that they report to the next corporation meeting."

This cautious delicacy, remarks Prof. Goddard, with which the corporation interfered with President Manning's existing relations, presents a somewhat grateful contrast to the unceremonious and otherwise questionable modes of procedure, which, under similar circumstances, are now sometimes adopted.

The final decision to locate the college at Providence, although a wise one, as the result has proved, seems nevertheless remarkable in view of the relative importance of the two rival candidates for the honor. Providence was then a town, with a population of less than four thousand, while Newport was the second city in New England, and the centre of opulence, refinement, and learning. In her extensive commerce and trade, her numerous manufactories, and her merchant princes, she excelled indeed all other cities in the American Colonies. As early as 1729, Bishop Berkley, in one of his letters to a friend in Dublin, described Newport "as the most thriving place in all America for bigness." The late Dr. Waterhouse, in a newspaper article published in 1824, thus writes: "The island of Rhode Island, from its salubrity and surpassing beauty, before the Revolutionary War so sadly defaced it, was the chosen resort of the rich, and philosophic, from nearly all parts of the civilized world." Among the arguments advanced in favor of Newport, was the advantage to be derived by the professors and students from the Redwood Library. This was at the time the second library in the country, containing about fifteen hundred choice books on the arts and sciences, and especially rich in classical and theological lore.

Providence, on the other hand, had no such literary advantages. But her situation was more convenient, and in case of any rupture with the British Government, of which there were strong probabilities at this time, she was much less exposed to an invasion or attack. Besides, here Roger Williams found his home and resting-place, and here was the centre of Baptist influence. Hence the "Baptist Society," as Manning designates the denomination at large, were not dissatisfied with the final action of the corporation. It will be observed that Providence, according to the records, offered a less amount in subscriptions and securities than her defeated rival.

One of the results of the location of this institution at Providence, was an application to the General Assembly, by another set of petitioners, for another college. At the February session, 1770, a charter for an academy and college, to be located in Newport, passed the lower house of the Assembly, by twenty majority. The application, says Judge Staples, was not favorably received in the upper house, where it was either rejected or indefinitely postponed.[1] The following action of the corporation, at a special meeting held in Warren on the 2d of April, is the probable explanation of the defeat of this project: —

"*Resolved,* That this corporation make application to the General Assembly, and pray that a petition now before the Assembly, for granting a charter to another college, be rejected."

"*Voted,* That the Chancellor, the President, Hon. Darius Sessions, Rev. Samuel Stillman, Col. Job Bennet, and the Secretary (Thomas Eyres), be a committee to draw a memorial to the General Assembly, pursuant to the preceding vote."

The said memorial or remonstrance having been prepared and approved, it was —

[1] Annals of Providence, p. 529.

"*Voted*, That the Hon. Stephen Hopkins, Hon. Samuel Ward, Hon. Darius Sessions, Job Bennet, Moses Brown, Daniel Jenckes, John Tillinghast, Oliver Arnold, and James Mitchell Varnum, be, and they or the major part of them are, appointed a committee to be present at the General Assembly, and enforce the said remonstrance."

The location of the edifice having thus been finally determined upon, the building committee prosecuted their labors with great energy and zeal. The lot selected for it comprised originally eight acres, including a portion of the "home-lot" of Chad Brown, the "first Baptist elder in Rhode Island." It was for this reason purchased by John and Moses Brown, and a deed of the same given by them to the corporation, that the college might stand on the original lot[1] of their pious ancestor. The plans which the

[1] This lot, extending from Main Street to Power Street, and also the home-lots of George Rickard and John Warner, which came into the possession of Chad Brown, descended, on the death of said Brown, to his eldest son, John, who, in 1672, gave a deed thereof to his brothers James and Jeremiah, reserving the family burial ground, situated a little west from the old Town House, on College Street. It was afterwards sold to Daniel Abbot, from whom it descended to his son Daniel, and from him, the middle part whereon University Hall now stands, to Samuel Fenner, of Cranston, a nephew of Abbot's wife. It was purchased of Fenner, in 1770, by John and Moses Brown, and by them sold to the corporation, for the sum of three hundred and thirty dollars, paid by a discount from their subscriptions, in order that the college "might stand on the original lot of the first Baptist elder in this State." (See papers of the late Moses Brown.)

The following extract from the Record of Deeds, Book 19, p. 108, will be interesting to the antiquarian. It presents a clear and accurate account of the southern half of the original college premises.

EXTRACT FROM DEED OF COLLEGE LOT.

"To all people to whom these presents shall come: We, John Brown and Moses Brown, both of Providence, in the County of Providence and Colony of Rhode Island and Providence Plantations, merchants, send *greeting*: — Know ye, that we, the said John and Moses Brown, for and in consideration of the sum of three hundred and thirty dollars, to us in hand already paid by the Trustees and Fellows of the college or university in the English Colony of Rhode Island and Providence Plantations, in New England in America, the receipt whereof, by a discount out of the sums we have severally subscribed to the college, we do

committee adopted for the building were, in the main, those of Nassau Hall, Princeton, which, as we have before remarked, was regarded as one of the finest structures in the country. They broke ground on Tuesday, the 27th day of March, 1770, and on the 14th day of May following, the

hereby acknowledge, have given, granted, bargained, sold, aliened, enfeoffed, conveyed, and confirmed, and by these presents do give, grant, sell, alien, convey, and confirm unto said Trustees and Fellows, and to their successors and assigns forever, one certain piece or parcel of land lying in the town of Providence, bounded . . . . . which said piece of land contains about four acres, and became the property of us, said Moses and John Brown, by a deed of bargain and sale from Samuel Fenner, of Cranston, who received it as one of the legatees of Daniel Abbott, Esq., late of said Providence, deceased, who received the northerly third part thereof from his father, Daniel Abbott, by descent, who purchased the same of James Brown, who received it of his brother John Brown, the present grantor's great-grandfather, who received it by descent from his father Chad Brown, who was one of the original proprietors after the native Indians of whom it was purchased, and is the middle part of that which was his houselot or home-share of land so called; the other two thirds being the middle part of the original houselot or home-share of George Rickard, since called John Warner's, which part was conveyed by the said Rickard to the said Chad Brown, from whom it descended to his aforesaid son John, who conveyed it to his brother Jeremiah Brown, who conveyed the same to the aforesaid Daniel Abbott the elder, from whom it descended to Daniel Abbott the younger, and became Samuel Fenner's as aforesaid: the whole of this piece of land making the southern half of the lot and highway leading to it whereon the college edifice is now erecting."

Signed Aug. 1st, 1770, by John Brown and his wife Sarah, Moses Brown and his wife Anna, and Stephen Hopkins, Chief Justice. Recorded Jan. 7, 1771, in book 19, page 108.

The northern half of the original college premises, consisting of about four acres of land, was purchased by the corporation, as per deed recorded in the aforesaid book, page 106, of Oliver Bowen, of Providence, one of the legatees of the aforesaid Daniel Abbott, Esq., for the sum of four hundred dollars. Mr. Abbott, says the record, "took it by descent from his father Daniel Abbott, who received two thirds part of it, being on the north side, from Robert Williams, by deed of gift, who purchased it by deed of bargain and sale of Robert Morrice, who purchased of Daniel Abbott the first, who was an original proprietor after the native Indians. The other third part the second named Daniel Abbott purchased by deed of bargain and sale from his brother John Brown, who took it by descent from his father Chad Brown." It will thus be seen that Chad Brown originally owned, or came into the possession of all the land which constituted he original college premises, with the exception of a small portion which at first belonged to Daniel Abbott.

corner-stone of what is now called University Hall was laid by John Brown. This stone is said by Mr. Howland to have been the first one laid in the foundation, at the bottom of the cellar wall, in the southwest corner of the building. Tradition adds that Mr. Brown, in accordance with the customs of the times, generously treated the crowd with punch, in honor of the joyful occasion.

Mr. Edwards describes the location selected by the committee as "remarkably airy, healthful, and pleasant; being the summit of a hill pretty easy of ascent, and commanding a prospect of the town of Providence below, of the Narraganset Bay and the islands, and of an extensive country, variegated with hills and dales, woods and plains," etc. Surely, he adds, "this spot was made for a seat of the Muses."

Meanwhile the President was prayerfully considering the sundering of his connection with the church in Warren; an event in which his tenderest and best feelings were involved. It is true that the compensation which he had thus far received for his various labors had been barely sufficient for his support. "While, however," says Prof. Goddard, "his outward man was thus a stranger to the luxurious accommodations of life, his inner man was sustained by the ennobling consciousness that he lived not in vain; that he was treading with cheerful alacrity the path of appointed trial; and that through his agency multitudes were becoming wiser and better, for time and for eternity. On this passage in the life of Dr. Manning it is delightful to dwell. It is delightful to turn aside from scenes of political ambition and ecclesiastical turbulence, which now mar our peace, and to repose for a while upon a bygone example of unaffected humility, of quiet duty, and confiding prayer. He had been elected President of

Rhode Island College; and the future prosperity of that institution was thought to depend on its removal to Providence. So affectionately desirous, however, was Dr. Manning of the people of his care, many of whom had, through his instrumentality, experienced the transforming efficacy of the religion of Christ, that he could not find it in his heart to leave them. To avoid a separation so painful to his sensibilities, he even proposed to resign the elevated station to which he had just been appointed. To this proposition his influential friends would not listen, and they persuaded him to abandon all thought of resigning the presidentship.[1] While we are compelled to think that his final decision was a wise one, we honor the feelings which well-nigh betrayed his judgment. Under similar circumstances, how few men would have faltered,— how few would have sought to renounce the pathway to literary and social distinction, for the unambitious career of a village pastor!"

After consulting with his family and friends, and corresponding with various members of the corporation, Manning, as has already been observed, decided to resign his pastoral charge, which he did on the 26th of April, 1770, "to the wonderment," in the language of the church records, "of his people; he being greatly admired and renowned." In May following he removed with his pupils and undergraduates to Providence. On taking up his

1 On this subject the Rev. Morgan Edwards wrote him from Philadelphia as follows: "I cannot help being angry with you when you talk of another President. Have you endured so much hardship in vain? We have no man that will do so well as you. Talk no more, think no more of quitting the presidency, unless you have a mind to join issue with those projectors and talkers who mean no more than to hinder anything from being done. If you go to Providence, the Warren people may have a supply; if they were willing to part with you, it is likely the college would have no reason to covet you."—*Howland's Biographical Sketch of Manning.*

abode here, he occupied, says Howland, the old house of Benjamin Bowen, on the lot at the corner of Bowen and North Main Streets, where Mr. Richmond's brick house now stands. Mr. Howell and the students boarded in private families, at one dollar and a quarter per week. There they studied, and at certain hours of the day met in one of the chambers of the brick schoolhouse, now the house of the Meeting Street colored school, for prayers and recitations. These details, trifling though they may appear, nevertheless afford an insight into the condition and management of the college at this period, and a view of Manning's position, better than more formal statements.

"Dr. Manning," says Goddard, whose chaste and expressive language we again quote, "now entered upon a theatre of enlarged and responsible action. The college was yet in its infancy, and demanded his parental supervision; its funds were scanty, and needed to be recruited; its actual system of discipline and instruction was imperfect, and required not only to be improved, but to be adapted to the new circumstances under which it was hereafter to be administered. To these important objects he devoted himself, with patience and energy, and with that spirit of self-denial which is essential to the success of great enterprises, and which great enterprises are apt to inspire. In the beneficent work of establishing, within the little Colony of Rhode Island, 'a public seminary for the education of youth in the vernacular and learned languages, and in the liberal arts and sciences,' he was aided by the efficient coöperation of the Rev. Messrs. Edwards, Smith, Stillman, Backus, Gano, and others of his clerical brethren. It is, however, perhaps not too much to say, that, but for the enlightened zeal and substantial liberality of a few Baptist laymen, citizens of Providence, the college would have been slow in winning its way to general repute. These public-spirited men, though strangers themselves to the discipline of schools of learning, knew how to prize the benefits of high intellectual culture. Though self-educated, they were without a particle of hostility to the distinctions of learning, or of that affected contempt for learned men with which the uncultivated sometimes seek to console their deficiencies. Moved by a generous ardor, they determined that their children and the children of their contemporaries should enjoy, to the remotest generations, opportunities for intellectual improvement denied to themselves. Well have they been repaid for their efforts in this good cause. Their activity and enterprise in the accumulation of wealth are now well-nigh forgotten; but still fresh is the memory of all their deeds in behalf of science and letters and religion."

A part of Manning's plan was to secure by correspondence the coöperation and assistance of friends in England. In pursuance of this plan, he addressed a letter to the Rev. Dr. Samuel Stennett, for thirty-seven years the faithful and affectionate pastor of the Baptist church in Little Wild Street, London. Mr. Stennett was regarded as one of the most eminent ministers of his own denomination. His connections too with Protestant Dissenters generally, and with members of the Established Church, were large and respectable. One of his constant hearers was the philanthropist John Howard, whom Burke has so highly eulogized. George III., it is said, was on terms of intimacy with him, frequently calling at his house on Muswell Hill. As a scholar and an author Mr. Stennett had no small repute. His Works, edited by the Rev. William Jones, were published in 1824, in three octavo volumes.

PROVIDENCE, June 7, 1770.

REVEREND AND DEAR SIR:

Although unknown to you, I take the freedom to trouble you with reading a letter from an unworthy friend. I was urged to this partly by the desire of our common friend, Mr. Henry Williams, merchant of New York, and partly because I have often heard that you are a lover of our nation, and are engaged to further the interests of the Baptist society; as also that you may be informed of the state of our college, the interests of which I am told you have at heart. Of this the late very acceptable present of your two volumes of Sermons is an additional proof. I heartily wish that your example may be followed by others of our friends who have written for the public.

It was resolved, after long deliberation, to place the college edifice in the town of Providence in this colony, as most conducive to the ends of its institution. This, however, has been attended with considerable difficulty; but I forbear to trouble you with the recital of our little affairs. The foundation of the college is now laid, and the building proceeds faster than could have been expected, its magnitude considered, which is one hundred and fifty by forty-six feet, with a projection in the middle, of ten feet on each side, for the public rooms. It is to be four stories high, with an entry of twelve feet through the middle of each, and is to be built of brick. It will contain fifty-six rooms in all. The town of Providence itself has nearly provided for the building, as they have raised by subscription near £4000, lawful money, at six shillings per dollar. The beneficence of a few Baptists in this place, their fortunes considered, is almost unparalleled. I should rejoice to find many elsewhere like-minded. We should then see the college properly endowed, as well as founded. This we must expect from abroad. Added to the sum collected by Mr. Edwards in Europe, our Brother Hezekiah Smith, of Haverhill, has collected and obtained subscriptions in South Carolina and Georgia, from whence he has just returned, to the amount of about £500 sterling.

It would be happy for us if we could find in England a family of Hollises[1] to patronize our college; but I fear the Baptists are not to expect

[1] Concerning the Hollis family, who for nearly a century continued their benefactions to Harvard College, we may here state in brief, what Pierce and Quincy have given at length in their histories of the University. Thomas Hollis, the father of the "benefactor," was born in 1634, and died in 1718. His son, called, by reason of his donations to Harvard, Thomas Hollis, 1st, died in 1731. A second son, Nathaniel, died in 1738. A third son, John, was a partner in

such an instance of public spirit in their favor, although I have heretofore indulged such hopes, and am yet unwilling to give them up.

Two young men have already engaged in the ministry who have been assisted by this institution, and both from their beginnings give promise of usefulness. Their first attempts have thus far been highly acceptable to the public. May the Lord of the harvest thrust out many more faithful laborers. In this part of the world the field for labor is very large, while the faithful and well-furnished laborers are truly few. To my great satisfaction, I lately received certain information of the conversion to Baptist principles of a young Presbyterian minister, eminent for his piety and success as a preacher. The manner in which this was, by Divine Providence, brought about, is somewhat singular. He was preaching upon John xiv. 15, when truth was let into his mind with such vividness as compelled him to open the nature of the ordinance of baptism so clearly as to convince the church, of which he was pastor, that believer's baptism by immersion *only* is a divine institution. In consequence of this, they sent a messenger to me to come and administer the ordinance to both minister and people, the most of whom expect immediately to submit thereto. As they, however, are more than one hundred miles distant from me, and near Mr. Smith,[1] he has engaged to supply my place. I am also told that God is do-

business with his brother Thomas. Thomas Hollis, 2d, son of Nathaniel, died in 1735. The total amount of the benefactions of this family up to this date, "exceeded," says Quincy, "£6000 currency of Massachusetts, which, considering the value of money at that period, and the disinterested spirit by which their charities were prompted, constitutes one of the most remarkable instances of continued benevolence upon record." Thomas Hollis, 3d, was born in 1720, and died in 1774. His donations to Harvard College during his lifetime exceeded £1400 sterling. Timothy Hollis died in 1791, at an advanced age. He gave £20 sterling for the library. Thomas Brand Hollis, the last of the benefactors, was born 1719, and died in 1804. His Memoirs were published in 1808, in two handsome quarto volumes, by his friend the Rev. John Disney.

[1] Rev. Hezekiah Smith. In his diary, now among the archives of the University, we find the following: "*Wednesday*, June 13th. Went to Deerfield, and preached from Acts xi. 23: 'Who, when he came, and had seen the grace of God, was glad, and exhorted them all that with purpose of heart they would cleave unto the Lord." After the sermon I examined the Rev. Eliphalet Smith and a number of his hearers for baptism. *Thursday*, 14th, I preached in Mr. Smith's meeting-house from Col. ii. 11, 12. After sermon I baptized fourteen persons, whose names are as follows: Rev. Eliphalet Smith and his wife Nancy, Dea. Wadley Cram and his wife Elizabeth, Samuel Winslow and his wife Jane, James Philbrick and his wife Elizabeth, Jeremiah Present, Moses Clough, William Tir-

ing marvellous things in Virginia and North and South Carolina amongst the Baptists, bringing multitudes to submit to baptism according to Christ's instructions. And we are not quite forsaken in New England. In several towns on Cape Cod God is at work, although in general we have reason to cry, "Our leanness, our leanness!"

My situation in the centre of American intelligence, especially as I have travelled through, and have correspondents in, most of the principal towns, furnishes me with an opportunity of knowing almost everything interesting to the Baptists; of whose affairs, should you be disposed to hear, you may depend upon receiving the best accounts I can collect, whenever you lay your commands in this way. However agreeable the like from you would be respecting affairs in Britain, yet, amidst your more important connections and engagements, the utmost I presume to ask is your indulgence for interrupting you by this tedious epistle, and beg leave to subscribe,

Dear sir, your most unworthy brother,

JAMES MANNING.

To this letter Dr. Stennett thus replies: —

LONDON, Aug. 10, 1770.

REVEREND AND DEAR SIR:

I received your favor of June 7th, and take this opportunity of returning you my sincere thanks for it, and of assuring you that a correspondence with Mr. Manning, for whose character, before I received this expression of his friendship, I had great respect, will afford me a particular pleasure. I write by Mr. Gordon,[1] a minister of the Independent persuasion of this city, who intends settling in America. He is a very sensible and worthy man, and has ample recommendations with him. His po-

rill, Hannah Polsiper, Nancy Folsom, and Isaac Blasdel, of Chester, the rest of Deerfield, who the same day were embodied into a Baptist church. A good day it was, indeed. The goings of the Lord were very evident." Two days afterwards Mr. Smith baptized seven persons, one of whom was Dr. Samuel Shepard, who, in 1771, was ordained as pastor over the church at Stratham. Mr. Stillman, of Boston, preached the sermon, Mr. Smith gave the charge, and President Manning the right hand of fellowship. Dr. Shepard became a very active and highly honored minister of the Baptist denomination. A sketch of his life appears in Sprague's Annals of the American Pulpit. He was converted to Baptist sentiments, it seems, by reading Norcott's work on Baptism.

[1] William Gordon, D.D. He settled in Roxbury, Mass., and afterwards wrote a history entitled "The Rise, Progress, and Establishment of the Independence of the United States of America," published in 1778, in four octavo volumes. For a more extended notice of Gordon, see page 387.

litical speculations in favor of America, and some little misunderstanding with his people occasioned by his not knowing how conscientiously to baptize *all* the children of those who attended his ministry, have engaged him to leave us, and spend the remainder of his life with you. Where he shall settle I believe he has not himself determined, but I imagine somewhere about Philadelphia or New York. Should he take a tour your way, I have no doubt he will meet with a friendly and brotherly reception at Providence. I was educated at the same academy with him, and have a great esteem and affection for him. Indeed, he is well known and esteemed by all denominations here.

I am glad your college is in such forwardness, and that the design, which is truly important, meets with so much encouragement among our friends on your side of the water. The groundless prejudices which have a long time prevailed among many good people of our persuasion, will, I hope, in time subside; and nothing will contribute so much to the removing of them as the zeal, good behavior, and, with the blessing of God, success of the first young persons you send out into the ministry. I look upon it as a very kind Providence that hath set you at the head of this college; and as I am sensible you must have many difficulties to contend with, so I heartily pray you may have strength according to your day. The success you have already met with is a circumstance which I doubt not affords you no small encouragement, and I hope you will still, my dear sir, meet with a great deal more. I shall rejoice to help forward your design in any way that I am able. But you are sensible we have not a great deal of wealth in our denomination, and few of the Baptists, as I hinted before, are very warm advocates for learning. Dr. Llewelyn is your very good friend, and I am persuaded would be glad of an acquaintance with Professor Manning. I speak not from any intimation on his part, but from the particular knowledge I have of his character, and his good dispositions towards your plan. We have had a great loss in Mr. Roffey,[1] who died in April last, and through whose further good offices I hoped your college would have been considerably benefited. But God will, I hope, raise up friends.

I cannot now be so particular as I wish, as I write in a hurry. By the

[1] Mr. Roffey, it appears, was a benefactor of Rhode Island College. From the records we find that at a meeting of the corporation held at Newport, Nov. 16, 1769, it was voted "That the thanks of this corporation be transmitted to Mr. Samuel Roffey, for his generous benefactions to this institution, by the secretary."

hand that conveys this I have written to Mr. Stillman, of Boston, whom I have, I fear, wearied with a very long scrawl. I rejoice in the agreeable account you have favored me with, of the success of the gospel in many parts, and that the truth with respect to baptism prevails. May the knowledge of Christ and of his ways spread far and wide. We are not without some instances of the power and grace of God among us; and I think the interest in many places revives. New associations of ministers and congregations are lately set up in the country where there were none before.

As to Dr. Moore's scheme, he has met with considerable success, though as yet but little has been collected among the Baptists. I believe about £1000 is raised; we have obtained also £1000 of the King. Trustees are appointed for the management of the moneys collected, among whom, of the Baptists, are Mr. Stead, Dr. Llewelyn, and myself, who consider ourselves as particularly obliged to look after the interests of our friends in Nova Scotia.

As to political matters, my time will allow me to say but little now. The sovereignty of Parliament over all the British dominions seems to be the great object of Government; and yet I believe they would be glad to have peace and harmony restored. I made use of the argument of policy, as well as of the goodness of the cause itself, in favor of the discussion in Nova Scotia, and it was duly attended to. I hope the discouragements the Baptists have lately met with in America are removed, and their grievances in some degree at least redressed. I am sure, however, it would be good policy, to say no more of it, in the other denominations with you, to treat them well. And our friends, I hope, see the importance and reasonableness of taking every united step that our divine religion teaches, before they proceed further. But I must not run out any further at present.

It will, I assure you, my dear friend, afford me a very sensible pleasure to hear from you quickly, and often; and you will oblige me much by favoring me with all the news you can. My sincere Christian regards to Mr. Hezekiah Smith, for whose character I have a high esteem, and all inquiring friends. I am, dear sir,

Your very affectionate friend and brother,

SAMUEL STENNETT.

The Rev. Hezekiah Smith, to whose efforts in behalf of the college Manning in his letter refers, was desired by the corporation "to solicit benefactions for their use in the Southern provinces." He left home on his important mission Oct. 2, 1769, and returned June 8, 1770, having been absent from the people of his charge a little over eight months. He travelled extensively through South Carolina and Georgia, preaching as he had opportunity, and prosecuting with energy and zeal the work to which he had been appointed. His fervid piety, his eloquence, his commanding presence, and genial manners, gained him hearers, and rendered him everywhere a welcome guest. He succeeded in obtaining subscriptions to the amount of £3710 17s. 6d., South Carolina currency, of which, £2287 5s. 7½d. he received, and remitted at sundry times to the treasurer of the corporation. His journal or diary, together with his accounts, list of subscribers, etc., form a document of rare interest and value, in connection with the early history of the college. For his "great and generous services" the corporation at their annual meeting, in September, returned him their "hearty thanks."

The following letter from the Rev. Oliver Hart shows how Mr. Smith was received, and the manner in which he performed the duties of his mission: —

CHARLESTON, April 17, 1770.

DEAR MR. MANNING:

As our good friend Mr. Smith is now almost ready to embark for your Northern clime, I embrace the opportunity of sending you a few lines, which I hope you will accept as a superadded token of my unfeigned regard. I am sorry that Mr. Smith is obliged to leave us so soon. His labors have been acceptable to my people universally, and many others have constantly crowded to hear him. Some, I trust, have received advantage by his faithful preaching. Two young men were to see him last night under soul concern. May the good work be carried on in their hearts, and may we yet hear of many more being awakened to a sense of their lost state by nature. As to his endeavors to serve the college, they have been indefatigable, and his success has been more than equal to what could have been expected, all things considered. I am sure he has merited the grateful acknowledgments of the corporation. No man could have done more, and few would have done so much as he has, to serve the institution. He has met with much opposition, and bore many reflections, but none of these things have discouraged him. I heartily wish the benefactions of this province may greatly promote the welfare of the college. Great grace be with you.

I am, yours, etc.

OLIVER HART.

The first Commencement in Providence was held in the meeting-house of the society now known as the Beneficent Congregational Society, on the west side of the river. In this house, then the largest in town, all subsequent Commencements were held, until the completion of the new Baptist meeting-house in 1776. But four young men graduated at this time; one of whom, Hon. Theodore Foster, represented Rhode Island for thirteen years in the Senate of the United States, and at his death left many fruits of antiquarian research connected with Rhode Island history. For the following account of this Commencement, we are again indebted to the *Providence Gazette:*—

SECOND COMMENCEMENT. 1770.

"PROVIDENCE, Sept. 8.

"On Wednesday was celebrated here the second Commencement in Rhode Island College. The parties concerned met at the courthouse, about ten o'clock, from whence they proceeded to the Rev. Joseph Snow's meeting-house, in the following order: First the grammar scholars; then the under classes, the candidates for degrees, the Bachelors, the Trustees of the college, the Fellows, the Chancellor, the Governor of the Colony, and, lastly, the President. When they were seated, the President introduced the business of the day by prayer; then followed the salutatory oration in Latin, by Mr. Dennis, and a forensic dispute, with which ended the exercises of the forenoon.

"Those of the afternoon began with an intermediate oration on Catholicism, pronounced by Mr. Foster; then followed a syllogistic disputation in Latin, wherein Mr. Foster was respondent, and Messieurs Nash, Read, and Dennis, opponents. After this, the degree of Bachelor of Arts was conferred on Messieurs John Dennis, Theodore Foster, Samuel Nash, and Seth Read; and the degree of Master on the Rev. Isaac Eaton, Messieurs William Bowen, Benjamin West, David Williams, Joseph Brown, and Abel Evans; also on the Rev. Messieurs Hugh Evans, Daniel Turner, Samuel James, Benjamin Beddome, Benjamin Wallin, John Reynolds, and Isaac Woodman. To which succeeded a valedictory oration by Mr. Read, and then a charge to the graduates.

"The business of the day being concluded, and before the assembly broke up, a piece from Homer was pronounced by Master Billy Edwards,[1] one of the grammar school boys, not nine years old. This, as well as the other performances, gained applause from a polite and crowded audience, and afforded pleasure to the friends of the institution. But what greatly added to their satisfaction, was an opportunity of observing the forwardness of the college edifice, the first stone of which was laid not longer since than the latter end of May last, and 'tis expected the roof will be on next month. It is a neat brick building, one hundred and fifty feet by forty-six, four stories high, with a projection in the middle of ten feet on each side, containing an area of sixty-three feet by thirty, for a hall and other public uses. The building will accommodate upwards of a hundred students. Its situation is exceedingly pleasant and healthy, being on the summit of a hill, the ascent easy and gradual, commanding an extensive prospect of hills, dales, plains, woods, water, islands, etc. *Who hath despised the day of small things?*"

The following letter was originally published in Judge Staples's Annals of Providence. It affords a good illustration of the early discipline of the college under the care and management of its first President.

PROVIDENCE, Dec. 12, 1770.

SIR: — You may think strange that I, a stranger to you, should address you by this epistle; but you will excuse me when I give the reason; which is, an information that I have received that one Scott, a youth

[1] Son of the Rev. Morgan Edwards. He graduated in the Class of 1776.

under my tuition, some time ago riding through Smithfield, in company with one Dennis, of Newport, rode up to, and in a most audaciously wicked manner, broke the windows of the Friends' meeting-house in said town, of which meeting I understand you are clerk. Upon the first hearing of this scandalous conduct, I charged him with the fact, which he confessed, with no small degree of apparent penitence; whereupon I thought good to inform you, and by you the meeting, that they shall have ample reparation of damages, and such other satisfaction as they shall think proper; being determined to punish with the utmost rigor all such perverse youth as may be intrusted to my care, as I hold such base conduct in the greatest detestation.

You will be so good as to let me know when the first meeting of business is held, that I may send him up to appear before them, and make not only reparation, but such a confession before the meeting as shall be fully satisfactory. I choose to mortify him in this way, and should be very glad that some of the heads of the meeting would admonish him faithfully and show him the evil of such doings, if this would be agreeable to them; but I speak this, not to direct them in the matter, but what would be agreeable to me. When this is settled, we shall discipline him with the highest punishment we inflict, next to banishment from the society, and with that if he does not comply with the above.

The youth has been but few months under my care, is a child of a respectable family in Kingston, Massachusetts Bay, and had his school-learning at New Haven. I am sorry for his friends, and that it happened to fall to my lot to have such a thoughtless, vicious pupil; but I am determined this shall be the last enormity, one excepted, of which he shall be guilty while under my care. I hope the meeting will inform me how he complies with these injunctions, if they think proper to take these or any other methods. Please, by the first opportunity, favor me with a line in answer to the above requests, and you will do a favor to

A real friend,

JAMES MANNING.

Mr. Thomas Lapham, Jr., in Smithfield.

The young man, Judge Staples adds, appeared before the meeting, according to the direction of the President, made a suitable acknowledgment of what he had done, paid the damage done to the windows, received some wholesome admonition and advice, and returned to his college duties, it is to be hoped, a better man. Whether his associate was the Dennis who graduated the September previous to this occurrence, we are not informed. It is certain that he was not a youth or person over whom Manning, at this time, had any special control.

It would seem proper to introduce here some account of Backus, Stillman, and Smith, the three Baptist clergymen of New England, with whom Manning was intimately associated, and to whose active coöperation in all his plans for the advancement of learning and religion, the denomination at the present day is so largely indebted for its prosperity and greatness.

ISAAC BACKUS.

The name of Backus, it will be observed, is of frequent occurrence throughout our work. The following brief sketch is compiled mainly from Prof. Hovey's Memoir, to which our readers are referred for a fuller account of his character and life.

The Rev. Isaac Backus was born at Norwich, Conn., on the 9th of January, 1724. His parents were members of the Congregational church. At the age of seventeen, during the excitement that prevailed in consequence of the preaching of Whitefield, he received his first permanent religious impressions, and united with the church. Subsequently he was led to devote himself to the preaching of the gospel. In 1749 the subject of baptism was agitated in the church of which he was the pastor, and several of his members became, in consequence, Baptists. Mr. Backus himself was soon afterwards baptized by immersion. On the 16th of January, 1756, the First Baptist

Church in Middleborough was constituted, and he became the pastor. This relation he retained until the close of life.

In 1772 he was chosen agent for the Baptist churches in Massachusetts, in place of Mr. Davis, whose ill-health had compelled him to relinquish his charge as pastor of the Second Church in Boston. This agency, which was designed for the promotion of religious liberty, and especially to secure to the Baptists an exemption from the burdens imposed upon them by law, he executed with great ability and success. In his labors in connection with this agency, he was greatly assisted by Manning, whose superior learning and more skilful pen proved invaluable aids in times of emergency.

Mr. Backus, besides his volumes of history, published numerous discourses, essays, treatises on religious liberty, and controversial tracts; a list of which is given in the account of him in Sprague's Annals of the American Pulpit. He died on the 20th of November, 1806, in the eighty-third year of his age, and in the sixtieth of his ministry.

"All New England," says the late Hon. Zechariah Eddy, "is indebted to Mr. Backus more, I think, than to any other man, for his researches in relation to our early ecclesiastical history. Mr. Bancroft bears the most honorable testimony to his fidelity, and considers his history, as to its facts, more to be depended on than any other of the early histories of New England. . . . In his own day, his labors were certainly appreciated. It is truly wonderful that, amidst the poverty and privations incident to the war of the Revolution, there could have been awakened interest enough to defray the expense of publishing large volumes, of history, at the high price which was then demanded for such works. . . . Mr. Backus was of a large, robust, and muscular frame, made firm, probably, by his early agricultural labors, and by his travels on horseback the greater part of his life. His large face and head appeared more venerable by reason of his very large wig — an adornment of ministers in the times in which he lived."

Mr. Backus, we may add in conclusion, was a Trustee of the college for a period of thirty-four years, resigning his place in 1799, in consequence of the infirmities of age, which prevented his attendance upon the meetings of the corporation.

SAMUEL STILLMAN.

To the success which the college had in the earlier periods of its history, the Rev. Dr. Stillman, it may truly be said, was one of the principal contributors. His name appears in the act of incorporation as one of the Trustees. In 1765 he was elected a Fellow, an office which he held until his death, a period of more than forty years.

He was punctual in his attendance upon all the regular meetings of the corporation; and the great influence which he exerted throughout the Baptist denomination was cheerfully given in aid of the various interests of the college. The following brief sketch of his character and life we have compiled from memoirs of him now extant.

The Rev. Dr. Samuel Stillman was born in the city of Philadelphia, Feb. 27, 1737. At the age of eleven he removed with his parents to Charleston, S. C., where, under the direction of Mr. Rind, a teacher of some celebrity, he received the rudiments of his education. He early gave promise of intellectual and moral superiority. Having become the subject of religious impressions, under the preaching of the Rev. Oliver Hart, he was hopefully converted, and was afterwards received into the church, upon a public profession of his faith by baptism. He pursued his classical studies in part at the Hopewell Academy, being one of the first beneficiaries of "The Religious Society," formed in 1755, for the purpose of aiding young men in preparing for the ministry. He also pursued his theological studies at Charleston, under the care of his pastor, Mr. Hart. On the 26th of February, 1759, at the age of twenty-two, he was ordained, in the city of his home, to the work of an evangelist. His first settlement in the ministry, which occurred shortly after his ordination, was at James Island, a beautiful place in the neighborhood of Charleston. About this time he married a Miss Morgan, daughter of a highly respectable merchant, and sister of Dr. John Morgan, who was distinguished as a surgeon in the Revolution. This marriage proved to them both the source of long-continued happiness. She was the mother of fourteen children, only two of whom, however, survived their father. On the 9th of January, 1765, he was installed as pastor of the First Baptist Church in Boston. This was a little less than two months after Manning had been installed as pastor of the church in Warren. Thenceforward these two distinguished men seem closely united in their efforts to bless the church, and to elevate the character and standing of the Baptist denomination. Dr. Stillman retained his connection with the First Church in Boston until his death, which occurred on the 13th of March, 1807, at the age of seventy.

Dr. Stillman's congregation at the time of his settlement was the smallest in town. He left it one of the largest and most respectable. As a popular preacher he had no superior in New England. Among his admirers were the elder President Adams, General Knox, and Governor Hancock; the latter of whom was for a season a member of his congregation. No clergyman of the day was so much sought after by distinguished strangers who visited the metropolis. His services were often required on public occasions, and he rarely if ever failed to meet the highest expectations. "In his person," says the Rev. Dr. Jenks, "he was slender, and very small in size (weighing less than one hundred pounds); agile in movement and erect in bearing; in address polite, combining dignity with condescending kindness, so as to maintain rank with the most eminent, though affable with the meanest. He was scrupulously neat in his dress, wearing, as in his painted and engraved portrait, a wig such as was in his day common, with a gown and bands." A volume of his sermons was published in 1808, with a portrait, and a biographical sketch of the author. In Sprague's Annals of the American Pulpit, Vol. VI., may be found a highly interesting sketch of Dr. Stillman, accompanied with letters or reminiscences from James Loring, Esq., and the Rev. Dr. Wm. Jenks; also a fine engraved likeness.

A view of the meeting-house in which Dr. Stillman preached may be found in Drake's History and Antiquities of Boston. It was built in 1771, and dedicated on the 22d of December of that year. Its dimensions were fifty-seven feet long by fifty-three feet wide. In 1791 the house was enlarged, this step having been rendered necessary by the great increase of the society. Its site having become valuable for stores and inconvenient for public worship, the place was sold in 1853, and the old building turned into shops for mart and trade. The proceeds of the sale have enabled the society to rear the most conspicuous spire in the city, upon the east point of Beacon Hill, overlooking the State House even, and commanding a view of the city and surrounding country, not surpassed, if equalled, by any other. "To such an eminence," says Drake, "has that church attained, whose foundation was obliged to be clandestinely laid by its original founders. The present grand and lofty steeple will, it is hoped, long stand, not only an ornament to the city, but as a beacon for the intolerant." The following is a list of the ministers of this church as recorded by Winchell and others: Thomas Gould, 1665–75; John Russell, 1675–80; John Miles, 1683; John Emblen, 1684–99; Ellis Callender, 1708–18; Elisha Callender, 1718–38; Jeremiah Condy, 1739–64; Samuel Stillman, 1765–1807; Joseph Clay, 1807–9; James M. Winchell, 1813–20; Francis Wayland, 1821–26; Cyrus P. Grosvenor, 1827–30; William Hague, 1831–37; Rollin H. Neale, 1837 ——.

HEZEKIAH SMITH.

The Rev. Dr. Hezekiah Smith, whose relations with Manning from early manhood down to the close of life were those of the closest intimacy, was born on Long Island, New York, on the 21st of April, 1758. In his youth he became pious, and at the age of nineteen joined the Baptist church in New York City then under the pastoral care of the Rev. John Gano. He commenced his classical education at Hopewell, entered the College of New Jersey at Princeton, and graduated in the year 1762, in the same class with President Manning. After leaving college he travelled through the Southern provinces, in order to recover his health, which had become somewhat impaired by too close confinement to his studies. In a single year he made a tour of four thousand miles, and laid the foundations of lasting friendship with the Rev. Messrs. Hart,

Pelot, and others of a kindred spirit, whose intercourse and correspondence proved a delight to him in his riper years. At Charleston, S. C., he was ordained by several ministers of the Charleston Association. The Baptist church in Haverhill, Mass., gathered through Mr. Smith's instrumentality, was organized on the 9th of May, 1765, and he was chosen the pastor. He was duly installed on the 12th of Nov., 1766. The ministers who officiated upon this occasion were President Manning, Dr. Stillman, and the Rev. John Gano. The relations which Dr. Smith thus assumed he sustained during a period of forty years. Under his ministry the church soon acquired great influence in the town, and indeed throughout all the surrounding country.

On Thursday, June 27, 1771, Dr. Smith, as we find it stated in his diary, was married to Miss Hephzibah Kimball, of Boxford, Mass. This most estimable woman was a stranger to religion at the time of their marriage. Her husband's letters to her during his service in the army express the most affectionate yearnings for her spiritual welfare. She survived him many years, dying Dec. 9th, 1824. They had four children, namely, three sons and a daughter.

In the year 1775, our struggle with the mother country commenced. The Baptists had always been the friends of civil and religious freedom, and at this critical period they were ready to pledge their fortunes and lives in the defence of their country. Their chaplains, as Washington himself testifies, were among the most prominent and useful in the army. True to his patriotic principles, Dr. Smith, notwithstanding the tender ties binding him to his people and home, left Haverhill immediately upon the breaking out of hostilities, and joined the American army. Here, as chaplain, he continued five years. He became, says his biographer, the intimate friend of Washington, and possessed the confidence and esteem of the officers and men of the whole army. Repeatedly he exposed his life in battle; and he was always among the foremost in encouraging the soldiers, and in soothing the sorrows of the wounded and the dying. On all occasions he reproved vice, with a boldness of tone and manner which, contrasting with his gentleness in the approval of virtue, awed the most hardened into respect and fear.

After the clouds of war had been dispersed, Dr. Smith returned joyfully to his family and his parish, and to the sacred duties to which he had consecrated his life. In his work at home and in his missionary tours abroad his time was fully occupied, and the even tenor of life flowed on. He died Jan. 22, 1805, in the sixty-eighth year of his age. An impressive discourse was preached at his funeral, by the Rev. Dr. Stillman, from Acts xiii. 36, which discourse was afterwards published. His ashes repose in the village graveyard at Haverhill, surrounded by the remains of his family and friends.

Dr. Smith was a man of commanding presence, large and well proportioned, inspiring respect by his dignity, and winning affection by his affability and grace. His voice was one of unusual compass and power, and his genuine eloquence opened a way for his message. His views of truth were strictly evangelical, and his ministry combined, in due proportions, the doctrinal, the practical, and the experimental. He never wrote his sermons, but uniformly went into his study on Thursday morning, and devoted the residue of the week to careful preparation for the duties of the Sabbath. As an illustration of his pastoral and missionary labors, it is stated in the journal to which we have already referred, that, from the time when he entered the ministry to Aug. 1, 1773, he baptized two hundred and ninety-four persons.

The following amusing instance of persecution which occurred to him is mentioned by his biographer, Dr. S. F. Smith, as an illustration of the times in which he lived. The constable of a neighboring town, where Mr. Smith had gone to preach, a weak and inferior-looking person, was moved to go, clothed in the majesty of the law, and "warn him out of the place." The little officer, on coming into the presence of one of such commanding person, and bearing all the airs of a consummate gentleman, on such an errand was very naturally much confused, and, on opening his mouth to deliver his message, said, "I warn you — off of God's earth." "My good sir," said the preacher, "where shall I go?" "Go anywhere," was the reply; "go to the Isle of Shoals." It may be presumed, says the narrator, that the expounder of law was scarcely aware of the indignity done to the inhabitants of those seagirt rocks in placing their geographical position so far out of the ordinary track of navigators.

Dr. Smith was one of the first Fellows of the college, retaining this position until his death, a period of nearly forty years. How zealously he labored, with Manning, to promote the welfare of the institution, these pages throughout abundantly show. He was conscientiously faithful in attending the annual Commencements, frequently preaching the sermon customary upon those occasions, and, on the ensuing Sabbath, occupying the pulpit of the Baptist church. His visits to Providence were hailed with pleasure, especially by his friend Mr. Nicholas Brown, whose hospitalities he shared, and at whose house he was a welcome and frequent guest. The last meeting of the corporation which he ever attended was in September, 1804, only four months before his death.[1]

Among the papers and correspondence of Mr. Smith are numerous letters written by him to his wife during his service in the army. From these we present a few extracts, as an illustration of the spirit and patriotism of the man, and as a valuable contribution to the history of the war.

CAMP WINTER HILL, July 31, 1775.

MY DEAR AND LOVING WIFE:

Last night and this morning we had several skirmishes with the regulars. Near the common, before you come to Charlestown Neck, was one, in which our people killed one regular, and got four or five of their guns, without losing a man. The second was at Roxbury Neck, in which we lost none, although we took three of the regulars, besides those that were wounded. The third was at the Lighthouse, which the regulars and Tories were rebuilding, in which we lost one or two men, and had a small number wounded. Our forces killed their captain of the guard, and took about twenty-five regulars and eleven Tories prisoners, besides the wounded. The pilot who pilots vessels in and out of Boston harbor was one of them. Thirty-six men were brought into Cambridge just before sunset, as I am informed. The Tories hang their heads.

CAMP WINTER HILL, March 11, 1776.

Since my last, the movements of the ministerial army give us reason to think they are about leaving Boston; but in what direction they will go from thence is uncertain. We expect they will aim for the Southern colonies. If so, our army will soon move, and be ready to attack them where they land. The general order of to-day is, for all the army to get ready for a speedy remove. The field officers of the regiments I serve, as well as others, insist upon my going with them; and, I must confess, the prospect of usefulness in the glorious cause of our country, joined with that of usefulness to souls, inclines me to yield to their request. And since my people as a body have not manifested their disapprobation of my being in the army, during the present campaign, I think they cannot justly blame me in struggling with others for the salvation of America, especially the

[1] Sprague's Annals of the American Pulpit.

United Colonies in America. Your zeal for the cause, united with consideration, will, I doubt not, cause you to yield to the disagreeable parting for a few months.

CAMP WINTER HILL, March 20, 1776.

This day I was in Boston, where I saw a number of houses destroyed by the regulars; but the damage in that town is not so great as I expected; and what they left amounts to a large sum, which is a proof that they left the town in great fear, and with much precipitation. We have no particular orders about marching to the southward yet, but I am confident we shall be obliged to go before long. If so, you will not expect to see me at Haverhill very soon, as my horse is low in flesh, and not so well fitted for a long journey as I could wish. You may well judge that so long an absence from home is equally disagreeable to me as to you; but as duty in the course of Providence requires it, we ought to be reconciled to it, and bear up under it with a becoming fortitude. Let us place our confidence in God, and take delight in him the Supreme Good. Then shall we be happy, and the time will not seem so tedious to us during my absence. . . . . I am sorry my good Deacon Shepherd discovered such a temper at my yielding to what I think is my duty. It will be the best for you not to say much about it; and if you hear reflections cast upon me, not to resent them, but to let them pass. The least said is the best.

CAMP NEW YORK, June 8, 1776.

We have expected something would be done before now by the ministerial troops in this city; but their exported army has not, I believe, yet arrived. Only a few vessels lay down at the Hook at present. Our men in general are healthy, and are daily at work in preparing for the enemy. If the enemy should take New York, I am persuaded they will find great difficulty, and sustain great loss in the acquisition. We received in this city the good news of our privateers' success in taking three large vessels, whose valuable cargoes we have sent to New England. I hope they will arrive safe. The Congress has greatly increased the American army, so that, with the blessing of God, I hope the ministerial army will be disappointed the present campaign. I long to see vital piety abound, and true godliness prevail; then would I pronounce America blessed, and her sons and daughters free.

CAMP NEW YORK, June 27, 1776.

In my last I informed you that there had been a plot formed in this city to destroy our generals and blow up the magazine, but that it had been providentially discovered. The Mayor of this city, amongst many others, is in confinement. I hope they will meet with their just reward. They are now under examination daily. The British fleet has not yet arrived. Our army is strong, and great preparations are making in this place for the enemy. . . . . Things are very dear here. I gave ten coppers yesterday for about one pint of strawberries. One may readily spend the most of his wages in this place. Some do spend the whole of their wages, I suppose, if not more. However, if we can but live and get the victory, it will be a favor; when we die, we shall not want any of this world.

CAMP STILLWATER, Aug. 5, 1777.

We came to this place last Lord's Day evening; but how long we shall tarry here I cannot say. Our State of Massachusetts Bay is shamefully deficient in the number of Continental troops. We have not one half our number here yet, and what will be the consequence I cannot say. Hope kind Providence will excite our people to a more vigorous exertion than heretofore, and that a glorious event in favor of America will yet take place this present campaign. I am yet sanguine in my expectations, and trust the American army will be victorious.

CAMP STILLWATER, Sept. 13, 1777.

We are now on our march up the river to meet Mr. Burgoyne with his boasted strength. Expect soon to engage him, unless he should retreat. Our army is in good spirits. We have a good commander, Gen. Gates, and a large body of troops; so that I don't doubt of success, unless we should put our trust in the arm of flesh, which is forever attended with a curse. With the blessing of Heaven, I expect our army will soon do something grand for the salvation of our country.

CAMP STILLWATER, Oct. 3, 1777.

Since the battle mentioned in a former letter, we have either taken prisoners, or had deserters come in from the enemy almost every day. I have expected a general engagement before now, but when it will take place I know not. From the best information we understand that the enemy's provisions grow short.

CAMP ALBANY, Oct. 22, 1777.

Although I sent you a letter since our total conquest of Gen. Burgoyne's army, in which I enclosed the articles of capitulation, yet I am loth to miss this opportunity by Mr. Chadwick to let you know that I am in a good state of health, ready to serve my country in the reduction of our enemies to the southward, if Gen. Washington should stand in need. We have no very late intelligence from him; but the last we had was favorable, and we daily expect to hear of a general battle. Hope the Lord will give success to our arms. The following is a list of the taken, killed, etc., of Gen. Burgoyne's army: —

British troops by capitulation,	2442
Foreigners,	2198
Prisoners sent to Canada,	1100
Staff,	12
Sick and wounded,	528
Prisoners of war,	300
Deserters,	400
Took at Bennington,	1220
Killed between Sept. 18th and Oct. 8th,	600
Taken at Ticonderoga,	413
Total,	9213

The number of killed and taken at Fort Stanwick I cannot ascertain. Gen. Burgoyne and three other officers taken were members of the British Parliament.

CAMP CONTINENTAL VILLAGE, July 14, 1780.

There are great preparations making to do something capital this campaign, and it is my opinion that a vigorous exertion will be made for New York, in which enterprise I expect many will lose their lives. Oh that they may be prepared by grace for such an event! I have reason to think that my poor endeavors have been blessed to the awakening of several persons in Peekskill since my arrival. Oh that conviction might terminate in conversion! Next Lord's Day I expect to preach to my brigade for the first time since I joined them this season; for I found the brigade so scattered, and taken up with guards, etc., that the brigade major said that he could not turn any out for public exercise, nor even furnish men to relieve the guards. But now the recruits have joined us we are able to have religious worship in camp again; and I pray that my preaching may be attended with power.

The present seems a fitting place to make special mention of the BROWNS, whose names so frequently occur throughout these pages. They were Manning's intimate friends. To their vigorous and united efforts the college is largely indebted for its early prosperity and growth, if not for its very existence. Their ancestors were among the founders and prominent members both of the colony and of the Baptist church. Their descendants, in pious emulation of their fathers, have nobly contributed of their abundant wealth to the present resources of the institution, — its spacious grounds, its buildings, its library and apparatus, and its endowments and funds, — and Brown University will transmit, to the latest posterity the many virtues and generous deeds of the family whose honored name it bears.

I. CHAD BROWN.

Concerning the remote ancestry of the Brown family in Rhode Island, but little is now known. That they are the descendants of some one of the hundred and fifty-five families bearing that name in England, Ireland, and Scotland, whose escutcheons, or armorial bearings, are described in Burke's Encyclopædia of Heraldry, is at least probable. The Rev. Chad Brown (or Browne, as the name was at first written) came over from England, according to Savage, in his recent edition of Winthrop's History of New England, in the ship Martin, during the month of July, 1638.[1]

[1] "Two ships," says Winthrop, "which came over this year (1638), much *pestered*, lost many passengers and some principal men." In a note upon this passage, Savage, after speaking of the Nicholas of London as one of the *pestered* ships, remarks as follows: "Another of the *pestered* ships probably was the Martin, coming nearly at the same time with the Nicholas. I know, at least, that the nuncupative will of Sylvester Baldwin, one of her passengers, who died on the ocean, was proved July 13th, of this year, by Chad Brown, and other fel-

Winthrop states that "there came over this summer twenty ships, and at least three thousand persons, so as they were forced to look out new plantations." It was during this period, also, that many of the inhabitants of Boston, "and others who were of Mrs. Hutchinson's judgment and party, removed to the Isle of Aquiday (Rhode Island); and others who were of the rigid separation, and savored anabaptism, removed to Providence, so as those parts began to be well peopled." In this latter class, thus described by Winthrop, may be included Chad Brown; who, with his wife Elizabeth and his little family, at once sought a permanent home in the land which had afforded a friendly shelter to Roger Williams and his companions. The precise date of his arrival at Providence cannot now be ascertained, as the early records of the town were loosely kept, and many of them were afterwards destroyed during the so-called King Philip's War. From the documents that have come down to us, it is evident that he soon exercised an important influence, as a leading man in the colony. The first written or civil compact of which

low-passengers, before Deputy Governor Dudley. His wife and children are named." It has been asserted that Chad Brown was "one of that little company who fled with Roger Williams from the persecution of the then Colony of Massachusetts." The epitaph on his tombstone, erected by the town of Providence, three quarters of a century ago, states that he was "exiled from Massachusetts for conscience sake." Prof. Gammell, in his Memoir of Nicholas Brown, says that he arrived at Providence in the year 1636, a few months after the arrival of Roger Williams. Dr. Hague, in his historical discourse delivered at the second centennial anniversary of the First Baptist Church, makes a similar assertion. Among the papers of the late Moses Brown, we find it stated that he came from Salem, Mass., in the year 1637. Edwards, Backus, and Benedict are equally confused in their brief notices respecting the early history of the great ancestor of the family from which the college derives its name. Mr. Savage, in his remarks as above quoted, proves conclusively that Chad Brown came to Providence in 1638, more than two years after the arrival of Roger Williams and his five companions. For a further illustration of this point, see Savage's Genealogical Dictionary of New England, Vol. I, p. 265.

we have any knowledge has his signature, with that of twelve others. A full account of this compact, which was probably entered into soon after Mr. Brown's arrival, may be found in Staples's Annals of Providence.

On the 8th of October, 1638, Roger Williams executed a deed, known as the "initial deed," granting to twelve of his companions an equal share with himself of the lands which he had purchased from the Indians. These, therefore, including the grantor, constituted the original thirteen proprietors of Providence. Soon after the execution of this deed, the proprietors divided the lands thus obtained into two parts, — one called "the grand purchase of Providence," the other "the Pawtuxet purchase." Great dissensions and difficulties grew out of this division, in allusion to which Roger Williams, in his plea before the Court of the New England Colonies, in Providence, in the year 1677, gives the following brief but comprehensive view of Mr. Brown's character and personal influence: "The truth is, Chad Browne, that wise and godly soul (now with God), with myself, brought the remaining aftercomers and the first twelve to a oneness by arbitration." In the first of the aforementioned divisions, "the grand purchase," are recorded in a small book, among the files of the city clerk's office, the names of fifty-four persons as the owners of "home-lots," as they were called, extending from the "town street" (now North and South Main Streets) eastward to Hope Street. Among the names thus recorded is that of Chad Brown. In addition to these lots, each person had a six-acre lot assigned to him in other parts of the purchase; some on the banks of the Seekonk, where Roger Williams's out-lot was located, and some on the Wanasquatucket river. We are thus particular in these details, because the college, as we have already seen, was located upon a portion of the home-lot of Chad Brown.

In 1640 Mr. Brown was appointed a committee, with Robert Cole, William Harris, and John Warner, to draw up a plan of agreement for the peace and government of the town; the growth of the colony having rendered the purely democratic government, adopted at the first, impracticable. To this plan, consisting of twelve articles of agreement, his name is the first signed, followed by the signatures of thirty-eight others. It went into immediate operation, and for several years constituted the only acknowledged government of the town. In 1643 he was employed, with three others, in making peace between the people of Warwick and the Massachusetts Government. The whole of this affair, which forms a painful chapter in our early New England annals, is told at length by the principal actor, Samuel Gorton, in his "Simplicity's Defence," which, with Staples's notes, may be found in the second volume of the publications of the Rhode Island Historical Society. In addition to his various public duties, he was also a surveyor of land, and thus rendered important services to the town. In 1660, as appears by the records, he was appointed, with John Throckmorton and Gregory Dexter, to compile a list of the first town lots, from Mile-end Cove, north of Fox Point, to Olney's Lane, and note the several divisions and grants of land made previous to that date. This list or record, much worn and defaced, is now on file at the clerk's office.

But it is as a minister of religion, as the "first elder" of the oldest Baptist church in America, that Chad Brown claims our especial attention. It is true that the distinguished honor of founding this church belongs to Roger Williams; who, having been baptized by Ezekiel Holliman, "a man of gifts and piety," baptized the administrator and ten others, in the month of March, 1639. But in a few months, says Scott,[1] a contemporary with Williams, and one of the thirteen original proprietors of the soil, "he broke from the society, and declared at large the grounds and reason of it,—that their baptism could not be right, because it was not administered by an apostle." He became what, in the history of New England, is denominated a *Seeker;* a term, says Prof. Gammell, not inaptly applied to those who, in any age of the church, become dissatisfied with its prevailing creeds and institutions, and seek for more congenial views of truth, or a faith better adapted to their spiritual wants. Those writers who desire to place Roger Williams at the head of the Baptist ministers of America, do not sufficiently regard the facts as recorded in history. He indeed was instrumental in planting and establishing the Baptist denomination in this country; but his true glory and greatness consist, not in his vocation as a Baptist preacher, but in his wisdom and benevolence as a legislator, in founding, says a distinguished German statesman and scholar,[2] "in 1636, a small new society in Rhode Island, upon the principles of entire liberty of conscience, and the uncontrolled power of the majority in secular concerns,"—principles, the same author continues, which have not only maintained themselves here, but have spread over the whole Union, superseding the aristocratic commencements of Carolina and of New York, the High-

1 Richard Scott. See his letter respecting Roger Williams in Fox's "New England Fire Brand Quenched," Part II., p. 247. He came to Providence in 1638. He was at first a Baptist, but afterwards became a Quaker. One of his descendants was married to Judge Jenckes, and thus became the grandmother of the late Hon. Nicholas Brown.

2 Professor Gervinus. See his recent "Introduction to the History of the Nineteenth Century."

Church party in Virginia, the theocracy in Massachusetts, and the monarchy throughout America; which have given laws to one quarter of the globe, and which stand in the background of every democratic struggle in Europe.

In the year 1642, Mr. Williams was appointed by the colonists to visit England for the purpose of procuring a charter; when Mr. Brown, having been formally ordained, assumed the pastoral office. Associated with him were the Rev. Messrs. Thomas Olney, William Wickenden, and Gregory Dexter. The terms of their ministry, and the nature of their relations to Mr. Brown, are not definitely known. It is certain that for more than half a century they had no meeting-house, the church being accustomed to assemble in a grove or orchard for public worship, and, when the weather would not permit this, in private houses. In those primitive times the ministers, or elders as they were more commonly called, doubtless exercised their gifts after the manner of laymen in our modern conference meetings. This they called prophesying. Mr. Wickenden, who, during the latter part of his life, resided at a place out of town which he called *Solitary Hill*, is said to have been ordained by Mr. Brown. Mr. Dexter was formerly a printer in London, in company with one Coleman. He came to Providence in the year 1643, and was at once received into the church, having been before his arrival both a Baptist and a preacher. He was not, however, according to Edwards, chosen to be their minister, until Mr. Wickenden's removal to his new residence rendered this step in a measure necessary. Mr. Olney, according to Savage, came from Salem, Mass., from which place he was banished in the year 1638. He was one of the original members of the church, having been baptized by Roger Williams at the time when it was constituted.

During Mr. Brown's ministry there appears to have originated a controversy, which was long agitated in the town, and throughout the colony. It had reference to the "laying on of hands" mentioned in Hebrews vi. 1, 2,—a doctrine which prevailed in the Baptist churches for more than a century. The principal leaders in this controversy were Wickenden and Olney, both of whom favored giving up the doctrine altogether. Indeed, the latter, not succeeding in carrying his point, withdrew, with a few others, from the fellowship of the church, and formed a new one called the "Five-principle Baptist." This last, says Callender, continued till about the year 1718, when, becoming destitute of an elder, the members were united with other churches. It is more than probable that Wickenden's removal from town was owing, in part, to the unpleasant relations growing out of this controversy.

Unmoved by the arguments of "Seekers" or "Separatists," Mr. Brown maintained his standing firmly in a church which he believed to be founded on the rock of eternal truth, even "the word of God, which abideth forever." The duties of his high calling he continued to discharge, with greater or less regularity, until his decease, which occurred about the year 1665. His death was regarded by the colonists as a public calamity; for he had been the successful arbitrator of many differences, and had won the not unenviable reputation of being a "peacemaker." His other services, too, for the public good, had been numerous, and scattered over more than a quarter of a century. His remains were interred in a part of his original "home-lot," lying on College Street, just west of the old town house, whence, in 1792, they were removed to the family lot in the North Burying-ground. A plain, simple stone, erected by the town of Providence to his memory, indicates his final resting-place.

Mr. Brown left five sons; namely, John, who married a Holmes; Judah, alias Chad, who died childless; James, who removed to Newport, about the year 1672; Jeremiah, who also settled in Newport; and Daniel, who married a Herenden.

"We may easily suppose," says Prof. Knowles, "that as Mr. Williams's connection with the church was very short, Mr. Brown was considered as the first pastor, even by his contemporaries, and that this impression was transmitted to their descendants. It was not unnatural, moreover, for the church to be willing to recognize Mr. Brown as the first pastor, rather than a man who soon left them, and who refused to acknowledge them, or any other body of men, to be a true church. It is possible that other causes had some influence in the case. It is certain, however, that Mr. Brown has been generally believed to have been the first pastor of the church. He was, unquestionably, the first regular and permanent pastor, and may be regarded as one of the chief founders. It is not probable that he contended for the honor while he lived; and we may be sure that there was no strife on this point between him and Roger Williams, who speaks of him in one of his letters as 'that noble spirit now with God,' and, on another occasion, as 'that holy man.'"

In a letter to Prof. Knowles, by the late John Howland, Esq., the author says:—

"The college was built in 1770. On the question among the founders of it, on what lot to place the building, they decided on the present site of the old college, because it was the home-lot of Chad Brown, the first minister of the Baptist church. Other land could have been obtained, but the reason given prevailed in fixing the site. Had the impression been prevalent that Roger Williams was the first minister or principal founder of the society, his home-lot could have been purchased, which was a situation fully as eligible for the purpose. If any doubts rested in the minds of the gentlemen at that time as to the validity of the claim of Chad Brown to this preference, perhaps the circumstance of Mr. Williams deserting the order, and protesting against it, might have produced the determination in favor of Brown."

II. JOHN BROWN.

John, the eldest son of Chad, was born in England, in the year 1630, being eight years of age at the time of his arrival in Boston. His mother's name was Elizabeth; but her maiden name we have not been able to ascertain. He married Mary, daughter of the Rev. Obadiah Holmes, of Newport. Mr. Holmes was the successor of the Rev. John Clark, M. D., the distinguished founder of Newport Colony. He was a native of England, and was educated, says Ross, at Oxford University. Formerly he was settled in Rehoboth, Mass. He is noted in history as the first martyr to Baptist principles in New England, having been apprehended in Massachusetts, in company with John Clark, and cruelly whipped "for conscience sake." Concerning Mr. Brown's life, but few memorials have come down to us. He appears to have been a man of influence in the colony, and to have inherited in a measure the character and spirit of his father. We first find his name on record in a document dated Jan. 19, 1646, which reads as follows: —

> "We, whose names are hereafter subscribed, having obtained a free grant of twenty-five acres of land, apiece, with the right of commoning according to the said proportion of lands, from the free inhabitants of this town of Providence, do thankfully accept of the same; and do hereby promise to yield active or passive obedience to the authority of (King and Parliament) established in this colony, according to our charter, and to all such wholesome laws and orders, that are or shall be made by the major consent of the town of Providence, as also, not to claim any right to the purchase of the said plantations, nor any privilege of vote in town affairs, until we shall be received as freemen of the said town of Providence."

This document has the signature of John Brown, followed by twenty-seven other signatures, including that of his brother Daniel. A few years after this transaction, commenced the most trying period in the early history of Rhode Island. In consequence of the ambition of Gov. Coddington, the local jealousies of the towns, and the refractory disposition of individuals, a spirit of disunion and misrule sprang up, which continued several years, and had well-nigh proved fatal to the peace of the colony. A happy settlement of all difficulties was at length effected by a full court of commissioners, six from each town, which assembled at Warwick on the 31st of August, 1654. One of the commissioners from Providence was John Brown, who was then twenty-four years of age. In the year 1662 he was appointed, with Roger Williams and Thomas Harris, Jr., to make up the town council. Mr. Backus, in his Church History, further adds that he was a minister in the church. These records, scanty as they are, give all the information that can be obtained respecting his character and life. At what time he died is not known. In the year 1667, we find his name as a witness to the signature of Roger Williams to the "initial deed," so called, which Williams originally granted on the 8th of October, 1638. He left five children; namely, John, born March 18, 1662; James, Obadiah, Martha, and Deborah. Martha was married to Gov. Joseph Venckes, "of happy memory," who was therefore the brother-in-law of Elder James Brown, and not a son-in-law, as erroneously stated by Dr. Benedict in his History of the Baptists.

III. JAMES BROWN.

James, the second son of John, was born in Providence, in the year 1666. He married Mary, daughter of Andrew, and grand-daughter of William Harris, one of the first five who came to Providence in June, 1636, in company with Roger Williams. Of him but little is known, save as pastor or elder of the Baptist church. He was a colleague of the Rev. Pardon Tillinghast, and his successor in the pastoral office; but the time of his ordination does not appear on record. Associated with him in this work was the Rev. Ebenezer Jenckes, who was ordained in 1719, soon after Mr. Tillinghast's death. During Mr. Brown's ministry, an event occurred which exhibits his character in a pleasing light. It was in relation to the doctrine of the imposition of hands, about which, in former years, there had been so much controversy, and which, during the ministry of his grandfather, Chad Brown, had divided and nearly rent asunder the church. It seems that a revival of religion was in progress at Newport, and Mr. Walton, a young minister of liberal education, had been invited to preach in Providence, with the hope of promoting one here also. He accepted the invitation, at the same time freely expressing his willingness to practise the laying on of hands, but not as a divine ordinance, necessary to church fellowship. Mr. Windsor, then a deacon of the church, was the leader of a party that urged the imposition of hands as a term or prerequisite of church communion. Gov. Jenckes, who was the leading member of the church, was then residing at Newport. He wrote to his pastor, Mr. Brown, on the subject, confirming Mr. Walton's view, that laying on of hands "should be no bar to communion with those who have been rightly baptized;" and saying that he had been informed by ancient members of the church that such had been the opinion of Baptists throughout the colony from the earliest times. This interesting letter of Gov. Jenckes, which is dated March 19, 1730, is published in the second volume of Backus's Church History of New England. Mr. Brown perfectly accorded with these views; for although himself a "Six-principle Baptist," holding and allowing with many of his brethren "the six principles in Heb. vi. 1, 2, to be the doctrine of Christ and the bounds of church communion," he nevertheless strongly remonstrated with Mr. Windsor and his friends against this rigid innovation. So far as the case admitted, he thus evinced a liberal and catholic spirit, eminently befitting a Christian teacher. The result was the following agreement, or compromise, which we here present, as an illustration of Mr. Brown's views and of the spirit of the times: —

May 25th, 1732. Whereas there was a meeting appointed by some of the Baptist church of Providence, this present day, at Elder James Brown's, the few of us that have met together to reconcile this woful breach or division that has happened of late about the bounds of our communion, we think it needful to bear each others' burdens, and so fulfil the law of Christ. The difference between us is this, that some of us have borne with larger communion than others. We shall endeavor, by the help of God, not to offend our brethren in this thing, nor any thing whereby it shall offend their consciences, but shall endeavor to be a building up of peace and tranquillity within the spiritual walls of Jerusalem. We do all further agree, that there be no contradictions, but that we may all speak the same things; for as we all agree and allow the six principles in Heb. vi. 1, 2, to be the doctrine of Christ, and to be the bonds of our communion, so we ought to be of one body, and not tearing one another to pieces. We further agree, that if any brother or sister shall join in prayer without the bounds of the church, they are liable to be dealt with by the church for their offending their brethren.

SAMUEL FISK,
JOSHUA WINDSOR,
ELDER PLACE,
THOMAS BURLINGAME, JR.,
JAMES KING,
JOHN DEXTER,
JOHN DEXTER, JR.,
JONATHAN JENCKES,
NICHOLAS SHELDON,
BENJAMIN CARPENTER,
EDWARD FENNER,
EDWARD MITCHEL,
EDWARD WANTON,
JAMES BROWN,
SAMUEL WINDSOR,
THOMAS OLNEY,
JAMES BROWN, JR.,
JOSEPH SHELDON,
EBENEZER JENCKES,
ELISHA GREENE,
DANIEL SHELDON,
JOSEPH WILLIAMS, JR.,
DANIEL SWEET,
DANIEL FISK.

Mr. Brown died on the 28th of October, 1732, in the sixty-sixth year of his age. He was, says Edwards, "an example of piety and meekness worthy of admiration." He had ten children; namely, John, James, Joseph Martha, Andrew, Mary, Obadiah, Jeremiah, Elisha, and Anna. John died in 1716, childless. The rest married into the Power, Field, Green, Knowlton, Harris, Comstock, Rhodes, Smith, and Barker families.

IV. JAMES BROWN.

James, the second son of the preceding, was born March 22, 1698. Very few memorials of his early life and subsequent career have been preserved. He engaged in active business, and became a successful merchant of Providence, thus laying the foundations of the wealth and prosperity of his descendants. During the year 1723 he married Hope, daughter of Col. Nicholas Power, and grand-daughter of the Rev. Pardon Tillinghast, one of the early pastors of the Baptist church. Mr. Tillinghast who came over from England in 1645, is said to have been a soldier under Cromwell. He built, at his own expense, the first meeting-house ever occupied by the church; a deed of which, and of the lot on which it stood, he executed to them and their successors in the year 1711. With the beloved wife of his choice he lived most happily until his death, which occurred on the 27th of April, 1739, in the forty-first year of his age. She survived him many years, dying June 8th, 1792, at the advanced age of ninety. Both she and her husband were worthy members of the church, and patterns of exemplary piety. She was remarkably amiable in her temper, and brought up her boys well; a proof, says one, of strength of character and mind, which few widowed mothers possess. They had five sons, and a daughter Mary. James, the eldest son, became master of a vessel. He died at York, Va., on the 15th of February, 1750, at the age of twenty-six. The daughter was married to Dr. David Vanderlight, a German, who practised medicine in Providence until his death, which occurred on the 14th of February, 1755, while in his thirtieth year. She survived him long, dying on the 6th of May, 1795. The remaining sons, Nicholas, Joseph, John, and Moses, familiarly known in Providence annals as the "Four Brothers," will form subjects for more extended sketches.

V.[1] NICHOLAS BROWN.

Nicholas, the oldest of the "Four Brothers," was born in Providence, on the 28th of July, 1729. At the age of ten he was deprived of a father's care, and in a measure thrown upon himself, as the senior representative of the family. To the good counsels and judicious training of his excellent mother, for whom he ever cherished a profound regard, he was, doubtless, indebted for many of those traits of character which rendered his life illustrious. At an early age he gave proofs of the singular goodness of his heart and of the benevolence of his disposition. Upon coming to man's estate, immediately after the death of his brother James, he could, as the eldest son, have inherited a double portion of his father's property, in accordance with existing colonial laws. Setting aside, however, all legal rights, and following only his generous impulses, he promptly divided with his brothers and his sister Mary so much of the paternal estate as fell to their lot. So auspicious a beginning of his career in life could hardly fail of a happy and successful termination. He at once engaged in mercantile business, and thereby acquired a very ample fortune. His success in trade was truly remarkable; but not more so than were his diligence and punctuality, — traits of character for which his descendants have ever been distinguished.

On the 2d of May, 1762, at the age of thirty-three, he married Rhoda Jenckes, fifth daughter of Judge Daniel Jenckes, whose name appears prominent in the history of the college charter. Her mother was Joanna Scott, a descendant of Richard Scott, one of the original proprietors of the colony, and an early member of the Baptist church. This union proved a source of great domestic felicity. They were blest with a numerous offspring; but of ten children, only two survived them; namely, Hon. Nicholas Brown, from whom the University derives its name, and the late Mrs. Hope Ives, wife of Thomas Poynton Ives, Esq. After more than twenty-one years of happy married life, this most excellent lady, whose special delight it was to aid her husband in his deeds of charity, and to cheer the gloomy mansions of poverty and pain, was taken from him. She died on the 16th of December, 1783, in the full assurance of a blessed immortality. During all her sickness she manifested a pious resignation to the divine will. For many days previous to her death she had expressed a desire to "depart and be with Christ;" and in this delightful frame of mind she continued, patiently waiting the summons for her to "come up higher."

On the 9th of September, 1785, Mr. Brown married for his second wife, Avis, daughter of Capt. Barnabas Binney, of Boston. She was a woman of superior worth, and was well versed in books and useful learning. Happy in her society, and in the esteem and good-will of his fellow-men, his remaining years glided peacefully on until his death, which occurred on the 29th of May, 1791, in the sixty-third year of his age. On the morning of this day, which was the Sabbath, he rode out, and on his return breakfasted with his family as usual. After sending his son and daughter to church, and declaring his intention, weak as he was, to go himself to the house of God, he was taken worse, and in a few hours, by an easy death, gently translated from this state of change and trial to the pure and blissful worship of the church above. On Tuesday following, his remains were carried to the Baptist meeting-house, where a most eloquent and impressive funeral sermon was preached by the Rev. Dr. Stillman, who for many years had been his intimate friend.

From this sermon, which was afterwards published, we make the following extract, as an illustration of the manner in which he was esteemed by those who had known him long and well: —

"Perhaps there is nothing more difficult than to give characters: we say too much for some, and too little for others; but in this instance the deceased was too well known, and his character too long established, to need any commendation from me. Yet I wish to gratify my present feelings, by saying that for twenty years I have enjoyed an intimate and pleasing acquaintance with him, and knew him well. He was the affectionate husband, the tender father, the compassionate master, the dutiful son, the loving brother, and the steady, faithful friend. He took much pains, by reading and by conversation, to inform his mind, and had acquired general knowledge. But religion was his favorite subject. To Christianity in general, as founded on a fulness of evidence, and to its peculiar doctrines, he was firmly attached. And from his uniform temper, his love to the gospel and to pious men, together with his many and generous exertions to promote the cause of Christ, we may safely conclude that he had tasted that the Lord is gracious. Therefore we sorrow not as they who have no hope. He was a Baptist from principle, and a lover of good men of all denominations. Blessed with opulence, he was ready to distribute to public and to private uses. In his death, the college in this place, this church and society, the town of Providence, and the general interests of religion, learning, and liberality have lost a friend indeed."

Mr. Brown, it is somewhat remarkable, never made a public profession of that religion which, from the tenor of his every-day life, was seen to be the animating motive of his conduct, and the source of his highest joys. He appears to have been distrustful of himself, and to have shrunk from a public avowal of his faith, from a too great timidity, perhaps, and a painful consciousness of imperfections and short-comings, which are but the common heritage of our fallen natures. Perhaps, too, his awful reverence for Deity prevented his taking upon himself the solemn vows involved in church covenant and membership. This reverence impressed every one who heard him speak, or saw him write the sacred name. It was his custom to write it in capitals, and he often desired others to do the same.

The following letter, addressed to his intimate friend, the Rev. Hezekiah Smith, of Haverhill, Mass., affords a happy illustration of his views and feelings in regard to his religious state. It is interesting also from its allusions to the college: —

PROVIDENCE, March 30, 1772.

REVEREND SIR:

This may serve to acquaint you and Mrs. Smith that we have not forgotten you. We have received none of your favors since 28th September, by Mr. Manning; yet we have no excuse for not writing to you before, except that of not having any particulars worthy your notice. Mr. Binney,[1] a worthy, humble, and meek young Christian, having been the evening with us, I engaged to forward these to you from Boston, as he is now going home the ensuing vacation. His conversation upon Christianity is really entertaining, and we sincerely wish, while we can say that we take knowledge of him that he has "been with Jesus," that

[1] Barnabas Binney, who graduated in 1774.

the same might be said of ourselves. This knowledge we are still waiting for. I hope, in the day of God's power, it will be made manifest in us; and I take this opportunity of requesting your fervent prayers that God would remove from us the veil of ignorance and unbelief, and that Christ in his fulness may be savingly applied to our souls through faith, which we believe to be the gift of God, as saith the Scriptures. It is a very dull time in religion here, though we have to rejoice that God has not left himself wholly without a witness. We are informed that in Swanzey, among the Baptists in Messrs. Mason's and Martin's societies, upwards of forty have been baptized since January came in. Some additions have been made to the Baptist churches in Newport. We have heard from Philadelphia that Rogers was much liked there, and that his preaching has been blessed. Mr. Edwards has gone to Carolina. I hope he may be able to promote the collection of your subscriptions got there, as they are much needed. There is nothing new here about the college. The lower rooms have been finished, so that the scholars have lived in them this winter. The enemies to the institution are doing what mischief they can, by discouraging scholars from coming here; which fact ought to stir up every friend to exert himself to the utmost. Should be glad to hear of some boys coming here from your quarter. Mr. President is well, but his wife is poorly, with her old complaints. Pray let us hear of your welfare by every opportunity.

Your most respectful and obedient servant,

NICHOLAS BROWN.

In a letter to Mr. Smith, written fifteen years afterwards, Mr. Brown further remarks: "I am as rationally convinced of the reality of religion as ever, and wish to live with a more lively sense of it in my own soul. I know there is a great work of duty to be attended to, without which we have no promise. And I feel assured that this line of duty, however straight and plain, we shall not pursue, without the supernatural aids of that *Spirit of love.*"

To this sketch we append the following remarkable epitaph, written by the Hon. David Howell, and placed upon the monument erected by his widow and surviving children. It is a fitting and eloquent tribute to his memory, and presents in brief a comprehensive view of his entire life: —

IN MEMORY OF

Nicholas Brown, Esq.,

WHO DIED MAY 29, A. D. 1791, ÆT. 62.

He descended from respectable ancestors,
Who were some of the first settlers in this State.
His stature was large, his personal appearance
Manly and noble,
His genius penetrating, his memory tenacious,
His judgment strong, his affections lively and warm.
He was an early, persevering, and liberal patron
Of the College in this town,
And a member and great benefactor of the Baptist Society.
His donations in support of learning and religion
Were generous and abundant.
His occupation was merchandise;
In which, by industry, punctuality, and success,
He accumulated a large fortune.
He was plain and sincere in his manners, a faithful
Friend, a good neighbor, and an entertaining companion.
His knowledge
Of books, of men, of business, and of the world
Was great, and of the most useful kind.
He loved his country,
And had an equal esteem of liberty and good government.
He had deeply studied the Holy Scriptures, and was convinced
Of the great truths of revelation.
He was a religious observer of the Sabbath,
And of public worship,
And trained up his household after him.
He was a lover of all men, especially of good men,
The ministers and disciples of Christ,
Who always received a friendly welcome under his hospitable roof.
As in life he was universally esteemed,
So in death he was universally lamented.
The conjugal affection of a mourning widow,
And filial piety of an orphan son and daughter,
HAVE ERECTED THIS MONUMENT.

V.[2] JOSEPH BROWN.

Joseph, the second of the "Four Brothers," was born Dec. 3d, 1733. At an early age he gave proofs of a superior genius. He engaged in merchandise and in the manufacturing business; and by his industry and skill acquired, if not affluence, at least a competency, which enabled him to indulge his natural taste for science. The first display of his philosophical abilities was in electricity, in which he became an adept. At his death he left an electrical apparatus of his own construction, equal, it is said, if not superior, to any then existing in the country. His researches, too, in other branches of science, particularly in astronomy, attracted the notice of the *literati.* But his favorite study was mechanics. The want of an early education was an obstacle in the way of his literary career, but the efforts of his genius in surmounting it excited the greatest admiration. In testimony of his merits, the honorary degree of Master of Arts was conferred on him, and he was elected a member of the American Academy of Arts and Sciences.

He was a warm friend of the college, of which he was a Trustee from the year 1769 until his death; and in all that pertained to its prosperity and growth he was thoroughly identified. In 1784 he was made a Professor of Natural Philosophy; and in consideration of the impoverished condition of the college, resulting from the war, he generously gave his valuable services to the institution without compensation. He was thus the second professor (aside from the President) ever appointed by the corporation; the Hon. David Howell being the first. He was a consistent member of the Baptist church, being the only one of the brothers who ever made a public profession of religion. The meeting-house of this venerable society, which for nearly a century has adorned the place, still stands, a conspicuous monument of his skill as an architect. In the year 1775, we find that he was appointed by the General Assembly, in company with the Hon. Esek Hopkins, to go through the colony and decide what places should be fortified, and in what manner. This shows the estimate which the public put upon his judgment and abilities as a man of science.

He died on the 3d of December, 1785, at the age of fifty-one. His funeral was attended by a numerous train of mourning relatives and friends, and a discourse suitable to the occasion was delivered by his pastor, Dr. Manning.

The following, which we copy from his tombstone, is a brief summary of his character and virtues: —

IN MEMORY OF

Hon. Joseph Brown, Esq.,

WHO DEPARTED THIS LIFE DEC. 3D, 1785,
IN THE 52D YEAR OF HIS AGE.

In the course of his life
He was a Representative for the Town of Providence,
An Assistant of the Governor in Council,
A Trustee of Rhode Island College,
A Professor of Experimental Philosophy therein,
A Member of the American Academy of Arts and Sciences,
And of the Baptist Church, etc.
He became an adept in Electricity,
And well versed in Experimental Philosophy.
But his great strength appeared in his
Favorite study of Mechanics.
He was a Patriot from principle,
And zealous for his country's freedom and independence.
In his life were exemplified charity and munificence,
Preëminently, with other virtues of an
Honest man.

Erected by his disconsolate widow
And four children.

Mr. Brown married Elizabeth, daughter of Nicholas Power, Esq. In 1774 he erected for his residence the elegant house now owned and occupied by the Providence Bank. Here, in happiness and peace, he spent the closing years of his life. Of his children, Mary, the oldest, was married, in 1799, to the Rev. Dr. Gano, who for nearly forty years was the esteemed pastor of the First Baptist Church. She died the following year, Dec. 8th, in the forty-first year of her age. A funeral sermon on the occasion of her decease was preached by President Maxcy, which sermon was afterwards published. She appears to have been a woman of great worth, possessing many and rare accomplishments. Obadiah, who was never married, died Feb. 14, 1815, at the age of fifty-three. Eliza, the third child, married Richard Ward, a merchant of New York, son of Gov. Samuel Ward, of Rhode Island. She died in 1845, without issue. Joseph, the youngest, died in 1791, at the age of sixteen. The only living representative of the family is Mrs. Eliza B. Rogers, wife of Joseph Rogers, and only daughter of Dr. Gano, by his wife Mary. At her death, therefore, she having no children, this branch of the Brown family becomes extinct. Mrs. Rogers has recently given to the University a scholarship, to be called the Joseph Brown Scholarship, in honor of her distinguished grandfather.

We close this sketch of Mr. Brown with the following extract from a pamphlet, published nearly a century ago, entitled, "An Account of the Observation of Venus upon the Sun, the third day of June, 1769, at Providence, in New England. With some Account of the Use of those Observations. By Benjamin West. Providence: Printed by John Carter, at Shakspear's Head, 1769." Mr. West, it may be added, was Professor of Mathematics, Astronomy, and Natural Philosophy in Rhode Island College, from 1786 to 1798.

"It remains now to give an account of the preparations that were made in Providence for the observation of this transit;[1] in doing of which I shall be as particular as possible, that the reader may the better judge of the merit of our work.

"When it became more generally known that there would be a transit of Venus in 1769, and the advantages that were like to accrue to astronomy, and consequently to navigation and chronology, from proper observations of it, Mr. Joseph Brown,[2] a very respectable merchant of Providence, being very desirous, if possible, to obtain an observation of it, was pleased to advise with me concerning an apparatus suitable for such an observation, and to know if we should be able to observe the transit with the necessary precision for answering the important design.

"As the proposal was new and unexpected, my answer was not direct, as it required some time to consider of it. At length I gave him my opinion concerning an apparatus proper for such an occasion; and that I thought we could observe the transit with that accuracy as would render it worthy of notice, provided we could have such an apparatus as was described. My answer gave him so much satisfaction in the matter, that he immediately sent his orders to his correspondent in London to procure the instruments. His orders were accordingly executed with fidelity and dispatch. They arrived in Providence about one month before the

[1] The street called Transit Street was named in commemoration of this event. The observations were taken on the hill where the street is laid out.

[2] "Mr. Brown is a gentleman of a solid, active genius, strongly turned to the study of mechanics and natural philosophy, which has induced him to construct and furnish himself with as curious and complete an apparatus for electrical experiments as any, perhaps, in America, and of which he well knows the use. Reading Mr. Winthrop's account of the transit in 1761, was what first occasioned him to send for a telescope, fitted in the manner Mr. Winthrop there describes. Afterwards, taking notice of the application of the American Philosophical Society to the Assembly of Pennsylvania for an apparatus for observing the transit of Venus, he found the orders he had sent were incomplete. He then advised with the author, as mentioned, and thereupon ordered a micrometer to be added. Mr. Brown's expense in this laudable undertaking was little less than £100 sterling, besides near a month's time of himself and servants in making the necessary previous experiments and preparations."

transit. Our apparatus was made by Messieurs Watkins and Smith, London. It consisted of a three-feet reflecting telescope, with horizontal and vertical wires for taking differences of altitudes and azimuths, adjusted with spirit-levels at right angles, and a divided arch for taking altitudes; a curious helioscope, together with a micrometer of a new and elegant construction, with rack motions, and fitted to the telescope. Such a noble disposition in Mr. Brown for promoting useful knowledge certainly merits the applause of the public; and, in justice to him, I must acknowledge, our work could not have been done with equal accuracy had it not been for his skill and contrivance therein."

V.[3] JOHN BROWN.

John, the third brother in age, was born on the 27th of January, 1736. He was the most active and energetic of the family; and in developing the industry and extending the commerce of the town, he has left his impress upon the entire community, in a degree seldom equalled. He was the first merchant in Rhode Island, it is said, who carried trade to China and the East Indies. He fostered the interests of the church over which his ancestors had been elders or ministers, contributing liberally of his wealth for the support of preaching, and in creating a permanent fund for the society. In founding, endowing, and sustaining the college, he was ever prominent and active, as our pages throughout show. Though a wealthy merchant, and having larger interests at stake than most men, he was a patriotic leader in the cause of the American Revolution;[1] and, at a later period, when his native State stood

[1] In reference to Mr. Brown at the breaking out of the war in 1775, we find the following, in a memoir of Elkanah Watson, published in the April number of the New England Historical and Genealogical Register for 1863. Mr. Watson was an apprentice to Mr. Brown at this period.

"Mr. Brown, finding the army desitute of every munition of war, particularly of powder, directed the captains of his vessels, on their return voyages, to freight

aloof from the Union, and refused to adopt the Federal Constitution, he was distinguished as a champion of the Federal party; and he without doubt did more than any other man towards securing the final adoption of the Constitution by the people of Rhode Island. In 1784 he was chosen a delegate to Congress, in place of Jonathan Arnold, who had removed to Vermont. While here he was appointed one of the commissioners for erecting the Federal buildings, which it was then proposed to locate on the banks of the Delaware. At the spring election in 1785, he was again returned to Congress as a delegate, and in 1799 he was elected a member, serving two years. This was about the last of his public life. He died on the 20th of September, 1803, in the sixty-eighth year of his age.

with that article; and when the army at Boston had not four rounds to a man, most fortunately one of Mr. Brown's ships brought in a ton and a half of powder, and it was immediately forwarded, under the charge of young Watson, to Cambridge, attended by six or eight recruits to guard it. . . . . Soon after this war, Brown, having contracted to supply the army of Washington with flour, sailed for Providence with a cargo from Newport. This vessel was seized, and Mr. Brown was himself made prisoner, and sent to Boston in irons, charged with heading a party, in 1772, which burned his Majesty's schooner Gaspee in Providence river.

"The whole community were indignant and exasperated at his seizure. A consultation was held immediately, and it was decided to send an express to Plymouth in order to fit out two armed schooners to intercept, if possible, the captured flour vessel, in her passage round Cape Cod."

Some sixty or eighty men embarked in two fishing schooners, equipped with two old cannon each; but after cruising about Cape Cod for ten days, they returned without success. Mr. Brown was soon after released, through the interposition of his brother Moses Brown. (Mr. Brown was taken prisoner Wednesday, April 26, 1775, and released the following week.)

As a further illustration of Mr. Brown's prominence and activity in the war, it may be stated that in the eighth volume (just published) of Bartlett's Colonial Records, including a period of four years (1776-79), his name appears, in connection with important committees and various public services, no less than twenty-six times. No other name has such frequent mention in the volume to which we have referred.

The following inscription on his tombstone describes briefly, but well, his character and worth: —

Underneath this stone
Are deposited the mortal
Remains of

John Brown,

The enterprising and accomplished Merchant,
The tried Patriot and wise Legislator,
The universal Philanthropist and sincere Christian.
Born January 27th, 1736.
Died September 20th, 1803.

Wife, SARAH, daughter of
Daniel Smith and Dorcas his wife.
Born, Providence, May 13th, 1738.
Married November 27th, 1760.
Died February 27th, 1825.

Mr. Brown has been happily described as "a man of magnificent projects and of extraordinary enterprise." Whatever he did was in accordance with his enlarged views, and oftentimes far in advance of the age in which he lived. In his day Main Street was a sandy and disagreeable walk. He first caused it to be paved; and although at that time he had twenty sail of ships abroad upon the sea, he might be seen busily engaged upon the work himself, in order to be sure that it was properly done. "University Hall," of which he laid the corner-stone, and in the planning and construction of which he bore so prominent a part, is even now one of the finest and best of the college buildings. No other man would have had the resolution and courage as "the committee man" to carry on the building of the Baptist meeting-house, at a time when Providence was comparatively a small town, and when hostilities between the colonies and the mother country seemed about to begin. His own stately mansion, built of imported brick and freestone, after English models, in the year 1786, was long noted as one of the largest and finest private residences in all New England. It was at his former residence on South Main Street that he gave, in honor of Gen. Nathanael Green, the greatest private dinner, it is said, that had ever been given in Rhode Island. His Commencement dinners, to which all graduates and friends were freely invited, at a period when public dinners were not provided by the college, as at present,[1] were remembered with pleasure years after the hospitable entertainer had passed away.

In appearance and manners Mr. Brown was not perhaps so prepossessing as his brother Nicholas. He was short in stature, and inclined to corpulency. In his bearing he was somewhat imperious at times, and seemed like one born to command. Had he entered the army, he would undoubtedly have attained to military distinction, possessing as he did the essential qualities of a great commander.

[1] Commencement dinners, so called, were first provided after the death of President Manning, as appears from the following entry in the records of the corporation: —

"COLLEGE HILL, Sept. 4, 1792.

"*Voted*, That the person who collects tuition from the students, in future charge each student with one dollar per year, to be taxed in his third quarter's bill for the year, to be applied towards furnishing a public dinner annually for the corporation and gentlemen of a literary character who may attend the Commencements; which dinner is to be provided by the steward on Commencement days, under the direction of a committee appointed by this corporation.

"*Voted*, That Dr. Enos Hitchcock, Mr. Welcome Arnold, and Col. Daniel Tillinghast be a committee for directing the steward in providing the public dinner the next Commencement."

From this time onward, as appears from the records, public dinners have been regularly furnished for the corporation and graduates of the college on Commencement occasions. Of late years, however, the tax therefor on the students has been confined to members of the graduating class.

As an instance of his wonderful influence over the people, his grandson, Gov. Francis, relates, that, while riding about the city with him, a fire broke out at India Point. He immediately hastened to the spot, and at once his stentorian voice was heard above the noise and din, giving commands with clearness and precision. Order took the place of confusion. The crowd looked to him as their natural leader in this emergency, notwithstanding the presence of several fire organizations; and soon the fire was extinguished. This was about a year before his death. Mr. Brown, as the inscription on his tombstone states, married a daughter of Daniel Smith, of Providence, by whom he had two sons and four daughters; namely, James, who died Dec. 12, 1834, aged seventy-three; Benjamin, who died July 7, 1774, aged ten; Abigail, who died in infancy; Abby, who married, Jan. 1, 1788, John Francis; Sarah, who married Charles F. Herreshoff; and Alice, who married James Brown Mason, a graduate of the college in the Class of 1791.

Mr. Brown is known in history by his connection with the affair of the Gaspee, without some mention of which our sketch of him would be incomplete. We have therefore compiled the following account from Judge Staples's "Documentary History of the Destruction of the Gaspee," published in 1845, and also from Lossing, Arnold, and other writers, as a fitting close to this brief biography. To his grandson, the Hon. J. B. Francis, we are indebted for some particulars of this transaction not found in the published accounts.

In March, 1772, the Gaspee, a British armed schooner, first appeared in the waters of Narragansett Bay, having been despatched thither by the commissioners of customs at Boston to prevent infractions of the revenue laws. Her appearance disquieted the people, and her interference with the free navigation of the bay irritated them. Thereupon a spirited correspondence ensued, between Deputy Governor Sessions and Gov. Wanton on the one hand, and Lieut. Duddingston and Admiral Montague on the other. On the 9th of June, 1772, Capt. Lindsey left Newport for Providence in his packet the Hannah. The Gaspee as usual gave chase, but ran aground on Namquit, since called Gaspee Point, below Pawtuxet, and the Hannah escaped, arriving safely at Providence about sunset. Capt. Lindsey at once communicated the fact of the grounding of the Gaspee to Mr. Brown, who thought this a good opportunity to put an end to the vexations caused by her presence. He immediately ordered the preparation of eight of the largest long-boats in the harbor, to be placed under the general command of Capt. Abraham Whipple, afterwards commodore, who was one of his most trusty shipmasters. Information of the enemy's situation was proclaimed by beat of drum; a man named Daniel Pearce passing along Main Street and inviting such of the inhabitants as were willing to engage in a perilous enterprise for the destruction of the Gaspee, to meet at the house of James Sabine, lately the residence of Richard J. Arnold, Esq. The boats left Providence between ten and eleven o'clock, filled with sixty-four well-armed men, and between one and two in the morning they reached the Gaspee. Two shots were exchanged, one of which wounded Lieut. Duddingston in the groin. This was the first British blood shed in the war of Independence. The schooner was now boarded without much opposition, and the crew and officers were compelled to leave with their effects, when she was set on fire and blown up. Mr. Brown was the last man to leave the deck, being determined that no one should carry from the vessel anything which might lead to the identification and detection of the parties. By so doing he narrowly escaped with his life, in consequence of the falling timbers and spars.

When the news of this daring feat reached England, the King's proclamation was issued, offering a reward of one thousand pounds sterling for the arrest and conviction of the two leaders of the affair, and five hundred pounds each for any other of the offenders, with a free pardon in addition, to any one concerned, except the two chiefs, who would implicate the rest. A commission of inquiry, under the great seal of England, was established, which sat from the 4th until the 22d of January, 1773. It then adjourned until the 26th of May, when it assembled and sat until the 23d of June. But not a solitary clew to the identity of the perpetrators of the deed could be obtained, notwithstanding they were well known to the people. Many of them were among the most prominent citizens of the colony. The price of treachery on the part of any accomplice would have been exile from home and country; and the proffered reward was not adequate to such a sacrifice. Moreover, those whose weak moral principles or strong acquisitiveness might have tempted them into a compliance with the terms of the proclamation, were bribed, it is said, to silence, by Mr. Brown and some of his associates. The principal actors, besides Mr. Brown, were Capt. Abraham Whipple, John B. Hopkins, Benjamin Dunn, Dr. John Mawney, Benjamin Page, Joseph Bucklin, Turpin Smith, Ephraim Bowen, and Capt. Joseph Tillinghast. Mr. Brown, says Gov. Francis, afterwards deeply regretted this affair, as foolhardy in itself, and resulting in so much needless apprehension to himself and family. For a long time he was accustomed to sleep away from home, lest he should be arrested during the night. The first booming of the guns at Lexington and Concord filled his mind with gladness. He was a stranger himself to fear, but he rejoiced when the anxieties and fears of others were merged in the open contest now commenced. History has given to the leader in this Rhode Island enterprise the fame which he so richly deserves.

V.[4] MOSES BROWN.

Moses, the youngest of the brothers, was born on the 23d of September, 1738. His father dying while he was in his infancy, his youth and early manhood were spent in the family of his uncle, Obadiah Brown, a wealthy merchant of Providence, whose daughter he married, and a portion of whose estate he inherited by will. In 1763, one year previous to his marriage, he engaged in mercantile pursuits, in connection with his three brothers; but after ten years of active life he withdrew from the bustle of trade to that retirement to which his feeble health invited, and which was more congenial to his early-formed taste for intellectual pursuits. Here on his beautiful estate in the environs of Providence, in rural quiet and simplicity, he spent a long and useful life, aiding by his judicious counsels and abundant wealth in the promotion of intelligence, piety, and freedom among men. In his religious sentiments Mr. Brown, like the rest of his family, was a Baptist. At the early age of thirty-five he became a member of the society of Friends; and from that time until the close of life, a period of more than sixty years, he was a firm adherent to the primitive doctrines of the society; exerted a strong influence in all its concerns, both secular and religious; sustained many of its most important offices with dignity and usefulness; was long regarded as the patriarch of the society; and was greatly respected and beloved for his many Christian virtues, not only by his own brethren, but by other denominations. He was the founder and patron of the excellent institution known as the "Friends' Boarding School" in Providence, — a school which, under the auspices of the yearly meeting of the society, has done much to diffuse the influences of intellectual culture among the members of that estimable Christian denomination. Among Mr. Brown's donations to this institution, may be mentioned one of forty-three acres of land, on which the school edifices now stand, and, at his decease, a house and lot near the school, a valuable collection of books, and fifteen thousand dollars in money. Besides these, his fatherly regard for the children of others induced him to appropriate one hundred dollars annually during life for their education. In this way he educated thirty individuals. He was, in accordance with the principles of the religious denomination to which he belonged, a friend of peace, and opposed to slavery in all its forms. He manumitted his slaves in 1773; was one of the founders, and for many years an efficient member of, the Abolition Society of Rhode Island, and was also an active member and liberal supporter of the Rhode Island Peace and Bible Societies. Though his constitution was originally feeble, yet he nearly completed his ninety-eighth year; until his last illness retaining in a remarkable degree the use of his faculties of body and of mind. He spent much of his time in reading and writing, maintained an extensive correspondence, and rarely made use of a clerk or an amanuensis. He made his will at the age of ninety-six; a long instrument, exemplifying, in an interesting manner, his attachment to his friends, and his desire to promote the cause of education, philanthropy, and religion. His death took place at Providence, September 6, 1836.

Mr. Brown was connected with the Masonic fraternity, being one of the earliest members of St. John's Lodge, Providence. He received his first degree on the 4th of October, 1758. In December following, he was elected secretary of the Lodge, an office which he retained eleven years. During this time the Lodge held ninety-seven meetings, at eighty of which he was present,— an instance, says the Rev. Dr. Randall, of fidelity to official duties well worthy the imitation of the generations that have succeeded him. The discipline of the society of Friends, with which he subsequently connected himself, forbade all union with Masonry; nevertheless, he continued to cherish a high regard for the institution, although compelled to withdraw from active connection with the fraternity. His brother John, it may be added, was initiated a member of the Lodge on the 29th of March, 1758, and his brother Joseph on the 6th of April, 1757.

A fine portrait of this venerable philanthropist has been placed in Manning Hall, with the portraits of other distinguished men. It was painted by Mr. Heade, from an original sketch by W. J. Harris. Mr. Brown was three times married; but he outlived all his family — lacking only two years, two weeks, and two days of being one hundred years old. By his first wife, Anna Brown, he had three children, — a son and two daughters. One of the latter died in infancy. His daughter Sarah, who was married to William Almy, died in 1794. His son Obadiah died in 1822, in the vigor and strength of manhood. His only grandchild was the late Mrs. Anna Almy Jenkins, whose untimely death, at the burning of her mansion, cast such a gloom over the entire community. To Moses Brown

Jenkins, the only son of this grand-daughter, he bequeathed the house and lands where, in peaceful retirement, he had spent sixty-five years of his life, and where he breathed out his latest breath.

In closing these imperfect sketches of the Browns, we can but express our regret that no painter's skill has transferred to canvas (except in the case of Moses Brown), the looks and features of these great-hearted men, to whose Christian activity and benevolence the present generation is so largely indebted. We know them only by their works.

CHAPTER IV.

1770–1773.

First Baptist Church of Providence — Founded by Roger Williams, in 1639 — Samuel Winsor — Manning's connection with the Church — Invited to preach — Controversy on Singing in public worship, and the Imposition of Hands — Becomes the Pastor in 1771 — Revival under his preaching — Letter to Dr. Stennett, of London, giving an account of his views and feelings as Pastor of the Church and President of the College, together with an account of the dispute between the Baptists and Congregationalists of Massachusetts, New Hampshire, and Connecticut — Circular Letter of the Warren Association, in 1770, recommending the churches to seek redress of their grievances at the King's Court in England — Letter to Rev. Hezekiah Smith in behalf of an oppressed Baptist Church in Richmond, N. H. — Letter to Rev. John Ryland, of Northampton, England — Bitterness of the New England Congregationalists in general towards the College — Ryland's reply — List of worthy men of learning and character in England deserving the honors of the College — Letter from Morgan Edwards illustrating the ill-feeling of the Congregationalists towards the College — Extract from Prof. Knowles's Memoir of Roger Williams respecting the expediency of unveiling scenes of intolerance and persecution — Account of the third Commencement, in 1771 — Letter to Dr. Llewelyn, of London, giving the condition and prospects of the College, and urging its claims upon his benevolence — Letter to Rev. John Ryland — Honors of the College — Spread of Baptist sentiments in New England — Manning suggests a Lottery to augment the funds of the College — His connection with the Latin School — Manning's Salary — Letter to Rev. John Ryland — Gift to the College of Dr. Gill's Works and fifty-two volumes of the Fathers — Ryland's letter to Manning — Character and early history of Ryland's friend, Rev. Augustus Toplady — Letter to Dr. Stennett — Letter from Rev. Isaac Woodman, of Thorp, England, suggesting a printed Narrative of the College and declining its honors — Manning's reply — Extract from a letter from Ryland respecting a History of the College — Playful letter to Rev. Hezekiah Smith — Letter to Rev. Benjamin Wallin, a wealthy Baptist of London — Wallin's reply — Letter to Ryland upon academic honors, and detailing facts illustrative of the ill-will of Congregationalists towards the College — Ryland's reply — List of Calvinistic Baptist Ministers in England able to read the Greek Testament — Letter from Rev. O.

Hart, of Charleston, S. C., thanking Manning for the discipline of the rod to his son — Letter to Ryland — Letter to Wallin — Letter to Rev. Abraham Booth, of London, author of "Reign of Grace."

THE connection of Dr. Manning with the Baptist church in Providence was an important event in his life, and is therefore deserving of special notice. This church was founded by Roger Williams, during the year 1639; and it is the oldest Baptist church in America. With its history prior to 1770 we have now no special concern. At that time it numbered one hundred and eighteen communicants, and was under the pastoral care of the Rev. Samuel Winsor, Jr. Residing at a distance from the meeting-house, and finding the duties of his office too arduous for him, he made known to his people his earnest desire to be released from services which he could no longer perform without infringing upon family obligations, which he regarded as paramount to all others. The settlement of Dr. Manning in Providence was hailed by the church as a happy event, supposing, as they did, that, by calling him to be their pastor, they could carry into effect the wishes of Mr. Winsor. He was at once invited to occupy the pulpit. He accepted the invitation, and preached a sermon on a Sunday which happened to be the day for the administration of the Lord's Supper. Several of the members of the church were, however, dissatisfied that "the privilege of transient communion" should have been allowed to Dr. Manning; believing that he held the doctrine of imposition of hands rather too loosely, and that he practised it more to accommodate the consciences of others than to meet the demands of his own. This dissatisfaction led to the formation of a party, and to a series of church meetings, in which the majority, however, was, in every instance, found to be on the side of Manning. With this party Mr.

Winsor himself sympathized and acted. This, however, was thought by some to be only "the ostensible reason" of dissatisfaction with Mr. Manning. The true cause of opposition to him was "his holding to singing in public worship, which was highly disgustful to Mr. Winsor." On this point the sentiments of the Quakers appear to have prevailed in the church, and singing was discarded as unauthorized by the New Testament. What diversity of opinion once existed touching a point which seems clear to us, may readily be seen by consulting the controversial works, on this subject, of Keach, Russell, Allen, Marlow, Claridge, and others, published in London towards the close of the seventeenth century.

Finally, adopting for the most part the language of the church records, Mr. Winsor, in April, 1771, presented to the church a writing, signed by a number of the members, stating that they were in conscience bound to withdraw from such as did not "hold strictly to the six principles of the doctrine of Christ as laid down in Hebrews vi. 1, 2." In May following he accordingly withdrew, and joined the "Separates." After advising with the Rev. Gardner Thurston of Newport, Rev. Messrs. Job and Russel Mason of Swanzey, and others, the church appointed a meeting to consider the propriety of calling President Manning to administer ordinances; whereupon the following resolution was passed:—

"At a meeting of the members of the Old Baptist Church in Providence, in church meeting assembled this 31st day of July, 1771, Daniel Jenckes, Esq., moderator: Whereas, Elder Samuel Winsor, now of Johnston, has withdrawn himself, and a considerable number of members of this church, from their communion with us who live in town; and we, being destitute of a minister to administer the ordinances amongst us, have met together in order to choose and appoint a suitable person for this purpose. Upon due consideration, the members choose and appoint Elder James Manning to preach and administer the communion according to our former usage."

To the above resolve Mr. Manning returned the following answer: —

" As the church is destitute of an administrator, and think the cause of religion suffers through the neglect of the ordinances of God's house, I consent to undertake to administer *pro tempore;* that is, until there may be a more full disquisition of the matter, or time to seek other help; at least, until time may prove whether it will be consistent with my other engagements, and for the general interests of religion."

Thus commenced a relation, which, through various vicissitudes and trials, incident to the disturbed times that soon followed, continued, with credit to the pastor and with great advantage to the church and congregation, down to a short period before Mr. Manning's death, in 1791. At first his preaching was not attended with marked results. But in 1774 a remarkable revival of religion attended his labors, as the fruits of which one hundred and four persons were added to the church. "It is delightful," says the Rev. Dr. Hague in his Historical Discourse, "to place ourselves in imagination amidst the scenes of that year, — to picture before us the able and faithful preacher who then officiated here as he stood up amidst the large assemblies of the people who thronged around him, listening, as they did, to the gospel with intense attention, as a message from the skies — the very word of God, which worketh effectually in them that believe, — to mark the lively interest which was kindled in every bosom and beamed from every eye, as one after another came forth 'on the side of the Lord,' and professed his faith in public baptism, — to contemplate the fresh springs of spiritual life which were then opened in many a house when the family altar was first erected there, and parents and children bowed together to worship the common Father and Redeemer in spirit and in truth."

The following letter to the Rev. Dr. Stennett gives a pleasing account of Manning's feelings in view of the responsibility of his position as head of the college and pastor of the church: —

PROVIDENCE, June 5, 1771.

REVEREND AND DEAR SIR:

Your most agreeable favor of August 10th, 1770, came to hand the 19th of January, 1771, after our ships had sailed for London; and consequently I have had no opportunity of acknowledging the receipt of it before. There are two ships from this town which make two voyages a year to London, besides others from the colony, by which letters will have a safe conveyance. The captains' names are Shand and Gilbert. I mention this that there may be the most direct conveyance.

I thank you for the expressions of kindness and respect in your letter, and am as desirous as before to keep up a correspondence as often as opportunity will admit. Mr. Gordon, the gentleman by whom you wrote, has never called on me, nor can I hear any direct account of him since his arrival in America. Your good wishes to the college are very acceptable, and we doubt not your readiness to contribute all in your power to its future growth and increase. The popularity, usefulness, etc., of our first sons, is to me an object truly desirable; but these things I leave to the wise conduct of the supreme Governor of the church. One of the youth,[1] graduated at our first Commencement, who is thought to be savingly brought home by grace, has joined Mr. Thurston's church in Newport, and appears eminently pious. As soon as his age will admit, for he is quite a youth, he will be called to the work of the ministry, with hopes of his making a distinguished figure in the pulpit. He bears the greatest resemblance to Mr. Hezekiah Smith of any person I know, and I hope will make such another son of thunder. I am constrained to think that Providence placed me at the head of the college; but for what end I cannot divine, I hope for good; for my ease and worldly advantage it could

[1] William Rogers.

not certainly be, for I have been constrained to forego these, and many more things desirable in life, on this account; and in the discharge of my office here I have found my way strewn with thorns hitherto.

Dr. Llewelyn's friendship for the college is highly satisfactory to us. He has it in his power, and, we have reason to believe, in his heart, to do it great service. I should highly prize a correspondence with a gentleman of his merit, were a door properly open for it; but to address him with a letter, uninvited, and without particular cause for so doing, might be deemed too great forwardness in me. I therefore choose to defer it at present. We were sensibly affected at the news of Mr. Roffey's death, as he promised usefulness to the public; but God can raise up men to carry on his own cause, in an unexpected way. The government is upon His shoulders; therefore we ought to rejoice. But nothing gives one such satisfaction as the account you give me of the success of the gospel in England. I firmly believe there are yet glorious days for the church militant, and that the doctrine of believer's baptism will prevail in proportion to the prevalence of the religion of the heart. I do not imagine this *only* from my own sentiments that it is an important and glorious ordinance of the Lord Jesus, but from facts; for I have observed for some years past that in this country it has been invariably the case where there has been a powerful moving of the Spirit of God upon the minds of men. I will give you a recent instance. God has been doing wonders in Virginia and North Carolina within these few years past. Thousands have been hopefully converted to God in these two provinces; and my Brother Gano, who travelled through these provinces last summer and fall, informs me that not less than two thousand have been baptized by immersion, upon profession of their faith. And it has been observed there, that persons were no sooner brought into the glorious liberty of the gospel than they followed the example of their Divine Master by going down into the water; and that, too, where the name of Baptist was scarcely known. This work, I am told, still continues, and extends five hundred miles in length through the country. Truly, light has risen to those who were in the region and shadow of death; for when I travelled through that country about ten years ago, I thought as Abraham did of Zoar, that the fear of God was not in that place. To me it seemed to be the rendezvous of devils. But what cannot God do? This indeed is all my consolation when I view the unpromising appearance of religion in many places, — that God not only can, but will work, and none shall let or hinder it.

There is a gradual increase of the work of religion in sundry places in

New England. Mr. Smith, I am told, is still marvellously owned in his labors, and that he was lately called to administer baptism to numbers at a distance from where he resides, and to constitute two or three Baptist churches. I can say but little of my success in the vineyard of the Lord, although I hope there are some promising appearances of conviction amongst us. The last Lord's Day there appeared an unusual solemnity in the assembly, and I trust God enabled me, though a worm, to speak with some happy degree of zeal and earnestness in warning souls of their danger; and if flowing eyes may be thought a presage of the return of wanderers to God, I am not without hope of some seals of my ministry. But alas my unprofitableness! — my unworthiness to be employed in so sacred a work! If ever one soul is converted by my instrumentality, it will clearly appear that the excellency of the power is all of God.

But I cease to trouble you with my unprofitable complaints, and proceed to give you some short account of the dispute between Baptists and Presbyterians in the provinces of Massachusetts Bay, New Hampshire, and Connecticut; in the latter of which, I am told, some of our brethren are now in jail for ministerial rates, and in the other two many are forcibly despoiled of their property for the same purpose. The Presbyterians, I believe, are determined, where they have the power, to use it against us to prevent our growth; for no effectual remedy can yet be obtained, though it has been carefully and industriously sought. They are afraid, if they relax the secular arm, their tenets have not merit enough and a sufficient foundation to stand. This has been so plainly hinted by some of the committees of the General Court, upon treating with our people, that I think it cannot be deemed a breach of charity to think thus of them. However, I will not pretend to justify everything which has been said and done by Baptists during this controversy. I fear there has been too great warmth in some publications; yet it is certain that there has been great provocation to write and speak some bitter things. However, I am far from believing that the cause of God requires acrimony in defending it, especially as the great Example of his people "reviled not again when he was reviled." Upon the whole, it is very uncertain what will be the issue of the matter, whether we must address the throne of our sovereign for relief, or not. The contention has been improved as an argument against sending scholars from that denomination to our college. How long this will continue I know not; but at present the clergy use all their endeavors to this purpose.

I am glad to hear that there are three Baptists in the trust of Dr.

Moore's fund who will see that the money is appropriated according to the original proposal; for our brethren of that denomination need good looking after in these matters, if we may judge from what has happened before.

I suppose you have heard that Dr. Wheelock has obtained a charter for a college in the province of New Hampshire, and about twenty thousand acres of land as an endowment, from the Governor and other gentlemen who are largely concerned in lands there. He has begun his business, and carried it forward with great rapidity. In short, from what I can gather, it is to be a grand Presbyterian college, instead of a school for the poor Indians. There were but two Indians there at school last fall, and they were Narragansetts from this colony, brought up like us. Moreover, it is more than a hundred miles distant from any number of Indians. I have conversed with two intelligent gentlemen from that part of the country, and, from what I can gather, the money raised in England by Whitaker and Oakam will be as greatly prostituted as ever the fund for propagating the gospel in foreign parts has been by another denomination of Christians.

As to political matters, all is peace and quietness with us, though we hear that the city of London and the House of Commons have proceeded to great lengths in opposing one other, and that the Lord Mayor and Alderman Oliver are committed to the Tower. We are anxious for the result of this procedure; but hope that God will order all matters for the best, and bring good out of evil.

We now proceed slowly with the college, as our succors from abroad fail. I hope we may have some more assistance from Great Britain as soon as may be.

If your patience is not quite gone, permit me to request the favor of a letter by our vessels this summer, in which you need not fear trespassing upon my patience, though I have reason to fear I have upon yours, and therefore subscribe, what I am in truth, dear sir,

Your very affectionate friend and brother in the Lord,

JAMES MANNING.

Allusion having been made in the foregoing communication to an effort on the part of the denomination to seek redress from their grievances by direct application to the "throne of our sovereign," or king, the following circular is presented as a sort of appendix thereto. Aside from its value in the connection, it will be read with interest as an illustration of the spirit and zeal of our fathers, among whom Manning was regarded as a "prince and a leader." It has never before, we believe, been printed.

CIRCULAR LETTER OF THE WARREN ASSOCIATION. 1770.

The Elders and Messengers met in association at Bellingham, September 11th, 12th, and 13th. To the churches they represent, and all others of the denomination of Baptists, send greeting:

We met in peace, and upon reading the letters from the several churches, found that they were generally at peace among themselves, some of them having had considerable additions, — the number of which, in all the churches, amounts to fifty-six. We find that God hath not left himself without a witness, but is still carrying on the work of grace in the churches. We would not despise the day of small things; yet at the same time desire you to unite in solemn prayer to the great Head of the church, that he would hasten the time when converts shall come as the clouds, and fly as doves to their windows. Oh happy period, which God in his wisdom has given us reason to expect, when the whole world shall be filled with the knowledge of the Lord! We have however to inform you, dearly beloved, that some of our churches are sorely oppressed on account of religion. Their enemies continue to triumph over them; and as repeated applications have been made to the court of justice and to the general courts for redress of such grievances, but as yet have been neglected, it is now become necessary to carry the affair to England in order to lay it before the King. It is therefore warmly recommended to you to endeavor to collect money to defray the expense which will arise from such a proceeding. Should you not contribute in this matter, some of our brethren must unavoidably be ruined as to this world; especially our brethren at Ashfield, some of whose lands have been taken from them and sold for a trifle. Brethren, make the case your own, and then do as you would be done by. We also recommend to you to search for promising gifts among yourselves, and bring them to the trial, as there is a great want of ministerial help in the churches. In fine, brethren, live in love; preserve the unity of the Spirit in the bonds of peace; keep your garments unspotted by the flesh, and may the God of peace and love be with you.

P. S. — The churches are requested to be expeditious in sending their contributions to the Rev. Samuel Stillman, of Boston, who is appointed treasurer, and to take his receipts. If our agent, Mr. Hezekiah Smith, should not go to England, the money will be returned when demanded. It is also requested that the churches will unite in keeping the first Thursday in October next as a day of fasting and prayer, to entreat God to favor our undertaking to obtain liberty of conscience, and to save our property, and consequently our families, from ruin; also that He will be graciously pleased to revive religion, and to deliver our nation from its present difficulties.

To his friend the Rev. Hezekiah Smith he thus writes. Manning, Edwards, and others, it will be observed, not unfrequently use the term Presbyterians for Congregationalists. The two denominations are much more distinct at the present day than they were a century ago.

NEWPORT, May 1, 1771.

DEAR SIR:

I perceive, by an application made to a neighboring Baptist church, that the people in Richmond, in Hampshire Government (I mean the Baptist church there), are in great distress on account of the taxes for the clergy; and so are the Baptists in sundry other towns thereabouts. The charter gave a farm to the first settled minister in that town; and Mr. Balow, the Baptist minister, was the first, though a Friend speaker was there before him. Now the Friends have united with the Presbyterians, and voted the farm for the use of the town. Upon the whole they seem troubled much, and some are likely to be totally ruined by the Presbyterians. Now if you can lend any aid or assistance, you will do them a singular favor; and I have been urged to write to you, that, if possible, you might make interest with the Governor, or some of the great men, to redress these grievances. I received a letter from Mr. Edwards, dated March, which informs me that he has a law of New Hampshire which obliges the Baptists to pay their ministers, — that is, Presbyterian ministers, — and he is greatly afraid they will fall into the snare. Pray do your utmost to prevent the Baptists from taking the benefit of that law; for the

Presbyterians will triumph in that case. Mr. Rogers, the bearer, will give you information of my affairs, and other matters in these parts; so that nothing remains but to desire you with Mrs. Smith to pay us a visit soon, to whom with yourself I give my sincere love, and remain, sir,

Your very loving friend,

JAMES MANNING.

The following letter was the commencement of a correspondence with the Rev. John Ryland, of Northampton, England, for many years principal of a flourishing academy in that place. Mr. Ryland was a distinguished scholar as well as a Baptist preacher, and was held in high esteem by Dr. Johnson and other eminent men of his time. He published "Contemplations on the Beauties of Creation," in three volumes octavo, "Essay on the Advancement of Learning," and various sermons and pamphlets. He died in 1792.

PROVIDENCE, June 1, 1771.

REVEREND SIR:

By the Rev. Morgan Edwards, last year, I was directed to draw upon you, the first of June, for five guineas, which you proposed to contribute annually to the support of the President of Rhode Island College during life, if your circumstances would admit of it. I drew accordingly in favor of Messrs. Joseph and William Russell, merchants of Providence; and, according to my instructions, have done the like this year, in favor of the same gentlemen.

Your zeal for the welfare of this young seminary, discovered in this as well as many other instances, has gained you the high esteem of all the true friends of the college here; but the particular favor done me herein has laid me under the strongest obligations of gratitude, of which I hope not to be unmindful, in any instance, when in my power to express a proper sense of them; and at present I can only do this by the strongest expressions of thankfulness, and fervent prayer to God that he would abundantly reward your beneficence in this and in the life to come.

I was particularly obliged in your favoring me with the patterns of the regular Greek and Latin nouns and verbs, etc., and find it the most easy method of leading boys into a general notion of grammar in a short time. The college in this place consists of twenty-three youths, five of whom are to leave us in the fall; though we hope to have some additions at that time. The institution calls for the vigorous exertions of all its friends, as well on account of the smallness of its funds as the unreasonable opposition made against it by Pedobaptists; especially the New England Presbyterians in general, who express the greatest bitterness on every occasion. The part I have had to act in the matter has exposed me to numberless difficulties hitherto; although I am cheerful under the hopes of its rising, at some future period, to be the joy of its friends and the denomination, as well as the mortification of its ungenerous enemies. The state of religion in New England is at a low ebb in general, except a few places, amongst which Mr. Stillman's of Boston is one, where there have been lately large additions to the church. Should there be any gentlemen of your acquaintance in England on whom diplomas might be well bestowed, we should always be glad to be advised thereof, and confer them accordingly. Forgive this unsolicited scrawl, and believe that it had its birth in the unfeigned gratitude and real friendship of, sir,

Your humble servant,

JAMES MANNING.

To this letter Ryland thus replies: —

TO MY WORTHY FRIEND, MR. JAMES MANNING,
PRESIDENT OF RHODE ISLAND COLLEGE:

REVEREND AND DEAR SIR: — I received your letter in due course by the post from London, and took care to pay your draft on me for £5 5s. when it came for payment, which it did in the beginning of December. Where it lodged all that time after you drew it, I know not.

Be assured that I have the interests of your college deeply at my heart; and in order to serve it I have picked out the enclosed list of scholars, for whom I solicit some of your academical feathers, to the end that we may attach as great a number of active and learned men to your seminary as we can. Who knows but some of them may do you more service in the long run than we can at present imagine? I am determined to send over some names every year as long as I live; but be assured I shall not recommend one that shall be a dishonor to your college, if I know it.

Have you had a short account of the ministers and churches of the Baptist denomination in England? If not I shall take care to send it. At present I would just observe that we have about two hundred and fourteen churches and ministers. About twenty-four ministers, perhaps twenty-six, can read the original languages in which the Bible was written. Amongst them I have a son (John), nineteen years of age, who was called to the ministry last year. He read his Greek Testament into English all through before he was nine years old, and is very ready at Hebrew, Latin, and French. Grace called him at fourteen years of age. I baptized him when he was about fifteen, and we received him into the church. He proves a good, zealous boy, and the people of God love to hear him preach. He has ventured to publish a volume of poems on experimental religion, the whole edition of which, five hundred, has gone off in less than a year. If I can procure a copy, I will send you one for your public library. Perhaps it may be a stimulus to some lazy student on your side of the water. My opinion, I am persuaded, is the same with yours, "that young boys and students need all sorts of motives to keep them in a steady, regular, resolute pursuit of learning and religion," and for this purpose academical honors were wisely instituted; and 'tis for this reason I desire for my brethren in the ministry who desire it the honors of your college, in order to incite others to the same diligence. I am sorry to say it, but 'tis too true, that above one hundred and seventy Baptist ministers in England have been kept from reading the Hebrew Bible and Greek Testament more by laziness and cowardice than by the difficulty of attaining it. I want to rouse these sluggards into diligence, and for that purpose I earnestly beg your assistance.

N. B. — Out of ten thousand clergy, we have seventy or eighty that preach the gospel. The Presbyterians are almost all gone off to Socinianism. We have a few in London that are excellent men; namely, Dr. Langford, Dr. Trotter, Geo. Stephens A.M., Mr. Hunter, and the Rev. Mr. Spilsbury. I cannot at present give you an exact list of our Independent ministers in London and the country, but shall try to send you an account. Let me be sure to hear from you four times a year; that is to say, once every quarter.

WORTHY MEN OF LEARNING AND CHARACTER WHO DESERVE THE HONORS OF RHODE ISLAND COLLEGE.

I. OF THE ESTABLISHED CHURCH OF ENGLAND.

These are most excellent men as scholars and divines.

1. AUGUSTUS MONTAGUE TOPLADY, A.B., Rector of Broad Hemburg, Devon.
2. HENRY FOSTER, A.B., Curate to the Rev. Mr. Romaine.
3. JOHN NEWTON, Curate of Olney; a man of uncommon wisdom, and a fine writer.

II. Independents.

1. William Porter, minister in Camomile Street.
2. John Stafford, successor to Dr. Guise.
3. John Pye, minister at Sheffield, Yorkshire.
4. William Hextall, successor to Dr. Doddridge, at Northampton.
5. Moses Gregson, at Rowell, Northamptonshire.
6. Joshua Symmonds, at Bedford. Preaches in John Bunyan's pulpit.
7. Rev. James Jennings, at Islington, near London.
8. Samuel Wilton, at Tooting, in Surrey.

III. Particular Baptists.

1. Robert Day, of Wellington, Somersetshire.
2. John Brown, of Kettering, Northamptonshire.
3. John Ash, of Pershore, Worcestershire.
4. John Poynting, of Worcester.
5. Benjamin Fuller, of Devizes, Wiltshire. (An old, rich, learned man, that can leave £100 to the college.)
6. John Oulton, of Rawdon, in Yorkshire.[1]

The "bitterness" of the Congregationalists of New England towards the college, to which Manning alludes, and their "unreasonable opposition" to it from its beginning, are illustrated in the following extract from a letter addressed to him by his friend Morgan Edwards. The writer supposes the President to have expected the friendship and help of the Congregationalists, had not the Baptists complained of the oppression of their brethren in New England, and threatened to carry their complaints to the throne of the King, in case the oppression should be con-

[1] The seventeen names mentioned in the above list all received the honorary degree of A.M. at the annual Commencement of the college in 1773 and in 1774. (See Triennial Catalogue.) It does not, however, appear that Mr. Ryland's good wishes in regard to the benefit which the college might thereby derive were ever realized, at least to any great extent. The unhappy feeling engendered by the war of the Revolution was, probably, the cause of this apparent neglect or indifference.

tinued. The letter, which is published in Staples's Annals of Providence, is a brief recapitulation of facts already stated in other forms. Mr. Edwards was evidently accustomed to express his opinions without reserve, and sometimes, perhaps, with a little too much pungency.

"I should not have ventured to oppose my opinions to yours, had not facts, recent facts, decided the matter in my favor, and shown that the goodness and candor of the President have imposed on his judgment. Remember you not the first charter? While the Baptist college was yet in embryo they very disingenuously opposed it, as such, and contrived to make it their own; since which disappointment Dr. Stiles would have nothing to do with it, though courted again and again to accept even a fellowship therein. And when the present charter was presented to the Assembly at South Kingston, remember you not what clamor they raised against it there? And what stout opposition they made to the passage of it, insomuch that its friends thought it best to desist? And how they triumphed afterwards? And when the affair was brought on again at East Greenwich, the next session, you can never forget with what heat and coarse expression the same oppositions were renewed, nor the mortification and murmurings which the passing of it occasioned. It is true, while the charter lay dormant they remained easy, and, as you say, appeared well pleased when you had set it on foot at Warren. But the reason of that is obvious. They knew that while the college stood friendless and moneyless, as it then did, they should have the pleasure to see it fall, and to mock those who began to build a tower and were not able to finish it. But seemed they good-humored when money came thither from Europe? or did they look as the man of Bristol did, at your first Commencement, and put the same invidious construction upon everything that he did on the complaisance you showed him that day? Their good affection toward the college edifice was but varnish; for while with specious arguments they would have it here, and anon there, and then in another place, they were only working to prevent it being anywhere; and soon as it had a locality and the beginning of its existence, at Providence, did they not, with some misled Baptists, attempt to get another college, to destroy yours, and actually carried their design through the lower house? This also failing, what remains but to prevent youth from resorting to it? Their slandering the officers of instruction, as insufficient; the town where it is in, as a lawless place; the college, as wanting government; their representing it as a nest of Anabaptists, calculated to make proselytes; their visiting grammar schools and tampering with masters and parents; their scolding Presbyterian youth when they enter with you, as your neighbor Rowley did, who is capable of nothing but what is gross and indelicate; their refusing to pay their subscriptions, etc., — are all intended to hurt what they could neither prevent nor destroy. Think you that their present opposition to the college is the effect of those newspaper complaints and threatenings of Presbyterian oppression in New England? Why, then, did they oppose it before those complaints and threatenings had existence? Think you they will be friends should we desist from these complaints and court their favor? It cannot be, except God should once teach them to love their neighbors as themselves, and do as they would be done by. Destroying the Baptist college will pacify them, and nothing else. The existence of that on the hill of Providence is a Mordecai in the gate. I told you, long ago, that if you could not do without the Presbyterians, you could not do at all. I need not inform you that I deal in generals. I except the honest, the trusty, and the good, and some such Presbyterians I have met with, in their connections with this college. God send us more, and mend the rest."

These ecclesiastical oppressions, and this sectarian bitterness towards the college, have all passed away, and are now forgotten; if occasionally recalled to remembrance, it is only in the spirit of kindness, as impressive admonitions to the fuller exercise of that charity which "beareth all things." As matters of history, they must of necessity appear conspicuous in any faithful account of the life and correspondence of Manning. They unveil, it is true, scenes of intolerance and persecution, which the enemies of religion may view with impious delight. On this point we may be allowed to quote the remarks of Professor Knowles, in his preface to the Memoir of Roger Williams. "We must not," he says, "in order to promote or defend religion, attempt to conceal events which history has already recorded, and much less to palliate conduct which we cannot justify. Let us rather confess, with frankness and humility, our own faults, and those of our fathers; learn wisdom from past errors; and bring ourselves and others, as speedily as possible, to the adoption of those pure principles by which alone Christianity can be sustained and diffused. The book of God records, among its salutary lessons, the mistakes and sins of good men."

On Wednesday, Sept. 4, 1771, was celebrated the third anniversary Commencement, at which six young men took their Bachelor degrees. From the account of this Commencement in the *Providence Gazette*, we present an abstract of the President's address: —

"A concise, pertinent charge was then delivered to the graduates, by the President; in which, besides many useful instructions and cautions, he remarked that this institution, though liberal and catholic in its foundation and government, despising the contracted views of a party, aiming at the good of mankind in general, and always studious to maintain a good agreement and harmony with others of the like nature, had not been so happy as to pass altogether without censure; and that not only from the ignorant and pedantic, but even from some of those whose friendship it has sought, and would highly esteem, could it consistently be obtained. He concluded by requesting their friendship and kind offices to that seminary of learning in which they had received their education; and with great energy exhorted them that if they could not, by their joint testimony of the generous, free, and impartial manner in which they had been treated in the course of their studies, silence the unreasonable clamors of ignorance and enmity, to give the world the same kind of proof of the usefulness of the institution which some of its first sons now do, who fill public stations with honor to themselves and advantage to mankind."

Among the graduates this year was Samuel Ward, son of Governor Ward, who, at the age of eighteen, commanded a company, under Arnold, through the wilderness of Maine to Quebec. He served with reputation in the army during the Revolutionary War, attaining to the

17

rank of lieutenant-colonel. Another graduate was Thomas Ustick, who was for many years the esteemed pastor of the Baptist church in Philadelphia, having succeeded the Rev. Dr. William Rogers.

The following letter, addressed to Thomas Llewelyn, LL.D., presents an idea of the condition and prospects of the college, and especially of the library, at this time. It affords an illustration of the author's skill in urging the claims of the institution over which he presided upon the attention of strangers of reputed benevolence and wealth. Mr. Llewelyn was a distinguished Cambro-British scholar of London. He published, in 1768, a History of the Welsh Versions of the Bible, and, in the following year, "Historical and Critical Remarks on the British Tongue." He died on the 7th of August, 1783, bequeathing to the Bristol Academy, where he pursued his early studies, his large and valuable library. Dr. Gibbons was accustomed, says Rippon, to speak of him "as the first scholar among the Protestant Dissenters."

PROVIDENCE, Feb. 21, 1772.

DEAR SIR:

I am emboldened to address you, both from the recommendation of Dr. Stennett to do so, and from my knowledge of your friendship to the college in this town, of which you would doubtless be glad to know the state.

The college edifice is erected on a most beautiful eminence, in the neighborhood of Providence, commanding a most charming and variegated prospect; a large, neat brick building, and so far completed as to receive the students, who now reside there, the whole number of whom is twenty-two. We have the prospect of further additions; yet our numbers will probably be small until we are better furnished with a library and philosophical apparatus. At present we have but about two hundred and fifty volumes, and these not well chosen, being such as our friends could best spare. Our apparatus consists of a pair of globes, two microscopes, and an electrical machine; to this we are desirous of making the addition of an air pump, if one reputable can be purchased for £22 10s. sterling; a sum which two young men informed me they intended to give towards an apparatus or library. If, therefore, it would not be too much trouble to inform me whether or not that sum is sufficient, I shall receive it as a particular favor; for if not, we shall appropriate it to some other use.

Our whole college fund consists of about £900 sterling, being the whole sum collected abroad; for no money collected without the colony is made use of in the building, but solely applied to endowing it, with the strictest regard to the donor's intent. The interest of this sum is quite insufficient to provide for tuition, as two of us are now employed, and we stand in need of further help. May we not expect some further assistance from our friends in England? or must we conclude that the Baptists, only, are inattentive, to their own cause, while seminaries of other denominations have the highest reason to extol their generosity? or is it because we use less industry to promote our common cause than others? If so, what might another personal application to England do on this head, could we find a person among us, of public spirit, who could forego the mortification of a beggar, etc.? Mr. Edwards happened in England at a most unfavorable juncture, or we should have expected far better success. If you imagine anything considerable can be done, we shall strive hard to obtain some person for this purpose; if not, permit me to solicit your interest, where you may be able to serve the cause. We have had the earliest proofs of your regard for the infant college, and retain a grateful sense of your unsought favors.

I shall take pleasure in communicating any intelligence in my power, whenever you please to lay your commands. My present situation is such as will furnish me with a general acquaintance with the state of the Baptist society in America, especially as I have travelled through the greatest part, and hold correspondence with some in almost all the provinces.

The ship by which this comes is bound directly back to Providence; and being owned by a zealous friend of the college, any books, or other things, should there be anything to send from any of our friends, would not only come directly, but free from the expense which might otherwise attend them.

The jealous eye with which other denominations of Christians behold this infant seminary leaves us without hope of any assistance from any but Baptists; and I think if we could but unite, and the whole body lend a helping hand, we should be able, without great difficulty, to rear the tender plant to a degree of maturity which might greatly subserve the cause of religion, especially in our society.

Craving your indulgence for giving you this interruption, and sincerely wishing you every felicity in this and a future world, I remain, dear sir,

Your unworthy brother and servant in the gospel,

JAMES MANNING.

TO THE REV. JOHN RYLAND.

PROVIDENCE, May 19, 1772.

REVEREND AND DEAR SIR:

On the 5th ult. I received your letter, as I judged from the contents, for it had neither your name nor any date to it. The contents gave me very great pleasure on various accounts, — as a testimony of your regard for me, the college, and the cause of religion in general, and especially for the zeal you discover in promoting the Baptist interests. The list of names you sent me shall be laid before the Faculty next September, and without doubt they will receive the honors of the college. We shall also be obliged to you for your proposed favor of sending us some names every year, and such, too, as are worthy of honor. I saw a paragraph in a letter to Rev. Isaac Backus, from Rev. Benjamin Wallin, of London, in which he intimated we had conferred degrees on some on your side of the water who would not do us honor. I shall therefore rely on you to pay particular regard to the literary qualifications of those whom you recommend, in order that our enemies may not have it in their power to reproach us on this head. I thank you for the hint given me concerning the number of our ministers and churches in Britain, and your offer of sending me a short account of them, which I have not seen. If there should be more than one on hand, it would gratify some of our friends if I could supply them. The present of the volume of poems will be very acceptable. Please to give my cordial love to the author, of whom I shall be mindful amongst others who deserve the honors of the college. I hope you will be happy in seeing him not only a faithful but successful laborer in Christ's vineyard. You may assure yourself that I will contribute all in my power to assist in "rousing the sluggards," etc. If the Presbyterians have let go the faith, I hope it is to promote the primitive ordinances of the gospel under the direction of a wise Providence. I think this has been and now is the case in New England; for many of the good people are following Christ into the water, who before quieted their consciences by the example of the fathers now with God; but they cannot find the same reason when they view the clergy of the present age. In short, if you hear of a work of God's Spirit among the Presbyterians of New England, you will soon hear that a Baptist minister is applied to to baptize them. God has been and is still doing marvellous things, in the outpouring of his Spirit on some of our churches; especially in Boston, Dighton, Rhehoboth, Swanzey, in the Bay Government, and in Warren, of this colony, under the ministry of Mr. Charles Thompson, one of the first class that graduated at this college. I am told that near three hundred have been baptized in these places since last September. Mr. William Rogers, a member also of the same class, about twenty-one years of age, has been called to the ministry, and is preaching in Philadelphia, where God appears to own his labors to admiration. He is a pious, warm Christian, and a very popular preacher in that city. All these things encourage me to believe that God regards this college with a favorable eye; especially as I have reason to hope that he has called by grace some who are now in college, since they came here, while others appear to be hopefully anxious about their salvation.

I shall make free to draw on you again the 1st of June, by Mr. Edwards's instruction, and continue to do so yearly until you forbid me. What think you of an application to England, by some suitable person, in order to augment our little and insufficient fund, as Mr. Edwards made but a partial application; or would a well-concerted scheme of a lottery [1] to raise £1000 or £2000 sterling meet with encouragement by the sale of tickets in England? Some method must be adopted, unless some generous, able benefactors should arise to assist us. I shall write frequently and long; and if you will do the same to me, you will greatly oblige,

Yours, etc.,

JAMES MANNING.

[1] Suggested perhaps by Mr. Manning's familiarity with the history of the College of New Jersey, the funds of which institution had been increased by lotteries which the legislatures of Connecticut, Pennsylvania, and New Jersey had granted for this purpose. Harvard and Yale Colleges, it may be added, were also aided by lotteries, the former even as recently as the year 1808. To show how common were lotteries in Rhode Island at this time, it may be stated, that, in the space of twenty-seven years, from 1752 to 1779, no less than fifty-four were granted by the General Assembly for the building of churches, parsonages, schoolhouses, bridges, streets, wharves, etc., as we find by looking over the "Colonial Records."

For a very interesting account of lotteries in behalf of the Rev. Dr. Hopkins's church in Newport, the reader is referred to Prof. Park's Memoir of the Life and Character of Dr. Hopkins, pp. 113, 114.

From the following notice, which was published in the *Providence Gazette*, it appears that President Manning still retained charge of the Latin school, it being without doubt the same which he commenced at Warren eight years previous to this date. Thus, in addition to his labors as pastor of the church and President of the college, he was engaged in teaching lads, directly or otherwise, the elements of knowledge, and in furnishing them, as also the college students, with school books, "at the lowest rate."

Whereas several gentlemen have requested me to take and educate their sons, this may inform them, and others disposed to put their children under my care, that the Latin school[1] is now removed, and set up in the college edifice; where proper attention shall be given, by a master duly qualified, and those found to be the most effectual methods to obtain a competent knowledge of grammar, steadily pursued. At the same time, spelling, reading, and speaking English with propriety, will be particularly attended to. Any who choose their sons should board in commons, may be accommodated at the same rate with the students, — six shillings per week being the price. And I flatter myself that such attention will be paid to their learning and morals as will entirely satisfy all who may send their children. All books for the school, as well as the classical authors read in college, may be had, at the lowest rate, of the subscriber.

JAMES MANNING.

PROVIDENCE, July 10, 1772.

[1] Where the Latin school was kept previous to this date we cannot positively state; it is, however, more than probable that it was in one of the chambers of the brick schoolhouse on Meeting Street. The other chamber, as has already been stated, was occupied by the officers and students of the college. This schoolhouse, as appears from Staples's Annals of Providence, was built during the year 1768, partly by the town, and partly by subscription. By this compound arrangement the town owned the lower story, while the upper story was owned by the subscribers, among whom the friends and guardians of the college were largely represented. As we have remarked in a previous chapter, this school, commenced by Manning at Warren in 1764, was for a long time connected with the college or university. In 1810 the corporation erected a brick building for its accommodation, at an expense of fifteen hundred dollars.

The following letter, addressed to Mr. Ryland, under date of Nov. 12, 1772, gives an account of the greatest donation the library had at that time received; namely, the works of Dr. Gill the distinguished commentator, and fifty-two folio volumes of the Fathers, presented through Dr. Gill's executors. From this letter we also learn the interesting fact that Manning's salary as President of the college was a little less than £68 sterling, or about three hundred and forty dollars. His salary as pastor of the church, according to Morgan Edwards, was £50. Whether this was £50 sterling or lawful money we cannot tell; probably the latter. This would make the sum total of compensation for all his services about five hundred dollars.

Reverend and dear Sir:

I have not received an answer to mine of May 19th, 1772, yet am not willing to let this opportunity pass without a line. The Faculty conferred the degree of A.M., at our last Commencement, on your son, the Rev. John Ryland, Jun.; but through my hurry, and absence from home since Commencement, I have not got his diploma written, and must therefore omit sending it until my next. Those other gentlemen you mentioned did not receive their degrees; the Faculty chose to know whether they have been consulted personally, and wish to receive the honors of our college; otherwise it might do us hurt instead of service. What suggested this reflection, in part, was a paragraph in a letter from Mr. Wallin of London to Mr. Backus, which I saw, in which he seemed to insinuate that we had been too lavish of our honors. If these gentlemen would accept diplomas from us, we should give them with pleasure; but we do not choose to give them to those who would not thank us for them, as I think has been the case with some even on your side of the water.

With this I send you a catalogue of those who have received the honors of the college from the first. Our last Commencement, I believe, acquired us considerable reputation amongst the *literati* in New England; and had we not to combat with the inveterate enmity of the New England clergy, it would have added to the number of our scholars; but they take unwearied pains to prevent any from coming if possible, and do not stick at the method of carrying their points; but, thank God, *they* don't govern the world.

Last month I returned from a journey through the western provinces, as far as Philadelphia. I found religion at an ebb in those churches in general, as is the case through the most of New England. Virginia is still in a flame, and hundreds are hopefully turning to God. I attended the Association at New York, and we had a very comfortable season. I herewith send you an Association letter.

I should be glad to know in what sense you give the five guineas which I have been directed to call upon you for annually. The reason is this: I have always rendered an account of it to the corporation as a part of my salary from the college, which is £67 13s. 4d. sterling, annually, and some of the members have found fault with me for so doing, alleging that, as my salary is inadequate, I ought to consider it as a free gift, or so much over the above sum; but this I would by no means do without an explicit account of your intention in the donation, according to which I shall be governed, and therefore I pray you to resolve me in this matter.

By the last ship we received the works of the great and good Dr. Gill, with fifty-two folio volumes of the Fathers, etc., the gift of Messrs. George Keith and John Gill, the Doctor's executors. This is by far the greatest donation our little library has yet had; but I hope their generous example will be followed by others on your side of the Atlantic. Do you think it would be worth while for an American Indian, as we are generally deemed, to visit England, on the errand of collecting some more money for our college? For we really need it. I have been mentioned, if my place in the interim could be supplied, for this purpose, provided the prospect promised anything worth while. But the inattention of the Baptists to their own interests disheartens me greatly.

I have written two letters to Dr. Stennett since I have had an answer, and I am afraid I have tired that good man with my nonsense, and that my letters have been mislaid or intercepted. Pray, have you heard of the Doctor's being addressed by Dr. Chauncey, of Boston, with a design to alienate him from the cause of the New England Baptists, by sending him reproachful accounts of them? I was told by one of our brethren this was suspected to be the case, from some extraordinary steps taken by that society. If that should be the case I should be glad to know; and if you are intimate with the Doctor, you may probably know through him. A minister of reputation gave me this hint but a few days past, or I would not have mentioned it, supposing them incapable of so low an artifice. I am told another[1] of my first class is to preach on trial next Lord's Day, which will make three of that class in the ministry.

With great respect, I am, sir, yours to serve,

JAMES MANNING.

RYLAND'S REPLY.

NORTHAMPTON, Feb. 9, 1773.

REVEREND AND DEAR SIR :

I have enclosed a few hints for your notice and consideration. If they are of any service to you, or to the cause of religion and to your college of learning, I shall be glad.

I have, in the midst of the cares of a family of about sixty persons, thrown out some thoughts concerning matters before us; and as you know I bear you a hearty good-will, I am not in any pain how you may receive and relish them. If you are that man of sense and honor I conceive you to be, you will like my blunt friendship better than drivelling flattery and nauseous palaver. (*Verba sit nenia;* for it is not in Dr. Sam. Johnson's Dictionary.)

I have filled a whole sheet of post-demy paper, so that you have rough and enough. The pamphlets and sheets which accompany this are a present to yourself, unless you think it worth while to put them in your college library, or in the fire, just as you please.

If you like my mode of correspondence, and take everything in good part, I shall soon hear from you. I am to you, and to the interests of religion and learning under your care,

A hearty and zealous friend,

JOHN RYLAND.

RYLAND'S HINTS FOR PROF. MANNING'S USE.

1. In January, 1772, I sent a box of twenty-five books to the Rev. Morgan Edwards, at Philadelphia, by the favor and care of Mr. Daniel Roberdean, merchant, who was then in London, and abode at my old lodgings, Mrs. Stephens's, No. 11, in Great St. Hellen's; and was about to return

[1] The Rev. William Williams.

to America. In a letter to Mr. Edwards I desired him to present some of those books to Rhode Island College, but have heard nothing from him, nor have you mentioned one word about the books.

2. Mr. Wallin had no right to reproach your college as being too lavish of its honors, unless he meant himself, and himself only.

3. For me to ask any of those gentlemen I nominated in my letter, whether he would please to accept of a degree from your college, would spoil all the honor and delicacy of conferring it. Its coming *unsought*, yea *unthought* of, constitutes its chief excellence and acceptableness to men of fine feelings. For my own part, I would not have given you a single farthing, or so much as a thanks, for a feather, if I had it not in my power with the utmost truth to say, "I neither sought it, nor bought it, nor thought for a moment about it" (Dr. Gill's saying on having his diploma from Scotland).

4. By your withholding these honors from the men I so well knew to deserve them, and not one would have refused them, you have done your college damage in its temporal interests. My design was to serve you by attaching men of grace, learning, property, and influence to you. But if you do not choose it in my way, it shall be let alone; for I assure you I never will ask one man whilst I live to accept of a degree.

I could find men enough in Britain that have learning sufficient, who would snap at your honors for the sake of some low ends and purposes; but their characters as divines, or their capacity or will to serve you, is nothing. In truth, I keep no such company. I form no connection with them, nor will I whilst I live. On the other hand, the Rev. Augustus Toplady is the first divine of the Established Church, or indeed of any church in England or in Europe. He is a man of fortune, of high genius, and learning. He is my intimate friend; and let me tell you, as a secret, of a mark of his regard for me. He put it to my choice, in case of his death before me, which part of his library I would have, the English, or the Latin and learned part. I chose the latter, and it is accordingly fixed. But I hope I shall never have the pain to accept them. He is a man of a prodigiously high spirit by nature, but 'tis so tempered and moderated by grace, and a noble and generous disposition, as renders him one of the boldest champions for the sublime truths of the gospel in the world. We have no writer amongst all our divines that comes near to him in energy and grandeur of thought, rich and daring imagination, masculine judgment, and glowing colors of style. He is about twenty-nine or thirty years old, but has been educated, from sixteen years of age, in all the grand essentials of the gospel. He had his classical education at Westminster School, and his academical at the University of Dublin; owing to an estate falling to his mother in Ireland, and she being obliged to go over and possess it, she took her only son, at sixteen, with her. Dr. Thos. Leland was his tutor. But he had the good sense and piety to go to the Baptist meeting on Lord's Days to hear an able preacher, now dead, his name Rutherford; and every year, when Mr. Toplady came over to England, he had the boldness and wisdom to sit under the stated ministry of Dr. Gill. He is a generous friend to Dissenters, especially to us poor Baptists. He commenced A.B. at Dublin. He scorns all honors, unless conferred like grace from heaven, — "unthought of, unimplored."

My other friends are of the same complexion; therefore I will never ask one of them to accept of a feather from your college. Mr. Isaac Woodman, of Sutton in Leicestershire, is a prince in his spirit and conduct. He is the father of our Midland Association, and a wise counsellor to us all. He has such a degree of modesty that he will not wear the feather you sent him, and wishes not to have it known on this side of the water. But what then? Has he done you any damage or dishonor? No. All that know him will revere him as a man of wisdom, benevolence, and learning in the Greek language and philosophy. As to damage, I will tell you. He is a man of substance, and has a fine library; he has no children; and you will have half, if not the whole, for your college when he dies. Will this hurt you? Perhaps some money into the bargain. And thus I should have attached others to your interests; but you would not let me, in your wisdom. Just as if you knew men here better than I do, who have lived forty years amongst them. As to the five guineas I pay every year, 'tis for yourself and nobody else. 'Tis because I like your character, spirit, and principles. If you die, and another succeed you whom I should not approve, I will stop my hand.

As to raising money by a lottery, I dislike it from the bottom of my heart. 'Tis a scheme dishonorable to the supreme Head of all worlds and of the true church. We have our fill of these cursed gambling lotteries in London every year. They are big with ten thousand evils. Let the devil's children have them all to themselves. Let us not touch or taste.

I sent two books to the Rev. Mr. Stillman, at Boston, last summer, by Mr. Story, of Boston. One of the books is a present to the library of your college. It is entitled "An Easy Introduction to Sir Isaac Newton's Philosophy." It was written by one of the clearest and most condescending good-natured philosophers in the world for the use of my school, Mr. James Ferguson, Fellow of the Royal Society. 'Tis adapted to your school-boys and junior students, to prepare them for larger treatises on the same subjects. I should be glad to find it meet with the approbation of your learned Professor of Philosophy.

Agreeably to Ryland's suggestion, the college the following year conferred on the Rev. Augustus Toplady the honorary degree of A.M. Mr. Toplady's works have been published in six octavo volumes, with an account of his life. To the Christian public he is known as the author of "Rock of ages cleft for me," and "Deathless spirit, now arise," regarded by many as two of the finest hymns in the English language.

TO THE REV. DR. STENNETT.

PROVIDENCE, Nov. 13, 1772.

REVEREND AND DEAR SIR:

As I have sent two or three letters since receiving one from you, I should not now write, as I have nothing of importance to communicate, had not the Rev. Isaac Backus, of Middleborough, requested me, on the following account: He has been up to Ashfield not long since, and found that the Congregational clergy there, as well as elsewhere, have been very busy in collecting all the scandalous reports they can hear of; and as they think, from some circumstances, sending them to Dr. Chauncey, of Boston, in order to transmit the same to you, to prevent you from interesting yourself in their cause. I confess this is a suggestion which would seem to flow from a bad heart, destitute of charity, to a person who is acquainted only with the fair side of their character; but to those who are conversant with them in New England, that they should conceive such a design is far from being a thing incredible. Now if this is the case, I have authority from Mr. Backus, a man of unblemished reputation, to inform you that, so far as he could judge, from being on the spot and viewing the lands, etc., wrested from those poor Baptists, he verily thought their complaints were lighter than their grievances, and that their sufferings have been extremely great. And as Mr. Backus is appointed by the body of the Baptists in New England to collect materials for their history, he prays and doubts not but you will, through my hands, favor him with intelligence respecting this matter, by the first opportunity, that he may have it in his power to undeceive you if they have sent you these accounts.

The state of the college is much the same as when I wrote last, as to numbers, and still wants powerful friends to patronize and endow it. Messrs. Keith and Gill, the Doctor's executors, by the last ship have sent us a set of the Doctor's works, and fifty-two volumes of the Fathers, etc., which is the greatest donation our little library has yet had.

I have visited the western provinces this fall, and find there but dead times in religion, except in Virginia, where God still continues to do wonders amongst the people; though, as of old, by instruments to the eye of human reason very weak; but God clothes them with power. I attended the Philadelphia Association, held in New York this year, and was very agreeably entertained with the company of a number of my fellow-servants, who seem zealous to promote the Redeemer's kingdom. One of them, Mr. David Jones, has been the last summer visiting and preaching to the western tribes of Indians between the Ohio and Mississippi; and, like an apostle amongst the Gentiles, was to set out on the first of this month, at his own charges, to pay his interpreter, and spend the winter among the natives. He says they give ear to the gospel, and importuned him to come again. He thinks there is a great prospect of many turning to God amongst them; and who knows but they may? I believe it is the first instance of the Baptists going among them for that purpose. The Association was highly pleased with the accounts he gave, and recommended it to the churches to set on foot a collection for him; but I fear he must exhaust his own little pittance, notwithstanding what they will do; for public spirit is a virtue rarely found in this country amongst good people. But lest I weary your patience, I subscribe myself, sir,

Your friend and servant,

James Manning.

REV. ISAAC WOODMAN, TO MANNING.

Thorp (or Sutton), near Leicester,
Feb. 20, 1773.

Reverend Sir:

By the favor of Mr. Ryland I have seen the New York Association letter, and have had some account also of yours to him. I am glad Christ's interest under our denomination has such a respectable footing in your parts, but sorry for the languor of religion in some places, whilst glad 'tis otherwise elsewhere. Amongst other things at the Association, the respectful notice taken of Mr. Edwards gives me pleasure.

As I am a well-wisher to the prosperity of the college, I would, if I could, advise to anything for its furtherance. If you were to come over, I fear your compass or scope for soliciting visits would be very narrow. There is no reasonable hope of success where congregations are unable to support the interest at home, and where there may be a prejudice against literature: a common but not universal case amongst us. I think it would be in vain to attempt it, unless you have encouragement from London, Bristol, and a few more of our opulent congregations.

But, whether you come or not, I have long thought that a good printed narrative of the state of the college sent hither, to be disbursed by its friends, would be of service. I doubt not some fruit would spring from such seed scattered by skilful hands.

You will be able, I hope, to let us know that our denomination in the Island, and especially the college, is loyal and obedient, disapproving the opposition made to Government in your neighborhood, if public reports of such opposition made, be indeed true. I am for liberty, regularly maintained.

Should any such narrative be sent, or brought by yourself, it is to be hoped the list of those you have honored with degrees will not be put into every hand, or at least that those who particularly desire it may have their names omitted. I esteem the honors of the college, and am obliged to the Faculty for putting my name amongst your worthies; pray please to present my grateful compliments; but I must not own the title. 'Tis an honor I cannot support. For your sakes, therefore, as well as for my own, I must decline it. I ought to say, indeed, in favor of my friends, whoever recommended me to your regards, they verily believed, I doubt not, that I was qualified; and it might have been so had I prosecuted my beginnings; but an inveterate headache, of above thirty years' standing, has disabled me from making much addition to what I set out with when I left Bristol. I am a hearty friend to your cause. My silence has not been from carelessness or ingratitude, and much less from contempt. I desired Mr. Ryland to make my excuse. I am not able to show the regards I wish to discover; howbeit, I have friendly designs. But the honor you have done me would, if known, as it is not yet in my neighborhood, block up my way to serve you, which I have much at heart to do.

I congratulate you upon your correspondence with and interest in Mr. Ryland. He is, I may say from long acquaintance with him, a worthy man, and a warm friend of the cause which he espouses. I do not know that you could have one more zealous in your affairs in all Old England. With sincere and hearty wishes that the honorable and important institution over which you preside may have its worthy ends answered in the furtherance of knowledge, virtue, and true religion, and yourself be greatly helped and blessed with all needful assistance in the good work of forming the minds of youth, I rest, esteemed and dear sir,

Yours, affectionately,

ISAAC WOODMAN.

MANNING'S REPLY.

PROVIDENCE, NOV. 26, 1773.

REVEREND AND DEAR SIR :

Yours of Feb. 20th, 1773, came to hand last week, in company with several others, agreeable letters from friends in England, to whom I write by this opportunity. I am heartily glad to hear your favorable disposition towards the college, and could heartily concur with you in your wishes for greater abilities to serve its interests ; though we have for our encouragement the commendation of the poor widow's contribution. I should think it a prodigy if all you English Baptists were friends to literature, while the case is so far otherwise in America. But I think your good, zealous people are mistaken in striking against it, when kept in its proper place, — I mean in making it an handmaid to religion.

I am sorry you are so scrupulous in point of confessing the honor we meant to confer on you, though you must be a better judge of the expediency of this, in your situation, than I can possibly be. But the infant state of literature in this new world, and the usages of the college here, lead us to conclude, from your known character, that you need not be so diffident of your abilities as to decline the feather, as our common friend Mr. Ryland calls it.

The history of the rise, present state, etc., of the college, will be done in some manner, and sent to England next spring, unless Providence should prevent it ; but I wish it could be done by an abler hand, or that I had more leisure than my present circumstances will afford for it. I know how to sympathize with you in your inveterate complaint (of the headache) ; for, while I write, I am distressed with this pain.

I highly prize Mr. Ryland's friendship, because I have found him a friend indeed. I revere his character, and place the highest confidence in him. The very small number of friends and the great number of enemies the college has, requires the greater exertion of the few friends of which it can boast, in its favor. I hope to see it on a more respectable footing, should I live to an advanced age; and if not, I hope posterity will reap great advantages from it. With the most hearty wishes for your highest welfare, I am,

Your friend and servant in the gospel,

JAMES MANNING.

N. B. — I hope those who know the little Colony of Rhode Island, and especially the Baptist society in it, will find that, though firm in the cause of constitutional liberty, we are as loyal subjects as any of which his Majesty King George can boast. I wish I could tell you more agreeable news of the state of religion among us, but it is indeed a dark day. Enclosed I send you a form of bequeathment, which we make use of this way. At Newport I find one of which I had no knowledge before.

J. M.

Concerning Mr. Woodman, and his suggestion in regard to a narrative of the college, Mr. Ryland, under date of Feb. 9, 1773, thus writes to Manning: —

"My good father in the ministry, and counsellor, Mr. Isaac Woodman, is earnestly desirous (and with him I concur) to hear from you. A clear narration of the rise, progress, and present state of the college at Rhode Island, with an account of the methods of education in the languages, sciences, and divinity; the exercises of the students, and the character of those who have distinguished themselves by their diligence, improvement, and piety, — this we think to reprint and disperse through all England amongst our best and richest friends of all denominations, in order to solicit subscriptions and donations. Had you done this already, and sent about twenty honors to the men I named, a way would have been paved for your coming over and making your appearance and personal applications this next summer. But for want of these two preliminaries, you have prevented yourself from coming with a good prospect of success for this year. If you will take our advice, and put it in our power to serve you by conciliating men's esteem and affection to your person and college, perhaps we can pave the way for you by next May come twelvemonth, 1774; and may do Rhode Island some service."

The following playful letter to his intimate friend, the Rev. Hezekiah Smith, shows that Dr. Manning could be merry, as well as serious. Indeed, he was noted above most men for his genial companionship and rare social qualities.

PROVIDENCE, May 5, 1773.

REVEREND AND DEAR SIR :

This is to give you the reason why I did not visit you at Haverhill, and invite you to come to Providence. I set out from Providence, intending to spend a week at Boston and Haverhill. We (for Mrs. Manning accompanied me) arrived at Boston Friday evening, and proposed to set out for Haverhill on Monday; but that and several succeeding days proving rainy, and Mrs. Manning being very poorly, to our very great disappointment, mortification, etc., we were obliged to return to Providence without going further. Now, therefore, as I am tied to college, pray take Mrs. Smith, and the heir apparent,[1] and the new chaise, and come and take your station for a week or two on the hill of Providence, where I will insure you excellent good water, the best my house affords, and our good company. Pray, what more would you have? If anything in my power to render the visit still more agreeable, depend on it, you sha'n't be wanting it.

I have made a tour into the hither parts of Connecticut this vacation, and preached fifteen times in fourteen days; seven of them in Presbyterian meeting-houses. What do you think of that? See what it is to be catholic like me, while you, with brandishing weapons, take the field of Mars like an old veteran that scorns to let his sword rust. Good success to you, if you must draw. I have received a packet from England, and our good friend Rev. John Ryland is angry enough because we did not give degrees to the gentlemen he recommended, and says that we have lost by it greatly. How happens it that not one scholar, through your influence, comes from you to our college I? fear you don't exert yourself. We have no late news from the westward. Friends here are generally well, and very desirous to see and hear Mr. Smith, as are your good friends at New London. Mrs. Manning joins in love to you and Mrs. Smith, as, also, to all our good friends at Haverhill, with, dear sir,

Your unworthy brother,

JAMES MANNING.

[1] Their infant son, born March 12, 1772.

Dr. Manning now begins a correspondence with the Rev. Benjamin Wallin, a prominent Baptist minister of London, and a gentleman of reputed wealth. He was also a religious writer of some note. "The Christian Life Described," "Discourses on various subjects," "Parable of the Prodigal Son," "Evangelical Hymns and Songs," and various other works by him are to be found upon the shelves of the college library, a gift from the author. Under date of May 18, 1773, Manning thus writes:—

DEAR BROTHER:

From Mr. Philip Freeman, of Boston, I received your agreeable present, on the third inst., and having perused with much satisfaction the several pieces, especially the Tribulation, I am rejoiced to find that it is not "another gospel." Had I capacity, to which I make no pretensions, to examine Mr. Wallin's productions with the eye of a critic, I feel no disposition, be assured, to do it. I import annually a few books from London, principally for the youth under my care, and should have sent for some of your publications; but as Mr. Backus has them by him, I have thus far deferred doing this, not wishing to interfere in any way with him. I should be glad to know whether you designed the books as a present to me personally, or to the college library, that I may return you thanks in a proper manner. In either case I am greatly obliged, and heartily thank you therefor.

The executors of Dr. Gill have followed the laudable example of Dr. Stennett, and made us a present of his works, which we deem a most valuable donation. These acts encourage us to hope for similar favors from our friends in Europe. Should any benevolent person be disposed to make a useful donation to our library and at a loss to know what books to choose, allow me to suggest the works of good Mr. Bunyan, than which none would be more acceptable.

Mr. Edwards has been your substitute for the gentlemen as desired. Through Messrs. Stillman and Backus I learn that the Lord has visited you sorely in the loss of your only daughter. But you need not be told by me that God is a portion infinitely preferable to that of sons or daughters. I doubt not but you find already a strong attachment to this earth broken, and that God leads by the right way. The discipline of the rod is often necessary, at least to such perverse hearts as mine.

Mr. Backus informs me that he has lately written to you, thus removing the necessity of my giving you a recital of affairs amongst us, or of detaining you longer than to crave your indulgence for obtruding upon you this letter, which assures you, dear sir, of the unfeigned affection of your unseen but very much obliged

Friend and servant,

James Manning.

P. S. — This day received letters from several of the western provinces. Find that religion is at a low ebb in general there, as, alas, it is too generally amongst us. If business would permit, should rejoice to see a line from Mr. Wallin, by our fall ships.

Mr. Wallin's reply is so excellent in spirit, that no apology need be offered for its introduction into our present work: —

London, July 30, 1773.

Reverend and dear Sir:

Your respectful lines by Mr. Keith very much obliged me; nor am I less indebted to your candor in perusing my endeavors, being sensible that they will not bear the eye of a critic. The disadvantages under which I was at length brought into a service, conscientiously declined in the very early part of my life, in consequence of which I deprived myself of an intended more liberal education, might plead some excuse; and were you to know by what solicitation and management I was prevailed on to repeat my visits to the press, you would rather pity than blame me, and cover my numerous defects with a mantle of love.

I thought it a venture to possess one of your character with such feeble and imperfect attempts, — they are at best only fit for children in Christianity, — how, then, could I think of proposing them to the most infant seminary of learning? Indeed, sir, they were intended only as an instance of respect to yourself, to be glanced at with the friendly disposition you express. It would have impeached your last, had not the ingenious discourses of my much esteemed brother, the Rev. Dr. Stennett, been universally admired among you. As to the works of that great man, the late Dr. Gill, who was truly a father, they may justly be accounted a considerable acquisition. I know not, upon the whole, an author more judicious and consistent. The compass of his writing is astonishing, from the labors of which he now rests until the Chief Shepherd comes, when it will appear that our endeavors for his name shall not be in vain.

But seeing you intimate that it may not be unacceptable, I presume, though with some reluctance, to send all I can collect of my publications, which together make ten little volumes, and possibly five entire pieces, and five of sermons, addresses, etc. Also the ordination of Rev. A. Booth, who sends a volume of the sermons of his predecessor, the late Mr. Wilson, and his own "Reign of Grace," etc. These will not be the less welcome for being accompanied by all the works of Mr. Bunyan, agreeably to your suggestion. These I present, with my most respectful compliments, to every member of the college, including their worthy President the Rev. Mr. James Manning. Have you, sir, any stated form of bequeathment? If not, permit me to move for a concise account of your institution, with a direction how to describe you in a will. Such a paper, neatly printed and disposed, may be useful. Be not sparing of copies to your friends. The difference in point of expense between one or two thousand is but trifling.

As to my own works, most of them have been out of print for some years. They are chiefly practical, and all very plain. The hymns, more especially, need an apology. They are no other than artless compositions, in which the substance of occasional discourses was drawn up in a suitable form. Such a one did not occur in our stated collection. At the time, they were sung with peculiar satisfaction, the people being unacquainted with the author; but at length many of them were stolen and mangled, which induced me, at the instance of some, to print them, and so obviate any apprehension of a conceit that they were deserving of public notice. It is my study, both in preaching and in writing, to lead to those inexhaustible treasures of wisdom and comfort, the Holy Scriptures; hence the tone of my naked lines. I must observe further, that in order to make up the set, I was obliged to put in a volume containing my sermon on the experience of the saints, which was bound up in another. You will therefore excuse a duplicate of them.

It is long since I have heard from my very worthy and agreeable correspondent the Rev. Mr. Backus. He usually much entertains me. I have often rejoiced at his accounts of the success of the gospel in your world, and am sorry to hear that at present in general it seems rather low. May the Lord of Jacob revisit it! Two things are threatening with us, — the growth of Anti-Trinitarians, in a variety of forms, for they cannot agree; nor can I forbear to say that I think a dereliction of, or indifference to the divine Sonship of our glorious Redeemer, has greatly contributed to the insolence of men against that foundation of the gospel. The other is a popular ignorance of the authority of Christ, in particular church fellowship, which some are bold enough to put on the footing of prudence and convenience among the disciples of Jesus. The one strikes at the doctrine, the other at the discipline of the gospel. But Zion is insured against the gates of hell.

I am now in the eve of my ministry and life; childless, and in a manner destitute of natural relation, having lost an excellent wife, two sons, and three daughters. It is good to be weaned from an undue attachment to the present state, but afflictions alone will not do it. My heavenly Father has been very gracious in helping me, I trust, to receive not only good at his hand, but also evil. He has given me a name and a place in his house better than that of sons or of daughters, and some spiritual children who are exceeding affectionate and dutiful.

May your valuable life be long spared, and all your instructions succeed to the advantage of mankind, and especially to the spread of the truth and the prosperity of Jerusalem. I remain, reverend and dear sir,

Your obliged and truly affectionate brother,

BENJAMIN WALLIN.

TO THE REV. JOHN RYLAND.

PROVIDENCE, May 20th, 1773.

REVEREND AND DEAR SIR:

Yours of Feb. 9th, 1773, came safely to hand, by the Charlotte, Capt. Jno. Rogers, about the 20th of April, containing your agreeable present of pieces, letters, etc., for all of which I scarce need tell you I heartily thank you. You need not for the future hesitate about sending anything to me in that way, or writing with the utmost plainness to one who believes not in the use of ceremony, even if he were master of it. To convince you that I am entirely suited with your plain dealing, I have embraced the earliest opportunity of returning an answer.

Your friendship to the interests of the college and religion here is very cordially accepted by many besides myself; and though you thought we slighted your friendship, I can assure you it was not so meant; I shall be glad to gratify you, and testify our respect for any of your friends, on every occasion. But I come to particulars.

The books ordered here from Mr. Edwards have not come; neither have I heard of them, except by your letter, though I saw Mr. Edwards at Philadelphia last October. He must surely have forgotten it entirely.

I have seen Mr. Backus since I received yours, and he thinks I mistook Mr. Wallin's meaning, and that he intended only himself. If so, I am sorry I mentioned anything of the matter. Indeed, Mr. Wallin, in his last letter, which I have seen, intimated as much.

I entirely agree with you respecting academical honors, and the mode of conferring them on gentlemen of taste; and as you are fully satisfied that the gentlemen mentioned would cordially accept them, you may be assured we shall take proper care of that matter next Commencement, and forward the diplomas as soon as possible. If we have been tardy, I know you will forgive us. An unforgiving friend is not worth having. Such I do not deem my very good friend Mr. Ryland. I am heartily sorry that the college should sustain damage, through what we meant only for precaution, and hope, if so, that it will be only temporary. We beg you not to remit an iota of your zeal in attaching gentlemen of grace and learning, property and influence, to the college. For amongst all our good friends in Britain, we consider your opportunities in this way, together with your zeal, as placing you foremost.

The character of the Rev. Mr. Toplady, which you have enlarged upon, is truly a rare one, and I shall think the college highly honored in his accepting a feather, and indeed in the least expression of his friendship.

I am sorry to hear that pious Mr. Woodman is so exceedingly modest as not to choose to wear his feather; but am glad to hear such a worthy character of him, and that he is so well disposed towards the college as to think of providing for it. May the Lord possess many others with the same spirit! I hope you may have it in your power to put many more in the way of leaving us some love tokens, when they are better employed than in enjoying terrestrial goods. This is what I have hoped for, though hitherto I have not seen cause to expect much from it soon.

I am much obliged to you for the annual contribution of five guineas. I have made free to draw a bill for them in favor of Mr. Geo. Keith, of London, hoping that the Lord may enable me to conduct worthy the gospel, so that you may not repent the donation.

Your opinion of lotteries coincides with mine; but some of our friends urged me to mention the subject, as they could not see a prospect of supplies in any other way. Besides, I believe there have not been such iniquitous methods used in this matter, with us, as in the State lotteries at home. They have been used to promote good designs.

The book from Mr. Stillman we have received, though lately, as Mr. Story did not do his errand to Mr. Stillman faithfully.

I have written to Mr. Edwards respecting the books in his hands, and expect an answer soon. Perhaps you may meet this in London. If so you need not mention the hint relative to Dr. Chauncey; for I believe he has not yet forwarded anything of that nature.

To give you a full detail of facts and instances of the ill-will of persons to the college[1] would require "*centum ora et ferrea vox,*" as sung the poet. Dr. Stiles, of Newport, gave as a reason to the corporation for not accepting a place in the Faculty, the offense he should give his brethren should he accept it. The manner of obtaining the charter, has, by the clergy of the Congregational society, been represented as highly iniquitous. (But the particulars of this affair you shall have as soon as the college history can be completed and sent to you, together with other particulars which you request.) Those gentlemen of that denomination who have spoken favorably of the institution have been reprimanded, as I have been credibly informed, and that by a convention, for showing us so much countenance as to attend the Commencement. I was lately told by a worthy minister of that order in Connecticut, that one of the same order in this town, a sour man, had done the college amazing damage by representing us as bigots, and our sole design to be that of proselyting to the Baptist sentiments; and that if they sent their children here they never could get into any employment in that Government; so that he had it not in his power to send us the scholars to whom he taught grammar, though he chose it. The same zeal has been used in the neighboring provinces, both by him and others; and both parents and tutors have repeatedly told me that everything except violence has been used, and almost that in some instances, to prevent them from sending their children here. Some of them have boasted that they have prevented persons from coming who designed it; and few scholars come but say every obstacle has been laid in their way to prevent them. The characters of the teachers, their abilities, and the character of the place even, have been aspersed to the highest de-

1 Mr. Ryland, in a letter to Manning, under date of Feb. 9, 1773, thus writes: "I wish you would give me a full detail of facts and instances of the ill-will of men to your seminary. I would make use of them for its benefit and advantage, without hurting you in the least."

gree for the same purpose. But I should tire you to recite a small part of our ill-treatment. They know that the low state of the college fund requires considerable tuition money to support the teachers, and that that depends on the number of scholars. If, therefore, they can prevent them from coming, they know they distress us. But, notwithstanding what I have said of our enemies, there are many valuable men in that society in these parts, some of whom are friendly to the college; but through their connections, or want of ability, few of them have it in their power to express their friendship.

You may expect a particular account of our mode of education, and of the students, their characters, proficiency, piety, etc., when we send you an account of the rise, progress, and present state of the college, which I intend to draw up as soon as I can, and forward it by the first opportunity. Our number of scholars is thirty, and amongst them are many pious, promising young men. Take them together, they are a set of well-behaved boys. I have a Latin school under my care, taught by one of our graduates, of about twenty boys. Amongst those who have left us are three eminent Baptist ministers, their age considered, and another just entered on the work, who, I am told, promises as fair as any of the others; one attorney-at-law, the most eminent at the bar of any in this colony, etc., etc.

I thank you for the list of ministers of the Church of England, and shall be glad to see that of the Calvinist Baptist ministers.

What treatise upon fluxions do you deem the best? The state of religion is generally at a low ebb amongst us. May the Lord revive it! Would your English people be scared at an American Indian? I remain, dear sir, your unworthy friend and brother in the gospel,

JAMES MANNING.

REV. JOHN RYLAND'S "MEMORANDA AND HINTS FOR PROF. MANNING, AT RHODE ISLAND.

[No date. Probably August, 1773.]

1. The Calvinistical Baptist ministers in England and Wales are about two hundred; but I have given away my printed lists, and forgot to ask Mr. Wallin for some more. Be so good as to mention it to him.

2. I cannot yet procure a complete list of the Independent ministers and churches. You know there are about thirty-two in London, and we have twelve or fourteen in Northampton.

3. I suppose you know that it was Dr. Stennett that procured an order from Government to put a stop to the oppression of the Baptists near Boston. I have not a perfect idea of that affair.

4. Two young men, of good parts and sound knowledge of the learned languages, and men of eloquence and piety, are lately come into the ministry from Mr. Evan's academy in Bristol; namely, Mr. Biggs, just going to be ordained over the Baptist church at Wantage, in Berkshire, and Mr. Dunscombe, at Coat in Oxfordshire, whose ordination is to be at the same time. You will do well to mark them down as men of uncommon merit, worthy of your feathers in a year.

5. The sooner you send over a clear, short, printed account of your college, in its rise and present state, the better. I beg you would pay due and equal attention to our leading men, in presenting each with a copy, that no jealousy or pique against you may arise. You know our chief ministers. We have about thirty or forty that can read Greek. Let not one be forgot. If you know not all of them, I will inform you, or take the trouble of giving them a copy in your name.

6. As to your visit to old England, I shall be glad to see you, and will do you all the service I can; but I wish you to attach some more of our ministers to your interest by your *pretty baubles* first, and also let your account of the college come six months before you.

7. As to your worthy Mathematical Professor, I wish him all possible success; but I must not presume to assist or direct him with respect to the best book on fluxions. The students at our Cambridge use chiefly an abridgment of Sanderson's Algebra, an octavo, price six shillings; and then we have such a number of books on fluxions, so good that 'tis hard to say which is the best. There are four of great note; namely, Maclaurin, Ditton, Thomas Simpson, and Emerson last of all, who is now living. He has published a noble course of mathematical learning, in about ten or twelve octavo volumes. He is an amazing genius in the north of England. His Mechanics, quarto, fourteen shillings, and Astronomy, octavo, six shillings, I have in my study. But the lovely humane philosopher, and my intimate friend, is James Ferguson, F. R. S. He has just now assisted me to complete my optical cards, which are engraving on copper plates. You will, I hope, approve of them, as the easiest introduction to optics ever seen in the world. By the way, Ferguson drew up the book you have in your hands with my name to it; for I could not persuade him to put his own, for fear of appearing ungrateful to Andrew Miller, bookseller, who had been his friend in a time of need.

CALVINISTIC BAPTIST MINISTERS IN ENGLAND WHO CAN READ THE GREEK TESTAMENT, ETC.

1. SAMUEL STENNETT, D.D.,
2. BENJAMIN WALLIN,
3. WILLIAM CLARK,
4. JOHN REYNOLDS,
5. ABRAHAM BOOTH,
6. DR. GIFFORD,

} London.

1. HUGH EVANS,
2. CALEB EVANS,
3. MR. NEWTON,

} Bristol.

1. BENJAMIM BEDDOME, Bourton, on the water, Gloucester.
2. JOHN ASH, Pershore, Worcestershire.
3. JOSHUA SYMMONDS, of Bedford, who has lately altered his sentiments from a Pedobaptist, and honestly is come into and submitted to believer's baptism; for which he is abhorred and despised by the Independent ministers. Give him your best honors.
4. DANIEL TURNER, Abingdon, Berkshire.
5. MR. ROBINSON, of Cambridge.
6. PHILIP GIBBS, of Plymouth.
7. MORGAN JONES, of Hampstead, Hertfordshire.
8. SAMUEL JAMES, of Hitchin, Hertfordshire. Now dying.
9. ISAAC WOODMAN, of Leicestershire.
10. JOHN BROWN, of Kettering, Northamptonshire.
11. BIGGS and DUNSCOMBE; excellent scholars.
12. ROBERT DAY, Wellington, Somersetshire.
13. BENJAMIN FULLER, Devizes.
14. JOHN POYNTING, Worcester.
15. JOHN OULTON, of Rawden in Yorkshire.
16. JOHN FAWCETT, of Wainsgate, Yorkshire; now keeps a seminary.
17. JOSEPH JENKINS.
18. BENJAMIN DAVIES, in Wales, keeps an academy at Abergavemry, about ten pupils. Give him a feather.
19. MR. JOHN RIPPON, at Dr. Gill's meeting-house.
20. RYLAND, Sen.
21. RYLAND, Jun.

President Manning, in his official relations, was not altogether unmindful of the wise man's injunction touching the rod. "John" to whom Mr. Hart refers below, was now, it seems, a Freshman in college. He had probably been one of Manning's grammar-school pupils. Whether he profited by the "discipline," we cannot say. As his name, however, appears among the graduates four years later, it is reasonable to draw the most favorable inferences.

CHARLESTON, Nov. 5th, 1773.

DEAR MR. PRESIDENT:

I have hardly time to say, yours of the 6th Sept., ult., came to hand two days ago. I am now preparing for a journey into Georgia, very high up, in order to assist my good Brother Pelot in constituting a Baptist church. The Lord has greatly owned the labors of our young Botfford; many are converted, baptized, and are now waiting for the enjoyment of church privileges. This intelligence, I know, will be agreeable to you; more so than the account you gave of my sad boy was to me. I am sorry John has conducted so as to give you so much trouble, and to forfeit the place he had under the management of Mrs. Manning. Had I been apprised of his unworthy conduct sooner, perhaps I should have remanded him back to Carolina; for I am not in such affluent circumstances as to throw away money in the education of one who has no view to his own advantage. I thank you, however, for all the pains you have taken with him, and that you have made trial of the discipline of the rod. Let me entreat you unweariedly to exert your best endeavors for his advantage. Who knows but God may give him a turn? I should be sorry he should return a worthless blockhead. When I return from my Georgia route, which will take me near a month, I shall use my utmost endeavors to remit you some more guineas. I have enough due me if I could collect it; but cash was never so scarce in Carolina as at present. This is an unfavorable circumstance, both for you and for me.

I should be glad to see an account of your late Commencement in print. Pray, how goes on the great man of Haverhill? I have heard nothing from him for a great while past; and I hear almost as little about Mr. Stillman, or our affairs in Boston. How is Mr. Davis's place supplied? Has that church any minister?

Could you not prevail on John to write to me? I have received but one letter from him for the space of twelve months past, although I have sharply reproved him for his neglect, over and over again. With kind love to Mrs. Manning, I remain,

Yours, with much esteem,

OLIVER HART.

TO THE REV. JOHN RYLAND.

PROVIDENCE, NOV. 25, 1773.

REVEREND AND DEAR SIR:

Yours by Capt. Shand I received last week. I am obliged to you for the number of Calvinist Baptist ministers in England and Wales, and for information where I may procure a complete list of Independent ministers.

I did not know before that it was Dr. Stennett who procured the repeal of the Ashfield law against the Baptists. I rejoice at the addition of Messrs. Biggs and Dunscombe to the number of laborers in the vineyard of our Lord. I shall remember and do honor to such worthy characters.

I expect we shall be able to send over a printed account of the college the next spring, together with diplomas to those in England who were graduated the last fall. The reason of our being so tardy in this matter is, the corporation, at their last meeting, ordered us to revise the form of our diplomas, and send it to England to be engraved in copper plate, and procure a quantity of good parchment, as we had none here fit to send abroad. Should you happen in London on the receipt of this, I should be glad to have you inspect the draught and design, and prescribe the best form of the plate, hands, etc.

I shall pay due attention to the literary gentlemen you mentioned, when the account of the college is sent over, and am obliged to you for your proffered kindness in distributing them. This I shall expect.

I know not whether I shall ever have the pleasure of seeing your face in the flesh; should my life be spared, though, it would be very agreeable. However, we shall omit nothing which is judged agreeable or necessary to pave the way for some future personal solicitation in favor of our college in England, should it be thought expedient. Am obliged to you for the account of books on fluxions and your optical card. I doubt not I shall approve of it when favored with a sight.

In company with yours I received a letter from that venerable man, Rev. Isaac Woodman, together with another testimony of his good-will towards us. He writes like an experienced, modest father. This letter I must answer, though I am greatly paralyzed with a crowd of business, and cannot do it as I would be glad to do. Also Rev. Benjamin Wallin, of London, sent me an agreeable letter, accompanied with all he has published, in ten volumes, neatly bound and gilt, with the most valuable works of John Bunyan, in six volumes, the Reign of Grace, by William Booth and Wilson's Sermons, — all for the college library. These I esteem valuable presents.

Enclosed I send you the Minutes of the Association at Philadelphia, and that called the Warren Association, in New England.

The last vacation I spent in riding three hundred and fifty miles, and preaching twenty-five times, to a number of our little Baptist churches and societies in New England; many of which I never had visited before. Was cordially received, and importuned to repeat my visit as soon as might be. In general found religion to wear a promising aspect; but in many places they met with a great interruption from the Establishment in New England. I wonder how men by human laws can establish a religion, and then have the effrontery to call it Christ's kingdom!

I should have sent to you before this for a number of your books, but understood you had sent some of them to Mr. Edwards, directed to me, which I have not seen. With my best wishes for your welfare, I am, sir,

Your unworthy brother in the gospel,

James Manning.

P. S. — I have seen Rev. Augustus Toplady's Treatise on Predestination, with his letter to Rev. Jno. Wesley, and deem them masterly performances, answering well the character you gave him.

TO THE REV. BENJAMIN WALLIN.

Providence, Nov. 25th, 1773.

Reverend and dear Sir:

Yours of July 30th, by Capt. Shand, together with the box of books, came safe to hand last week; for which I return you many thanks, as well in the name of the corporation of our college as in my own. I have not had leisure to peruse many of the pieces, since their arrival, but from my prepossession in favor of the author, and from what I have read of his works, I am confident they will be highly agreeable; so that you might have spared everything said by way of apology for them on that account.

I am, however, greatly obliged to you for the information you give concerning your entering the ministry, your age, situation in the world and in the church of God, etc., etc. Your present of the venerable Bunyan's works were not the less welcome for being accompanied with the agreeable present from the Rev. Abraham Booth, of his Reign of Grace, and of Mr. Wilson's Sermons. I must trouble him with a letter too.

We expect next spring to send over a printed account of the rise and present state of the college, in which we shall give an account of the manner of donations to the college by wills; but lest that should come too late, I here send the name by which it is known in law, and by which it is to hold donations, until some more distinguished benefactor shall give it a new one, for which the corporation have liberty in the charter.

"Item. I give to the the Trustees and Fellows of the College or University in the English Colony of Rhode Island and Providence Plantations, in New England in America, the sum of ——."

The Society for the Propagation of the Gospel in Foreign Parts, last year or the year before, prescribed a form of bequeathment to them, in which they say: "To be raised and paid by, and out of my ready money, plate, goods, and personal effects, which, by law, I may or can charge with the payment of the same; and not out of any part of my lands, tenements, or hereditaments, and to be applied towards," etc. The particular design must be expressed, or it must be left to them to dispose of as they shall think proper. I suppose the statute of Mortmane, or that of 9th of George II., made this precaution necessary. But as our friends in Great Britain will be always able to advise with those who are skilled in these matters, they will doubtless put it out of the power of any to defeat their benevolent intentions, after they are gone to the eternal world. Pardon my being so particular on this point: the loss of sundry donations to the society above mentioned, published in their extracts, suggested the thought.

When our account of the college comes, we shall not be sparing in numbers to be distributed, as our friends judge proper.

I wonder that Mr. Backus is behindhand with you, as he is not commonly tardy in this way. He is an excellent man, and though unfurnished with the knowledge of letters, has been an eminent instrument in the hands of God to spread the truth in this country, as well by his publications as by his preaching. He has lately published an appeal to the public in favor of the Baptist society in New England; and he is now collecting materials for the history of the Baptists. I will forward Mr. Edwards's list by the first safe conveyance.

Your information of the low state of religion amongst us is but too true! May the Lord in mercy visit us. I travelled this fall about three hundred and fifty miles, and visited many of the Baptist churches. In several places there were, I thought, evident marks of the power of God attending gospel means. While on that journey I baptized four persons. I am sorry to hear of the decline of vital godliness in old England, and of the prevalence of Anti-Trinitarianism, or, if you please, infidelity. I believe no arguments will effectually refute that, in men of corrupt minds, short of the power of divine grace, for a day of which I need not solicit you to help with your prayers.

I am glad to hear you express that happy degree of resignation to the will of God in your bereaved, afflicted state. Oh that blessed word! "Our light afflictions," etc. May God grant you an experience of its full import, make your last days your best, and late, very late, call you home from earthly labors to mansions of glory. This is the sincere prayer of

Your most unworthy brother in the gospel,

JAMES MANNING.

We close this chapter with a letter to the Rev. Abraham Booth, of London, proposing an "exchange of some letters." Mr. Booth was an eminent Baptist minister in his day, and an author of no little celebrity. His "Reign of Grace," "Pedobaptism Examined," "Apology for the Baptists," "Essay on the Kingdom of Christ," and numerous other religious and polemical writings, may be found upon the shelves of the college library. Most of them were republished in 1813, in three octavo volumes, with a memoir of the author. An account of him, compiled from this memoir, is given in Rose's General Biographical Dictionary.

NEWPORT, Nov. 26, 1773.

REVEREND AND DEAR SIR:

The last week brought your agreeable present of the Reign of Grace, and the Rev. Mr. Wilson's Sermons, a present to our college library; for which the corporation have ordered me, in their name, to return you their thanks: an agreeable task, as it not only gives me an opportunity of expressing my gratitude for the donation, but opens a door for me to address a gentleman and brother in Christ whose character has often been represented to me in so amiable a light that I should think it a happiness to maintain a correspondence with you, if agreeable on your part.

It gives me peculiar pleasure to find our friends in Great Britain mindful of this infant seminary. It greatly needs and most cordially accepts their patronage, and wishes too an increase of benefactors. I hope in our turn we shall show all proper respect to all its friends who can justly have any claim upon us.

Should it be agreeable to you, sir, to exchange some letters, you will always find me ready to execute your commands, as far as I am able. May you experience in your soul the dominion of that grace you have so agreeably described, is, dear sir, the devout wish of

Your obliged but unworthy brother,

JAMES MANNING.

FIRST BAPTIST CHURCH, PROVIDENCE, R. I.

Erected A. D. 1775.

CHAPTER V.

1774–1779.

Description of the Baptist meeting-house at the time of Manning's removal to Providence — Church and Society prosper under his pastoral care — Resolve to build "a meeting-house for the public worship of Almighty God, and also to hold Commencements in" — Committees appointed — John Brown — Lottery to assist in defraying the expense — Raising of the house — Dedication — Description of the building and grounds — Letter to Rev. Benjamin Wallin — Baptists imprisoned for the non-payment of rates — Letter to Rev. John Ryland — Manning's illness — His narrative of the college — Commencement in 1774 — Barnabas Binney — Valedictory oration — Letter to Thomas Ustick — Manning's efforts in behalf of civil and religious freedom — Congress of Delegates meet at Philadelphia, Sept. 5, 1774 — Address to the same from the Warren Association — Backus an agent to said Congress — Meeting of the Baptists in Philadelphia — Conference between them and members of Congress — Manning addresses the Conference and reads a Memorial — Results — Increase of Baptist sentiments throughout the land — Extract from letter giving Dr. Stiles's statements in regard to said Conference — Petition from the Senior Class — Manning's reply — No Commencement in 1775 — Reasons — Commencement in 1776 — Newport taken by the British forces — Providence under martial law — College studies suspended — College building occupied by the American, and afterwards by the French troops—Manning's duties at this time — Letter to John Ryland, giving a picture of the war and an account of the progress of religion in the land — Letter to Rev. Benjamin Wallin, giving an account of a remarkable revival of religion in the church and College —Wallin's reply — Letter of sympathy and counsel to Miss A. Howard, of England — Controversial letter on Infant Baptism, to Rev. John Berridge, of London — Conduct of the Episcopal clergy in reference to the war — Meeting of the Corporation in 1777 — Instance of Manning's humane disposition — Important civil function confided to him — Anecdote of Manning in relation to the "Dark Day" — Letter to Rev. Thomas Ustick, urging him to open a Latin school with a view to aiding the College — Letter from Judge Howell resigning his Professorship.

At the time of Dr. Manning's removal to Providence, the Baptist church were worshipping in a small house, thirty-five by forty-one feet in dimension, erected in the year 1726, on the corner of North Main and Smith Streets. The lot, which was seventy-seven by one hundred and twelve feet, was partly the gift of the Rev. Pardon Tillinghast, a former pastor, and partly the purchase of the society. The following description of the building, and of the mode of worship, which we take from Stone's Life and Recollections of John Howland, will be found interesting:

"At high water the tide flowed nearly up to the west end of the building. There were no pews. From the front door, opening on Main Street, an aisle extended to the pulpit, which was raised three or four steps from the floor. On each side of the aisle benches extended north and south to the walls of the house, and there were benches in the gallery, which was entered by narrow stairs from a door on the south side of the house. . . . . They did not approve of singing, and never practised it in public worship. When more than one elder was present, and the first had exhausted himself, he would say, 'There is time and space left if any one has further to offer.' In that case another and another would offer what he had to say; so there was no set time for closing the meeting. . . . .The house could not contain a large congregation, nor did the number present seem to require a larger house, as they were not crowded though many of them came in from the neighboring towns, on horseback, with women behind them on pillions."

Under the pastoral care of Dr. Manning the church and society greatly increased in numbers and efficiency, so that ere long it became necessary to erect a new house of worship. With a view to the accommodation of the college, it was determined to build it in such a style of elegance, and of such dimensions, as should surpass any edifice of the kind connected with the Baptist denomination in the colonies.

In looking over the records of the society, we find that, at a meeting held at the house of Mr. Daniel Cahoon, on Friday evening, Feb. 11, 1774, it was —

"*Resolved,* That we will all heartily unite as one man, in all lawful ways and means, to promote the good of this society; and particularly attend to and revive the affair of building a meeting-house for the public worship of Almighty God, and also for holding Commencements in."

In accordance with this resolve, the society, with unanimity and promptness, entered upon the prosecution of their labors. A committee of two persons, Messrs. Joseph Brown and Jonathan Hammond, were immediately appointed to proceed to Boston, "in order to view the different churches there, and to make a memorandum of their several dimensions and forms of architecture." The old house and lot were sold at public auction, and the present spacious lot, bounded by Thomas, Benefit, President, and North Main Streets, was purchased by Mr. John Angell. In this latter transaction very important service appears to have been rendered by Mr. William Russell.

On the 25th of April, 1774, at a meeting of the society, of which Dr. Manning was moderator, and Benjamin Stelle clerk, it was resolved —

1. That a petition be presented to the honorable General Assembly, praying that a charter, containing certain privileges and immunities, may be granted to the Baptist society in Providence.

2. That the Rev. James Manning, Ephraim Wheaton, Nicholas Brown, David Howell, and Benjamin Thurber be a committee to draft a plan of a charter, and present the same to the society for approbation as soon as may be.

3. That Mr. John Brown be the committee-man for carrying on the building of the new meeting-house for said society.

4. That Messrs. John Jenckes, Daniel Cahoon, Ephraim Wheaton, Nathaniel Wheaton, Daniel Tillinghast, Joseph Brown, William Russell, Edward Thurber, Nicholas Brown, Christopher Sheldon, and Benjamin Thurber, they or the major part of them, be a standing committee to assist and advise with Mr. John Brown in locating and carrying into execution the building of the new meeting-house.

Thus, while a large committee of eleven was chosen for assistance and advice, the carrying on of the building and the execution of the plans was wisely left to a committee of one. There was hence a unity of purpose, and a success in the final results, which a large and divided committee could never have attained. In this matter our fathers have left on record an example which societies of the present day may do well to imitate. It is pleasing to notice, in this record, the unlimited confidence reposed in the abilities and discretion of Mr. Brown. Had there been informers in those days of trial and peril, the large reward offered by the British Government for the apprehension of the author of or leader in the destruction of the Gaspee, two years previous, might have seriously interfered with the plans of the society.

In order to defray the additional expense of purchasing a lot and of building a house sufficiently large to accommodate the college, recourse was had to a lottery. This, as we have already remarked in a previous chapter, was in accordance with the universal practice of religious societies, in Rhode Island and elsewhere, at this period. The lottery was divided into six classes, the time and place of drawing which were notified from time to time in the *Providence Gazette.* Eleven thousand nine hundred and seventy tickets were sold, at prices ranging from two and one half to five dollars each. The sum proposed to be raised by this scheme was two thousand pounds lawful money, or about seven thousand dollars. The managers appointed by the General Assembly, were Nicholas Brown, John Jenckes, William Russell, Benjamin Thurber, Edward Thurber, Nathaniel Wheaton, Daniel Tillinghast, William Holroyd, James Arnold, and Nicholas Power. In their announcement of June 25, 1774, they ask for the "cheerful assistance and encouragement of the public, especially when it is considered that this is the first time the Baptist society have solicited their assistance in this way, which they can assure them would not now have been the case had they not purchased as much more land, and designed a house as much larger than the society required for their own use (purposely to accommodate public Commencements), as will amount to the full sum proposed to be raised by this lottery."

On Monday, Aug. 29, was the "raising" of the new meeting-house, due notice of which had been given in the papers. A large crowd assembled, and the occasion seems to have been made a general holiday throughout the town.

During the following year the house was so far completed that it was occupied by the society. It was opened for public worship on Sunday, May 28, 1775, when President Manning preached the dedication discourse, from Gen. xxviii. 17, — "And he was afraid, and said, How dreadful is this place! This is none other but the house of God, and this is the gate of heaven." On Tuesday, June 6, the raising of the steeple, which occupied nearly four days, was finished. The plan of this most elegant piece of architecture was taken from the middle figure in the thirtieth plate of Gibbs's "Designs of Buildings and Ornaments," representing the steeple of St. Martin's in the Fields, one of the finest churches in London.[1] It measures one hundred and eight feet from the top of the tower, and one hundred and eighty-five feet from the ground to the top of the vane. The total height of the steeple is one hundred and ninety-six feet. The house itself is eighty feet square. The roof and galleries are supported by twelve fluted pillars, of the

1 See Knight's "London Illustrated," Vol. V. p. 195.

Doric order. The weight of the original bell was two thousand five hundred and fifteen pounds, and upon it was the following motto: —

> "For freedom of conscience the town was first planted;
> Persuasion, not force, was used by the people;
> This church was the eldest, and has not recanted,
> Enjoying, and granting, bell, temple, and steeple."[1]

Fronting three of the four streets that surround the house is a door, and fronting Benefit Street are two doors. Thus on Commencement days, and on other public occasions, it can be easily and readily vacated. Mr. Joseph Brown, a member of the church, was the principal architect, and Mr. James Sumner superintended the building. The entire expense of the edifice and lot was upwards of twenty-five thousand dollars. When we consider the value and scarcity of money in those days, the perils and dangers of an impending war with the mother country, and also the fact that Providence was then a small town, containing, when the building was commenced, a population of only four thousand three hundred and twenty-one, according to the official numeration of the inhabitants, we are amazed at the genius which could conceive, and the energy, enterprise, and skill which could successfully complete so great an undertaking. Even at the present day, the venerable structure, with its tall, graceful spire, and its spacious enclosure, shaded by stately elms, constitutes one of the chief attractions of the city. In the beginning and progress of this enterprise, we have an illustration of the remarkable influence which Manning must have exerted over the people of his care.

1 Dissenters in Great Britain were not allowed to have steeples or bells to their churches. To this prohibition reference is undoubtedly had in this inscription.

Returning now to our correspondence, we find under date of May 25, 1774, a brief letter addressed to the Rev. Benjamin Wallin:—

REVEREND AND DEAR SIR:

Yours of February, now before me, was very acceptable, as also the two pamphlets; for which I return you my hearty thanks. Hope the separation in Dr. Gill's church, although attended with some circumstances in themselves disagreeable, may eventually prove to the furtherance of the gospel.

Any apology in behalf of your productions, dear sir, is perfectly unnecessary. Mr. Booth's piece has not yet come to hand. Please to make my compliments to him, and to any others who may inquire after your unworthy friend.

Mr. Backus is now raking into the rubbish of time to collect materials for a History of the American Baptists, and prosecutes his design with great assiduity.

* A very considerable number of Baptists were last winter imprisoned, for the non-payment of their rates to the Presbyterians, in the Colony of Massachusetts Bay;—very ill-timed, considering their contest with the British Parliament respecting the right of taxation, and the measures they might have guessed would have been pursued. But, alas! how blind are we to our own faults!

I expect the account of the college will be complete this summer, and hope you may not be disappointed in the manner of its execution. We are not accustomed to write for the public eye. When done they will be forwarded to England with all speed. A grievous diarrhœa, for several months past, has put it out of my power to contribute my assistance, or it would have been more forward at this day. I heartily thank you for your good wishes for me and for the seminary, and hope the institution may prove a public blessing. Religion is in a flourishing state in several of the places around us, but low in Providence. May the Lord revive his own work. With sincere regards, I am, dear sir,

Your unworthy friend,

JAMES MANNING.

* The Baptist committee are to meet at Boston to-morrow on this business. If no redress is granted from government, they will, I suppose, apply to the King and council through their agents in London.

TO THE REV. JOHN RYLAND.

NEWPORT, May 27, 1774.

REVEREND AND DEAR SIR:

Though I had no letter from you by the last vessels, I cannot omit sending you a line. The college papers have been retarded by my indisposition through the past winter. An obstinate diarrhœa, for several months together, took away almost all hopes that I should ever recover my health, and prevented my attention to business in a great measure; but through the goodness of God I am happily recovered. The Anecdotes of the college will be drawn up and forwarded as soon as may be, and the other papers. But I could not get them ready by this opportunity. This spring I received from Philadelphia your Cause of Deism Ruined Forever, etc.; and according to the directions, forwarded one to Harvard College, Mr. Stillman, etc. Return my hearty thanks for the one presented me, and, in the name of the corporation, present their thanks for that given to our college library. The college is in much the same state as when I wrote last. Religion is on the revival in some places in New England; but great calamities seem to threaten us, in consequence of the dispute relating to taxation; and the Lord only knows when this dispute will end. I think it incumbent on all who have any interest at the throne of Grace, to employ it, both in Britain and America, that God would pour out his Spirit on us all, and heal the breaches sin has made.

I have taken the liberty to draw on Mr. Ryland, in favor of Mr. John Brown, for five guineas, as usual. My Brother Gano has returned to New York from a tour of six or seven months through the Carolinas. Have not yet seen him, but am informed that he brings good tidings respecting the state of religion. With great respect, I am, sir,

Yours, etc.,

JAMES MANNING.

We find no further meniton by Dr. Manning of his "Anecdotes" or "Narrative" of the college. His ill health at this time, the cares and anxieties of a pastor in seasons of revival, and the breaking out of the Revolutionary War, prevented the final completion of his literary undertaking. It is to be regretted that his manuscript papers have not been more carefully preserved.[1] Doubtless there

[1] For an account of Manning's papers, see Preface.

was among them at his death a sketch of the college, which, if not completed, would at least have thrown light upon much that pertains to its origin and early progress.

This year the Commencement was held for the last time in Mr. Snow's meeting-house. Six young men took their Bachelor's degree, "delivering their respective parts with that dignity and propriety which acquired them the applause of a very numerous, judicious, and polite assembly." "The company of cadets," says the *Chronicle*, "in uniforms, made an elegant and truly military appearance; and both in the procession and in the manoeuvres which they performed on the college green, procured universal approbation, and convinced the spectators that Americans are no less capable of military discipline than Europeans."

Among the graduates on this occasion was Mr. Barnabas Binney, who received the valedictory honors of the class. He was born in Boston, Mass. In early youth he discovered a ready and prolific genius, which gave promise of usefulness in the clerical profession. But the liberality of his ideas, says his biographer, rendered it incapable for him to attach himself to any particular sect, and hence he could never be prevailed upon to assume the vows and duties of a professed teacher of religion. He therefore perfected himself in the various branches of medicine, and finally established himself as a physician in the city of Philadelphia. Here he died, in the month of June, 1787. His son, the Hon. Horace Binney, is now the Nestor of the Pennsylvania bar, and ranks among the most distinguished lawyers and jurists of the day. The valedictory oration of Mr. Binney, which was immediately published,[1] was universally regarded as a splendid produc-

[1] A copy is still preserved in the University library. The following is the title: "An Oration delivered on the late public Commencement at Rhode Island

tion. After the usual addresses, it discussed fully the politics of that eventful period, and was listened to with the most profound attention. The merits of this production were greatly enhanced in the delivery by the gracefulness of the orator, and the uncommon elegance of his manners.

Judge Dorrance, of Providence, was a member of this class. Immediately after graduating, he was appointed a tutor, and for many years during the latter part of his life he was one of the Trustees of the University. Dwight Foster, whose name also appears in this connection, was a brother of the Hon. Theodore Foster, the senator from Rhode Island. He settled as a lawyer in Brookfield, Mass., and represented his native State as a senator in Congress from 1800 to 1803.

The following letter, directed to "Thomas Ustick, schoolmaster, New York," has reference to this Commencement. Mr. Ward, we observe, delivered an oration for the Master's degree, but the other candidates for this honor took no part in the public exercises.

PROVIDENCE, May 30, 1774.

SIR: — This is to let you know that Messrs. Ward and Arnold, your classmates, spent this evening with me to determine their Commencement exercises, and they desired me to ask you what you propose to do for Commencement, when you expect to be at Providence to prepare, etc., etc. These things you are desired to answer by the first opportunity. I had from Ashford in Connecticut, this day, an application for a Baptist minister. I mentioned you to them; and desire you to confer with Mr. Gano on the subject, that he may bring over word, when he comes. Their

College, in Providence, September, 1774; being a plea for the right of private judgment in religious matters, or for the liberty of choosing our own religion; corroborated by the well-known consequences of priestly power; to which are annexed the valedictions of the class then first graduated. By Barnabas Binney, A.B. Boston: 1774." The oration, with the illustrative notes, makes a small quarto of forty-four pages.

start for a Baptist minister is a new thing; but they subscribed last week near £500 lawful money towards building a meeting-house. The town is large and rich, and I am told that full one third have declared for the Baptists; and that, in case they can get a minister of abilities, it is the general opinion that much above half the town will attend the meeting, though there are three parishes in it. The richest men are on our side, and they say they believe in supporting the minister handsomely. What say you of visiting them, at least, as soon as you can with convenience? I want you to send me, by the first opportunity, two dozen grammars, and I will satisfy you for your trouble. Show this to Mr. Gano, and tell him we expect him over very soon, and also Mrs. Gano and the children, to spend the summer with us. Tell them not to disappoint us. All are well with us, and at Middleborough. Mr. Hinds went from here this day. Enclosed I send two proposals, etc., which I received this evening from poor Boston. Please hand them to Mr. Gano, to use as he thinks proper. It is now almost midnight, and I can hardly see; besides, I have told Mr. Gano all I know in a letter written since I received any from him, or I would write him now. There are thirty-five or thirty-six students in college, and many of them fine young men. Tell friends they are remembered by

JAMES MANNING.

The correspondence of President Manning, it will be observed, abounds in allusions to the oppression of his brethren in Massachusetts and elsewhere, on the part of the "standing order." This oppression he felt called upon to resist to the extent of his ability. To his intelligent and active exertions in behalf of religious liberty and equality, we of the present day and generation are greatly indebted for what we now enjoy as our birthright.

To set forth in detail the efforts of Manning and his contemporaries in this direction, would require more space than can be allotted to our present work. For full information on the points involved in this controversy, the reader is referred to Backus's Church History of New England, and especially to Prof. Hovey's Memoir of the Life and Times of Backus. One effort of Manning demands special mention. During the present year, which was a year of marked importance in the history of the country, the spirit of resistance to the unjust claims of England had greatly increased among all classes throughout the land, until it was at length determined to unite the separate colonies in defence of their common rights. For this purpose a congress of delegates met in Philadelphia, on the 5th of September, 1774. To this meeting it was resolved to send Mr. Backus, the agent of the Baptist churches, to see if something could not be done to secure rights and liberties from the government at home, as well as the government abroad. Accordingly, at the anniversary of the Warren Association, held the week after Commencement, the following certificate was given: —

To the honorable Delegates of the several Colonies in North America, met in a general Congress at Philadelphia:

HONORABLE GENTLEMEN: — As the Anti-pedobaptist churches in New England are most heartily concerned for the preservation and defence of the rights and privileges of this country, and are deeply affected by the encroachments upon the same which have lately been made by the British Parliament, and are willing to unite with our dear countrymen, vigorously to pursue every prudent measure for relief, so we would beg leave to say that, as a distinct denomination of Protestants, we conceive that we have an equal claim to charter-rights with the rest of our fellow-subjects; and yet have long been denied the free and full enjoyment of those rights, as to the support of religious worship. Therefore we, the elders and brethren of twenty Baptist churches, met in Association at Medfield, twenty miles from Boston, Sept. 14, 1774, have unanimously chosen and sent unto you the reverend and beloved Mr. Isaac Backus, as our agent, to lay our case, in these respects, before you, or otherwise to use all the prudent means he can for our relief.

JOHN GANO, *Moderator.*
HEZEKIAH SMITH, *Clerk.*

The idea of sending a representative to this congress

originated with Dr. Manning, Hezekiah Smith, John Gano, and others, who proposed it to Mr. Backus, at the college Commencement. Mr. Backus, having thus been duly appointed by the Warren Association, set out for Philadelphia on the 26th of September. His journey occupied nearly a fortnight. This circumstance is here mentioned to show what travelling facilities were in those days, and what sacrifices were sometimes made by those ministers who attended from a distance the meetings of the college and of the associations. Upon his arrival in Philadelphia he immediately conferred with President Manning, and with the Philadelphia Baptist Association, then holding its sessions in that city.

In the evening of Oct. 14, says Backus, "there met at Carpenter's Hall,[1] Thomas Cushing, Samuel Adams, John Adams, and Robert Treat Paine, Esqrs., delegates from Massachusetts; and there were also present James Kinzie of New Jersey, Stephen Hopkins and Samuel Ward of Rhode Island, Joseph Galloway and Thomas Miflin, Esqrs., of Pennsylvania, and other members of Congress. Mr. Rhodes, Mayor of the city of Philadelphia, Israel and James Pemberton, and Joseph Fox, Esqrs., of the Quakers, and other gentlemen; also Elders Manning, Gano, Jones, Rogers, Edwards, etc., were present. The conference was opened by Mr. Manning, who made a short speech, and then read the memorial which we had drawn up."

[1] "On the morning of the 5th of September, 1774, the 'old Congress,' as it is now familiarly known in our history, commenced its sessions, in Carpenter's Hall in Philadelphia. The place but ill corresponded with the real magnitude of the occasion. No tapestry bedecked its walls, no images of sages and heroes of other days looked down upon the scene. Yet, to one who could read the future, it would have presented a simple grandeur, such as we may now look for in vain within the majestic halls of the Capitol, and amidst the imposing forms of the Constitution." —*Prof. Gammell's Life of Governor Ward.*

This memorial, which may be found in Hovey's Memoir, after an eloquent plea in behalf of both civil and religious freedom, recounts in brief the various acts of oppression which the Baptists had suffered in the province of Massachusetts Bay, commencing with the charter obtained at the "happy restoration." What part Manning had in the drafting of it we cannot now determine. It was probably the joint production of several hands. The introductory plea and the closing remarks may very properly be attributed to his skilful pen. A copy was afterwards delivered to each of the delegates, together with Mr. Backus's "Appeal to the Public."[1] The result of the conference was not at all satisfactory, John Adams remarking that we might as well expect a change in the solar system as to expect that they would give up their Establishment; or, as he himself gives the account,[2] "they might as well turn the heavenly bodies out of their annual and diurnal courses, as the people of Massachusetts at the present day from their meeting-house and Sunday laws." This effort of Manning and his associates was nevertheless the means indirectly of accomplishing great good. It opened the minds of the people generally to a knowledge of their true position and principles, and prepared the way for the astonishing increase of the Baptists,[3] and for the remarkable spread of their sentiments throughout the land. Doubtless it was one of the impor-

[1] The following is the title of this pamphlet, which Backus had prepared and published the previous year: "An Appeal to the Public for Religious Liberty, against the oppressors of the present day. 'Brethren, ye have been called unto liberty; only use not liberty for an occasion to the flesh, but by love serve one another.' Gal. v. 13. Boston: Printed by John Boyle, in Marlborough Street, 1773." pp. 62. A copy of this rare pamphlet is in the library of the University.

[2] See Works of John Adams, Vol. II. p. 399.

[3] In 1764, when the college was founded, the Baptists in all America numbered only sixty churches, with five thousand members or communicants. The lapse of a century finds them, with a single exception, the largest denomination of evan-

tant agencies which slowly and silently effected a change in the public sentiment of Massachusetts herself, until, in 1833, the Bill of Rights was so amended, that church and state were separated in the old Commonwealth, and soul-liberty, as maintained by the Baptists of every age, was finally and perfectly secured.

How this conference of the Baptists with the members of Congress was regarded by their opponents, may be seen from an extract from a letter of President Manning, dated Dec. 2, 1774, which we quote from Hovey's Memoir of Backus. The writer states that the following assertions in reference to said conference were made by the Rev. Dr. Ezra Stiles; namely: —

"That the Baptists had made an application to the Congress against the Massachusetts Bay; that the delegates of that province expected only a private interview with some of the Baptists; but instead of that, when they came they found a house full, etc.; that they were attacked and treated in the most rude and abusive manner; that the Baptists pretended they were oppressed, but, after all their endeavors, they could only complain of a poor fourpence; that they were ashamed of their errand, and gave up their point, except one or two impudent fellows, who, with Israel Pemberton, abused them in a most scandalous manner; that all the delegates present were surprised at and ashamed of them, and thought they complained without the least foundation," etc. Then Dr. Stiles added: "*When we have the power in our own hands, we will remember them.*"

gelical Christians in the United States, — having 588 associations, 12,648 churches, and 1,037,576 communicants; also 35 colleges or universities, upwards of 100 academies, 13 theological schools, and 26 weekly, monthly, semi-monthly, and quarterly periodicals. If to this we add 71,767 Baptists in Nova Scotia, New Brunswick, Canada, and the West India Islands, and 499,941 in the United States who practise immersion, but are not included among the regular Baptists, we have a total of 1,609,284 members, being an increase during the past century of more than a million and a half. (See the American Baptist Almanac for 1863. Also, the excellent article on Baptists in the "New American Cyclopædia," by the Rev. Dr. J. N. Brown, of Phhiladelpia, and a paper on the "Growth of the Baptist Denomination in this Country during the last half Century," read by the Rev. Kendall Brooks, at the recent Jubilee Meeting of the American Baptist Missionary Union.)

The following communication, which we copy from the *Providence Gazette*, sufficiently explains the position of affairs in reference to the Commencement for 1775: —

To the reverend President, honorable Professor, and rest of the honorable Corporation of Rhode Island College, — the dutiful petition of the Senior Class:

MOST WORTHY PATRONS: — Deeply affected with the distress of our oppressed country, which now, most unjustly, feels the baneful effects of arbitrary power, provoked to the greatest height of cruelty and vengeance by the noble and manly resistance of a free and determined people, permit us, gentlemen, to approach you with this our humble and dutiful petition, that you would be pleased to take under your serious consideration the propriety of holding the ensuing Commencement in a public manner, as usual; whether such a celebration of that anniversary would be in conformity to the 8th Article of the Association formed by the grand American Congress, and which all the colonies are now religiously executing; and that you would be pleased to signify unto us your resolution respecting the same, that we may govern ourselves accordingly.

JOSIAH READ,
ANDREW LAW,
JAMES FULTON, } Committee in behalf of the Senior Class.

COLLEGE IN PROVIDENCE, June 8, 1775.

To this communication the President and Professor thus reply: —

TO THE COMMITTEE OF THE SENIOR CLASS:

GENTLEMEN: — Your dutiful and reasonable petition has been duly attended to; and permit us to assure you, that it gives us no small satisfaction that the present members of this institution, and particularly the respectable Senior Class, are so sensibly affected with the distresses of our country in its present glorious struggles for liberty. We rejoice that you are so ready to sacrifice that applause to which your abilities would entitle you at a public Commencement; and though by this means you may be deprived of an advantageous opportunity to give proof of your abilities in pleading the righteous cause of liberty, for which your predecessors in this institution have been justly celebrated, yet you have hereby given us a convincing proof of your inviolable attachment to the true interests of your country. Be assured that we shall most heartily concur in this, and every other measure which has been, or may be, adopted by the grand American Congress, as well as the Legislature of this colony, in order to obtain the most complete redress of all our grievances; and deem it the greatest honor to which a noble and generous mind can aspire, to contribute in any degree towards a restoration and reëstablishment in our country of all those liberties and privileges, both civil and religious, which the Almighty Father of the universe originally granted to every individual of the human race, and which all ought to enjoy till by law forfeited; which reason claims, which the right of soil, obtained of the natives by free purchase, settles upon us; which our charters insure to us, and which have been recognized by Great Britain, and guaranteed to us by the faith of the English nation. These inestimable rights and privileges our country has for many years enjoyed, — the source of its present wealth and strength, more than its fertile soil or healthy climate: by the cruel and wanton invasion and violation of these, she now bleeds in almost every vein; and finally it is these that her noble sons, the illustrious American patriots, prompted as well as justified by the examples of heroes in all ages, are now prepared to defend, by the same means which have hitherto preserved the liberties of Great Britain, and raised to royal dignity the House of Brunswick.

And though the din of arms and the horrors of a civil war should invade our hitherto peaceful habitations, yet even these are preferable to a mean and base submission to arbitrary power and lawless rapine.

Institutions of learning will doubtless partake in the common calamities of our country, as arms have ever proved unfriendly to the more refined and liberal arts and sciences; yet we are resolved to continue college orders here as usual, excepting that the ensuing Commencement, by the advice of such of the corporation as could be conveniently consulted, will not be public.

JAMES MANNING, *President.*
DAVID HOWELL, *Philos. Professor.*

COLLEGE LIBRARY, June 9, 1775.

In accordance with the decisions of the college authorities thus announced, and for the reasons assigned, there was no *public* Commencement, although the graduating class consisted of ten, — a larger number than any heretofore. The battles of Lexington and of Bunker Hill had electrified the public mind, and turned away its attention from the literary performances of the stage to the sterner duties of the field and the camp. A prominent member of this class was Pardon Bowen, who afterwards became one of the most distinguished physicians of Providence. He was an active member of the Rhode Island Medical Society, and for seven years was its presiding officer. Prof. Goddard, in Thatcher's Lives of Eminent Physicians, has paid a just tribute to his genius and worth. In this class also was Robert Rogers, who was elected to the fellowship in 1788, and who is said to have attended nearly every Commencement until his death, in 1835. For several years he taught a classical school in Newport, which became one of the nurseries of the college. In this class also was Andrew Law, a clergyman who, in 1820, received the degree of LL.D. from another college. The meeting of the corporation this year was rendered memorable by the election of John Brown as treasurer, the duties of which office he discharged with great ability and acceptance for a period of twenty-two years.

The next year Commencement was held as usual, and, for the first time, in the new Baptist meeting-house. Nine young gentlemen graduated and received their diplomas, among whom was Daniel Gano, eldest brother of Dr. Stephen Gano, Mr. Manning's successor in the pastoral office.

This was the last public Commencement held during the war. On Saturday, Dec. 7, following, Sir Peter Parker, the British commander, with seventy sail of men-of-war, anchored in Newport harbor, landed a body of troops, and took possession of the place. Providence was hence all in confusion. Troops were massed throughout the town, martial law was proclaimed, college studies were interrupted, and the students were dismissed to their respective homes, as appears from the following notification of the President, published in the *Providence Gazette:* —

This is to inform all the students that their attendance on college orders is hereby dispensed with, until the end of the next spring vacation; and that they are at liberty to return home, or prosecute their studies elsewhere, as they think proper; and that those who pay as particular attention to their studies as these confused times will admit, shall then be considered in the same light and standing as if they had given the usual attendance here. In witness whereof, I subscribe,

JAMES MANNING, *President.*

PROVIDENCE, Dec. 10, 1776.

The seat of the Muses now became the habitation of Mars.[1] From Dec. 7, 1776, until May 27, 1782, the course of studies was suspended, and the college edifice was occupied for barracks, and afterwards for a hospital, by the American and French forces.

Dr. Manning having thus far discharged his arduous and responsible duties with unwearied assiduity and the most gratifying success, now employed this interval of relaxation from collegiate service in the labors of the ministry, and in various acts of social benevolence which the perils and distresses of that period in our national history prompted him to perform. A letter to his friend the Rev. John Ryland, written a few days before the closing of the college, gives a vivid idea of the war, regarded by a Christian and a philanthropist: —

PROVIDENCE, Nov. 13, 1776.

REVEREND AND DEAR SIR:

After a long interruption of our correspondence, an opportunity again offers of sending you a line, by some of our captive brethren, who have

[1] Up to this time the number of college students had steadily increased from year to year. In 1769 there were thirteen students; in 1770, twenty-one; in 1771, twenty-five; in 1772, thirty; in 1773, thirty-three; in 1774, thirty-four; and in 1775, forty-one students. These facts we learn from a paper preserved on file by Judge Howell.

liberty to return directly to England. The bearer, Mr. Thomas Mackaness, partner with Mr. Thornton, can give you many more particulars of our affairs than I can by a letter.

Since I wrote you last I have seen both glorious and gloomy days. The winter before last it pleased God to pour out his Spirit upon the people of this town in a most glorious manner. I believe about two hundred persons were converted within the space of a few months. I baptized more than half that number in less than a year. But the fatal 19th of April, the day of the Lexington battle, like an electric stroke put a stop to the progress of the work, as well in other places as here. Oh horrid war! How contrary to the spirit of Jesus! May you never be alarmed, as we have been, with the horrid roar of artillery, and the hostile flames, destroying your neighbors' habitations. These I have repeatedly seen and heard, sitting in my house and lying in my bed. I desire to bless God, these scenes of carnage always appeared peculiarly shocking to me, and I feel no disposition to destroy or injure my fellow-men. May the Lord turn the hearts of all to himself! and then I know war will instantly cease. The scene of action, in a hostile way, has been at the distance of more than two hundred miles from me this campaign, and I could wish it had been more than ten thousand, if it must be at all. You will not think strange that the colleges have suffered greatly by this tremendous convulsion; though I believe we have not suffered more than our neighbors. Our number is about thirty; but the high price of everything amongst us, I fear, will drive some of the students away.

For more than a year the state of religion has been truly lamentable, except in some places in Connecticut. But there are pleasing prospects opening in several places around us; I think there are some favorable symptoms in my congregation. May the Lord increase these. There have been seven Baptist ministers ordained in New England since last April, and about that number of churches constituted within about a year. These are encouraging circumstances amidst our troubles.

My dear Brother Gano[1] has suffered greatly by the war, and where he now is with his distressed, numerous family, I cannot learn, as I have never had a line from him since he was obliged to quit New York.

[1] Rev. John Gano. He served as chaplain during the war, and by his patriotic counsels and earnest prayers did very much to encourage the officers and privates of the American army. After the occupation of New York by the British, he retired with his family to a farm within five miles of Warwick, near the New Jersey line. Mr. Manning visited his family in May, 1779, as we learn from his diary or journal. (See Chapter VI.)

There was a glorious revival of religion, last winter, at Hopewell in the Jerseys. Ninety were baptized and added to that church in seven months. I have heard nothing of the state of religion from the southward for a long time; but I fear that politics and war have not promoted it. If they have, they have fared better than New England.

Mr. Mackaness informs me that there is a glorious revival in many parts of England, especially in the Establishment. I heartily rejoice to hear the news. May the kingdom of the Redeemer come throughout the world!

The gentlemen you recommended to me as worthy of the honors of the college were all graduated; but as the communication was shut up their diplomas were never written; and as I have but short notice of this opportunity, and as there is no parchment in the country, I could not forward them now. But I hope it may not be long before these obstructions may be removed.

I wish you great success in your labors in the gospel, and many crowns of rejoicing in the day of Christ Jesus. If possible, let me have a line from you. If not, grant me an interest in your prayers at our Father's throne, that I may be kept in the day of temptation, and be enabled to fulfil the ministry which I have received. With great respect, and many obligations, I remain, dear sir,

Your unworthy brother in the gospel,

JAMES MANNING.

The religious awakening to which Dr. Manning here refers is more particularly described in a letter to the Rev. Benjamin Wallin, dated Nov. 12, 1776: —

REVEREND AND DEAR SIR:

It is long since I have had the pleasure of hearing from you, or an opportunity of writing to you, in consequence of the perilous times in which we live. But I hope, though Great Britain and America are at war, that the saints of God do not mean to wage war against each other, or suffer their love and affection towards each other in the least to abate, because a wise Providence has cast their lot in the respective contending countries. I do not think it the business of the ministers of Christ to meddle much with politics, as they are concerned to promote a kingdom not of this world. You will not, therefore, expect anything from me on this subject, except so far as the cause of the Redeemer appears to be affected by the alarming aspect of public affairs.

In the beginning of the winter of 1774, it pleased the Lord in a most remarkable manner to revive his work in the town of Providence, and more especially among the people of my charge. Such a time I never before saw. Numbers were pricked to the heart. Our public assemblies by night and by day were crowded, and the auditors seemed to hear as for the life of their souls. It was frequently an hour before I could get from the pulpit to the door, on account of the numbers thronging to have an opportunity of stating the condition of their minds, — some exulting in the love of God and speaking of a precious Jesus, and others bewailing their awful, ruined state, and asking, "What must I do to be saved?" My dear sir, never until now did I so effectually feel the insufficiency of instruments to afford the poor sinner the least help. How glorious now to view the all-sufficient Saviour! There I would stand pointing to him, and saying, "Behold the Lamb of God, which taketh away the sin of the world." This was all I could do. Never before did I experience such happy hours in the pulpit. Day and night my dear people resorted to my house to open to me the state of their souls, insomuch that it was with difficulty I could at any time attend to secular business; and I think I may say with truth, that I had as little inclination as leisure for it, further than the absolute demands of duty required.

And what added peculiarly to my happiness was, that the Lord visited the college as remarkably as the congregation. Frequently, when I went to the recitation-room, I would find nearly all the students assembled, and joining in prayer and praise to God. Instead of my lectures on logic and philosophy, they would request me to speak to them of the things concerning the kingdom of God. But your experience in the service of the dear Redeemer will enable you to form a more adequate idea of the concomitant circumstances of such a work of grace than I can here communicate. In a word, the mountains seemed to melt at the presence of the Lord; the pride and haughtiness of man were laid low; and the Lord alone was exalted. In the space of about six months, I baptized more than one hundred persons.[1] Many were also added to the other churches of the town, who, I believe, were first added to the Lord. Thus the glorious work continued, and rather increased, until the fatal 19th of April,

[1] Among those who became religious at this time was Mrs. Manning, whom her husband baptized in the month of January, 1775.

when the affair at Lexington happened, which, like an electric shock, filled every mind with horror and compassion. When one would have thought this would have promoted seriousness amongst us, it, strange to tell, operated the very reverse; for since the fatal day languor and abatement of zeal for God seem greatly to have obtained, and instances of conversion to Christ are rare. Yet I hope our affairs are now somewhat improving. I have often labored to investigate the cause of the almost universal decline of vital godliness amongst us since the commencement of this unhappy war, but can find no other than that war is in its nature a hardening judgment. I have heard of and know many places where the Lord by his Spirit appeared to be at work when hostilities commenced, and in every instance the work immediately abated. In one instance only were they made the means of any considerable awakening. Yet, blessed be God! the dews of divine grace have distilled gloriously in many places, and reformations are commencing. I know you will heartily join at the throne of grace that Christ's kingdom may so come in both countries, yea, in all the world, that war may cease from the ends of the earth. I expect Mr. Thomas Mackaness, merchant in partnership with Mr. Thornton, will hand you this. He has been a great sufferer by having been taken on his voyage to Quebec, in consequence of which he lost vessel and cargo. He can give further information concerning me, if you desire. With sincere regards, I am, dear sir,

Your friend and unworthy brother,

JAMES MANNING.

The following reply, the last letter from Wallin ever received by Manning, shows that war had not alienated all our English friends. This fact is delightfully evident in the correspondence of a later period.

MAZE POND, SOUTHWARK, Aug. 30, 1777.

REVEREND AND DEAR SIR:

I embrace the opportunity of acknowledging your very acceptable favor, which came to hand in January last. Oh the wonders of Omnipotent love! Peace on earth and good-will to men, dispensed by the everlasting gospel in a rebellious world, like the antediluvian, corrupt before God, and filled with violence! It is the Lord's doings, and marvellous in our eyes. Your striking account of the heavenly visitation on the church and college over which you preside filled me with gratitude and joy, as it did my people, and indeed many others, ministers and respectable individuals, from whom I could not conceal the glad tidings. They proved as cold waters to a thirsty soul. Dear sir, if you would have such good news a secret, you must not trust a man with it who wishes to spread abroad the salvation of God, that all who love it may have continual occasion to glorify his name. Many thanksgivings redounded to the King of all grace upon a rehearsal of this glorious display of his mercy, — an evidence this of a genuine love among the saints whose lot is cast in the respective contending countries, originally united, now waging war, to the grief of all who wish well to Great Britian. What stronger proof of this divine grace than a free communication and an unfeigned great joy in each other's prosperity!

It would be pleasing to return a similar account from the mother country, but the state of religion is not so delightful and promising. Indeed, many preachers go forth, and the number of hearers increases, but it is not so strictly in the way of the Lord as I could wish. It seems to me vainglorious, and in some respects tending to confusion, of which God is not the author. Among the Episcopalians who have any idea of gospel truth (though I think for the most part they are rather superficial), their way is to open a chapel, as they style it, and, having drawn an audience, they are fixed at a custom-rate for their seats. On this plan many, and some of them sumptuous buildings have been erected, to which, by report, great numbers resort. I would hope by this means some may be led into a saving knowledge of Christ, and so far I rejoice; yet I cannot but lament the tending and the effect of this carnal contrivance and vague kind of social religion to the accommodation of man and the neglect of all gospel order. A becoming zeal for this is now a matter of reproach with many among us, insomuch that the enlightened, who wish to be conformed to the positive institutions of the Redeemer, are under great discouragements, and few join the regular churches of any denomination; so that a godly discipline in particular communion is in a manner out-of-doors. The consequence of all this will, I fear, be a still greater declension from real and practical piety. The Baptists more especially are obnoxious to these popular gentlemen, of which a specimen has lately transpired in an abusive pamphlet, by a warm-spirited young clergyman. Irritated by some altercations on a late baptizing in the parish of his vicarage, he has fallen foul on me for my little address to the churches of the Congregational order, — the first edition of which you have in a volume of mine. This piece has nothing to do with the point in debate, and, being anonymous, was by many ascribed to a person of the Independent persuasion before the author was discovered. This man holds me up to the public as a masterpiece of bigotry, and an enemy to all Pedobaptist communion, and at the same time pretends to much candor.

This newly-adopted mode has already emboldened some froward men to set up for themselves, under the color of Protestant dissenters; and, among the rest, lately, one Mr. Dawson, a Sabbatarian Baptist, not long since in New England. Alas! these men make a trade of religion! It likewise favors party divisions in church, too frequent, and which now for the most part end in grievous and shameful separations, to the prejudice of brotherly love; it being the taste of the day to follow new societies and teachers. This is a melancholy case; for we know by the disciples at Corinth that in this carnal spirit there is little regard to the power and grace of God in the increase of his church.

As to my congregation, they are in general steady, and our church state gradually advances. Of late we have been favored with some remarkable instances of conversion; among others, last month I baptized four young persons of one family, brothers and sisters in the flesh, the children of a deacon lately deceased, who was the second person that passed under my hands. This was in the year 1741. Their grandfather and grandmother were also valuable members of the church some years after I succeeded my honored father in the pastoral charge. The Lord will not *fail*, but may exceed the terms of his promise. His grace is not bound. You will not wonder at the joy of the brethren on this singular occasion.

I fear the Papists take advantage of our civil and religious confusion. According to some there are alarming symptoms of their increase in our nation and cities. Indeed, unknown and disorderly societies but too much favor their design, while the political sentiments of many Protestants are a hinderance, at least, to their social prayers. But with our God nothing is impossible. May he pour out the Spirit from on high on both countries, and graciously restore our public tranquillity on an honorable and permanent foundation; and may you, dear sir, enjoy many happy hours in the closet and in the pulpit, and again be employed in a field white for harvest, as in the year 1775.

As for me, my age and infirmities promise little further capacity for usefulness. Infinite are the obligations upon me for the grace by which I have been sustained thirty-seven years in the arduous work of the ministry. Our great Divine Master doth not cast off his old servants; yet the prayers of my brethren may subserve to a finish with joy; a request, I am persuaded, you will not deny me.

Having the honor of a place in your library, it seemed decent to present a copy of another attempt since my last. Parents, you know, sir, oft show their vanity in dressing up their children. Excuse the uniform of the eleventh volume. It comes in expectation of the same kind reception with that of its preceding companions. If any hints concerning parables in general, or that in particular which is the subject in hand, prove pertinent and useful, the author flatters himself that some other pen may improve them to public advantage.

For an increase of the church's prosperity and a period to the national trouble, we unite in our prayers to the Most High, with which I conclude.

Dear sir,

Your very obliged and affectionate Brother,

BENJ. WALLIN.

P. S.—The copy on The Prodigal presented to the college with my most respectful compliments to the venerable members, if it be needful to mention so trifling a matter to them, was bound in readiness soon after the publication. My notice of this opportunity was short, which it is hoped will apologize for the mourning dress of those directed to you and the other gentlemen, on whose candor in perusing them I rely. If by any means you can inform me of the arrival of these, it will be acceptable. Before the present interruption to our intercourse took place, I was in expectation of soon receiving a digested and authentic account of your college, which, I hope, will survive the civil commotions, and prove a flourishing seminary of learning under your direction. If this design is carried into execution, I hope to be presented with some copies the first opportunity.

The following letter, addressed to Miss A. Howard, in Scarboro, England, illustrates the peculiar tact and delicacy of Dr. Manning in his efforts to alleviate the distressed, and to give sympathy and counsel to the bereaved and unfortunate. In a footnote he remarks that the letter actually sent to Miss Howard was greatly altered and enlarged from this, which seems to be the first copy. Capt.

Bell, it appears, was taken with his vessel, by some of our cruisers, and brought into Providence, where he died. He was engaged to be married to the lady in question, who, as will be observed, was an entire stranger to Manning.

PROVIDENCE, NEW ENGLAND, Nov. 19, 1776.

DEAR MADAM:

I hope you will excuse the forwardness of a stranger in addressing a line to you, when I inform you of the amiable character given you by my dear unfortunate friend, Mr. Thomas Mackaness; as also from the sympathetic feelings of my heart under the distress which the news of the unexpected and truly lamentable death of the dear Capt. Bell must occasion, especially considering the endearing relation which, I am informed, he soon expected to stand in to you. Horrid war! What havoc dost thou make! To glut thy rage, must the youthful, amiable, virtuous, and what exceeds all these, must the singularly pious *Bell* fall a victim to thy relentless stroke! Must the hearts of tender parents bleed? Must more than half of all your happiness on earth perish? Must the dear bereaved church at Hull be bathed in tears? Must the tender orphans, his peculiar care, bewail the loss of their kindest benefactor, under thy unnatural domain?

But why do I open afresh the wounds which, long ere this arrives, have often bled? You, doubtless, have oft portrayed the bliss of the intended conjugal relation, and recounted the joys of such a virtuous connection, which, by a stroke, is now all blasted, and you sit solitary as one forsaken, and, in the plaintive strain of the sweet singer of Israel, cry, *Lover and friend hast thou removed from me, and mine acquaintance into darkness.* "I shall no more see good in the land of the living." But stop, my friend! Why these unavailing sighs? For whom do you thus lament? Is it for him who was so fully ripe for heaven, that earth was no longer for him a fit habitation, — for him whose heart and conversation were so in heaven, that the Redeemer chose to receive him to that society where, unmolested, he might sing those songs of praise, and give full scope to that ardor of spirit, which he had here so oft attempted, and so uniformly felt? True, the loss to you is great; but greater far, to him, the gain. And could you wish to disengage him from that blessed employment, — from that glorious society for which you long, and where you hope to bear a part in those anthems of praise to God and the Lamb forever?

Can you desire that he, disengaged from every earthly clog, should again, for many painful years, groan under the weight of a body of death, and see the object of his highest love through faith's dim medium, as we do now, and mourn his absence from our Father's house, — and all this to gratify and assist you through this painful journey home to glory? No, madam; both reason and religion forbid this selfish passion; and, painful as the thought of separation is, I know your generous soul can't wish it. You only mourn that you are left behind, and that our degenerate world has lost his bright example. But remember that he has left you in better hands, — that the swift-revolving years will soon land you at the same peaceful haven, where not only he but Jesus waits to welcome travellers home. Instead of pensive sadness, then, cheer up, and, as the poet sung, let us go singing on. It will render the journey less painful; and perhaps more than half the way is passed. Remember that now your attachment to heaven is stronger than ever. *There your best friend, your kindred dwell, there God your Saviour reigns.* May he grant you his divine presence to support you under the sore affliction, and abundantly sanctify his hand to you, that you may be more and more prepared for glory. Had I great interest at a throne of grace, you should not want a share of it; for I think if joining in your sorrow and mingling a friendly tear will alleviate your grief, I have borne a part for you.

Since the ship was taken and brought in here, I have often thought I should have been peculiarly happy had it been the will of Heaven to have spared the life of the dear man whose untimely death more than British friends lament. But here I find my want of submission to the will of God; for I am only happy when from the heart I can say to God, Thy will be done.

Probably I shall never see your face in the flesh; but should this happiness be denied me, I hope to see you where there shall be no more sorrow nor sighing; where God shall wipe away every tear from our eyes; where we shall see, not only the dear man whom we lament, but all the saints on earth, with those uncalled as yet, with Abraham, Isaac, and Jacob, with the apostles and prophets, and the general assembly of those whose names are written in heaven, with Jesus, the mediator, at their head, and God the Judge of all. Oh! what a glorious day when we shall rise to this exalted station! My dear friend, let us, then, walk worthy of such a calling; that whether we are absent or present in body, we may be present with the Lord. And here, I recollect, we may have an interview;

I mean at the throne of grace. Wishing you the highest possible happiness, I subscribe myself, madam,

Your friend and servant,

JAMES MANNING.

The following letter to the Rev. John Berridge, of London, shows Dr. Manning in the light of a controversialist. How skilfully he could handle the weapons of polemic warfare, will best be learned from its perusal. The pungency of its wit, the force of its argument, and the excellence of its style and spirit, amply compensate for its unusual length.

PROVIDENCE, NEW ENGLAND, NOV. 19, 1776.

REVEREND AND DEAR SIR:

Lately, through the kindness of my friend Mr. Thos. Mackaness, of London, I had the perusal of the "Christian World Unmasked. Pray, Come and Peep. By John Berridge, A.M., etc." 8vo. Lond. 1773. I accepted the invitation, and found the book in general corresponded well to the titlepage, until I came to pp. 223-5, inclusive, when I peeped again, but could not discover the least gleam of light, and therefore concluded the mask was in the way; when, lo! I turned to my New Testament, and found that light which is concealed by a veil while we search the Old for New Testament ordinances. Ay, Baptist, Baptist; I thought you was a water-fowl when you referred to the pages. Well, be it so; if he can be an instrument to pick open your eyes a little wider, I hope you will have no objection to him on that account. You say, "I would hate no man, and do condemn no man for *thinking* differently in this matter." Now if you mean to place the emphasis on *thinking*, I think I shall not fare well for *saying* differently. However, as you have made very free with the Grazier, I hope I may with the Doctor, upon the same principle, without offence.

You say that you have no doubt that infant-baptism is attended with the same blessing now that infant-circumcision was formerly. Both the ordinances are of God's appointment, etc. Till now, I find you producing plain Scripture warrant for the glorious doctrines you advance. And must we *only* rely upon the Doctor's bare word for the truth of this last assertion? What shall I say, then, to that voice I hear from Heaven, "*This is my beloved Son, hear ye him,*" and that, too, in the presence of Moses and Elias? Pray, Doctor, have me excused till you point me to the page where this great prophet authorizes you to say this. I have carefully examined the dispensatory, but can find no such prescription between the lids of it. You ask why Christian children may not be received into the church's fold by baptism, as were the Jewish by circumcision. Answer: The former was by God's special appointment, but not the latter. Surely, then, wide is the difference in their case. To say *nothing is said to forbid them,* is not sufficient to a truly Christian Protestant doctor; for if it is necessary, *totidem verbis,* for the Scripture to forbid everything practised under the name of Christianity, which is, notwithstanding, contrary to the true genius of the gospel, it would require a Bible ten times as large as Dr. Gill's Exposition of it. And then what should we field-preachers and the recruiting sergeants of the country do? But pray, Doctor, is baptism a moral precept, or an institution purely positive? If the latter, why need we wreck and torture our brains to find a reason for either mode or subjects, time or place, or anything further than what the New Testament simply informs us concerning it, as there is the only place where we should look for it? Or why need we be distressed how little children should be brought to Christ, while he has not seen fit to teach us the way in which it should be done?

In the next paragraph, you say that children dying unbaptized are left to God's uncovenanted mercy; and what that is, no mortal can tell. But I think I will undertake to tell what it is when the Doctor gives me a satisfactory account how baptismal water, through the grace of Christ, does wash away the *guilt* of original or birth-sin (so that dying before they can discern between good and evil, etc., they will be saved), consistent with the whole tenor of the rest of this performance, where the merits of Christ, applied by the Spirit of God, *alone* cleanses from sin; especially at the top of page 223, where the Doctor asserts that right to pardon, and a claim to eternal life, are wholly treasured up in Christ, and *only* are attained through faith in him; — I say, when the Doctor gives a solution of this Gordian knot, I will undertake the other part promised. Will the Doctor assert that infants, who are not capable of discerning between good and evil, are capable of believing in a gospel sense? If not, will he assert that they will be *saved* without a *right to pardon, or any claim to eternal life, which are blessings treasured up in Christ?* I cannot see how this difficulty can be solved, without recourse to believing by proxy, which I think the Doctor will not recur to, lest the Grazier should learn the trick, and get the curate to believe, in his stead, that he might follow more agreeable business and yet be safe, and after all vanquish the Doctor with his own weapon. But if there is so much efficacy in baptism, it is a pity everybody should not partake of it. And pray, can anybody administer it that pleases ? or must he be a clergyman ? If so, alas! what shall our poor American church-people do ? For since the King's naughty ministers undertook to enslave the colonies, the rebel congresses, conventions, committees, etc., have forbid the clergy to pray for the King, and they are so sulky that they will neither preach, pray, baptize, nor anything else.[1] And now must the poor infants who may happen to die all perish through their obstinacy, the wickedness of the congresses, and the King's ministers ? If this be the case, I hope the Doctor's patriotism will furnish the minority with a new argument, to urge at the next sitting of Parliament the repeal of the laws ; and which must be very forcible, for I do not believe that administration ever intended to kill our souls. I know pious Lord Dartmouth will turn about; for it is storied in America that he was very squeamish when they determined to kill only their bodies. I was glad, however, to find, with the Grazier, you was not "forgetting Jesus Christ to help out some defects," in which you put the grace of Christ together with "baptismal water," — especially as a man of a plain understanding might conclude the former quite sufficient of itself; though the Doctor seems to have given baptismal water the preference, agreeable to the Grazier's method of discharging sinful debts, or paying a decent part of the shot himself, and leaving Jesus to discharge the rest of the reckoning. But how will this comport with the sentiment advanced in page 176 : "It matters not at all whether the work be ritual or moral, while we seek to be saved by it. If we seek at all to be saved by any work of our own, we fall from grace." Pray, Doctor, is not baptism as much a work as circumcision ?

On page 224 you quote God's declaration to Abraham, long before Jesus

1 Perhaps Dr. Manning is too sweeping in his remarks touching the loyalty of the Episcopal clergy. It is certain, however, that there was ample foundation for such remarks. In the chapter of Staples's Annals devoted to ecclesiastical history, we find that the Rev. John Graves, who was the rector of the Episcopal church in Providence until July, 1776, declined to officiate after that period, because he could not be permitted to read the usual and ordinary prayers for the King, which he considered himself bound by his ordination vows to offer. The church was in consequence closed, most of the time, during the war of the Revolution. For a clear account of the relations of the Church of England to the American Colonies, see Thornton's "Pulpit of the American Revolution."

was given, "That an uncircumcised child shall be cut off from his people; he hath broken my covenant" (Gen. xvii. 16), and say the covenant here spoken of is not the Sinai covenant, but the covenant of grace. Circumcision was the outward sign of this covenant to Abraham, as baptism is to us. The outward rite is different, but the covenant the same. This I compared with pp. 33, 144, where I find it thus written: "If you desire benefit from the covenant of grace, you must be baptized, and if you seek advantage from the covenant of works, you must be circumcised. A rite of initiation is appointed to both the covenants, and you cannot enter into both without partaking of the double rite." "In a covenant of works a man must work for life by his own will and power," etc. "The tenor of this covenant is, do and live, transgress and die," etc. "In the covenant of grace all things are purchased for us, and bestowed upon us generously and freely. These two covenants are called the old and the new; no more are noticed in Scripture; and a suitable law respecting both is mentioned, — the law of works and the law of faith (Rom. iii. 27). All other laws are cobwebs of a human brain, such as the law of sincere obedience, the law of love," etc. And pray why not the law of infant-baptism? Now if the covenant made with Abraham was the covenant of grace, and circumcision was the sign of it, why are we told that if we desire benefit from the covenant of works we must be circumcised? It cannot be because these two very different covenants have the same rites of initiation; because the Doctor says their rites are different, unless the covenant of grace in Abraham's days is a covenant of works in ours; for there are but two covenants, the old and the new, noticed in the Scriptures.

But I will leave you to compare these passages yourself, without further insisting upon their inconsistency, and come to the dernier resort: "That no harm can possibly arise from baptizing an infant." Stop, Doctor, stop; these expressions are very strong, — I fear much too strong. For did not the Doctor say, page 222, "That much people, who are strangers to the work of regeneration, suppose the new birth is only their baptism, and that every one is born again who is baptized?" And is it strange they should think so when they hear thanks returned to God on its performance, that it is so by the doctors appointed to that service? Surely, to lead such multitudes into error in such an important article as that of regeneration, cannot be such a harmless thing, especially if we believe our Saviour's account of it (John iii. 3). Besides, it makes great doctors contradict themselves when they write or talk about the covenants. If I was one of those doctors, I should think this was some harm. But, most of all, it is invading the kingly office of the great Redeemer; for I can see no reason why the merits of saints may not be mingled with the merits of Christ to save the Christian, as the laws or ordinances of men with those of Christ to rule and govern it. Shall we, like Uzzah, not trust the Lord *wholly* with his ark, but must have a meddling finger? I forbear to recite the following part of your sentence. I must mention one more evil which arises from baptizing infants, which is this: The practice constrains those servants of God who practise it often to wrest and explain away the plain, obvious sense of Scripture to vindicate it; especially to give such representations of the covenant of grace as mars its glory, and encourages the opposers of the glorious doctrines of grace in rejecting the pure gospel of Jesus Christ. This has often grieved my heart, and in no case more than in reading your book, where the glorious Redeemer is exalted in his office, nature and grace, and the pride of man stained, until you get hampered, as I think, with infant-baptism, which neither we nor our fathers are able to prove was ever the mind of Christ. Upon this principle I concluded to address to you a line; not under the notion of a disputation, but in a friendly way to hint at what I thought mistakes in your performance.

You may probably esteem me rigid, from this specimen, and greatly attached to externals; but I think otherwise of myself. I think I love the followers of the Lamb, under whatever denomination they pass amongst men. I esteem them my brethren, and feel disposed to make all proper allowances for the prejudices of education, and the weaknesses of human nature, knowing that I myself also am in the body, and peculiarly need the candor of my Christian friends. I hope, therefore, that the benevolence of my intentions will apologize for the rudeness of my manner. I shall always rejoice to hear that dear Mr. Berridge is alive for God, — is held as a star in the right hand of Jesus, and is honored with many seals of his ministry, even though he should continue to think and practise very different from myself relative to the mode and subjects of baptism; though I sincerely pray that you may be set entirely right in this matter. And blessed be God, he has left us a rule which is able to make wise unto salvation through faith in Jesus Christ. May all our doctrines and practices be governed by that; and may the Spirit of truth lead us into all truth, and ever keep us humble, solely relying on the Lord for those sup-

22*

plies of grace and help which we always need. May the God of Blessing bless you. I am, reverend and dear sir,

Your friend and servant in the gospel,

JAMES MANNING.

On Wednesday, Sept. 3, 1777, the members of the corporation, as appears from the records, met in the new Baptist meeting-house, and conferred degrees upon seven members of the Senior Class, who had been examined the day previous, in accordance with the following, which we take from the *Providence Gazette*. There was no Commencement: —

As the term of vacation in the college is now expired, the students are hereby informed, that, in the present state of public affairs, the prosecution of studies here is utterly impracticable, especially while this continues a garrisoned town. It is therefore recommended to them to prosecute their studies elsewhere for the present, to the best advantage in their power. The Senior Class are desired to meet at the college, to pass their examination, and receive their degrees at the usual time, being the 2d day of September next, unless the college should be called together sooner. In behalf of the corporation,

JAMES MANNING.

PROVIDENCE, May 16, 1777.

There was no further meeting of the corporation held until May 5, 1780, when an attempt was made to revive the instruction of the college.

The years following the breaking up of the college were seasons of great distress. Many families left the town, unable to obtain a subsistence. The records of the church show that members of influence and property, some of them warm personal friends of Manning, were really objects of commiseration. It was the delight of the pastor, in this hour of trial, when members of his flock were scattered by the war, and the influences of literature seemed paralyzed, to aid the needy, and to throw the sunshine of Christian sympathy around the path of the afflicted. His knowledge of the world, his courtly manners, his Christian meekness, combined with his extraordinary energy of character, enabled him to move at ease in every class of society, and thus to promote the good of all. The following instance of his humane disposition is thus related by Howland, in his brief memoir of Dr. Manning, published in the year 1815 in the *Rhode Island Literary Repository*: —

"He enjoyed the confidence of the general commanding in this department, and in one instance in particular had all the benevolent feelings of his heart gratified, even at the last moment, after earnest entreaty, by obtaining from General Sullivan an order of reprieve for three men of the regular army who were sentenced to death by that inexorable tribunal, a court-martial. The moment he obtained the order revoking the sentence, he mounted his horse at the General's door, and, by pushing him to his utmost speed, arrived at the place of execution at the instant the last act had begun which was to precipitate them into eternity. With a voice which none could disobey, he commanded the execution to stay, and delivered the General's order to the officer of the guard. The joy of the attending crowd seemed greater than that of the subjects of mercy; they were called so suddenly to life from the last verge of death, they did not for a moment feel that it was a reality."

In the same memoir Mr. Howland thus relates the history of an important civil function which was confided to Dr. Manning, and by him most skilfully discharged: —

"The repeated calls of the militia, while the enemy remained in this State (Rhode Island), operated with peculiar severity. In some districts the ground could not be planted, and in others the harvest was not reaped in season; the usual abundance of the earth fell short, and he who had the best means of supply frequently had to divide his store with a suffering neighbor. In addition to this, laws existed in several States prohibiting the transport of provisions beyond the State boundary. The plea for these restrictions was that there was danger of the enemy being supplied; but the real cause was to retain the provisions for the purpose of furnishing their State's quota of troops, as the war was generally carried on by the energy of the governments of the individual States. These restrictions came with double weight on the citizens of Rhode Island, as a great part of the State was in the possession of the enemy, and the remainder was filled with those who had fled from the islands and the coasts for safety. These restrictions and prohibitions were variously modified; but under all their variations, which referred chiefly to the mode of executing the law, the grievance was the same. The Governor and council of war of Rhode Island, wishing to give their language of remonstrance a power of impression which paper could not be made to convey, commissioned Doctor Manning to repair to Connecticut, and represent, personally, to the government of that State our peculiar situation, and to confer with and propose to them a different mode of procedure. The Doctor in this embassy obtained all that he desired; the restrictions were removed, and, in addition to this, on his representation of the circumstances of the refugees from the islands, contributions, in money or provisions, were made in nearly all the parishes in the interior of Connecticut, and forwarded for their relief."

In this connection we cannot refrain from quoting another anecdote of Manning, as an illustration of his readiness to use every opportunity to benefit the souls of his fellow-men. We find it in Stone's Life and Recollections of Howland. In May, 1780, occurred "the dark day," so often referred to by the chroniclers of that period.[1] At noon all ordinary business was suspended. Fowls sought their roosts, cattle retired as at night, and men stood appalled at the dread appearances. "I went," says Howland, "into the street, where many persons were assembled, and among others Dr. Manning. A powerful man, but profligate, advanced up to the President, and said, 'How

[1] For an account of the "Dark Day," by Prof. Williams, see Memoirs of the American Academy of Arts and Sciences, Vol. I. See also Holmes's Life of Stiles, p. 265.

do you account for this darkness, sir? what does it mean?' The President, with great solemnity of manner, replied, 'I consider it, sir, as a prelude to that great and important day when the final consummation of all things is to take place.'"

A letter which we find addressed to his friend and former pupil the Rev. Thomas Ustick, now in Ashford, Connecticut, shows that the college was uppermost in all his thoughts and plans, even though the fortunes of war had suspended its public exercises: —

PROVIDENCE, Nov. 17, 1778.

DEAR SIR:

I am told that Mr. Kelly has entirely quitted Pomfret, to their great disappointment. There was a large gathering of people attended, and the prospect was encouraging of great good to be done there. In a letter to Brother Thurber, I mentioned the probability of your supplying them, at least for the present, and perhaps of settling amongst them for life, if you and they are blessed together. Should that be the case, it would be a good place for a Latin school, a nursery for the college, which I wish you immediately to engage in, and endeavor to influence as many as you can of our people to educate their children. The present state of the Baptist society in New England must convince us all of the importance of having men of education in all parts of the country. I am very sorry that I did not think to mention something of this to the Association; but I have written and am about writing to all our ministers capable of teaching Latin, to immediately engage in the business. I hope, from present appearances, that college orders may be again revived next spring. I think you ought at least to visit Pomfret, and help them under their present disappointment, as I understand you do not preach statedly at Ashford, and that you are nearly convinced that it will not be best for you to settle at that place. With respects to you and yours,

I remain, etc.,

JAMES MANNING.

A letter from Judge Howell, resigning his place as Professor of Philosophy in the college, may fitly close this chapter: —

PROVIDENCE, March 11, 1779.

SIR: — Having ever been impressed with a just sense of the honor conferred upon me in my appointment to the place of Professor of Philosophy in Rhode Island College, it becomes me, with much freedom and sincerity, to acknowledge it.

I have ever admired the liberal and catholic plan of this college, and esteemed it worthy of the State that gave it birth and patronage, which has induced me for many years assiduously and cheerfully to contribute towards establishing it on a footing, with respect to credit and finances, which might entitle it to more able teachers. That our young seminary had well-nigh attained this state of maturity, all circumstances conspired to afford us the most flattering prospect, before the commencement of the present war.

Although experimental philosophy was the direct object of my profession, yet other branches of learning were devolved upon me. How far my honest endeavors to initiate my pupils in the rudiments of classical learning, and instil into their minds the elementary principles of law, the parent of science, and my favorite theme, have been attended with success, and answered the good purposes of my appointment, is submitted to your honor, the corporation, the sons of the college, and the public to determine.

Having at length given over all hopes of a revival of classical instruction in this college during the continuance of the war, and not feeling disposed so far to take advantage of public munificence as to continue to avail myself of the emoluments of an office without discharging its duties, I have thought fit, not without weighty deliberation, to resign the professorship.

I am, sir, your most obedient humble servant,

DAVID HOWELL.

Chancellor Hopkins.

CHAPTER VI.

JOURNEY TO PHILADELPHIA.

APRIL 29 — SEPT. 29, 1779.

Distressed condition of the people of Rhode Island in 1779 — Probable reasons for a journey to Philadelphia — Diary or Journal — Manning sets out from Providence Thursday, April 29 — Sunday, May 2, preaches at Mr. James Thurber's in the forenoon, and at Mr. Thompson's in the afternoon — Thursday, May 6, Continental Fast — Preaches in the afternoon for Rev. Dr. Nathan Strong, of Hartford — Saturday, May 8, preaches to Seventh-day Baptists in Farmington — Description of the country — Sunday, May 9, preaches for Rev. Judah Champion, pastor of the Congregational church in Litchfield — Monday, crosses chains of tremendous mountains — Tuesday, May 11, preaches in the evening at Mr. Waldo's — Wednesday, 12, crosses Continental Ferry — Thursday, 13, reaches the family of his brother-in-law, Rev. John Gano — Sunday, 16, preaches twice for Rev. Mr. Randall's people — Tuesday, 18, assists his nephews in planting — Sunday, 23, preaches again for Mr. Randall at Warwick — Monday, 24, sets out for the Jerseys — Reaches Mrs. Manning's home in the evening—May 27, visits Elizabethtown, his native place — Sunday, 30, preaches at the Scotch Plains Church — Meeting interrupted by the march of the American forces — Sunday, June 6, preaches with Mr. Stelle, to a large audience — Saturday, 12, preaches at the Scotch Plains Church — Sunday, 13, preaches again and administers communion — Sunday, 20, preaches at Lion's Farms — Monday, June 21, sets out for Philadelphia — In the evening preaches at Samuel Randolph's — June 24, visits Dr. Vankirk, and preaches in the evening — Accounts of Grain and Indian Corn — June 27, tarries with Rev. William Van Horn at Southampton, and preaches — Fruit in this neighborhood cut off by the frost — Crops fine — Monday, June 28, reaches Pennepek, and tarries with Rev. Dr. Samuel Jones five days — Sketch of Dr. Jones — July 2, Manning arrives at Philadelphia — Puts up at William Goforth's — Calls on Samuel Davis, William Rogers, Mr. Watkins, Mr. Westcot, Dr. Rush, Mr. Moulders, Mr. Hart, and Robert S. Jones — Financial embarrassments of the country — Mr. Joseph Hart of the Executive Council spends the evening at his lodgings — July 3, breakfasts with Dr. Rush — Inquires of Mr. Collins, a member of Congress, relative to the money question — Dines at Mr. Redwood's with Hon. William Ellery — Sunday, July 4, preaches twice — General

Spencer, a member of Congress, spends the evening with him — Monday, July 5, importuned by a Committee of the First Baptist Church to tarry with them a long time — Sets out in the afternoon for Dr. Jones's — July 7, sets out for Bordentown — July 9, preaches in the evening — July 11, preaches at Cranberry — Sick with diarrhœa — July 13, preaches at the Baptist meeting — July 16, sets out for Piscataway — Mrs. Manning ill — July 17, preaches at Sabbatarian meeting — July 18, preaches for Mr. Stelle twice — July 19, returns to the Farms — Report concerning General Wayne and Stony Point — July 23, sets out for Hopewell — July 25, preaches twice and administers the communion — July 26, preaches in the afternoon — July 27, dines at John Hart's, Newtown — July 29, sets out again for Philadelphia — July 30, visits in town — Sees the prisoners taken at Stony Point — Aug. 1, preaches twice — Letters from friends — Aug. 5, call from Rev. Morgan Edwards — Aug. 7, visits Capt. Falkner, in company with Edwards — Aug. 8, preaches in town three times — Aug. 10, visits Col. Miles, in company with Edwards and Jones — Description of his country-seat — Weather — Crops — Aug. 14, preaches in the evening — Aug. 15, preaches twice, and attends funeral of a child — Aug. 16, sets out for Mr. Jones's at Pennepek — Finds Mr. Edwards there — Aug. 17, sets out for the Jerseys — Visits his family and friends — Sept. 8, sets out for Providence — Sept. 11, reaches the home of his brother-in-law, Mr. Gano, and next day preaches twice at Warwick — Sept. 14, meets Lieut. Hubbel on the road, who had come from Newburgh with an invitation from West Point — Sept. 16, goes down to West Point by water in Lieut. Hubbel's boat — Description of the Fort and Grounds — Introduced to Sergeon McDugal — Dines at General Green's quarters with his family — Is introduced to General Washington, General Knox, Baron Steuben, the French Ambassador, and others — Returns up the river — Sept. 17, sets out from the Continental Ferry — Journey through Connecticut — Description of the country — Character of the inhabitants — Manner of conducting town meetings — Ravages of the war — Reaches home, Sept. 29.

THE year 1779 was one of great trial and of severe suffering to the inhabitants of Rhode Island. For nearly two years Narragansett Bay and all the island towns, at least one fourth of the State, had been in possession of the enemy. External trade was almost entirely suspended, and the people were unable to procure any adequate supply of the necessaries of life. Nearly every able-bodied man was in service, either in the State militia or the Continental army, and even the negroes and Indian slaves were enlisted as soldiers. The price of labor and of all articles of merchandise was fixed by legislative decree. The taxes imposed by the State were enormous; amounting this year to £495,000, and in the year following to four times this sum. Paper money, which had greatly depreciated in value, was made a legal tender in the payment of debts; and so easily was it counterfeited, that not even the Secretary of State could distinguish the genuine from the spurious. In addition to all this, the national cause had encountered reverses, Congress was reduced to a very low ebb, the ablest members having left it, and the prospect of independence and peace was overcast with shadows and doubts.

It was in reference perhaps to this alarming state of the currency of the country, and in the hope of aiding by counsel or otherwise his distressed-fellow townsmen, that Dr. Manning set out on a journey to Philadelphia, visiting on the way his relatives in New York and New Jersey. In company with his wife he left Providence on the 29th of April, returning on the 29th of September. He was thus absent just five months, having passed through the States of Rhode Island, Connecticut, New York, New Jersey, and Pennsylvania. The following diary or journal was kept by him as they travelled from day to day. It abounds in historical incidents and allusions, and presents an excellent daguerreotype view of the author's private life. As an illustration of the times in which he lived, and of the general condition of society, it is an exceedingly valuable document. We have therefore devoted to it an entire chapter, illustrating it with such notes as seemed desirable for the better understanding of the text. As an evidence of Dr. Manning's popularity as a preacher, and of his love for this kind of work, it may be added, that his services were called into requisition forty-eight times during this journey to Philadelphia and the Jerseys. He preached in meeting-houses of different denominations, in private dwellings, and even in stores and places of business, as the reader will observe.

MANNING'S JOURNAL.

Set out from Providence Thursday, 29th of April, at six o'clock P. M. Reached Col. Abraham Winsor's in the evening; began to rain; were hospitably entertained; ten miles. *Friday morning, 30th.* A cold north-east storm; broke away at eight o'clock A. M., but remained showery and very blustering. Travelled to Mr. John Brown's farm at Chepachet, six miles. Refreshed ourselves and horse, and proceeded to Capt. Corlis's, Killingly, twelve miles. The roads extremely bad. Spent the afternoon and evening, and the next forenoon of May 1, in visiting them and Mr. Jones's family. Set out after dinner and visited Gov. Sessions, who has a most excellent farm in good order. After tea travelled to Mr. Benjamin Thurber's in Pomfret, six miles. The roads better; tarried over Lord's Day.

Sunday, May 2. Preached at Mr. James Thurber's, three miles back, in the morning, and at Mr. Thompson's in the afternoon. Preached a lecture at Mr. B. Thurber's at five o'clock; the house crowded and the audience very attentive and affected. Visited Paul Tew, Esq., at Woodstock, Monday, May 3, A. M. and P. M. Mr. Cahoon's family, and dined; also Mr. Lee's, Thompson's, B. Lindsey's, and Esquire Frink's. Borrowed Mr. Lindsey's trunk; left ours, a jacket, pattern for breeches, white gown, black wool hat, Hart's Hymns, and some valuable papers, in Mr. Thurber's care. Set out Tuesday morning, May 4, and visited Col. Nightingale, three miles. Spent the forenoon and dined. He lives most elegantly; has a grand farm; entertained us hospitably. Then proceeded to Mr. Jeremiah Brown's, two and one half miles; ascended a tremendous hill, refreshed, and proceeded two and one half miles to Capt. Bowles's, Ashford. Tarried all night, well entertained, and set out on the morning of the 5th. Travelled six miles to Stephen Snow's, refreshed, and then reached Mr. Robinson's, a pious Baptist gentleman, who bids fair to be useful in the ministry, in Mansfield, passing through a corner of Willington; six miles. Were received with great kindness; dined. Set out and reached an inn in Coventry, seven miles. Fed the horse, and travelled fifteen miles through Bolton into East Hartford, to the widow of Capt. Bidwel, a pious Baptist lady, and a good liver. Were kindly entertained, tarried all night, and went on for Hartford. Three miles to meeting, it being Thursday, the 6th of May, the Continental Fast; but a severe northwest wind prevented our crossing the ferry for several hours. Passed at length, and put up at Bull's Tavern, opposite the town house; were unknown to them. In the afternoon went to Mr. Strong's[1] meeting, who insisted that I should preach, which I did to a very large and attentive audience. After service Mr. Strong took us to his house to lodge, and entertained us like a friend, and Capt. —— took our horse from the tavern and kept it well; both insisting that we should call on them again on our way back, as did Dr. Smith. Till within ten or twelve miles of Hartford the way is in general mountainous and rocky, but the people live well by their industry, of which there are striking indications. The season at Hartford appears nearly or quite a fortnight earlier than at Providence. Except Sunday, Monday, and Tuesday, the weather very blustering and cold, but no frost. The winter grain looks exceeding promising, and a vast quantity of summer grain is put in; abundance of land prepared for Indian corn; the fruit not injured by frosts. *Friday morning, May* 7. Set out for Farmington; reached Mr. Joseph Woodruff's, ten miles, and tarried to dinner; kindly entertained; then proceeded to a settlement of Seventh-day Baptists in the northwest part of Farmington, ten miles. Tarried at Mr. Covey's, where we were kindly treated, and preached Saturday, the 8th inst., to their society, to great acceptance; after passing the meadows four miles, the road rough, and an exceeding high mount of difficult ascent. The weather cold, and frost at night. The fruit here killed. After meeting proceeded through Farmington; oated at Mr. Baldwin's tavern, and reached Mr. Philips's tavern at Litchfield at sundown. The whole of this way exceeding mountainous and rough, but the land fertile and well improved; fine fields of grain and good buildings all the way. The people here live exceeding well. One tedious mountain two and one half miles from Litchfield; the day warm; the distance thirteen miles. This town is situated on a cold hill, the water bad, and the season near a fortnight backward of Hartford. Good lodgings and entertainment at the tavern; the landlady very agreeable.

[1] The Rev. Dr. Nathan Strong, pastor of the First Congregational Church. He graduated at Yale College in 1769, with the highest honors of his class. He was a remarkable man in his day, and exerted among his own denomination, especially, a very important influence. He originated the "Connecticut Evangelical Magazine," and in the organization of the "Connecticut Missionary Society" had a primary agency. He died in 1816, in the sixty-ninth year of his age.

Sunday, 9th. Was waited on by Mr. Champion,[1] the Congregationalist minister, whom I found to be a worthy, friendly man, and a good preacher. He invited me to preach, which I did in the afternoon, to a large audience, with great freedom and to good acceptance. The people solemn and attentive. After meeting called on Lawyer Reeve, who lives here. Dined with Mr. Champion; lodged with Dr. Smith; an agreeable, genteel family. *Monday, 10th.* Set off at 8 o'clock, accompanied three and one half miles by Mr. Champion, whose company was very agreeable. He insisted if we ever came that way again we should make his house our home, as did Dr. Smith and Mr. Reeve. The road good this distance, but soon becomes exceeding rough, especially Mount Tom, a tremendous precipice near a mile long; at six or seven miles after this better to Rawmagin Iron Works, in Washington, eleven miles from Litchfield; Landlord Morgan's. After dinner set out to Bull's Iron Works, in Kent, ten miles, stopping to oat at Tirril's tavern, half way. Here we crossed successive chains of the most tremendous mountains I ever attempted to travel over, and which it was just possible to ascend. The whole distance over there is but a barren country, and the season very backward, until we come to the Works, where the soil and climate seem very different, as the season is much earlier. Refreshed at Landlord Beach's, a pretty good house; set off and arrived at Col. Morehouse's, four miles, in the evening. Had good entertainment and bed. The last stage a fine country, well improved, good buildings, and a good road. Passed Mr. Waldo's meeting-house, one half mile. This part of the country greatly divided in politics; the Tories have done great damage by robbing, etc., in this neighborhood. The York line one half mile this side of Bull's Iron Works. Through the mountains observed the grasshoppers as in summer. The country here full of good wheat fields, and also their first great preparations for a summer crop. *Tuesday, May* 11. Came to Mr. Waldo's, two miles; out of the road one half mile. Being both unwell and greatly fatigued, and our horse also, by yesterday's journey, concluded to tarry all day and night. This is in Dutchess County, Pawling's Precinct. Between this and Bull's Works passed a considerable river, along the banks of which fine and pleasant. Had good lodgings. Mr. Waldo has a good tract of land, two hundred acres, patent land, the lease for three

[1] Rev. Judah Champion. He graduated at Yale College in 1751; was ordained pastor of the church in Litchfield, July 4th, 1753; died in 1810. He preached the Connecticut Election Sermon in 1766, which was published.

lives. At night preached at his house, from 2d Cor. iv. 17. The state of religion remarkably cold, and the congregation much divided in politics. *Wednesday, 12th.* Set out, after being very hospitably entertained, and crossed a tedious and long mountain, two miles, before we fully got up; the descent easy and the road fine to the westward; the country full of good wheat fields. To Capt. Storm's, thirteen miles. Here a genteel tavern and good entertainment. The militia assembled to send every twelfth man to the frontiers against the Indians. Travelled five miles to Capt. Griffin's; fed my horse, and then five miles to Fishkill, and fed again. This but a small village, the buildings poor, and much injured by the troops. The whole of the road from Capt. Storm's remarkably fine, and the country good and well cultivated, especially with wheat. From hence to the Continental Ferry the road and country not equally good as before. No horse-keeping at the Ferry. No wind, and the tide unfavorable. Two hands rowed over, and were rowing until quite dark; rained steadily: this had been threatened all day by small sprinklings. Had a pleasant day for travelling; but now we are landed, in a dark rainy night, on a strange shore, and no tavern that had horse-keeping. With much difficulty found Col. Hansbrook's, but the kitchen people were in bed; were taken in, had good entertainment, horse-keeping, and a good bed. *Thursday, 13th.* Rose, but a storm from the northeast and a heavy rain determined us to tarry all day. The family very agreeable — high Whigs, and wealthy. *Friday, 14th.* Cleared away in the morning; set out at eight o'clock, and passed through New Windsor, a small village, under a disagreeable hill. The road bad here, as it is seven miles, to Mr. Cross's. Stopped and rested, but he not at home. From thence to Mr. Owen's, who married Lizzy Burden, six miles. There dined. From thence travelled seven miles, and at the tavern gave six shillings lawful money for two quarts of oats. From thence reached Mr. Gano's,[1] five miles, a little before night. He lives in a small log house, on a good farm, belonging to a refugee Tory, but much out of repair. Large quantities of wheat and rye on the ground along this road, which look tolerably well, but all the fruit killed by the frost in April. The cherry trees are again coming out in blossoms,

[1] Rev. John Gano, his brother-in-law, pastor of the First Baptist Church in New York, but now engaged as chaplain in the army. His family resided here probably until the close of the war. In the summer of 1776 the British took possession of New York and its environs, which they evacuated Nov. 25, 1783. During this time most of the loyal or Whig families were of course away from the city.

though not full. Think there will be no fruit for twenty miles east of the river. Tarried Saturday, 15th.

Sunday, 16th. Preached twice for Mr. Randall's people. A handsome congregation out, and very attentive. *Monday, 17th.* Visited Esquire Burt, a good liver, and genteel people. *Tuesday, 18th.* Assisted the boys in planting and dunging their farm; the afternoon and evening was sick; took a sweat, and was better. *Wednesday, 19th.* Nothing but a northeast storm prevents our setting out for the Jerseys. Mr. Gano had gone to the army before we arrived here, which is marching to the northward. This is a very hilly country, and much good meadow land. Warwick lies within about five miles of the Jersey line. The mountains to the southeast are infested with Tory robbers, who greatly terrify the inhabitants; thirty of them, or thereabouts, and their harborers, have been lately apprehended, and many more have fled, it is supposed to New York. A species of grasshoppers were discovered in the wheatfields, by men of undoubted veracity. From Wednesday to Saturday rain continued from the northeast. Tarried till Sunday, 23d.

Preached again at Warwick; the audience crowded, and much affected. Had great liberty in preaching. After meeting set out and dined at Col. Hathhorn's, one mile on. Proceeded fifteen miles over the mountains to Col. Soward's and lodged. Met kind people, and good livers. The house here fortified against robbers, and all sleep armed. I rested scarce any all night, through the importunity of a troublesome insect. *Monday, 24th.* Set off before sunrise, and reached Davenport's at Newfoundland to breakfast, ten miles; was kindly treated. They refused anything for our eating, as they did at Col. Soward's. From thence, ten miles, we reached Esq. Tuttle's. Fed our horses, refreshed ourselves, and set out for Morristown, twelve miles, where we arrived, between four and five o'clock, at Arnold's tavern. This is an extremely hot day, and the travelling excessively tedious, as well on that as on account of the rocky mountainous country, which extends from Warwick within about three miles of Morristown. The greatest part of this country unsettled, and consequently in general, till within about ten miles of Morristown, all this part of the country full of grain. Set out about sundown, and reached Mr. Stites',[1] about 11 o'clock, very much fatigued. Found the old people somewhat indisposed, but all very glad to see us. From 25th to 27th,

[1] John Stites, Esq., father of Mrs. Manning.

tarried at the farm; then went to Elizabethtown[1] and tarried till the 28th, at Brother Woodruff's. The town and suburbs less damaged by the enemy than I expected.[2]

Sunday, 30th. Preached at the Plains,[3] but the meeting much interrupted by the march of the Pennsylvania line, under General St. Clair, towards the North River.[4] Went to Sister Tingley's, and tarried till Tuesday. *Tuesday, June 1st.* A fine rain on Monday; went to Brother Joseph Manning's,[5] and tarried all night. Wednesday, accompanied by him and wife, visited Uncle Joseph Randolph, and reached Jeremiah Manning's at Bordentown. Tarried till Friday, June 4. There heard the cheering account of the Charleston victory,[6] and the moving of the whole army to North River. Afternoon crossed Crown Ferry, and lodged at Capt. Morgan's, Chester Quakers; ten miles. *Saturday, 5th.* Set out early, and reached Mr. Buckalaw's, two miles, to breakfast. Met with Messrs. Stelle[7] and Coles,[7] and proceeded to Bray's meeting-house. Mr. Stelle preached. Lodged at the widow Holmes's; an agreeable family.

Sunday, 6th. Mr. Stelle and myself preached. Had a large audience. *Monday, 7th.* Messrs. Coles and D. Jones[8] preached, and also had a large

1 Dr. Manning's native town, the capital of New Jersey at this time, and the principal place in the State; noted for its good schools, and the general culture and intelligence of its inhabitants.

2 On the 28th of February, 1779, a party of British troops, sent by Clinton from New York, landed at Elizabethtown Point, for the express purpose of taking "the rebel governor," as they called him, Livingston, whose residence was here at Elizabethtown. Not finding him at home, they seized his papers, burned a few dwellings, and departed for New York.

3 The Scotch Plains Baptist Church, of which Manning had been a member.

4 A large portion of Washington's army had been encamped, or hutted, as Hildreth terms it, at Middlebrook and vicinity, near Elizabethtown, during the previous winter and spring. The encampment broke up at this time; hence the disturbance of public worship caused by the marching of the troops northward, of which the Pennsylvania line under St. Clair formed a part.

5 Joseph Manning was a ruling elder of the Scotch Plains Church, having been elected to this office on the 10th December, 1777.

6 Referring to the invasion of Charleston by the British under Prevost, in May previous, and their repulse by the Continental troops and militia under Moultrie and Rutlege.

7 Rev. Isaac Stelle, pastor of the Piscataway Baptist Church, and Rev. Benjamin Coles, pastor of the church at Hopewell.

8 The Rev. David Jones, formerly of New Jersey, but now a distinguished chaplain in the army under Gen. St. Clair.

audience. Lodged this night at the widow Molly Holmes's; a fine family. This is a most excellent part of the country for land and excellent crops; but the shores are greatly infested, and the inhabitants robbed, by Tories, who have fled to the enemy. *Tuesday, June* 8. In company with Messrs. Stelle and Jones came to Mr. Dennis's at Spotswood, to dinner, thirteen miles; agreeable people. Nine miles to Brunswick, where at Capt. Dennis's we tarried Tuesday night. *Wednesday, 9th.* Crossed the river at the landing, and came to Uncle Ephraim's and tarried. Brunswick much injured by the British. *Thurdsay, 10th.* Visited Mr. Stelle, Aunt Manning, and tarried at Uncle Joseph Randolph's. *Friday, 11th.* Returned to the Farms; found parents ill. *Saturday, 12th.* Preached at the Plains, and returned.

Sunday, 13th. Preached again, gave out the communion service, and tarried at Rev. Mr. Miller's. A fine rain this day, though the meetings not interrupted. 14th. Returned to the Farms. A great rain, followed by a succession of thunder-showers, to-day. Sister Tingley and Joseph Manning's wife came and tarried the night. Went to town, and brought Sister Woodruff, upon the 15th. The season remarkably good, and the grain extraordinary, as well as grass, through the country. *Wednesday, June* 16. Fine weather. Rain in the afternoon. 17th, 18th, and 19th, tarried at Papa Stites's.

Preached at Lyon's Farms, the 20th, two sermons. The people in the morning service very attentive and affected, and the meeting tolerably full. Returned, and on Monday, the 21st, set out for Philadelphia. Visited Messrs. Miller and Joseph Manning, and dined. Preached, at 6 o'clock, with great freedom, at Capt. Samuel Randolph's, and tarried all night. Set out the 22d and visited Capt. William Manning, Jacob Martin Esq., Major Edgar, and Benjamin Manning Esq., who, with his lady, accompanied us to Brother Jeremiah Manning's, where we tarried. 23d. Accompanied with brother and wife, kinsman and his, went to Mr. Stelle's; thence to Brunswick. Heard Mr. Miller preach from the words of Hannah. Dined at Mr. Wall's. Called at Mr. Dennis's, and set out at four o'clock for Hopewell; reached Mr. Barton's at nine o'clock in the evening. The day hot. Next day, 24th, visited Dr. Vankirk's, to see aunt, and preached at the meeting-house at six o'clock. But few out. Next morning, Friday, 25th, visited Messrs. Coles and Blackwell, and reached John Hart's,[1] Esq.,

[1] Perhaps a son of the Rev. Oliver Hart. If so, he graduated under Manning, in the year 1776. The "discipline of the rod" seems to have been at-

at Newtown, two o'clock P. M.; were detained the night by a seasonable heavy rain, and treated most hospitably. The weather most intensely hot. English grain the best and in the greatest quantity from Brunswick here that I ever saw; but the Indian corn backward and poor in general, owing to the cold and wet of the former part of the season. 26th. Set out to Neshaminy Ford, but impassable by the great fall of rain. Went four miles up the creek to the bridge, which, being taken up, we were detained till four o'clock P. M. at Mr. Cozens's, when the water subsided, and we passed. The road from Newtown here very bad, but the creek to Southampton good, where we reached, before sunset, Mr. Van Horn's.[1] Found the family well.

Stayed the 27th, and preached at the meeting-house. But few people out. Mr. Coles was expected. After meeting returned, and tarried till Monday. On June 4th a report prevailed in Woodbridge that the British army at Charleston were totally defeated, with the loss of fourteen hundred killed and wounded, and seven hundred taken. Repeated reports somewhat similiar, though not making their loss so great, have been constantly brought from the South; but no official account confirming it has yet come to hand.[2] All the fruit nearly cut off by the great frost in these parts. The crops incomparably fine, but some fields near the river struck with the red rust, though but little hurt. Rye harvest begun, and wheat will be here this week.

tended with good effects, if we may judge from the little information respecting him here given.

[1] Rev. William Van Horn. He was born in 1746; educated at Dr. Samuels Jones's Academy at Pennepek; ordained as pastor over the Baptist church at Southampton, Pa.; honored with the degree of Master of Arts from the Rhode Island College 1774; and during the Revolutionary war was an efficient and honored chaplain. He died in 1807 in the sixty-first year of his age.

[2] Reports then must have quite equalled if not excelled the telegraphic news of the present day. The simple facts as recorded in history are as follows: The British in 1779 made a second invasion of South Carolina under General Prevost, and were eventually repulsed. On the 11th of May, Prevost with nine hundred regulars crossed the Ashley, leaving his main army on the south side of the river. During the forenoon Count Pulaski with his legion attacked the British advanced guard, and was repulsed with great slaughter. Prevost now advanced to the American lines, but in the night, after summoning the city to surrender, withdrew to James Island, fearing the approach of Gen. Lincoln with an army of four thousand men. On the 20th of June the British were attacked by about twelve hundred of Lincoln's men, and the assailants were repulsed. Loss about

Monday, June 28. Set out and travelled to Pennepek, Mr. Jones's.[1] Arrived in the evening, and found the family well and glad to see us. Tarried here until July 2d. Spent the time agreeably in viewing the farm, its products, harvest, etc., and in conversation. The season here extremely hot; height of wheat harvest; the grain struck with the red rust, though little injured, except the rye, which is much blasted. The greatest part of the harvest between here and Philadelphia, where we arrived at eleven o'clock A. M., July 2. Put up at Mr. William Goforth's, and my horse across the way, in Second Street, between Race and Vine Streets. Visited Samuel Davis, but he was out of town; also Mr. Rogers. Called at Mr. Watkins's, then at Mr. Westcot's; from thence to Dr. Rush's,[2] who treated me politely; from thence called on Messrs. Shields

three hundred killed, wounded, and missing on each side. Three days afterwards the British evacuated the island. (See Lossing's Field-Book, etc.)

[1] Rev. Dr. Samuel Jones, one of Manning's intimate friends. He was three years his senior, having been born in the year 1735. Of the church of Pennepek, afterwards called Lower Dublin, he was the honored and esteemed pastor upwards of fifty-one years. He was also an educator of youth, and in this latter capacity was greatly distinguished, being especially judicious and considerate to such young men under his care as had the ministry in view. On the death of Manning, in 1791, he was named by many of the Trustees and Fellows of the college as his successor in the presidency. (See letters of Stillman and Howell at the close of our last chapter.) He, it will be remembered, was one of the committee to remodel the college charter.

Dr. Jones was one of the most useful members of the Philadelphia Association. "Here," says Sprague in his Annals, "he is appointed to frame a system of discipline, and there to compile a book of hymns, and then to draw up a map representing the various associations; one year he holds the office of moderator, and the next writes the circular letter to the churches, and the next performs some other important public service; — indeed, it is impossible to look through the minutes without perceiving that he was always one of the master spirits of the body. Few men could manage more adroitly than he a difficult and involved case; and sometimes, by a single suggestion, in a deliberative body, he would bring light out of the thickest darkness, and order out of the wildest confusion." In 1807 he preached the century sermon of the Association, which was published. He died Feb. 7, 1814, in the eightieth year of his age.

Dr. Jones was a ready writer and a fluent speaker. In his person he is described as a large and firmly built man, six feet or more in height, and every way well proportioned. His face was the very image of intelligence and good-nature; which, with the air of dignity that pervaded all his movements, rendered his appearance uncommonly attractive. He possessed an ample fortune, which he used with signal grace and hospitality.

[2] Benjamin Rush, one of the signers of the Declaration of Independence; dis-

and Moulders. Called at Mr. Hart's lodging, but he not within, which was also the case at Mr. Robert S. Jones's. The evening of July 2, Mr. Joseph Hart, of the Executive Council, spent at my lodgings. *Saturday, July* 3. This morning came out a paper, in which Congress was handled pretty severely, under the signature of Leonidas.[1] Breakfasted at Dr. Rush's, and received two hundred dollars, Dr. Finley's draft on him. Spent the forenoon chiefly in writing to Providence, by Mr. Ellery, who sets off this afternoon. Went to the State House. Met Mr. Collins, and

tinguished for his learning and piety, as well as for his great professional skill. He was educated at the College of New Jersey, graduating in 1760, two years before Manning.

[1] The financial embarrassments of the country were exceedingly great at this period, in consequence of the rapid depreciation of the paper currency, of which Congress had emitted, on the 1st of September, 1799, one hundred and sixty millions. A spirit of discontent, of speculation and of fraud was everywhere manifest. "The honest and patriotic were impoverished, while rogues and Tories grew rich." As an illustration of the perils and difficulties of this crisis, we print the following handbill, which was posted up in the streets of Philadelphia about this time. Similar bills were posted in other cities.

"FOR OUR COUNTRY'S GOOD.

"The depreciation of our money, and the high price to which everything is got, is one and the same thing. We ask not who introduced the evil, how it arose, or who encouraged it. In the midst of money we are in poverty, and exposed to want in the land of plenty. You that have money, and you that have none, down with your prices, or down with yourselves; for, by the ever-living and eternal God, we will bring every article down to what it was last Christmas, or we will down with those who oppose it.

"We have turned out against the enemy, and we wish not to be eaten up by monopolizers and forestallers.

MOVE ON COOLLY."

"It gives me very sincere pleasure," writes Washington to his friend Reed, now President of Pennsylvania, "that the Assembly is so well disposed to second your endeavors in bringing those murderers of our cause, the monopolizers, forestallers, and engrossers, to condign punishment. It is much to be lamented that each State, long ere this, has not hunted them down as pests of society, and the greatest enemies we have to the happiness of America. I would to God that some one of the more atrocious in each State was hung in gibbets upon a gallows five times as high as the one prepared for Haman. No punishment, in my opinion, is too severe for the man who can build his greatness upon his country's ruin." When Washington wrote in this way, what, says Hildreth, was to be expected of the inconsiderate multitude?

inquired, without much satisfaction, what was on foot in Congress relative to the money. Dined at Mr. Redwood's with Mr. Ellery, and returned to my lodgings, where were Messrs. Shields and Conolly, who spent the afternoon with us.

Lord's Day, July 4. Preached twice with some freedom; the morning congregation thin; more in the afternoon. Both church and society here in a broken state. The people urgent for my tarrying a considerable time, which did not suit my affairs. In the evening visited one of the members of the church near her end. Appeared to be in a happy frame of mind. Attended a religious society composed of Baptists, Presbyterians, and Church people. They appeared very serious, and somewhat engaged in religion. Found Gen. Spencer[1] at my lodgings, now a member of Congress. It being the Fourth of July, the anniversary of Independence, the chaplains of Congress preached suitable to the occasion, and Congress attended. High mass was celebrated and Te Deum sung at the Romish chapel. The gentlemen of the town were invited by billets from the French minister to attend. I suppose these causes rendered the Baptist meeting thinner than otherwise. The lowering of prices by the committee is considered by the town as a violent measure and only a temporary relief, but think it will share the fate of former State bills.[2] The suburbs of this city greatly destroyed by the English, but the body of it not much damaged. A fine rain on the night of the 4th of July. Some more apples in these parts than in the Jerseys, though but few. *Monday, 5th.* Break-

[1] Joseph Spencer. He was born in Connecticut, in 1714. He was a major in the colonial army in 1756, and was one of the first eight brigadiers appointed by the Continental Congress in 1775. He was appointed a major-general in 1776, and in 1777 was in command of the American forces on Rhode Island. After his resignation he was elected a delegate to Congress from his native State. He died in East Haddam, in January, 1789, aged seventy-five.

[2] A short time after this (Oct. 4), a riot took place in Philadelphia in consequence of this attempt of a committee to regulate the prices of flour, rum, sugar, molasses, coffee, salt, etc. Robert Morris and other leading merchants refused to conform to the regulation. Wilson, Clymer, Mifflin, and their friends were threatened with banishment to New York, as abettors and defenders of the Tories. Soon afterwards (Oct. 20), a convention of the five Eastern States was held at Hartford, at which a plan was elaborated, which Congress adopted, regulating prices on the basis of twenty paper dollars for one of specie. Dr. Manning's visit to Philadelphia doubtless had reference to some measures of relief of this kind from the oppressive laws of Rhode Island and other States, passed by recommendation of Congress, which made paper money a legal tender.

fasted at Mr. Shields's, where a committee from the church met and importuned me to tarry with them some time, or come again and make them a longer visit. I gave them hopes of the latter after the four Sabbaths of this month. Went to Mr. David Bowers', and thence to Mr. Moulders'; then to hear the oration at the Dutch church. The performance indifferent. Congress and the French Ambassador present, and a large assembly. Here met Mr. Merchant, and called at his lodgings. Received an invitation to dine at Prof. Lawrens's, but we dined at Mr. Westcot's. Returned to our lodgings. Were visited by Messrs. Shields, Britain, and Gen. Spencer. Set out in the afternoon for Mr. Jones's, where we arrived in the evening. The weather intensely hot. *Tuesday, 6th.* Tarried at Mr. Jones's, and set out on the 7th for Bordentown. Dined at Bristol, and reached Mr. Alison's before night. Passed the ruins of Mr. Kirbright's buildings; the river three fourths of a mile wide; the ruins of the vessels burned by the English on the east shore, as also the stores, and the dwelling-house of Mr. Joseph Borden, treasurer.[1] There met Mr. Stites, from Cranberry, which detained us until Saturday, July 10. Were hospitably treated by the family, Col. Hogland, Dr. Moore, Mr. Borden, and Mr. Kirbright. Preached on Friday evening, and set out in the morning for Cranberry, in company with Col. Hogland and Mr. Stites. Reached Cranberry to dine. Found the Doctor well, and glad to see us.

Preached for Mr. Smith Sunday the 11th. The day rainy and few people out. At night had a severe diarrhœa, which continued the 12th, so that I kept house in much pain. 13th. The diarrhœa abated; the weather fine and cool, as there fell a vast quantity of rain on Lord's Day and evening, accompanied by abundance of thunder and lightning. This morning Mr. Stelle called on us on his way to Philadelphia, and informed us that accounts are received of the burning of New Haven by the British, and that they are destroying all in their way in that quarter.[2] Preached to-day at the Baptist meeting. Tarried the 14th and 15th. Still much

[1] On the 7th of May, 1778, six or seven hundred British troops left Philadelphia for the purpose of destroying vessels which were lying in Barnes's and Crosswick's Creeks at Bordentown. They burned two frigates, destroyed several smaller vessels, burned several residences and buildings on their return, and seized considerable property.

[2] Referring to the invasion of Connecticut by the British, under Governor Tyron of New York, and Brigadier-General Garth, in the early part of July, 1779, during which they plundered New Haven, and burned Fairfield and Norwalk.

indisposed. 16th. Set out for Piscataway, called at Brunswick, and reached Bonham Town. Mrs. Manning very ill since the 12th; scarce able to ride. My brother in great fear of the enemy. Was interrupted till midnight by the seizure of a trunk of goods. 17th. Went to Mr. Benjamin Manning's. Left my spouse, and preached at the Sabbatarian meeting; returning to our lodgings at Benjamin Manning's, Esq.

Sunday, July 18. Preached for Mr. Stelle twice, dined at lodgings, and came on to Brother Joseph's. 19th. Returned to the Farms. To-day heard that the British fleet at Stony Point was taken by General Wayne, with five hundred prisoners.[1] Found our parents as well as usual, and tarried there, Mrs. Manning being very unwell, 20th, 21st, and 22d. Set out Saturday, July 23, for Hopewell. Left my mare with Swan's horse. Called on Mr. Miller, who was in ill health. Stopped at Capt. Randolph's, dined at Benjamin Manning's; called at Mr. Stelle's, but he was not at home; met him at Mr. Hall's in Brunswick. Reached Mr. Prince's, at Rocky Hill. The day very hot and dusty, and my horse travelled hard and greatly fatigued. Distance thirty-two miles. *Saturday, 24th.* Was unable to find my horse until late in the morning. Reached Mr. Barton's at Hopewell, ten miles, much fatigued. The meeting opened by a sermon from Mr. Pitman, to good acceptance. Peter Smith also attended.

Lord's Day, 25th. Preached twice, and gave out the communion to a part of the church, as they are unhappily divided about their minister, Mr. Coles. The day exceedingly rainy, but the house full. *Monday, 26th.* Mr. Joshua Jones came and preached in the morning; a good sermon. I closed the meeting in the afternoon. *Tuesday, 27th.* In company with Mr. Smith reached Samuel Jones's, thirty miles; caught in a thunder-shower and got very wet; dined at John Hart's, Esq., at New Town. Tarried Wednesday, 28th, and set out, after a rainy morning, Thursday, 29th, for Philadelphia, twelve miles. Put up my horse at Mr. Shields's; called on some friends, and took quarters at Mr. Samuel Davis's. *Friday, July* 30. Visited some friends in town. *Saturday, 31st.* Saw the British pris-

[1] This, says Lossing, in his Field-Book of the Revolution, was regarded as the most brilliant achievement of the war, and raised the hero Wayne to the highest point in the admiration of his countrymen. The fortress, which was regarded as impregnable, was taken on the night of July 16. Conversing with Washington on the expedition and the obstacles to be overcome, Wayne is said to have remarked with emphasis, "General, I'll storm hell, if *you* will only plan it."

oners taken at Stony Point march in; fine-looking men. Dined at Mr. Goforth's.

Sunday, Aug. 1. Preached twice. The congregation pretty large, — more so than usual here, — and very attentive. Spent the evening at a religious conference, where there seemed a degree of quickening and freedom. *Aug.* 2. A storm of rain from the northeast, which continued the next day; heat intense. I tarried mostly at my lodgings. *Aug.* 4. Wrote letters to Providence, to the church and Nicholas Brown. *Aug.* 5. The account of the defeat of the British by the French fleet in the West Indies arrived. Spent the evening at Major Goforth's, in company with several gentlemen. Here I met Major Somner, ten days from Providence, who tells me that things are agreeable in that quarter, which I was also informed of by a letter from General Varnum, received yesterday. G Brigade is come to headquarters, which I heard by a line from Van Horn, at the same time. *Friday,* 6*th.* Delivered my letters to Mr. Somner. This day Mr. Edwards called upon me, and tarried in town several days. Saw General Spencer and Mr. Collins. Abundance of rumors concerning the West India affair. Visited in town in the forenoon. *Saturday,* 7*th.* Went with Mr. Edwards to Capt. Falkner's, five miles, and spent the afternoon agreeably.

Sunday, Aug. 8. Preached three times. The assembly full, and the people so importunate for another Sabbath that I concluded to stay. 9th. Messrs. Jones, Blackwell, and Nathaniel Stout came to town; the former tarried with me one night. *Tuesday,* 10*th.* Mr. Edwards, in company with Jones and myself, set out for Col. Miles's. Distance thirteen miles. Arrived in the evening, and he and lady next morning, from town. He has a most elegant seat, gardens, meadows, etc., and a most remarkable spring, which turns three wheels in one fourth of a mile from its source. Spent three days very agreeably, and on the 13th set out for town, Mr. Edwards returning with Mr. Jones. The weather extremely hot, and abundance of rain. The Indian corn incomparably fine, the buckwheat forward, and the second crop of grass cutting. This is an agreeable part of the country. Preached this evening, Saturday, 14th. Visited Major Goforth's; paid my barber; received one hundred dollars of Mr. Rogers, as per order; called at Mr. Morris's, and dined at Mr. Ball's.

Sunday, Aug. 15. Extremely hot. Preached twice, attended the funeral of a child, and drank chocolate at Mr. Turner's. Richard Lemon and both the McKims, from Baltimore, at meeting. *Monday,* 16*th.* Visited Mr. Moulders', and attended the meeting of the church and society, who unanimously agreed to get the pulpit supplied. Chose a committee of eight, half from the church and half from the society, to raise the necessary supplies for that purpose, and to call Mr. Gano for one year. At two o'clock set out for Mr. Jones's. Preached at Pennepek at five o'clock. Tarried with Mr. Jones and Mr. Edwards. The weather intensely hot; though the season uncommonly wet. *Tuesday, Aug.* 17. Set out for Bordentown, where I dined. Reached Cranberry, Dr. Stites's, at night, 18th. Reached Brunswick, and dined at Robert Huder's, where I met with Mrs. Gano and John. Reached Mr. Stites's in the evening, and found all well. The Indian corn incomparably fine through the whole country. *Thursday*, 19*th*. Went to Elizabethtown, and returned in the evening. Dined at Dr. Dayton's. Spent the 20th and 21st at the Farms. The weather rainy.

Sunday, 22*d*. Preached at the Plains with Mr. Stelle, who preached at six o'clock at Morristown. Tarried at Brother Joseph's. A terrible rain at night. My brother very sick with the bilious fever. Jeremiah and son and daughter tarried there also. *Monday*, 23*d*. Visited Uncle Joseph Randolph; in a deep consumption, to all appearance, but comfortable in mind. From thence, through Samptown, I visited Sister Tingley, who has broken her right arm by a fall, and dislocated her wrist. Dined and went to Dead River to Brother Jno. Manning's and tarried the night. His eldest daughter sick. His farm is much improved since I saw it, and he lives comfortably. Visited Uncle William Stites, Mr. Tingley, Cousin Jno. Manning, Mr. Miller, Mr. Brooks, and returned to the Farms on Tuesday evening, 24th. Wednesday went to Elizabethtown, visited friends, and tarried two days, returning to the Farms Thursday evening. Admiral Arbuthnot's fleet said to have arrived at New York, but the particulars not come to hand. *Friday*, 27*th*. Tarried at home. The season very sickly, but not mortal yet. Yesterday the weather cleared up cool and fine. Continued at home Saturday.

Lord's Day, Aug. 29. Peached at Lyon's Farms. The audience serious and attentive. Tarried at home till Thursday, the 2d of September, and then, accompanied by parents, visited Stites, Woodruff, dined, and then proceeded to Bonham Town, calling on two of the sisters on the way, and observing the desolations at Woodbridge. *Sept.* 3. Rainy, but in the afternoon went to Joseph Manning's; a heavy rain on the way; found him and two children sick. *Sept.* 4. Went to Joseph Tingley's; found my sister better; preached at the meeting-house, Lord's Day. Saw many old friends and acquaintances, and all my brothers but Joseph. After bidding the last farewell, returned to the Farms in the evening, calling on Mr. Miller on the way, who is much recovered. Tarried at home Monday, 6th, and were visited by Sister Woodruff. The season remarkably sickly throughout the country, but the mortality not very great. The complaints are intermitting fevers and agues. *Tuesday, 7th.* Tarried at home and rested; in the afternoon preached. Mr. Miller came, and we had something of a comfortable season.

Wednesday, Sept. 8. Set out for Providence. Were accompanied by parents four miles. Left Sister Woodruff at papa's; called and rested at Dr. Smith's at Chatham, seven miles. Dined at Col. Dunham's in Morristown, seven miles. Were kindly treated. The family sick, and himself indisposed. Set out at four o'clock and reached Rockaway, nine miles. Tarried at Jackson's, at the Forge. A thunder-shower in the night, and bedbugs, prevented sleep; otherwise good entertainment. Paid six dollars. The road much better this way than over the mountains. Set out on the morning of the 9th, to Esquire Moses Tuttle's, five miles. The road bad. Breakfasted and reached Davenport's to dinner; the road extremely bad; distance ten miles. Afternoon visited Col. Soward's, ten miles. The road bad; tarried the night, and were kindly entertained. 10th. Travelled to Col. Hath Horn's, fourteen miles, and dined; afternoon reached Mr. Gano's, three and one half miles. The road better over the mountains, though the mountains exceedingly bad. *Saturday, 11th.* Tarried at Mr. Gano's.

Lord's Day, preached at Warwick twice. The assembly full and very solemn. After meeting dined at Mr. Beard's, who had prepared an elegant dinner, and were treated very hospitably. Tarried at Mr. Gano's Monday. Took a very great cold. Mrs. Manning but indifferently well, and Sally and Dicky sick. *Tuesday, Sept.* 14. Set out, dined at Mr. Owen's, and reached Mr. Fought's in the evening. Met Lieut. Hubbel on the road, who came out from Newburgh for this purpose. Met also Capt. Wily from Providence, who informs me they are well in general. We were received and treated very kindly at Mr. Fought's, where we lodged; and Wednesday, 15th, I visited Isaac Belnap, and was visited by Mr. Edmonds. Preached in the afternoon at the Continental store. The people attentive and affected, and very desirous of another sermon. Visited Dea. Lawrence at the Landing, and returned in the evening to our lodgings. Ever since Sunday the wind fresh at the northeast, cloudy and very cold; at its first rising a boat was upset in this ferry Sunday morning, and two young ladies were drowned.

Thursday, Sept. 16. Went down to West Point by water in Lieut. Hubbel's boat. The French Ambassador's secretaries in company. One of them spoke English ; a most accomplished gentleman, and the handsomest Frenchman I ever saw. The other was agreeable, as were their attendant gentleman, but could not converse much in English. We had an agreeable passage, and were greatly entertained by the highlands through which we passed. Those huge, vast mountains, with their cloudy tops, approach near together as the river narrows. At about eleven o'clock we reached Gen. Washington's quarters, — a beautiful, level spot one mile north of the Point, surrounded by those precipices. His Excellency, the Ambassador, with a number of the generals, were gone to reconnoitre the fort. There I met Dr. Cochrane, Surgeon General of the army, who seemed very glad to find me in camp. After examining a correct map of this fort, shown us by one of the General's aids, and taking a drink, we sailed over to the Point, which is fitted by nature to form an exceeding strong port. Up to the top of the Point is a great ascent, and there a plain on which stands Fort Arnold, at the last part of the Point. A very strong fortress, with excellent bomb-proofs, and bastions below to defend the great chain stretched across just after the river turns west. The opposite shore is also strongly fortified to defend the chain, from what is called the island, and all the heights also on the east side of the river, to prevent their landing and bombarding the fort. These works, viewed from the Point, look most beautiful. These were shown us by Gen. McDugal, who commands this fortress. Fort Putnam stands on a great eminence at half a mile distance west from this, and commands Fort Arnold. This is the strongest work ever raised in English America, and is utterly, from its situation, inaccessible but on the northern side, where all the force of art is exerted to strengthen it by walls without walls, the outermost of which is laid with lime and stone, with bomb-proofs, etc., etc. This is also defended by all the commanding heights. The approach of an army by land is next to impossible from the west side of the river, as there are but few ways, and those almost impassable, and all strongly defended. The troops were encamped on both sides of the river on the most convenient grounds. I dined at Gen. Greene's quarters with his family, Mr. Olney, Col. Morris, Major Littlefield, and Col. Webb, as the General had not returned. Soon after, he, with Gen. Knox, returned, with whom had a little chat. Shortly afterward, his Excellency, the French Ambassador, and Baron Steuben, with their retinues, returned, to all of whom I was introduced by Gen. Greene. The Ambassador is a good-looking, ruddy-complexioned man as I ever saw for a Frenchman. His family are extremely polite.[1]

Having viewed the works, we returned up the river, had a good time, and arrived at New Windsor after sunset, and at Newborough in the evening. *Friday, Sept.* 17. The morning was foggy, which prevented our setting out early. Crossed the river with an easy time, and set out from the Continental Ferry between ten and eleven o'clock. Passing Fishkill, took the Danbury road, stopped at a private house to oat, and then reached Col. Luddington's, twenty-two miles; then reached Esquire Patterson's, four miles, at Fredericksburg. The road good fifteen miles, and then exceeding bad, over rocks and mountains. *Saturday*, 18*th*. Set out at sunrise. The road good three miles, and then exceeding bad to Danbury, fourteen miles, where we arrived at eleven o'clock. Put up at Capt. Clarke's. Good entertainment. The ruins of the town are affecting, marked with the traces of British inhumanity.[2] This town was considerbly large, and prettily situated between the mountains, with a good soil. Apples are plenty here. Some few were to be seen at the river, and a gradual increase. The Indian corn excellent on this side of the river, and the pastures good. Very difficult to get good entertainment. At two o'clock set out through Bethel, to which is a good road three miles. Then we ascend the shocking mountains which reach to Reading, five miles, Bitt's Tavern. This is a pretty village on a hill. From thence we reached North Fairfield, five miles, to Esquire Wakeman's, a private house. Had good entertainment.

Sabbath morning, 19*th*. Reached Greenfield, Mr. Tennent's,[3] six miles.

[1] This invitation to visit West Point, as extended to Manning and his wife, through Lieut. Hubbel, and the attention shown them by the generals and officers in command, afford a pleasing illustration of Dr. Manning's high character and personal influence. He associated with the first men of his times, and on terms of equality. Few persons of his day could be called his superiors, save in the externals of worldly prosperity.

[2] On the 26th of April, 1777, about two thousand British troops, commanded by Gov. William Tyron, reached the village of Danbury between one and two o'clock in the afternoon, for the purpose of destroying the military stores in that town. They left the next morning, after committing various excesses, burning the new meeting-house, nineteen dwellings, twenty-two stores and barns, and an immense amount of stores and provisions for the American army.

[3] Rev. William MacKay Tennent, a distinguished Presbyterian minister. He graduated at the College of New Jersey in 1763, one year after Dr. Manning. In 1772 he became pastor of the church in Greenfield, resigning in 1781 to take charge of a church near Philadelphia. He was one of the trustees of New Jer-

Were most kindly received. I preached twice. A large congregation, and attentive. Drank tea at Dr. Rogers's, Mr. Tennent's sister, an agreeable people, who spent the evening with us at our lodgings. The road stony, but not so bad here. The husbandry very good through all this rough country, in which are raised good crops of wheat. Great crops of flax are raised in these parts, though not so good this year. The husbandry in Greenfield is good, and the inhabitants very good livers. Mr. Tennent well settled. *Monday morning, Sept.* 20. Went to Fairfield, three miles, and viewed the ruins of that once beautiful place, which shocked me exceedingly. Very few buildings remain. Ninety-six houses, besides barns and stores, were burned. From thence reached Esquire Hubbel's at Stratford, three miles, to dinner. Visited Mr. Ross, who is sick with the fever and ague. There I saw Mr. Elliot, of Fairfield, who is also sick, as indeed are a great part of the people in this neighborhood. Peggy not at home. The family very kind; tarried here all night. She arrived in the evening; is kindly treated by the family, who are plain, good-living farmers. I took a walk to the southward of the road, and viewed a most beautiful, level country, suited to wheat, and the inhabitants very good livers; their buildings very good, and their crops excellent. Spent the evening at Esquire Brother's, a likely, agreeable man. *Tuesday, Sept.* 21. Set out at nine o'clock, through Stratford, five miles. The inhabitants here had moved out their effects, expecting a visit from the enemy. An agreeable town, situated on a river navigable twelve miles above the town. Crossing the ferry, reached Milford, five miles, and dined at the Rev. Mr. Sherman's. This town large and rich, but their buildings old and in bad order in general. Their husbandry through here good, and their crops excellent: plenty of apples. Visited the other minister of the town; was kindly treated, and invited to dine. Here met Mr. Elliot again, with the ague on him, on his way to Boston. Went in company with the ministers to the Freeman's meeting, to prox for deputies to nominate their council, etc., for the election next spring. Was importuned to open the meeting by prayer, which is their usage. Attended in order to observe their manner of proceeding. The clergy in this State vote for their

sey College from 1785 to 1808. He received the degree of Doctor in Divinity from Yale College in 1794; was moderator of the General Assembly of the Presbyterian Church in 1797. His wife was a daughter of the Rev. Dr. Rogers, of New York. Dr. Alexander speaks of him as having a very sweet temper, and distinguished for his hospitality.

officers, and often speak to direct in the choice of men. They have great influence on the people. When the meeting is opened by the constables, the people are requested to bring in their votes for their first deputy; which done, if one has not more than all the rest, it is declared that he is not chosen; and after declaring the numbers for the respective candidates, they are requested to bring in again, and so continue to do until he is elected. Twenty names at most are put in by each voter for general officers, out of which the twelve highest are chosen by the assembly for the spring choice. After gratifying my curiosity here, returned to Mr. Sherman's, dined, and set out for New Haven, ten miles, where we arrived in the evening. The road bad most of the way. Went to Mr. Sabin's, who was ill, and his wife from home. Was put to difficulty to find lodging and keeping for our horse, as the town had been sacked by the enemy, and the people had their effects out of town. Tarried at Mr. Lyman's. Indifferent quarters, but a high price. The town shows but few marks of outrage to travellers passing through, as the British did not burn here. *Wednesday, Sept.* 22. Set out at seven o'clock, having taken breakfast. Took the road to Durham, crossed the bridge, and the long causeway one half mile over the marsh. The first six or seven miles very sandy, then a good soil, and well improved to and through Paug, a pleasant village, nine miles. Mr. Williams, minister, invited me to his house, but we could only stop to oat. From hence to Durham, excellent land and husbandry, and the buildings uncommonly elegant. Durham a considerable town, situated on a hill; the buildings good; distance nine miles. Dined at Landlord Camp's. The people agreeable. After setting out was stopped by General Wadsworth, and invited to call, but time would not admit. Reached Middletown, seven miles, at five o'clock. Put up at Capt. Warner's. Was visited by Major Otis. Most kindly entertained; tarried Thursday, visited Mr. Otis, Mr. Hunting, and Capt. William Warner's lady. Tarried all night, and set out Friday, 24th, for Weathersfield. Crossed the Great Meadows, but the bridge having fallen down, were obliged to ferry over, with difficulty. The upper houses form a pretty village. It began to rain moderately, which lasted to Weathersfield. The town here is beautiful, and the inhabitants appear to live well, as the soil is exuberant. Vast quantities of onions are raised here for importation. Dined at the tavern, next south of the meeting-house, and then examined their fine structure; dimensions eighty-four by fifty feet, neatly finished with an elegant pulpit, and the most elegant steeple I have seen on the journey. Set out in the rain to Hartford, four miles. Called at Capt. Bull's, and found them well, and at Mr. Strong's and Dr. Smith's, but found them gone a journey. Passed the ferry, and reached the Widow Bidwel's, in East Hartford, where we lodged. Were kindly entertained. Set out Saturday, 25th, at seven o'clock. The road sandy from the river ten miles. Oated there ; found the road wet seven miles, to Kimball's, where we again oated. Dined at Mansfield, at Mr. Ephraim Rolins's, a Christian friend, seven miles. The road bad, and from hence, six miles, to Mr. Snow's tavern, in Westford, where we fed. Were hailed by Mr. Welch on our way, and invited to tarry and spend the Sabbath ; but we meant to reach Capt. Bowles's, which is six miles from Snow's, where we arrived in the evening, much fatigued. Mrs. Bowles brought forth a son this night.

Lord's Day, Sept. 26. In company with Capt. Bowles, went to Woodstock to Elder Ledoyt's meeting. Preached in the afternoon. The audience solemn and affected. The day being very rainy, tarried all night, and thereby disappointed a number who had assembled for meeting at Capt. Bowles's. Heard of Mr. Ledoyt a pleasing account of their journey into the northern parts last spring, and of the remarkable spread of the gospel and of the work of God in various parts. *Monday, Sept.* 27. Set out in company with the Elder. Found Mrs. Bowles better. At ten o'clock proceeded to Jeremiah Brown's, three miles, dined, and reached Mr. Thurber's before night, five miles. Were visited by several friends. Tarried the night, and on Tuesday to dine ; then reached Capt. Corlis's, six miles. The Indian corn but indifferent through these parts, but apples plenty. Throughout our whole journey the earth remarkably well clothed with grass. Visited Jno. Jones's family in the evening. *Wednesday, Sept.* 29. In the morning set out for Mr. John Brown's in Gloucester, twelve miles, where we dined. Reached Providence at six o'clock, the road better than usual ; being just five months to an hour absent from home, and having experienced the abundant goodness of God in the journey, in that we had never been molested by ill-disposed persons, nor maimed by the extremely bad roads and dangerous mountains over which we passed. May the Lord fill our hearts with true thankfulness for his abundant mercies through our whole life, and enable us to devote to his service lives which have been peculiarly his care !

CHAPTER VII.

1780–1783.

Meeting of the Corporation in 1780 — College instruction revived — Manning's perseverance — Second interruption — Meeting of the Corporation in 1782 — Resolution to apply to Congress for damages done to the College edifice during the war — First meeting of the Warren Association in Providence — Illustration of the efforts made by our fathers to educate and improve the "rising generation" — Letter to Hon. David Howell — Letter to Rev. Benjamin Wallin — Brief view of the Religious Condition of the Country — Public exercises of Commencement resumed — Manning's purpose to proceed to England to solicit funds for the College — His memorial to the Corporation on this subject — Second letter to Hon. David Howell, giving an account of Commencement and of the proceedings of the Corporation — Petition to the King of France for his patronage of the College — Sketch of Dr. Benjamin Waterhouse — Letter from Thomas Jefferson in regard to the aforesaid petition to the King — Extracts from a Digest of the College Laws by President Manning — Remarks of Tristam Burgess in regard to evening speaking on the chapel stage — Manning's ideas of college government and discipline — Letter to Henry Kane, of London — Letter to Rev. John Ryland — Influence of the College in favor of civil and religious liberty — Letter to Manning from Rev. Dr. Stennett — Anecdote of Thomas Mullet, Esq., respecting George Washington — Reply to Dr. Stennett, giving a history of the times during the war; John Murray; Jemima Wilkinson; The "Elect Lady"; increase of religious toleration in New England; calamities of the war; condition of the College; its influence in promoting Baptist sentiments; character of its library; plan for an Education Society, etc. — Origin of the Rhode Island Baptist Education Society — Letter to Dr. Thomas Llewelyn, urging him to endow the College, and thus give it his name, according to a provision of the Charter — Extract from an address of the Warren Association pertaining to education, and especially to the College.

IN the *Providence Gazette* for the year 1780, we find the following notice: —

The members of the Corporation of Rhode Island College are earnestly requested to meet on Friday, the 5th of May next, at nine o'clock

A. M., at the College Hall, to transact business of the highest importance to the institution, which will then come before them. It is not doubted but that every gentleman who has the welfare of the seminary at heart will attend if possible.

STEPHEN HOPKINS, *Chancellor.*
JAMES MANNING, *President.*
JABEZ BOWEN,
THOMAS EYRES.

PROVIDENCE, April 28, 1780.

At the meeting of the corporation, held agreeably to the foregoing advertisement, there were present, of the Fellows, the President, Hon. Jabez Bowen, Dr. Thomas Eyres, and David Howell; of the Trustees, Chancellor Hopkins, Henry Ward, Nicholas Brown, Joseph Russell, Daniel Cahoun, William Russell, Hon. Nicholas Cooke, Joseph Brown, John Jenckes, and John Brown.

The object of the meeting appears to have been the revival of college instruction, with a view to the commencement of the exercises, which, since Dec. 1776, had been suspended. President Manning presented a proposal, stating on what terms he would instruct such youth as might apply to him for this purpose. The proposal received the approval of the corporation, and he was accordingly, in the language of the record, "ordered to begin." In consideration of the times, and the great scarcity of money, his salary, which had formerly been £100, was fixed at £60, or $300. Few persons, like Manning, would have had the courage and perseverance to revive and carry on the instruction of the college, amid the uncertainties of the war, the general poverty and distress that filled the land, and the despondency and gloom into which the nation, at this period, was plunged. In this instance we have an illustration of his peculiar fitness to lead in an enterprise which, eighteen years before, his friends at Philadelphia had intrusted to his hands.

"President Manning," says Backus, "now engaged again in the work of education. But further interruptions were in store for him. On the 25th of June, 1780, while he was preaching at the church, it being Sunday, the college edifice was a second time seized, by the order of the council of war, for a hospital for the French troops, who held it until May 27th, 1782."

The next meeting of the corporation was held on the 4th of September, 1782, and was fully attended. Among the clergymen present from Massachusetts, we notice the familiar names of Backus, Stillman, and Smith. The following young gentlemen, who, amid all the embarrassments of the college, had prosecuted and completed their course of studies under President Manning, were examined, and duly admitted to the degree of Bachelor in the Arts; namely, Obadiah Brown, John Morley Green, Joseph Jenckes, Alexander Jones, William McClellan, Samuel Snow, and Levi Wheaton.

Of this number, Green and Snow had served with credit in the army. Wheaton, who died in 1851, was made a trustee during the Presidency of Dr. Maxcy. In 1815 he was appointed Professor of the Theory and Practice of Medicine. He was distinguished, says one who knew him well, for his learning and skill as a physician, and for his taste and varied acquirements in literature.

At this meeting of the corporation, says the chronicler, "the deplorable situation of the seminary was *particularly* taken into consideration; whereupon it was resolved that the edifice, which had been long occupied as a barrack and a hospital by the American and French troops, should be directly repaired; and ample provision was made for the immediate instruction of youth in all the branches of polite and useful literature."

It was also *Resolved*, "That Joseph Brown, Henry Ward, William Russell, and Ebenezer Thompson, Esq., be a committee to draft a petition to the Continental Congress, stating the account of the rents due and the damages done to the college edifice during its occupancy by the American forces and the troops of his most Christian Majesty; that they report the same to the Chancellor and President; and that on their approbation of it, they sign the said petition, in behalf of this Corporation, and forward it, together with the former petition, which was prepared some time since by the Hon. Jonathan Arnold, Esq.; and the delegates in Congress for the State of Rhode Island are requested to use their influence to get the same granted."

The week following, the Warren Association convened for the first time in Providence. Fifteen years had now elapsed since its organization at Warren, and notwithstanding the efforts of Manning and others, the parent church of the denomination had, during this period, withheld its coöperation as a body, and refused to join the Association. The opposition of many of its members to singing in public worship, and their adherence to the doctrine of laying on of hands, were the principal reasons, doubtless, why they did not, at an earlier day, coöperate with the neighboring churches, in united efforts for the public good. From the minutes of this meeting we copy the following extracts, as an illustration of the efforts made by our fathers for the education of the youth of the "rising generation": —

"As the instruction and morals of the rising generation are objects of very great importance, *Voted*, That a spelling-book, containing a good

English grammar and the Baptist catechism, be published; and Elder Foster is desired to prepare said book for the press, in conjunction with President Manning, Elders Backus, Stillman, and Skillman, to be presented at our next annual meeting for examination; and in the interim, for the encouragement of this undertaking, it is recommended to the churches to raise by subscription what moneys they can, and send the same to the Association next year."

"The Association, from a representation made to them, by the corporation of the college in Providence, of the low state of the funds of said college, and the urgent necessity of increasing them in order to support suitable instructors therein, and from an idea of the great importance of good education, have taken into consideration, as the most probable method to accomplish this valuable end, the recommendation of a subscription throughout all the Baptist societies on this continent, as well as to all the friends of literature of every denomination, on the following conditions:

"We, the subscribers, promise and engage to pay the several sums affixed to our names, to ——, to be by him paid to John Brown, Esq., of Providence, treasurer of the corporation, or his successor in said office, or order; to be placed at interest, and the interest only to be applied for the above purpose.

"N. B. — The several churches are desired to insert in the above blank the name of the most suitable person in the society for this service."

To his early associate in the instruction of the college, Manning thus writes:—

PROVIDENCE, Nov. 19, 1782.

TO THE HONORABLE DAVID HOWELL,
DELEGATE IN CONGRESS:

SIR: — This will come to hand too late to announce to you the good news concerning the fate of five per cent. This was forwarded before I reached here; but my letter may serve to congratulate you on the important event. You will not think strange that I have been at home twelve days and have never attempted to write until now, when I inform you that eight days before I reached here I was seized with a severe fever, with which I travelled, though in great distress, near two hundred miles, and of which I have been ever since confined. Though it has in a measure left me, yet I am still very weak.

On my arrival, I sent and delivered your letters and those of Dr. Arnold, desiring Mrs. Howell, by Jeremiah, to come and see me, as I could not go to her, which she would have done, but the French army are here, encamped on the lands of Jeremiah Dexter, and those of his brother's heirs. The town is full of officers, and she is crowded with them as well as others. The family, however, are all well. I found my family well, and am told that the town is healthy in general. I am exceeding sorry that the committee appointed to prepare and forward the papers relative to the college, have not yet done this. Joseph Brown tells me he has done everything in his power, but Mr. Ward has still disappointed them, by one means or other. When it will be accomplished, I know not. The edifice has been cleaned, and is now undergoing repairs. It is tenable for students. A steward has moved in, Mr. Foster. A tutor is also engaged, one Mr. Robbins, of Wethersfield, who is daily expected. The number of students is very small as yet. I still retain the idea of travelling and soliciting donations for the college; and I believe the corporation will approve it. But whom we shall get to supply my place in the interim, I know not yet. I am unable to attend even to my own business. The active executor of my father-in-law's estate, Dr. Dayton, could not collect any money for Dicky, son of Richard, who came with me, before I came away, but expected to get some before you return. I have desired him to have it in readiness by the middle of December, and left at my mamma's, and informed him that I expect you to bring it. I wish you to come that way and take it if there; if not, please to call on the Doctor at town for it and bring it, and I will cheerfully make good any expense it may cause you.

Dr. Randal is now here, and informs me that he has written Dr. Arnold by this conveyance fully upon all matters relative to the family, etc. Mrs. Manning joins in cordial respects to you and the Doctor, with, sir,

Your very humble servant,

JAMES MANNING.

P. S. — I expect Sister Woodruffe will be in your city before this reaches you. I should esteem it a particular favor if you and the Doctor would call to see her as you have opportunity.

The following letter, addressed to his friend the Rev. Benjamin Wallin, of London, of whose death he had not been informed, presents at this time a striking view of the religious condition of the New England during the war: —

NEW JERSEY, May 23, 1783.

DEAR SIR:

I feel happy that an intercourse is again opened between the two countries, after an eight years' interruption by a most calamitous war, and that I can again address a letter to my much esteemed friend and father in the ministry, with hopes of its reaching him before his dismission from the field of labor. Three years ago the past winter, I received a letter from you, accompanied with a small box of books, a very agreeable present, for which you have my most cordial thanks. It came safe, except the "Prodigal" for Mr. Stillman, and your poetical composition directed to me, which were lost by the way. The rest were delivered as directed. Your view of the parable of the prodigal son is to me the most satisfactory that I have met with. It has been perused by many here with great pleasure.

I have never written to England since the opportunity in 1776 by Mackaness and Shakspear. By yours to me, as mentioned above, I find it was received, and am happy that the short sketch given of the revival at Providence, and of the country round, furnished an agreeable entertainment for my English brethren and friends. But days of tribulation have succeeded those happy ones. The calamities of the war fell heavy upon us. First a dispersion of our church and congregation upon the coming of the King's army, which is in sight of my house. This was immediately followed by the evils attendant on a garrison, as we became a frontier. The dreadful effects of this upon the morals of the inhabitants who remained, I need not mention. But what of all things was the most distressing to me, was the lukewarmness of almost all professors of religion, and the total apostasy of many. The contagion became general. The places of worship were almost abandoned. Alarm upon alarm destroyed all tranquillity, and every day and night threatened us with that desolating devastation which spread with such rapidity along our coasts. The college was quite broken up, and the edifice was occupied by a rude and wasting soldiery, first for barracks, and then for a hospital, until they threatened its almost total demolition.

But language would fail to paint in proper colors the horrors of these days. About this time one John Murray, *alias* Murphy, supposed to be a fugitive from justice in Great Britain, with great address undertook to propagate the doctrine of universal salvation, as held by a Mr. Relly, in his book on Union, of which Murray was a mere retailer. In this work he was too successful in the towns and counties through New England. The avidity with which this error was imbibed greatly contributed to the decline of the morals of the people, and to unsettle the minds of professors. Soon after this, two women, who pretended to a participation of Deity, set up new kinds of superstition. One of them pretended to be Jesus Christ in the form of a woman. In her preaching and praying she considered herself as the Mediator. The other pretended to pardon sins, and to be at the head of a new dispensation, of which the form of worship is dancing, turning round on one foot, pretending to speak in unknown tongues, etc., etc. She interdicted all intercourse between the sexes, so that separations between man and wife became common, among those who would attain to a state of absolute perfection. The fruits of this *ex parte* religion you will easily conjecture. She, with her attendants, came to America from Liverpool, or its vicinity, about the commencement of the war. But what will astonish you most of all is that great multitudes are ensnared by these delusions, and follow their pernicious ways.

Yet notwithstanding these discouraging circumstances, a glorious reformation has progressed, during the past three or four years, in many parts of New England, and about two thousand persons have in consequence received believer's baptism, and several Baptist churches have been constituted. The good effects of this work are yet visible. Several places have been visited during the past year, and in these the good work of grace still continues. Dear Mr. Thurston, of Newport, and his people, have had a blessed shower, between thirty and forty of their number having lately been baptized. The attendance on public worship with us at Providence has of late inspired me with hopes of better times.

The college is again revived ; but our exhausted state will enable us to make only a partial repair of the edifice, and that by borrowing money. We have been so happy as to preserve our little fund amidst the wreck of public credit, but the present exhausted state of the treasury prevents our commanding the interest when due. The return of peace will, we hope, remedy this inconvenience ere it be of long continuance. The prospect of students grows more encouraging, though at present the number is small.

I write this from New Jersey, whither I have come *via* New York, for the first time in seven years. Last Lord's Day I preached here, and expect to preach for two Sabbaths to come. The Baptist meeting-house is still occupied for a hospital, and greatly out of repair. The people seem much disposed to hear the word, although attendance at church has long been out of vogue among them. Rev. Messrs. Miller and Stelle, of the Scotch Plains and Piscataway churches, two eminent Baptist ministers, died nearly two years ago. Their people have not yet found Elishas to take their places. Political contentions have proved exceedingly mischievous in many of our churches. A spirit of toleration, however, is vastly more prevalent among the Pedobaptists since the war. To this our friend Mr. Backus, who is well and still active, has contributed much. I fear I shall not have time to write by this opportunity to any of my English brethren except yourself. Please to present my best respects to all inquiring friends; for I will presume that I have some who will inquire for me. Let me be favored with a letter by the first opportunity. With sentiments of the highest respect,

I am, etc.,

James Manning.

In 1783 the public exercises of Commencement were resumed, on which occasion the Rev. Dr. Stillman preached an animating sermon from Luke xv. 32: "It was meet that we should make merry and be glad; for this thy brother was dead and is alive again, and was lost and is found." An account of this Commencement, and of the proceedings of the subsequent meeting of the corporation, may best be learned from a letter to Mr. Howell. It will be observed that Manning again alludes to his purpose to proceed to England to solicit funds for the college. In reference to this matter we make the following extract from the records of a meeting of the corporation held on the 27th of January, 1783: —

"President Manning laid before them a memorial setting forth the smallness of the college funds, and the necessity of augmenting them to preserve the institution from dissolution, and offered his services to travel abroad to solicit donations for augmenting them as per memorial on file; which being duly considered by the members present, it was agreed to recommend to the President to proceed to solicit donations, as soon as a proper person can be found to superintend the college in his absence; and that the secretary make out for him proper credentials, sealed with the college seal and signed by the secretary."

The following is the "memorial," to which reference is here made: —

To the Honorable the Chancellor and the Members of the College in Providence, convened by special request on Wednesday, the 25th of December, 1782:

GENTLEMEN: — The present low state of the funds of the college, and the consequent embarrassment of this corporation in conducting and advancing the institution, are matters of too great notoriety to need elucidation. Any plan, therefore, which renders an augmentation of them probable, I presume must meet your warmest approbation. The only one which I can conceive can at present be adopted is, to appoint some person, whom you shall judge qualified, to solicit benefactions of whom and wheresoever he shall think proper, for the sole purpose of endowing the college or making suitable provision for tuition therein,— withal assuring the donors that the corporation have pledged their faith that the interest only of the net proceeds of the money so collected shall be appropriated, and that the principal shall be reserved as a perpetual fund.

Looking around amongst the friends of the college, I can find no one who will undertake this arduous service unless I do it myself; and though, at my time of life, encumbered as I am with the cares of a family, the congregation, and the college, together with the mortifications which must unavoidably attend the execution, I find it exceeding difficult to enter on the design; yet my strong attachment to the interests of the college has induced me, for the want of a more suitable person, in the face of every difficulty to offer my services, on the following conditions: That the corporation shall, while on this service, discharge me from all duty in the college; that they furnish me with a proper authorization, and, out of the moneys I shall collect, pay me the sum of one hundred pounds lawful money per annum, besides defraying all my necessary expenses; that they allow me the use of the college estate [1] as when at home, and leave it to

[1] The house occupied by President Manning, and by his successors Maxcy and Messer, and for a while by Wayland, was built at the time of the erection of

my judgment in what places and how long to pursue this object. And should any difficulty arise concerning taking the moneys out of the governments where collected, it shall be left to my judgment how to dispose of them to the best advantage of the corporation.

Should the above propositions be acceded to, as soon as I can adjust my private concerns I engage, by divine permission, to begin and faithfully pursue the business as long as there is, in my opinion, a prospect of success. If it should be said that the state of war in which we are involved, the desolations of many parts of the country, the weight of taxes, scarcity of money, and drought of the last summer, all militate against this proposal, I freely grant the great force of all these arguments; but in my opinion matters are come to a point, and the question is not whether there have not been and may probably hereafter be more favorable times to collect money, but whether the college can be continued with any degree of reputation without some speedy exertions. I confess I think it cannot, and therefore necessity impels this measure. Besides, the Baptist Associations, held the last fall in this town and in the city of Philadelphia, lent a favorable ear to some proposals for augmenting the college revenue; but withal concluded that the only method to succeed would be for me to follow them by a personal application. And I conceive the only time to obtain their money is when the people are willing to part with it, whatever difficulty they may find in obtaining it. These proposals, however, are cheerfully submitted to your better judgment, by, gentlemen,

Your humble servant,

James Manning.

This plan of President Manning, which was never carried into effect, owing doubtless to the difficulty in finding a suitable person to take his place in the college and in the church, is another of the many proofs of his ardent desire to promote the interests of "religion and sound learning," and of his willingness to make sacrifices in behalf of the institution over which he presided. But to the letter: —

University Hall. It stood where now is the old college pump, directly in front of Manning Hall.

PROVIDENCE, Sept. 13, 1783.

TO THE HONORABLE DAVID HOWELL,
DELEGATE IN CONGRESS:

DEAR SIR: — Last night brought me your favor of the 17th ult.; by some means it has had a long passage. Am much obliged for the intelligence you communicate. I with you hope our happy Constitution may be preserved entire, and that place-men and pensioners may figure small under it, whatever raised hopes may have been entertained by candidates. I wish to know the event of the examination you mentioned, which was so full of expectation on the part of the examined. I am glad to hear that you are so happy in your colleague. I shall not be wanting in seconding your wishes with respect to your son. He does not make a rapid progress in language, but does much better than heretofore. He performed very well the last public speaking.

Our public Commencement met the highest approbation of a most numerous assembly, amongst whom were the high Consul of France, the Count dal Verme of Milan, and several English and Dutch merchants, who were very liberal in their encomiums on the performers and performances. It is generally thought, both by the friends of the college and others, to equal if not exceed any we have ever had. And I am happy to inform you that it seems to have inspired its friends with new life. Mr. John Brown requested the corporation to ascertain the sum necessary to procure a complete philosophical apparatus and library, and offered to advance, forthwith, one half the sum, provided the corporation would advance, or find ways and means to advance, the other half. It was found impracticable to ascertain this exactly. He then offered to equal any sum they could raise. A subscription was immediately set on foot, and pursued by Mr. Smith in the town the succeeding days, which amounted to better than £340; and will, with Mr. John Brown's, equal, if not exceed, £700 lawful money. A catalogue of the library and apparatus is ordered to be made out immediately. If you can assist us, by procuring from your friends any large catalogues of books, or can yourself furnish one both of the library and apparatus, we shall be happy to receive your assistance, as soon as possible. Governor Hopkins, Joseph Brown, Doctors Waterhouse and Drowne, Mr. Stillman and myself are appointed to this service; and we mean to have them prepared as soon as practicable.

Messrs. Stillman and Waterhouse, with the President, are appointed to draft an address and petition to the King of France for his patronage of the college, and a donation similar to that offered to Yale College, and forward it to you to use your influence with the Minister of France to get his sanction of it, and to point out the proper way of access to his most Christian Majesty, as soon as may be. And while it is preparing I am to request you to feel the pulse of the Minister relative to it, and advise us accordingly. This matter is ordered to be kept a secret, and by the corporation, lest we should be interrupted. President Wheelock, on this business for Dartmouth College, writes that he is likely to succeed equal to his expectations. It was also voted that Mr. William Van Horn should solicit benefactions to the southward of Pennsylvania, the President in the Middle States, Rev. Benjamin Foster through New England, and Rev. William Rogers go on the business to Europe. Mr. Foster I have since seen. He informs me that he cannot accept his appointment. Mr. Rogers has also intimated as much to me, in consequence of the ill state of his wife's health, and I am again in the question for this service. The great objection to this is, to have the college provided for in the interim. All agree, if you should return at the beginning of winter, and will undertake, that the objection will be removed; and I wish a line from you on this subject as soon as possible, as it is thought necessary to proceed to Europe this fall. In short, we are determined to make every possible exertion to make the college respectable if possible. Dr. Drowne is chosen Fellow in the room of Dr. Babcock; Dr. Waterhouse[1] has qualified also; Welcome Arnold is chosen in the room of Governor Cook.

[1] Dr. Benjamin Waterhouse was chosen a Fellow of the college in 1782. This gentleman, says Prof. Goddard, whose brief sketch of him we in the main quote, distinguished in the medical history of our country as "the American Jenner," was born in Newport, R. I. His father, originally a Presbyterian, embraced the religious opinions of the Society of Friends, after he had reached mature life; and to those opinions he remained sincerely attached till his death, at an advanced age. His son, to borrow his own language, "was born and educated in the principles of liberal Quakerism." He never, however, adopted the peculiarities of that quiet and useful sect, nor was he accustomed to unite with them in their religious worship. Dr. Waterhouse never received a college education; but few of our countrymen have been more frequently honored by distinctions from literary and scientific bodies, at home and abroad. That his early academical training was not neglected, is evident from his various publications, some of which evince a familiarity with the learned languages. He was a pupil of the celebrated Dr. Fothergill, of London, and he subsequently pursued his medical studies at the famous schools of Edinburgh and Leyden. From the Leyden school he received the degree of Doctor in Medicine. In 1783 he was appointed Professor of the Theory and Practice of Medicine in Harvard University, and he continued to perform the duties of that chair for the period of nearly thirty

Last Tuesday I attended the Association at Charlton. The convention was large and unanimous. I discover a growing attachment to literature, though by reason of the drought last year, etc., they had not complied with the request to raise money for the college, except Mr. Gair, who produced £13. Several more had begun, and the recommendation is still continued, with some additional stimulus. The plenteous crop of the present year, I hope, will enable the well disposed to lend us some assistance.

We have chosen the device for a seal, which Dr. Drowne exhibited, with the alteration of an enclosed instead of an open temple. Probably we shall employ you to get it engraved at Philadelphia, if you will take the trouble, as we expect it will be your winter residence. The subscription I mentioned was in books, apparatus, and money.

Mrs. Anthony is here, who, with Mrs. Manning, was at your house yesterday. They inform me your father is there, in a low state of health. Your mamma Corlis also continues to decline. Mrs. Manning presents her most respectful compliments to the honorable delegate, and Mrs. Anthony requests me to do the same to the old gentleman. She returned here from Boston last Monday. I had quite forgot to tell you we did not take up the consideration of our address to Congress for damages, etc., done the college. We wish you to feel the pulse of your acquaintance relative thereto; and if there should be an opening, to give us the earliest advice, that we may improve the opportunity to apply. With sentiments of esteem, I am, sir,

Your very humble servant,

JAMES MANNING.

In reference to the Count dal Verme, to whom allusion is here made, we find the following anecdote from the Hon. Asher Robbins, quoted by Prof. Goddard, as an illustration of the dignity and grace with which Dr. Manning was

years. This was among the earliest medical schools established in America. In 1784 Dr. Waterhouse was elected Professor of Natural History in Rhode Island College, and while occupying this chair he delivered, in the State House in Providence, the first course of lectures upon that science ever delivered in the United States. The benevolent and intrepid agency of Dr. Waterhouse in introducing vaccination into this country, is too well known to the public to need more than a passing allusion. He died at an advanced age, in the year 1846.

accustomed to preside at the annual Commencements. "I recollect," he says, "that at one of our Commencements, a French gentleman of distinction (I think he bore some title of nobility) was present. He sat by Dr. Waterhouse, and was, I think, introduced and presented by him. They conversed together in Latin, either as, being learned men, they chose to converse in a learned language, or as the Frenchman being less perfect in English and the Doctor in French, they found it more easy to converse in Latin. Struck with the natural dignity and grace, the Frenchman whispered to the Doctor, '*Natalis præsidere*' (born to preside). I heard this from Dr. Waterhouse himself the next day."

In looking over the records, we find that at a special meeting of the corporation, held on the 7th of January, 1784, the address to which Manning in his letter to Howell refers, "drawn up by the Rev. Samuel Stillman and Dr. Benjamin Waterhouse, was read and approved."

It was also at this meeting voted, "That the Chancellor, the President, Hon. Jabez Bowen, and Dr. Solomon Drowne, be a committee to draft a letter to Dr. Benjamin Franklin, to accompany the address to his most Christian Majesty."

The following is the address, which we copy from an original document now on file among the archives of the University. The penmanship of the document, it may be added, is remarkably clear and handsome, and the signatures to it are genuine. Some slight verbal alterations rendered it necessary to prepare another, and hence this is retained. A first draft, also, in the handwriting apparently of Dr. Stillman, is on file.

SIRE: — The Rhode Island College, studious of promoting literature, and of disseminating that kind of knowledge which tendeth to impress the minds of youth under their direction with such sentiments of benevolence as are circumscribed in no less bounds than the whole bulk of mankind, look up to your Majesty, not only as a friend and promoter of such knowledge, but also, like many of your illustrious ancestors, a patron of those arts which polish humanity and exalt our natures.

With these sentiments we regard the monarch of France, and with all deference beg leave to express our wishes of having a professor of the French language and history in this our infant seminary, — a thing we ardently desire, but are unable to accomplish.

Ignorant of the French language, and separated as we were by more than mere distance of countries, we too readily imbibed the prejudices of the English, — prejudices which we have renounced since we have had a nearer view of the brave army of France, who actually inhabited this college edifice; since which time our youth seek with avidity whatever can give them information respecting the character, genius, and influence of a people they have such reason to admire, — a nation so eminently distinguished for polished humanity.

To satisfy this laudable thirst of knowledge, nothing was wanting but to encourage and diffuse the French language; and that not merely as the principal means of rendering an intercourse with our brethren of France more easy and beneficial, but also for spreading far and wide the history of the so celebrated race of kings, statesmen, philosophers, poets, and benefactors of mankind which France has produced.

As no king will be held by us in so lasting and so dear a remembrance, so there is no name we are more desirous of repeating as the founder of the French language and history in this country than your Majesty's, and that too as much from gratitude to your Majesty as profit to ourselves.

From the scarcity of French books, our youth can at present only draw their information from English writers, and not from the more pure source, the French themselves. Our wish has therefore been to procure a proper collection of the best French authors, and to establish a professorship of the French language and history in the College of Rhode Island and Providence Plantations; but such have been the obstructions to learning during the war, and the course of education so impeded, that the edifice erected for the reception of the studious youth was granted by the governors of the college as a hospital for the troops. These, together with the calamities of the country, render it impossible for us to carry our design into execution respecting French literature.

Regarding, therefore, your Majesty as a monarch endowed with qualities that add lustre to a crown, ever ready to patronize what is good and useful, we presume to solicit your Majesty's assistance; firmly believing that whatever tends to make men wiser, better, and happier will meet with your royal assistance and encouragement.

May the common Father of the universe bless our endeavors, and make your Majesty the happy instrument of raising *to us* the literary genius of France in ages past as from the dead. May sacred and unerring wisdom ever be your guide, adorn you with every virtue, and crown you with every blessing, that future ages may commemorate the happiness of your reign with grateful admiration.

Signed by order and in behalf of the corporation,

STEPHEN HOPKINS, *Chancellor.*
JAMES MANNING, *President.*

PROVIDENCE, STATE OF RHODE ISLAND, Jan. 9, 1784.

This address was eventually put into the hands of Thomas Jefferson by the Rhode Island Delegates to Congress, the matter having been intrusted to them. We may be allowed to anticipate somewhat, and give the result of the application, by publishing the following letter, which we find in the second volume of Jefferson's Works.

PARIS, July 22, 1787.

TO THE DELEGATES OF RHODE ISLAND:

GENTLEMEN: — I was honored in the month of January last with a letter from the honorable the delegates of Rhode Island in Congress, enclosing a letter from the corporation of Rhode Island College to his most Christian Majesty, and some other papers. I was then in the hurry of preparation for a journey into the south of France, and therefore unable at that moment to make the inquiries which the object of the letter rendered necessary. As soon as I returned, which was in the last month, I turned my attention to that object, which was the establishment of a professorship of the French language in the college, and the obtaining a collection of the best French authors, with the aid of the King. That neither the college nor myself might be compromitted uselessly, I thought it necessary to sound, previously, those who were able to inform me what would be the success of the application. I was assured, so as to leave no doubt, that it would not be complied with; that there had never been an instance of the King's granting such a demand in a foreign country, and that they would be cautious of setting the precedent; that, in this moment, too, they were embarrassed with the difficult operation of putting down all establishments of their own which could possibly be dispensed with, in order to bring their expenditures down to the level of their receipts. Upon such information I was satisfied that it was most prudent not to deliver the letter, and spare to both parties the disagreeableness of giving and receiving a denial. The King did give to two colleges in America copies of the works printing in the public press. But were this to be obtained for the College of Rhode Island, it would extend only to a volume or two of Buffon's work still to be printed, Manilius's Astronomicon, and one or two other works in the press which are of no consequence. I did not think this an object for the college worth being pressed. I beg the favor of you, gentlemen, to assure the corporation that no endeavors of mine should have been spared could they have effected their wish, and that they have been faithfully used in making the preliminary inquiries which are necessary, and which ended in an assurance that nothing could be done. These papers having been transmitted to me through your delegation, will, I hope, be an apology for my availing myself of the same channel for communicating the result.

I have the honor to be, with sentiments of the most perfect esteem and respect, gentlemen,

Your most obedient and most humble servant,

THOMAS JEFFERSON.

The most important business transacted at the annual meeting of the corporation in 1783, was the confirming and ratifying of a new digest of the college laws, which had been carefully made by President Manning. A few extracts from this digest may serve to illustrate the character and liberal tendencies of the college, as also the spirit of the times: —

1. No student shall be admitted into this college until he shall have written out a correct copy of the laws of the college, or have otherwise obtained them, and had them signed by the President and one or more of the tutors, as the evidence of his admission; which copy he shall keep by him during his residence in college.

2. Both before and after noon, and before nine o'clock in the evening, the tutors in their turn shall duly visit the rooms of the students to observe whether they be within and pursuing their studies; and shall punish all those who are absent without liberty or necessity.

3. The President and tutors, according to their judgments, shall teach and instruct the several classes in the learned languages, and in the liberal arts and sciences, together with the vernacular tongue.

The following are the classes appointed for the first year, namely: In Latin, Virgil, Cicero's Orations, and Horace, all in usum Delphini. In Greek, the New Testament, Lucian's Dialogues, and Xenophon's Cyropædia. For the second year, in Latin, Cicero de Oratore, and Cæsar's Commentaries; in Greek, Homer's Iliad, and Longinus on the Sublime, together with Lowth's Vernacular Grammar, Rhetoric, Ward's Oratory, Sheridan's Lectures on Elocution, Guthrie's Geography, Kaimes's Elements of Criticism, Watts and Duncan's Logic. For the third year, Hutchinson's Moral Philosophy, Doddridge's Lectures, Fenning's Arithmetic, Hammond's Algebra, Stone's Euclid, Martin's Trigonometry, Love's Surveying, Wilson's Navigation, Martin's Philosophia Britannica, and Ferguson's Astronomy, with Martin on the Globes. In the last year, Locke on the Understanding, Kennedy's Chronology, and Bolingbroke on History; and the Languages, Arts, and Sciences studied in the foregoing years to be accurately reviewed.

4. Two of the students, in rotation, shall, every evening, after prayers, pronounce a piece upon the stage; and all the members of the college shall meet every Wednesday afternoon in the hall, at the ringing of the bell at two o'clock, to pronounce before the President and tutors pieces well committed to memory, that they may receive such corrections in their manner as shall be judged necessary.[1]

[1] In reference to this custom, which was continued down to a very late period, with some modifications, the Hon. Tristam Burges, in his Address before the Federal Adelphi, thus speaks: "You all remember the elevated advanced stage where the speaker took his stand, when, under the supervision of the whole authority, surrounded by the entire collegiate assembly, awed by the continued and pervading spirit of the hour and the occasion, he gave utterance to his own, so soon as the last echo of the voice of devotion had ceased to whisper in the ear of the listening audience. It was not to all the assembled Greeks, it was not at the Olympic Games that he spoke; but the pupil who passed through this ordeal under the eye of Manning or Maxcy, has never since that time, with more anxiety prepared himself for any other, or gone through it with more fear and trembling."

5. It is not permitted any one, in the hours of study, to speak to another, except in Latin, either in the college or college yard.

6. The Senior Class, when required, shall read a chapter out of the Greek Testament into English, before morning prayers; the President or tutors calling on whom they think proper of the class to perform this duty.

7. Every student shall attend public worship every first day of the week, where he, his parents, or his guardians shall think proper, provided that any who do not attend with any officer of instruction produce vouchers, when demanded, of his steady and orderly attendance.

N. B. — Such as regularly and statedly observe the seventh day as a Sabbath, are exempted from this law, and are only required to abstain from secular employments, which would interrupt their fellow-students.

8. Agreeably to the charter of this college, which enacts that Christians of every denomination shall, without the least molestation in the peculiarities of their religious principles, enjoy free liberty, etc., it is ordered, that if any student of this college shall deny the being of a God, the existence of virtue and vice, or that the books of the Old and New Testaments are of divine authority, or suggest any scruples of this nature, or circulate books of such pernicious tendency, or frequent the company of those who are known to favor such fatal errors, or harass and disquiet the minds of his fellow-students respecting any of the peculiarities of their Christian faith, by ridicule, sneers, scoffing, infidel suggestions, or in any other way, and shall continue obstinate therein after the first and second admonition, he shall be expelled from the college.

Young gentlemen of the Hebrew nation are to be exempt from this law, so far as it relates to the New Testament and its authenticity.

9. No student, except those who statedly attend the Friends' meeting, is permitted to wear his hat within the college walls; nor when speaking to, or spoken to by, or is in company with an officer of instruction, unless he be permitted by them to put it on.

10. The times of vacation shall be from September 6 to October 20, from December 24 to January 24, and from the first Monday in May three weeks.

11. And whereas the statutes are few and general, there must necessarily be lodged with the President and tutors a discretional or parental authority; therefore, where no statute is particulary and expressly provided for a case that may occur, they are to exercise this discretionary authority according to the known customs of similar institutions, and the plain gen-

eral rules of the moral law. And in general the penalties are to be of the more humane kind, such as are at once expressive of compassion for the offender and of indignation at the offence, such as are adapted to work upon the nobler principles of humanity, and to move the more honorable springs of good order and submission to government.

As a distinguished writer well remarks, the character of institutions, and alike of nations, is best known from their laws. We should be glad, therefore, did space allow, to present further extracts from this interesting digest. In the last paragraph, as above quoted, President Manning may be supposed to have embodied his ideas in respect to college government and discipline, which, says his pupil and successor, Dr. Maxcy, "was mild and peaceful; conducted by that persuasive authority, which secures obedience while it conciliates esteem."

The old stock, so to speak, of students, having now become exhausted, there were no more public Commencements until the year 1786, at which time the Freshman Class of 1782 were prepared to graduate. The progress of events during this period can best be learned from Manning's correspondence, which we present in chronological order. From the following letter to Mr. Kane, it appears that his friend and former correspondent, the Rev. Benjamin Wallin, had made a bequest to the college. How large this bequest was we cannot readily determine, as no mention of it is to be found in the records of the corporation.

TO MR. HENRY KANE, WALWORTH, NEAR LONDON.

PROVIDENCE, Nov. 8, 1783.

SIR: — I sympathize with you in the loss of your late venerable and pious pastor, the Rev. Mr. Wallin. I hope the church may find some Elisha to take his mantle, who, under the great Head of the church, may build you up. I am pleased to find that in his last will and testament he remembered the college. Mr. Mullett showed me the letter from you to him on the subject of discharging or receipting the papers. Mr. John Brown, our treasurer, who is empowered by the Trustees and Fellows to conduct all the money-matters of the corporation, has settled with Mr. Mullett, as you will see by his receipt, attested by the Chancellor and President. You may rely upon receiving his receipt at an early day.

The college has been dispersed during the war, but is again lifting up its head. The damages it has sustained, and the low state of its funds, call aloud for the assistance of its friends who are able to establish it. It has not yet received a name, for want of some distinguished benefactor. Such a person we should be glad to find amongst our friends in England unto whom God in his providence has given wealth and influence. We are making an effort to do something here in America, but the burdens of the war leave us but a gloomy prospect. The corporation have subscribed near seven hundred pounds lawful money, six shillings to a dollar, towards augmenting our little library and furnishing an apparatus, besides advancing near one half of this sum out of their own pockets for the repairs of the edifice. Every testimony of regard for it will be most thankfully received and acknowledged by the corporation, and especially by him who has the honor to be, sir,

Your humble servant,

JAMES MANNING.

TO THE REV. JOHN RYLAND.

PROVIDENCE, Nov. 8, 1783.

MY DEAR FRIEND:

It is long since I have had the pleasure of receiving a line from you, but I congratulate you on the return of peace and the opening again of a communication between England and America. I shall not at present trouble you with my reasoning on this surprising revolution, but shall only say that I am convinced that it is of God. To recount the distressing trials through which we have passed during the war, would but open again the wounds and cause them to bleed afresh. I suppose Mr. Ryland has no less affection for his American brethren than hithertofore, and therefore take the liberty of addressing a line to him with the same freedom as before.

The state of religion throughout America has been on the decline for several years, and the most destructive errors have prevailed, excepting a revival three or four years since in New England, and some favorable appearances of late. I should have excepted, however, the frontier parts of the country, for the wilderness has blossomed like the rose, and the Baptist principles have greatly prevailed there. The college was broken up for nearly six years, and the edifice devoted to the uses of the army. It is again revived, and twelve students now belong to it. More are expected. The edifice received great damage, but has been partially repaired, at the private expense of the corporation, who have also subscribed near £700 lawful money to augment our little library and procure an apparatus. The catalogues are making out, and when ready will be forwarded to England to give our friends, with you, an opportunity of testifying afresh their attachment. We are making application also through this continent to get what endowments we can for the college, but our exhausted state promises little favorable. The college has the reputation of contributing not a little to the interests of religion, not to say civil liberty. This has interested the Baptist society in general to look with a more favorable eye upon literature. But the burden of taxes, with their losses through the war, furnish them with arguments to withhold their pecuniary assistance which the most able logicians cannot confute. Can you find no gentleman of fortune among you who wishes to rear a lasting monument to his honor in America? If you can, direct his attention to the Hill of Providence, in the State of Rhode Island, whereon an elegant edifice is already erected, which waits for a name from some distinguished benefactor. The corporation are determined to do this honor to its greatest benefactor. Should some English gentleman deign to become such, it may serve to cement that union which I wish ever to see cultivated between the two countries, notwithstanding our independence. I promise myself your interest in finding such an one, if in your power. I must refer you to a letter to Dr. Stennett of this date for a more particular account of the state of affairs amongst us, as I have not time now to be particular. I should be happy to receive one of your old-fashioned long letters by the return of this vessel or the first which may come. It is probable there will be opportunity of transmitting letters as usual twice a year, as the trade from Providence is again opened directly to London. I should have written in the spring, but was absent when the vessel sailed. Our dear friend Mr. Wallin is released from the field of labor, as I learn by my letter from Dr. Stennett, who has done me the honor to begin a correspondence, and requested me to continue it. With this request I shall with pleasure comply. Please to present my Christian salutation to your worthy family, especially to your son, Mr. John Ryland, Jr., from whom a letter would be most acceptable to him who wishes you the highest felicity, and is with every sentiment of esteem, dear sir,

Your unworthy brother and servant in the gospel,

JAMES MANNING.

The Rev. Dr. Stennett, to whom Manning here refers, thus writes under date of May 14, 1783: —

DEAR SIR:

It is a long time since I had the pleasure of hearing from you. Among other evils that have been suffered from the late unhappy and unnatural condition between this country and North America, the embargo that has been laid upon epistolary correspondence is no inconsiderable one. But this evil is now removed, and you will give me leave to congratulate you on the event. We won't at present enter into the various political reasonings concerning this extraordinary revolution. God is no doubt bringing about his great purposes, and it is to be hoped that even during the late perilous times the temple of the Lord has been building with you as well as with us.

This letter my friend Mr. Mullett,[1] brother-in-law to Mr. Caleb Evans of Bristol, puts into your hands. He is a very worthy, sociable man, goes over upon very considerable affairs of a mercantile kind, and will be capable of giving you a variety of information. My brevity now, there-

[1] Thomas Mullett, Esq., a merchant of the first respectability. He was a native of Taunton, England, and died at Clapham, Nov. 14, 1814, in the sixty-ninth year of his age. He possessed, says his biographer, an excellent understanding, and was a firm friend to civil and religious liberty. The following anecdote is related of him in Evans's Life of Richards: —

"Thomas Mullett, Esq., was soon after the American war at Mount Vernon, the seat of General Washington. Besides other flattering marks of attention, Washington, when alone with him in his library, asked him if he had seen any individual in that country who was competent to the task of writing a history of the late unhappy contest. Mr. M. replied, with his usual presence of mind, 'I know of one, and one only, competent to the task.' The General eagerly asked, 'Who, sir, can that individual be?' Mr. M. remarked, 'Cæsar wrote his own commentaries!' The General bowed, and replied, 'Cæsar wrote his own commentaries; but, sir, I know the atrocities committed on both sides have been so great and many that they cannot be faithfully recorded, and had better be buried in oblivion.'"

fore, you will excuse. It will be an opening, I hope, to a familiar, happy correspondence between us. The state of religion with you, and of the college in Rhode Island, I should be glad to understand. Be so good as to remember me affectionately to all our Christian friends, the ministers in particular, Mr. Backus, etc., etc.

We have had many changes in our congregation by death; but I hope religion in our denomination is not on the decline. Of good Mr. Wallin's death you have no doubt heard. His place is not yet supplied. My health has of late been but indifferent, but through the goodness of God it is now better.

I am just publishing a volume of discourses on domestic duties, one of which either Mr. Mullett, or Mr. Stillman — who, I take it, is still at Boston — will put into your hands.

You will excuse my hurrying manner at present, and be assured that I am, very dear sir,

Your affectionate friend and brother,

SAMUEL STENNETT.

Manning's reply is one of unusual length, and seems to have been written with special care. It is of itself a history of the times during the American war: —

PROVIDENCE, Nov. 8th, 1783.

REVEREND AND DEAR SIR:

Yours of May 14th was lately handed me by Thomas Mullett, Esq., whom I find to justify, and more, the excellent character you gave him; though we have had but a small share of his agreeable company, owing to his attention to his widely-extended mercantile concerns. I most heartily rejoice to have a free communication again opened between England and America; for this I have earnestly wished ever since its first interruption. May heaven forbid its ever being again shut! But I feel peculiarly happy in the honor you have done me in the renewal of our correspondence. I congratulate you on the restoration of your health, and hope you may be long continued, a rich blessing to the church of God. The flourishing state of our society with you is pleasing.

During some of the first years of the war, God was pleased to display his power, in many parts of New England, in a glorious manner, and thousands embraced the Baptist principles; but those halcyon days soon ended, since which has ensued an amazing apostasy. The delusion of Relley,[1] in his book called the Union, etc., has been propagated with the most astonishing success by John Murray. This doctrine of universal salvation has been licked into various forms by its numerous zealous advocates; and as it so exactly coincides with the carnal mind, has been sucked in by multitudes, among whom are not a few professors of religion, with great avidity.

About the same time one Jemima Wilkinson,[2] near this place, who had been educated amongst the Quakers, pretended that she had been dead, reanimated with a celestial spirit, and endowed with an extraordinary commission from heaven to preach the gospel. She sometimes called herself the Comforter; and sometimes, when in an audience of great numbers, pointing to herself, said that when Jesus Christ first appeared, he came in the flesh of a man, but that he was now come in the flesh of a woman. She has continued to traverse the country and publicly preach ever since, accompanied with a number of disciples who do her homage on their bended knees. Many have been carried away with her delusion, and believe her to be the Saviour. But to close the rear, a number of people, who came from the west of England about the commencement of the war, under the direction of an old woman whom her adherents call *the Mother, the Elect Lady*, etc., etc., pretend that the new dispensation has taken place, and that they are the only and true church. They pretend to absolve the sins of their disciples, and of course require particular confession to be made to them. Their particular worship consists in dancing, turning round on the heel, jumping, singing, and embracing each other, while they pretend to talk in unknown tongues, work miracles, etc., etc. They interdict all intercourse between the sexes, declaring the marriage contract void, and pretending to a state of absolute perfection. Some carnal fruits, however, have inadvertently resulted from their chaste embraces. And — would you believe it? — vast numbers of those who once

1 "Doctrine of union between Christ and his Church. By James Relley." 8vo. London, 1731.

2 Jemima Wilkinson was born in Cumberland, R. I., about the year 1753. In 1789 she and her followers removed to Yates county, New York, where they founded a colony. She exacted from her adherents the most complete submission and the most menial services. After her death, which took place in July, 1819, the colony was broken up. A narrative of her life and character, by David Hudson, was published at Geneva, N. Y., in 1821, making a duodecimo volume of two hundred and twenty-eight pages.

appeared serious, well disposed-persons, have followed their pernicious ways. They are not to be reasoned with; alleging that they know they are right, and they will rave like madmen when opposed, calling this the effect of the Spirit of God. While these delusions on the one hand attack the truth of the gospel, growing infidelity on the other lends all its aid totally to subvert and destroy it, whilst the professed friends of it seem too generally overwhelmed and in a deep sleep. This, you say, is a dismal picture, but not more so than true. Yet there are those who stand fast in the truth, and some late revivals encourage us to hope for better days. One thing, however, is favorable, — a spirit of toleration more universally prevails throughout New England, and the doctrines of religious as well as civil liberty are better understood by the people at large, against any infractions of which they are determined to guard.

It was a glorious time of revival in our church when the war first commenced, but when the town became a garrison, on account of the vicinity of the royal army on Rhode Island, the apprehensions of an attack, and the daily alarms to which we were subjected, induced numbers of families to retire into the more interior parts of the country, not only for safety but subsistence. This scattered our church and congregation abroad, which has never been collected since, near fifty of our members not having yet returned. These things, with the disinclination of many to attend public worship from the example of the army, have greatly reduced us. It has been a season of heavy trials with great numbers of our churches, several of which have been almost totally dispersed. After all, when I view the last eight years, and reflect on the amazing anxiety and distress through which we have waded, and the astonishing goodness of God in preserving so many of us to see the return of peace, I am lost in wonder; especially when I consider the ingratitude of our hearts towards our glorious Benefactor. Thousands and thousands of families, once living in affluence, have, by the war, been reduced to beggary. Sometimes famine, and several times pestilence, as well as the sword, threatened to combine for our destruction. But language fails in communicating my ideas. I heartily wish you may never know by experience what it is to live in the midst of war.

In the fore part of December, 1776, the royal army landed on Rhode Island, and took possession of the same. This brought their camp in plain view from the college with the naked eye; upon which the country flew to arms and marched for Providence. There, unprovided with barracks, they marched into the college and dispersed the students, about forty in number. After this the college continued to be occupied for a barrack and a hospital alternately until June, 1782, when it was left in a most ruinous situation. The corporation advanced out of their own pockets near one thousand dollars for the most necessary repairs, and ordered the course of education to recommence; but under these circumstances the number of students was small, as the former number had mostly completed their education at other colleges, or turned their attention to other objects. Last September, five young gentlemen, who had studied with me in private, were admitted to the honors of the college at a public Commencement. Their performances met such a universal approbation of a numerous audience, as inspired the corporation with fresh zeal to promote the institution. Mr. John Brown, the treasurer of the college, offered to give a sum equal to what all the other members would subscribe, towards procuring an addition to our little library, and a philosophical apparatus. By this means we obtained subscriptions for near £700 lawful money, six shillings to the dollar, and the catalogues are being made out. This we propose to follow with an application to Europe, as well as throughout America, for further benefactions. We have nominated persons to this service, but we fear few if any of them will engage in the work, on account of the difficulty of leaving home, and the fears of not meeting a cordial reception in Great Britain. But I rejoice to find, from late accounts, that our friends remain friends to the college, and wish to know the state of it. This encourages us to solicit every assistance they can give, all of which we greatly need. I have the satisfaction to find that it has, under all its disadvantages, been instrumental in greatly promoting Baptist principles, and the spread of civil and religious liberty throughout New England. Our number of students is twelve, and more are expected soon; but the great objections which operate against us are the want of an apparatus and library, and the want of professors. Of these advantages the old colleges amongst us can boast. Our library consists of about five hundred volumes, most of which are both very ancient and very useless, as well as very ragged and unsightly.[1] Our prospects to remedy this, in America, are at present very unpromising. Last fall the state of the college was laid before the Associations in New

[1] The friends of the college will observe the contrast between these five hundred "very ancient, very useless, and very ragged and unsightly volumes," and the noble library of the present day, with its thirty-five thousand standard books of approved editions, in choice and substantial bindings.

England and Philadelphia, which strongly recommended to all the churches to make collections for endowing it; the same has been done this year, — from all which not £20 sterling has been raised, such is the scarcity of money, the burden of taxes, and the reduced state of the country. The society at large never before appeared so disposed to assist if it were but in their power; but, generally speaking, the Baptists here are the poor of this world.

Several pious youth, who promise fair for the ministry, having picked up some grammar learning, have applied to me to know whether any way can open for their assistance in getting an education. This has led me to think of a plan to assist such, and I have sketched out the following: That the Rev. Messrs. Samuel Stillman, Gardner Thurston, Isaac Backus, John Gano, Hezekiah Smith, with the President, be a standing committee of the corporation, and in case of the demise of any of them their number to be filled up from time to time by themselves, who, or the major part of them, shall examine and approve of such as shall be candidates to receive the assistance which may be proffered to worthy characters in that way, and to say in what proportions it shall be dealt out to them. It will be easy to procure a vote of the corporation to invest this committee with all necessary powers to discharge this trust; and I have fixed upon men whose doctrinal and practical principles, as well as their character in this country, will entitle them to the highest confidence of benefactors to this fund. I was long since convinced that a plan of this kind would be vastly serviceable, and proposed it to some of my friends, whose only objection against it was its interference with endowing the college, which was an object of the greatest importance; but I am of opinion that many would be induced to give for this purpose who would not on any other consideration. Should a donation be offered, and these persons be mentioned for the trust, in this way I have suggested, by some gentleman out of the corporation, I am convinced that it would immediately take, and that something considerable could soon be raised, which would be of standing benefit to our churches, and more widely disseminate the knowledge of truth.[1] Such has been the feeling, through New England, in favor of

[1] The system of scholarships, inaugurated by President Sears, is based upon the same general principles which Manning here develops; with this difference, however, — that the scholarships are not of necessity Baptist in their character, or confined exclusively to students who have or who may have in view the Christian ministry. These points are left for the respective founders of scholarships to determine. The majority of them, it may however be added, serve in carry-

a college education, that our pious illiterate ministers are greatly circumscribed in their sphere of usefulness, of which many of them are sufficiently sensible, and heartily wish their successors may be enabled to obviate this objection. A great and effectual door is opened for the labors of Baptist ministers throughout our vast, extended frontiers, and many new churches have been lately constituted in that howling wilderness; and indeed the labors of our society seem there generally preferred.

I fear I have already trespassed upon your patience; but you wished for various information; and you must consider this letter contains the substance of a ten years' correspondence. I shall be happy to have your assistance and patronage of the college, and your opinions on the subjects proposed by the first opportunity. I had forgot to mention that, amidst the wreck of public credit, we have been so fortunate as to preserve, undiminished, our little fund, though as yet, from the exhausted state of the treasury, which has operated greatly to my personal disadvantage, we

ing into effect precisely these views of President Manning. At the meeting of the Warren Association held in the year 1791, the Rev. Dr. Stillman presented a plan, which, he stated, he had received from a friend, for establishing a charitable fund, "for the purpose of assisting such young men of the Baptist denomination as may appear to be suitably qualified for the ministry, with a collegiate education." Who this friend was we cannot positively state, but we have no doubt whatever in regard to the source whence the plan itself originated. After a second reading it was unanimously adopted by the Association, and a board of trustees, consisting of twelve, was chosen. This board was styled, "Trustees of the Baptist Education Fund." It was required that "so many of the Baptist Fellows of Rhode Island College who are members of churches shall be trustees of this fund," the remaining number to be chosen by ballot from and by the Warren Association. Of the college Fellows on the board, were Dr. Stillman of Boston, Dr. Smith of Haverhill, Rev. William Williams of Wrentham, Dr. Maxcy, President of the College, and Robert Rogers, Esq., of Newport. Those elected by the Association, were Dr. Backus of Middleborough, Dr. Baldwin of Boston, Rev. Joseph Grafton of Newton, Rev. Noah Alden of Bellingham, Rev. Thomas Green of Cambridge, Rev. George Robinson of Bridgewater, and Rev. Isaiah Parker of Harvard.

In February, 1794, the society thus commenced was duly incorporated by the Legislature of Massachusetts. In 1816 a separate organization was formed, which, in 1823, was incorporated under the name of "The Baptist Education Society of the Warren Association." At this time the funds, now amounting to $3600, were equally divided between this society and the Boston Association, which had been formed in the year 1811. Hence the origin and present funds of the society now known as the Rhode Island Baptist Education Society.

have not been able to command any interest. I have the assistance of a tutor, and a grammar master keeps school in the college edifice.

I cannot say in what light you view the American Revolution, but to serious people here it appears to be of God; and if the counsels of Great Britain are conducted with wisdom and moderation, it will in the issue be of no disadvantage to her in a national view. In a religious view I am certain it should not operate to produce any discord among the subjects of that Prince whose kingdom is not of this world. As far as my acquaintance extends, I am convinced that, on our part, the former attachment still continues; and I am sure I have as little reason to doubt it on yours.

Mr. Mullett was kind enough to put into my hands your volume on domestic duties, and I heartily thank you for the pleasure which the perusal of it gave me. I wish there were more of them in this country. They are greatly needed, and I think would sell. Before the war, for supplying the college and my friends, I kept a small assortment of books, which I yearly imported from London. I still mean to do the same, and have thought of getting a number of our Baptist authors for the supply of our society in different parts of the country. I think there has not been sufficient attention paid to our own writings by our own people. Should you think proper to send any of your works for that purpose, on the same terms which booksellers with you have them, I shall exert myself to sell them, and directly remit you the money. I have mentioned my letter to you to Dr. Llewelyn, to whom, if you please, you may show it, and also to Mr. Ryland, and any other friend who may, in your opinion, be disposed to serve the college, or wish for the information which it contains. By every opportunity I shall be happy to receive letters from Dr. Stennett. With sentiments of esteem, I am, dear sir,

Your brother in Christ,

JAMES MANNING.

The distinguished scholar to whom the following letter is addressed died on the 7th of August, three months previous to its date. What he would have done for the college had he lived, cannot of course be determined. It is certain that his feelings towards the institution were friendly. In the original subscription book of Morgan Edwards, his name appears as the largest subscriber on the list. Among the duplicate books presented to the library by the Bristol Education Society, we notice a fine uncut copy of the "Biographia Britannica," in seven volumes folio, a gift from Llewelyn, who bequeathed his library to that society. It contains his book-mark, and states the time of his death.

TO THOMAS LLEWELYN, LL.D., LONDON.

PROVIDENCE, Nov. 8, 1783.

SIR: — By Thomas Mullett, Esq., for whose agreeable acquaintance I am indebted to an introductory line from Dr. Stennett, I had the pleasure of hearing that you are yet alive, and, though in a declining state of health, are still protracting your usefulness in the cause of the Redeemer and the best interests of mankind. Your known zeal in promoting the Baptist society for a series of years, your ability to serve it, and the desire you expressed, in his hearing, of knowing the state of the college at Providence, have encouraged me to address you on this subject, at once to give that information and to solicit your patronage of an institution which has already, in the minds of unbiased judges, greatly disseminated the knowledge of civil and religious liberty through this country, and added respectability to the Baptist profession. Bleeding with the wounds of war, it now solicits the relief which the benevolent and opulent alone can afford.

From its first establishment until the commencement of the late unnatural war, it gradually increased in the number of students, which at that time was about forty. It then began to attract the attention of the public, and bid fair to have been greatly augmented in numbers, as many were then preparing with a design to complete their education here. This town becoming a frontier, in the year 1776, the troops took possession of the edifice, to which purpose it continued to be appropriated until June, 1782. Great waste and destruction, you will naturally conclude, were made upon it by men whose profession has destruction for its object. To repair the edifice the corporation advanced money out of their own pockets, as also to fit up some rooms for the accommodation of students who are likely to enter soon. The number of these is now twelve, and more are soon expected. In short, we want nothing but a proper endowment to enable us to furnish a suitable library and apparatus, and properly support able instructors, to render the college very respectable; the grand objection against it is the want of these things, of which they can boast at other colleges. Those inimical to our profession are exceeding vigliant to prevent its growth, from an idea of its importance to the Baptist cause. Hitherto a very great part of our society in this country have been by no means friendly to it; but many have altered their opinion, and would assist if they could; but, reduced by the war and the weight of taxes, at present they can only wish it well. Cambridge college was so fortunate as to attract the attention of a Hollis, New Haven of a Yale, and New Hampshire of a Dartmouth, who have given their names to these seats of learning. We should think ourselves no less happy in the patronage of a *Llewelyn. Llewelyn College* appears well when written, and sounds no less agreeably when spoken. Nor do I know a name which it would please me better to hear extolled on our public anniversaries as the founder of the institution. The charter, one of which I beg leave to present to you, empowers the corporation to give the college a name in honor of its most distinguished benefactor, which they are resolved to do. I know your philanthropy and principles of liberty would not suffer you to object that we are now become independent of the British empire. You too well know that necessity, dire necessity impelled to this measure a people whose feelings revolted at the idea upon any other ground. Besides, subjects of the Prince of peace cannot approve of strong local attachments. It is the ardent wish of the human mind to establish a permanent fame. As this appears to be a passion natural to man, so it is doubtful whether he feels a stronger, or one that ceases to influence him later. And what can more effectually gratify this predominant affection, than the grateful recollection of the latest posterity that we have laid foundations for improving the human intellect, disseminating useful knowledge, and propagating the gospel of peace over almost half the globe? If we consider the rapid progress of religion, letters, government, and arts in this new world, where on earth can a theatre be erected, from which the human character can be exhibited to better advantage (in largely contributing to the progress of religion, society, and manners) than in America? But you, sir, need only consider that patronizing this college will directly contribute to the propagation of the gospel of Christ in its simplicity to bestow upon it your friendship. Of the prospects of this I have given some hints to Dr. Stennett, in a letter of this date, to which I refer you, as I have desired him to communicate the contents of it to his friends, and those of the college, particularly requesting him to show it to Dr.

Llewelyn. Therein I have mentioned the state of our library, apparatus, fund, etc. The whole interest of the latter does not amount to more, if so much as £60 sterling per annum. We propose to forward our catalogue as soon as it is ready, and invite our friends to lend us their assistance in purchasing the books. Should your views be different from mine in reference to the premises, I beg your forgiveness for troubling you on this subject through my zeal for the college; but should you think favorably of the proposal, you will do a singular favor to a grateful corporation, the Baptist society in America, and I doubt not to remote posterity, but to none more than to him who, with every sentiment of esteem, has the honor to subscribe himself, sir,

Your friend and servant in the gospel of Christ,
JAMES MANNING.

The Warren Association, at its meeting this year, to which Manning in his correspondence alludes, prepared an address to their "friends and countrymen," which presents a faithful picture of the times at the close of the war, and exhibits in a pleasing light the views and prospects of the Baptist denomination. We cannot resist the temptation to introduce here the closing paragraphs. They have special reference to the college, and show how intimate, formerly, were the relations which it sustained to the churches: —

"Permit us to add a word concerning education, and we shall have done. In Genesis xvii. God made a covenant with Abraham, which constituted a church in his household, who had a large grant of choice lands that in due time they were to take possession of by destroying the heathen inhabitants; and as long as that state continued, they were to make a visible difference in commerce and government, as well as worship, between the circumcised and all other people in the world. In the same church the priests were to have the whole government in worship, and were also to declare what the sentence of the law was in capital cases; and the judges were to carry the same into execution (Deut. xvii. 8–12). When Christ came he fulfilled the law, and abolished those distinctions among men; and constituted his church upon a better covenant — established upon better promises. His word calls said covenant with Abraham the covenant of circumcision (Acts vii. 8), but in after ages deceitful men took away that name, and called it the covenant of grace; into which they essayed to bring children before they believed, or could choose for themselves. And all colleges and superior places of learning were entirely under the command of such men for many centuries; by which means, natural affection, the force of education, temporal interest, and self-righteousness, all conspired together to bind people in that way; wherein the orthodox have claimed a right to treat all others as others have not a right to treat them. But a college is now erected at Providence upon a plan of equal liberty, where education is to be had without any sectarian or party tests. Other colleges have been erected and much of their expense borne by governments; but this has been done entirely by personal generosity; and some men of influence have tried to crush it; therefore it calls loudly, to all lovers of knowledge and liberty, to contribute their mite towards its necessary support."

CHAPTER VIII.

1784-1785.

Letter to Manning from the Rev. Dr. Rippon, of London — Most of the Baptist ministers in England on the side of America in the war — Manning's reply to Rippon — Apostasy of Rev. Elhanan Winchester — Sketch of Hon. Asher Robbins — Baptists compelled to contribute to the support of Pedobaptist worship in Massachusetts and Connecticut — Resolution of the Warren Association in reference thereto — Letter to Rev. Thomas Ustick on the subject — Sketch of Rev. Elhanan Winchester — His troubles with the Baptist church in Philadelphia — Letter to Rev. Dr. Smith — William Wilkinson and the College Grammar School — Extract from the *Providence Gazette* respecting the transfer of the school from the College to the brick schoolhouse — Letter to Rev. Dr. Caleb Evans, of Bristol, England — Condition of the College — Efforts to add to its funds and to increase its library — Evans's reply to Manning — Illustration of Manning's numerous and perplexing cares — Letter from Rev. A. Booth — Manning's reply — Letter to Rev. John Ryland, Jr. — Letter to Rev. Dr. Rippon, introducing Dr. Solomon Drowne, of Providence — Sketch of Dr. Drowne — Letter to Hon. David Howell, in Congress — Letter to Rev. Thomas Ustick — Degree of Doctor in Divinity conferred on Manning by the University of Pennsylvania — Second letter to Hon. David Howell — Letter to Thomas Mackaness, Esq., of London — Manning's plan to establish a library for the Baptist Association in Kentucky — Letter to Rev. Dr. Evans — Manning's philanthropic efforts to enlighten the illiterate Baptist ministers of Kentucky and Virginia — Letter to Manning from Hon. Granville Sharp, of London — Manning's reply — Ecclesiastical matters pertaining to the Episcopal Church — Letter to Rev. Dr. Rippon — Biographical sketch of Rev. Stephen Gano — Character of Hon. Stephen Hopkins, the first Chancellor of the College — Letter from Rev. Dr. Evans announcing a donation of books to the College Library from the Bristol Education Society — Character of the donation and of the aforesaid Society — Letter to Hon. David Howell, in behalf of the Corporation, urging him to use his influence with the members of Congress in favor of a petition for indemnity for injuries which the college building sustained during the war — Death of Hon. Joseph Brown — Correspondence between Manning and John Gill, of London, respecting the publications of Rev. Dr. John Gill — List of Dr. Gill's published works — Pleasant bibliographical "morceau" respecting the first volume of Backus's Ecclesiastical History.

THE following letter is from the Rev. Dr. John Rippon, of London, successor of the Rev. Dr. Gill. The remarkable statement which he makes, that all the Baptist ministers in London but two, and most of the Baptist clergy in the country, were on the side of the Americans in the "late dispute," as he mildly terms the war, is as gratifying to us of the present day as it doubtless was to Manning and his friends. The reader of the correspondence now begun will readily perceive that Dr. Rippon, from his character and position, was well qualified to judge of the views and feelings of his brethren in matters of public moment.

GRANGE ROAD, SOUTHWARK, May 1, 1784.

REVEREND AND DEAR SIR:

I have long wished for an opportunity of introducing myself to you, and to several other brethren on your side of the Atlantic. And as God in his wisdom has now put an end to the late bloody and unrighteous war, and opened a free communication between this country and America, I take the liberty, by the hands of your neighbor Mr. Chase (who speaks in the highest terms of you, Messrs. Stillman Gano, etc.), of soliciting such a Christian correspondence as your wisdom may suggest, and your large connections and many avocations may permit.

To describe myself is a work *less proper* than what I wish to be employed in; but as it is probable my name has never reached your ears, it may not be altogether *improper* to hint that I was born at Tiverton, in Devonshire, about forty miles from Plymouth, and about sixteen from Upottery, where my father is minister. I was called by grace, I trust, when about sixteen years of age, became a student at Bristol under the Rev. Messrs. Hugh and Caleb Evans when I was between seventeen and eighteen, and continued there between three and four years. After the death of Dr. Gill, I was invited thence to town as a probationer amongst his people, and with them have been comfortably settled as pastor for more than eleven years. The church now consists of about three hundred members, many of whom are very lively, affectionate, and evangelical. The declaration of their faith and practice, which they made at their admission, is at the close of the three volumes of sermons and tracts accompanying this, your acceptance of which will do me an honor, if you consider them as a small token of the great affection I bear you as a faithful and honored servant of our illustrious Master.

Whatever scepticism attacks my mind, of this I am certain, that there are brethren in your country "whom not having seen I love." This has frequently turned to me for a testimony of my having passed from death unto life. Nor did I least of all experience this in the year 1780, when Mr. Wallin (who left earth for heaven in the beginning of the year 1783) received a letter from Boston containing an account of a great revival through New England, and in which it was said Mr. Winchester was very instrumental. I sent this account to Mr. Evans, of Bristol, and he printed an extract from it in the following Western Association letter. It afforded a joy amongst many churches better felt than described. Some of us thought with pleasure on Isa. lix. 19. But, alas! the next account we hear is that this useful man has wofully changed his sentiments. Lord, what is man! A sermon of Mr. Wallin's, called the "Outcasts Comforted," on Isa. lxvi. 5, has been reprinted here, with an appendix said to be written by one Clarke, a mystic. It contains observations on the seventh trumpet, and a dissertation on the altar of brass called Ariel, etc. My heart has been grieved for the good man, and I have wept in secret places on his account. Is it true that Mr. Morgan Edwards, to whom I intend writing soon, has printed a book in vindication of him?

I believe all our Baptist ministers in town, except two, and most of our brethren in the country, were on the side of the Americans in the late dispute. But sorry, very sorry were we to hear that the college was a hospital, and the meeting-houses were forsaken and occupied for civil or martial purposes. We wept when the thirsty plains drank the blood of your departed heroes, and the shout of a king was amongst us when your well-fought battles were crowned with victory. And to this hour we believe that the independence of America will for a while secure the liberty of this country; but that if the continent had been reduced, Britain would not long have been free.

The last Warren Association letter that I have seen is dated 1779. It came with Mr. Backus's History. Since then many important things must have happened, and it may be there is much good news to be conveyed to us respecting our sister churches in the wilderness. Glad should I be to hear of the success of the gospel and of the prosperity of the college. When shall the priests of Zion be clothed with salvation, and her saints shout aloud for joy? O Lord, let "thy kingdom come," let it spread through all the world, and particularly let it come in my heart, and in the heart of thy honored servant for whom these lines are designed.

If I am not mistaken, the Baptist interest in this country is more flourishing than the Presbyterian or Independent. In most of our churches there is a cordial attachment to the truth as it is in Jesus, attended with a greater liberality towards others who differ from us than was formerly expressed. May a Christian contention for the truth and a general catholicism forever walk hand in hand, that unconverted men may have reason again to say, "See how these Christians love!"

This afternoon I have been employed in packing books as follows: Gill's Sermons and Tracts, 3 vols., blue boards, for yourself; do., in sheets, for that much respected man, Mr. Stillman, of Boston; a dozen of Watts's Hymns and Psalms, and half a dozen Bibles and as many Testaments, to be disposed of as you think best. Gill should have been bound neatly; but as Mr. Chase is likely to sail Monday morning, it cannot be done. Will you do me the favor of making this apology to Mr. Stillman if I have not time to write him, as I fear I shall not, for it is Saturday evening, nine o'clock, now, and it was past eight before I began this hasty scrawl.

With the above I have sent three prints, — one of the Rev. Dr. Gill, another of the late Rev. Hugh Evans, my much esteemed tutor, and another of myself. I have not time to get them glazed and packed. The first two deserve a respectful place in the college, and the last courts no situation but a place of solitude under your hospitable roof. I shall be much obliged to you to circulate the proposals which relate to Saurin and Claude, and to notice the advertisement of Gill's books which I have sent. If any of your friends want any of them, I can procure them at bookseller's price, considerably cheaper than the printed list. It will rejoice me to be of any service to them, and more especially if they are poor ministers. I have not time to read this over now, as a person has been waiting for it while I write. Excuse my haste. Remember me respectfully, if you please, to Mr. Howell, your assistant. Pray for me, write me the first opportunity, and be assured I think it a great felicity to have any good reason to subscribe myself,

Your affectionate brother and servant,

JOHN RIPPON.

P. S. — I am this week thirty-three years of age.

To this letter Manning replies: —

PROVIDENCE, Aug. 3, 1784.

REVEREND AND DEAR SIR:

I have now before me your most acceptable favor of May 1, for which I return you many thanks, as well as for the package and its agreeable contents. I felicitated myself on a large and free correspondence with Christian friends in England on the return of peace, and accordingly wrote to Mr. Wallin, from New York, at the first dawn of it, but soon after received information that he had rested from his labors. By the first vessel from the State this was followed by letters to Drs. Stennett and Llewelyn and Mr. Ryland; but these, I conjecture from your letter, never reached them, since they contained such information as I judged would be wished for by our brethren on your side of the water, and such as in your letter you request. Nothing could be more agreeable than the correspondence you propose, which I shall endeavor to keep up with the greatest punctuality. Your letter did not give me the first information of your name, etc., as Mr. Wallin had favored me with the sermon and charge delivered at your settlement. But the interruption of all intercourse by means of the war, left me in a great measure ignorant of the state of our churches and ministers in England, until Dr. Stennett's letter, last fall, by Mr. Mullett, and a short acquaintance with Capt. Thomas Mesnard last May in New York, who gave me such a pleasing idea of Mr. Rippon, that I requested him to present my Christian salutation, and inform him that a letter would be highly pleasing to your unknown friend.

Your letter, it appears, was then written in consequence of Mr. Chase's recommendation, to whom I am obliged for his favorable opinion. As soon as the package of books and the prints came safe to hand, Mr. Stillman's were sent forward, together with his letter, and I shall distribute the Bibles, Testaments, Psalms and Hymns as I think will be most serviceable to the poor. The proposals for Dr. Gill's, Saurin's, and Claude's works I have circulated; but the impoverished state of the country, and the disinclination to reading books on religious subjects, presage but a small sale at present. Some, however, will, I expect, be wanted, for which I shall expect your kindly proffered services. I most heartily rejoice at your success in the ministry, and the happy state of the church of which you are pastor. May the Lord continue to strengthen you for his service, and honor you with many more seals of your ministry. You speak the language of my heart towards brethren in your country when you express your affectionate regard for us. I conceive this results from the very nature of the religion of Jesus. Often has this prompted me to plan a voyage to Europe; but such have hitherto been, and most probably will continue to be, my embarrassments, that I shall be denied this privilege; but I hope to meet the whole family at home, and forever enjoy their improving society above when our labors on earth are finished. The prints of Dr. Gill and Rev. Hugh Evans shall have a respectful place in the college, and as I daresay Mr. Rippon loves good company, he will excuse me for placing his there also. Not that I am unwilling to furnish it, and its agreeable original, with the best accomodations my house can afford, for this I should esteem a peculiar favor; but as I promise myself your future patronage of the college, I know of no place so suitable as that.

The apostasy of Mr. Winchester has been for a lamentation amongst us. Self-exaltation was the rock on which he split. Though he had from the first been remarkable for instability of character, he inflicted a grievous wound on the cause, especially in Philadelphia; but I think he is now at the end of his tether. His interest is declining, which will most probably prove a deadly wound. I saw him last May, and from his appearance think he has nearly run his race. His state of health will not admit of his preaching, and by a letter last week from the Rev. Thomas Ustick, who now supplies the pulpit in Philadelphia, I learn that Winchester and his friends have lost the case in their suit for the meeting-house and the property of the church. It really appeared that God owned his labors in the revival in New England. Perhaps for attempting to take the glory to himself, He has laid him aside as an improper instrument for his work, who justly challenges the whole of it as his own. From common fame, and from what I myself saw, I really think this to be the case.

Mr. Morgan Edwards has not printed in vindication of his principles, but he read me a manuscript more than a year since on that subject, which he did not own, though charged then with being the author. He did not deny it; whereby he was entreated not to add the printing of this to the long list of imprudent things which had already so greatly grieved his friends and so injured his reputation. This plainness did not please him, but I thought the use of it was duty.

Enclosed I send you the minutes of the Eastern Association since the year 1779; and as I flatter myself that my letters must have reached Dr. Stennett, etc., before this, I refer you to the information which they contain, observing in general that at the commencement of the war the glorious revival in which the college and the town of Providence, as well as many places adjacent, had so largely shared (during the continuance of which, in the course of a year, I baptized more than a hundred persons), began to decline; and except the visitation you refer to in your letter, the state of religion, saving in the frontier parts, has been on the decline until about the close of the war, since which public worship is better attended, and many souls have of late been hopefully converted. On a visit to New York and the Jerseys, the last spring, I found the people anxious for the word, and hopeful appearances in almost every place where I was called to preach. By a letter the last week I find the work increases, especially under the ministry of Mr. Wilson, a young minister resident at Bordentown in West Jersey, and my Brother Gano in New York. As Mr. Backus is here, I prevailed on him to give a sketch of the reformation between two and three hundred miles east of us, of which he has had some direct and late accounts. This, for your satisfaction, I also enclose. Lord's Day sennight I conversed with a person from there, who professed to be a subject of the work. He gave a most remarkable account of the display of God's power and grace amongst them. In general our churches appear to stand steadfast in the doctrines of grace; and indeed the Baptist churches are almost left alone in defending them against Arminians and Universalists, as our brethren of other denominations who are sound appear much discouraged. I believe I may say with truth, that the Baptist society in America increases more rapidly than any other religious denomination; but in general we are the poor of the world. God grant that we may be rich in faith.

I rejoice to hear that our Baptist brethren in England sympathized with us in our deep affliction. Our blood indeed was wantonly shed, — of this I have been a deeply interested spectator, — but I trust God meant it for good. I think I can say that I never in one instance doubted the justice of our cause, and I desire to bless God that I never thirsted for the blood of those who were shedding ours. But I wish to banish from my mind those scenes of horror.

Brotherly kindness prevails more amongst the several denominations throughout New England than heretofore, and of course the prejudices against the Baptists are greatly abated. Nothing is more common than the most cordial invitations into the pulpits of the Pedobaptists when I travel through the country. I rejoice to hear that the same spirit prevails with you. Union in Christ, in my opinion, should lead his disciples to the strongest expressions of love towards one another.

The college edifice suffered greatly by the troops, who had it in possession nearly six years. To repair these damages has been a difficult task, while denied compensation from the public, and destitute of funds for that purpose. The members of the corporation have repeatedly submitted to make such partial repairs as were absolutely necessary to its preservation. With all these difficulties to combat, it begins, however, again to revive. It now consists of twenty-two members, and we expect an addition of several more this fall. Mr. Howell, my former colleague, has been for several years in the civil departments, and is now in the Continental Congress, where he has been upwards of two years. Mr. Asher Robbins,[1] an alumnus of Yale College, in Connecticut, is now a tutor.

Sept. 16. As no opportunity presented to forward the above, I beg leave to add that at the anniversary meeting of the corporation of the 1st instant, the Faculty testified their regard for Mr. Rippon by conferring on him the degree of Master in the Arts. I should have herewith sent the diploma, but could not get it written in time. Hope by the next opportunity to have it ready. Last week I attended the Association at Mr. Hunt's place in Middleborough. We had a most harmonious meeting; and though the addition to our churches is not so great as in some former

[1] Hon. Asher Robbins, LL.D. He was born in Connecticut, and was graduated at Yale College in the year 1782. Soon after completing his collegiate course, he was elected a tutor under Manning, which office he held for eight years. While thus occupied in quickening the diligence of his pupils, and in imbuing their minds with a genuine relish for the varied forms of classical beauty, he sought every opportunity to cultivate his own taste for the classics, and indeed for every species of elegant learning. After resigning his tutorship, he studied law under the Hon. William Channing, of Newport, at that time the Attorney General of Rhode Island. Here he established himself in the practice of the law, where he resided during the remainder of his life. From 1825 to 1839 he was an honored and useful member of the United States Senate. He seldom engaged in the debates of that body, but on no occasion, says Prof. Goddard, did he address the senate without leaving on the minds of all who heard him a decided impression of his high intellectual powers and accomplishments, of his ability as a statesman, and his acquisitions as a scholar. He died at Newport, in 1845, having lived, "by reason of his strength," fourscore years and more.

Mr. Robbins was the first librarian of Brown University, as we learn from a letter respecting its early history in which he thus writes: "At the reorganization of the college, in the autumn of 1782, I was appointed to the office of tutor, and took charge of the library as librarian. It was then kept in the east chamber, on the second floor, of the central building." A good likeness of Mr. Robbins is among the collection of portraits in Rhode Island Hall.

years past, yet there are many promising appearances of a revival in them. There were present some ministering brethren from the eastern part of New Hampshire, and Mr. Case, of whom Mr. Backus makes mention, as being signally blessed as an instrument in turning many to God in the northeastern parts of Massachusetts. They assured us that God was working wonders through a great extent of that newly-settled country, that gospel laborers were much wanted there, and that in the revivals great numbers embraced the Baptist principles. The most sorrowful accounts we received were from several places in the Massachusetts and Connecticut States, where Pedobaptists are again taxing our people, and seizing their persons and property, to compel them to support their worship. Poor men! They grudge their neighbors that liberty which they themselves enjoy, and for which, by their sides, they have fought and bled. This, however, in the issue may operate favorably. The whole body of Baptists seem determined to maintain their rights, and support those who may be called to suffer. This you will see by a resolution[1] entered into at the Association, the minutes of which I should have now sent had they been printed. Probably Mr. Stillman may obtain and enclose them before Capt. Scott sails. Last Lord's Day our church received in two persons. I had not been called on to administer baptism before in near two years. Others appear under serious impressions. May the Lord graciously revive his work. I forgot to mention that the Hon. Joseph Brown, a member of the corporation, a philosophical genius, was at our last meeting chosen Professor of Experimental Philosophy in this college; and Dr. Benjamin Waterhouse, M.D., of Leyden, was chosen Professor of Natural History, — both of whom engaged to give lectures in

[1] The following is an extract from the minutes of this meeting of the Warren Association, held at Middleborough, Mass., Sept. 7, 8, 1784, of which meeting President Manning was moderator: —

"Accounts were received from various parts of our country, that distress has lately been made upon a number of our brethren and friends for the support of a way of worship which we conscientiously dissent from; which is not only a violation of the law of God, but also directly against the fundamental principles of the late revolution in America; — therefore this Association are resolved to unite in the most prudent and vigorous measures for putting a stop to these oppressions, and to maintain the just rights of our brethren and friends; and for that end do make choice of the following committee of grievances, to act in this cause according to their best discretion; and we will recommend it to our several societies to communicate their proportion of the necessary expense hereof. The committee chosen for this purpose are our beloved Elders Stillman, Skillman, Smith of Haverhill, Backus, and Blood."

their respective branches, without any expense to the college while destitute of an endowment.

I fear I have wearied your patience, and therefore, with every sentiment of esteem, rest, dear sir,

Your unworthy brother and fellow-laborer in the gospel,

JAMES MANNING.

P. S. — The enclosed packet I beg you to forward to Mr. Evans, free of expense, if you can conveniently, besides a letter to him containing a catalogue of the books in the college library. He has encouraged us to hope for those duplicates which they have by a late donation, and of which we are destitute.

President Manning's reply to a letter from the Rev. Thomas Ustick, to which reference is made in the foregoing, gives more in detail the persecutions of the Baptists under the oppressive laws of Massachusetts and Connecticut: —

TO THE REV. THOMAS USTICK, PHILADELPHIA.

PROVIDENCE, Sept. 17, 1784.

REVEREND SIR:

Yours of July 11th ult. came to hand; but having no good opportunity of sending an answer, and being much engaged otherwise, I omitted an answer until now. I am glad your long suit has determined in favor of the church. I hope God will dispose you to make a proper improvement of so distinguished a favor, and the people be disposed to employ their property to his glory. I have communicated the contents of your letter, agreeably to your request. Last week I attended the Association at Elder Hinds's, Middleborough. Had an agreeable meeting, but find the Congregationalists in Cambridge, Brookfield, Woodstock in Connecticut, with some other places, have made distress on the Baptists this last summer. Some went to jail; from others they took their stock, land, etc. This does not look much like liberty. The Association recommended the paying not the least attention to their ecclesiastical laws, and resolved that they were determined to maintain their claims of equal liberty, etc., and would recommend to the churches to support the sufferers. I am surprised that they are not ashamed to hold up their heads, in this enlightened age, in such a shameful cause. But perhaps God means it for good.

We had several ministering brethren from New Hampshire and the northeastern parts of Massachusetts, who refreshed us much with good tidings from that quarter. Many have there been turned to the Lord, and the good work still goes on. The subjects of it generally adopt believer's baptism. There are great calls for gospel ministers in that quarter. I think the aspect of things is more favorable in our churches, public worship better attended, the ministry better supported, and some appearance of a revival of God's work. Even poor Providence seems to share a little. I baptized one young man last Lord's Day, and some more are under serious impressions. Mr. Ingalls preaches at Grafton. He told me the other day the people retained a great affection for you, and recently wished to hear from you. I think the college is in a growing state. I expect our number will exceed thirty at the close of vacation. At the last corporation meeting the Faculty conferred the degree of LL.D. on Governor Hopkins our chancellor, and of A.M. on Mr. John Rippon, Dr. Gill's successor. Mr. Joseph Brown was chosen Professor of Experimental Philosophy, and Dr. Benjamin Waterhouse, Professor of Natural History. They have both engaged to lecture without salary from the college until there shall be proper endowments for those chairs. Miss Joey, daughter of Nicholas Brown, is in a decline. I believe the rest of your friends are well as usual. With sentiments of esteem and respect to Mrs. Ustick and friends,

I am, etc.,

JAMES MANNING.

The Rev. Elhanan Winchester, to whom reference is made in the preceding correspondence, had been a Baptist clergyman of great repute in New England. He was born in Brookline, Mass., on the 30th of September, 1751. At the age of nineteen he became pious, and united with the church in his native town. Soon afterwards he commenced the public work of the ministry. Subsequently experiencing a change in some of his views of religion, he visited Canterbury, Ct., where he was baptized by Elder Ebenezer Lyon, and received as a member of the Baptist church. In the spring of 1771 he removed to Rehoboth, Mass., where he remained one year. He afterwards preached in various parts of New England and South Carolina. His extraordinary memory, his eloquence, and apparent zeal, excited great interest, and multitudes flocked to hear him. Unusual success attended his ministry, and his name became celebrated in all the churches. In the year 1781 he removed to Philadelphia, where he advocated the doctrine of universal restoration, and was excluded in consequence from the fellowship of the Baptist denomination.[1] He preached for several years to his adherents

[1] An account of this affair may be found in a little pamphlet entitled " An Address from the Baptist Church in Philadelphia, to their Sister Churches of the same Denomination, throughout the Confederate States of North America. Drawn up by a Committee of the Church appointed for said purpose." 18mo. Philadelphia: Printed by Robert Aitken, 1781, pp. 16. A few extracts from this rare pamphlet may fitly appear in this connection.

" In the beginning of October, 1780, Mr. Elhanan Winchester, a native of Massachusetts Bay, New England, came as a messenger from the Warren Association to ours, which was then nigh at hand. Many of the members having, previous to this, repeatedly heard him preach, not the least suspicion existed but that he continued an advocate for that faith which we look upon as the *faith once delivered to the saints*. Accordingly, at a meeting for business the 9th of said month, it was agreed to use our best endeavors to prevail on him to stay, and preach for us a limited time. In two or three days after this, the Rev. Oliver Hart arrived in town from South Carolina; we were, therefore, from many considerations, prevented doing anything decisive, until the 23d, when, at an assembly both of the church and congregation, it was, by the majority then present, deemed most consistent with the resolution of the 9th (a deviation therefrom carrying with it an appearance of injustice) to give Mr. Winchester an invitation to tarry with us during the space of one year. Being waited upon, and made acquainted with the circumstances attending the choice, he answered, ' That he was sorry we were not entirely unanimous therein; but, nevertheless, consented to supply our pulpit for six months, at least, and longer if everything should prove agreeable.'

. . . .

" Popular applause, the idol which too many worship, was soon discovered to be an object zealously sought for and courted by Mr. Winchester. To accomplish this, persons were every week hastily admitted to baptism, upon the slightest examination; though we really believe that among the number are several sincere Christians, who, during this season of trial, have not been ashamed openly to discountenance his errors. Various innovations, contrary to our established discipline, were introduced through his means. The church undertook

in Philadelphia, among whom his biographer includes the celebrated Dr. Benjamin Rush, and Dr. John Redman, first President of the College of Physicians in Philadelphia. In 1787 he removed to London. He published many religious and controversial works, the most important of which are, Dialogues on Universal Restoration; Lectures on the Prophecies, 2 vols. 8vo.; Letters on the Divinity of Christ; Defence of Revelation; Oration on the Discov-

a reform. In some respects success attended us; in others, an obstinate adherence marked his character.

"The principal foundation of the greatest uneasiness we shall now proceed to consider. Early in the winter it was whispered to a few, that Mr. Winchester, notwithstanding his artful endeavors to conceal the same in his public discourses, held the doctrine of a final restoration of bad men and angels from hell; that the whole of Adam's progeny, yea, the devils themselves, at certain different periods, would be delivered from their torment, and made completely happy; in other words, that he peremptorily denied the endless duration or perpetuity of future punishment. The method taken by him, at first, to propagate this wicked tenet, was by 'creeping into houses, and leading captive persons of weak capacities,' wherein he met with too much encouragement. Alarmed at this authenticated report, he was at different times privately conversed with on the subject by several of the members. He did not presume to contradict it fully, and yet his confession was by no means satisfactory. Upon these occasions he would frequently intimate his intention of going away, provided the smallest division took place on his account; while at the same juncture, as opportunity served, he failed not to use arguments in order to gain proselytes."

The result of all this, the Address goes on to add, was the introduction of the whole matter at a church meeting held on the 5th of March, 1781. Much debating ensued; the members became divided into two distinct parties, and finally a protest against the doctrine of universal restoration, as a dangerous heresy, was signed by sixty-seven of the most substantial and influential members of the church. This number was afterwards increased to eighty-six. Upon a motion made to wait on Mr. Winchester, and inform him that he could not, with propriety, be allowed to preach for them any longer, the protestors found themselves in a small minority, Mr. Winchester's adherents, including many of the "sisters" and younger members of the church, "being *rather* the most numerous." The church at this time numbered about one hundred and seventy. The protestors, however, conscious of having truth and justice on their side, viewed themselves as fully authorized to act independently of the new party. They accordingly appointed a committee of two to wait on Mr. Winchester at his lodgings. This committee, failing to find him at home, addressed him a letter, which

ery of America, with an Appendix; Reigning Abominations; various sermons, etc. Mr. Winchester died on the 18th of April, 1797, aged forty-six years. He appears to have been a man of sincere piety, notwithstanding the change in his theological opinions. His biography, by the Rev. Edwin M. Stone, of Providence, was published by Brewster of Boston, in 1836. The book, which contains an excellent portrait of Winchester, is now extremely rare.

From the following letter it appears that the college at this time, notwithstanding the financial embarrassments of the people in consequence of the war, promised better than at any former period of its existence: —

TO THE REV. DR. SMITH.

PROVIDENCE, July 3, 1784.

DEAR SIR:

By some means I mislaid your last to me in which you mention some buddings of a spiritual nature amongst you. I rejoice to hear it. Hope

he returned at once, unopened. On Thursday evening, March the 8th, his friends broke into the meeting-house, and took forcible possession thereof, Mr. Winchester preaching notwithstanding the confusion. On the ensuing Sabbath he administered the Lord's Supper. A council of ministers was now called, and committees representing the two parties were appointed to meet them, with a view to an amicable adjustment of the difficulties. Failing in this, the members of the New Party, so called, were, by advice of the council, formally excluded from the church. Subsequently Mr. Winchester was, by the action of the Philadelphia and Warren Associations, formally excluded from the fellowship of the Baptist denomination.

The Address, of which we have given the substance, was dated May 14, 1781, and signed by Samuel Miles, William Rogers, Thomas Shields, and John M'Kim. The suit for the possession of the house and property was, as we have already seen, finally decided in favor of the Protestors, as they were then called. We have devoted more space than could be well spared to this matter, because of its importance, and also because it is frequently alluded to in Manning's correspondence. Indeed, Manning was himself prominent in the affair. Mr. Ustick, Winchester's immediate successor, was received by the church on his recommendation; and he was a member of a committee appointed by the Philadelphia Association, in 1781, to investigate and report to said body the proceedings of the church in reference to Winchester and his doctrines.

it may gloriously increase. I returned the 27th ult. Mrs. Manning sailed that day sennight to enjoy the last interview with her dear mamma, just about to leave us by a consumption, and very desirous of seeing her. She arrived at New York last Tuesday. Your friends, as far as I could hear, are in usual health. The Plains are destitute of a minister. They intend to try for Sammy Jones. Mr. Runyon is settled at Piscataway, where are some appearances of a revival. The general meeting was crowded, ten or eleven ministers present, and amongst them Mr. Hart, who, I think, will settle at Hopewell. Cranberry is visited with a revival, as are some other places in some small degree, especially under the ministry of Mr. Wilson, of Bordentown. Mr. Gano's meeting-house is completely repaired and his congregation very full. Things look rather promising in New York, though the people are poor after their exile. I never enjoyed more freedom in preaching in any journey in my life, nor was I ever more attended to. The college consists of twenty-three students, nine being added since the vacation. More than a dozen are expected to enter in the fall. We have a number of promising youth, and amongst them is my nephew Jimmy, son of Jeremiah. Mr. Wilkinson[1]

[1] William Wilkinson, who was graduated in 1783. He immediately took charge of the college Latin school, which charge he retained until 1792. He was eminently successful as a teacher, and fitted for college many of its distinguished alumni. In 1785 he was appointed librarian of the college. As the history of the Latin school forms a part of our college history, we may be pardoned for introducing here an advertisement from the *Providence Gazette*, by which it appears that the connection which had existed between the school and the college was for a time dissolved: —

"William Wilkinson informs the public, that, by the advice of the school committee, he proposes removing his school from the college edifice, on Monday next, to the brick schoolhouse; and, sensible of the many advantages resulting from a proper method of instruction in the English language, he has, by the committee's approbation, associated with him Mr. Asa Learned, as an English instructor. Those gentlemen and ladies who may wish to employ them in the several branches of the Greek, Latin, and English languages taught grammatically, arithmetic, and writing, may depend on the utmost attention being paid to their children. Greek and Latin at twenty-four shillings per quarter; English at sixteen shillings.

WILKINSON AND LEARNED.

PROVIDENCE, Oct. 20, 1786."

In tracing further the history of this Latin or grammar school, we find in the records of the corporation, under date of Sept. 4, 1794, the following: "*Voted*, That the President use his influence and endeavor to establish a grammar school in this town, as an appendage to this college, to be under the immediate visitais a good master. The school is nearly up to twenty. All the rooms in the two lower stories are now full, and we must go directly to finishing the two upper ones, at least the third, if we can possibly devise ways and means; which I expect will be very difficult. I think the advice you gave Mr. Wood was right, and he will doubtless fare as well on the subject of advancement with us as at Jersey College. The institution promises better now than at any period of its existence. Had we about one or two thousand pounds more to provide for a suitable tuition, I should rejoice. Secure of your interest in sending us scholars, I shall say nothing on that head, but as the bearer, Capt. Thivell, is waiting, must conclude with best wishes to you, lady, and all friends.

Yours, as ever,

JAMES MANNING.

P. S. — Miss Joey Brown, daughter of Nicholas, is fast declining. Her disorder is thought to be the consumption.

President Manning now begins a correspondence with the Rev. Dr. Caleb Evans, President of the Baptist academy in Bristol. His father was the Rev. Hugh Evans, one of the most distinguished Baptist ministers of his day. Dr. Evans proved to be a warm friend of the college, and was the means of securing valuable books for the library. He died on the 9th of August, 1791, in the fifty-fourth year of his age. He published a collection of hymns, and numerous sermons and addresses, the greater part of which are to be found in the library. "Our Baptist college in America," says Dr. Rippon, "was proud to confer on him her highest honors, in which she was followed by the principal and professors of the King's College, Aberdeen, in the year 1789."

tion of the President, and the general inspection of the town's school committee, and that the President also procure a suitable master for such school." This resolution was doubtless carried into effect. Fifteen years afterwards, as we have already stated in a previous chapter (see page 198), the corporation erected a brick building for the accommodation of the school, at an expense of fifteen hundred dollars. This building, which has since been enlarged, is the one now occupied as the "University Grammar School."

PROVIDENCE, Sept. 13, 1784.

REVEREND SIR:

I have long wished for a favorable opportunity of introducing myself to you, and am happy that one has at length offered, by answering your request in a late letter to my friend and brother Rev. Samuel Stillman, of Boston. Enclosed is the catalogue of all the books now belonging to the college. Nearly one half of them have their bindings much broken, as they were old when presented. Besides the enclosed we have ordered out from London this fall about fourteen hundred volumes, a catalogue of which we sent to Dr. Stennett, requesting his advice to the merchants, Messrs. Champion and Dickinson, in the purchase of them, hoping that he may point out where they can be had second-hand, etc. Of this you may obtain a sight by applying to the Doctor. Together with that we sent a catalogue of books which we are not able to purchase, but which we should be glad to receive by way of donation, should any of our friends be so disposed. Were I not oppressed with cares, and at present destitute of assistance, I would send them to you also. If, however, I can make out a copy of these catalogues before the ship sails, they shall accompany this. The above-mentioned fourteen hundred volumes are a donation from our treasurer, John Brown, Esq., of Providence. The amount of two hundred pounds sterling was also ordered to be expended in the purchase of a necessary philosophical apparatus, in addition to what we already have, consisting chiefly of a telescope, an air-pump and its apparatus, globes, and a thermometer. The money for this order was subscribed by other members of the corporation last fall. A list of these articles was also forwarded to Dr. Stennett.

Your kind attention to the interests of the college, and the proffer of your services, were sensibly felt by the corporation at their annual meeting this present month; and it is in obedience to their commands, imposed by the following vote, that I now write: "*Voted,* That the Rev. Messrs. President Manning and Samuel Stillman be a committee to write to the Rev. Hugh Evans of Bristol, and other gentlemen in England, and enclose the catalogue of books belonging to the college, and endeavor to procure such donations in books, apparatus, and money as may be obtained from thence; and also consult Dr. Stennett on the expediency of sending a person to England to solicit donations for the college."

At the commencement of the war the college was in a growing state. The number of students was about forty, and there was a good Latin school in the edifice. In 1776 it was delivered up, or rather taken possession of by the troops as a barrack and hospital, and continued to be occupied by the militia, Continental and French troops, and seamen, until June, 1782. During this period the house sustained great damages, for which we have received no compensation yet, nor have we much prospect of it in future. This has thrown a heavy burden on the corporation, and greatly embarrassed them in making the necessary repairs, especially as our fund is small. This we have made many efforts to augment by collections, etc., in this country, but to so little purpose that our whole fund produces but about sixty pounds sterling per annum. The distressed and exhausted state of the country by war, leaves us little room soon to hope for much from this quarter, especially as money is become so scarce that our people in the country, although possessed of property, cannot command sufficient to pay their taxes. We are unwilling however to relinquish our design, as it is evident that the institution has already greatly contributed to the perpetuity of our denomination, and begins again to attract the public attention. The number of students already in college, and of those we expect in the course of the fall, is upwards of thirty. In teaching I have the assistance of one tutor. A small Latin school is kept up in the college. Any services you can render in endowing it will be most acceptable to the corporation.

Last week I attended our Association at Middleborough, and though several of the remote churches did not send messengers, a great number of Christian friends met and enjoyed a harmonious and agreeable interview. Were the minutes printed I would enclose them. In several places there is a happy revival of religion, especially in the eastern parts of Massachusetts, and I am not without encouragement under my poor ministry. The doctrine of religious, as well as civil liberty, is in general better understood in New England than before the Revolution notwithstanding in places the persons and property of several of our friends have been seized on for ministerial rates. I think it not improbable that the rapid increase of our society will provoke some of our neighbors to give us much trouble; but it affords encouragement that the whole body are determined to maintain their rights and support the burden which may first fall upon individuals. Possibly the knowledge of this resolution entered into at our last annual meeting may deter our oppressors. If not, may the great Head of the church furnish us with grace to suffer like Christians.

I have often heard of your Education Society, and of its great utility in training up young men for the ministry. My highly respected friend and your brother-in-law, Thomas Mullet, Esq., gave me the best account of it which I have yet received ; still, if it be not too troublesome I should be glad to receive further information respecting it, and I will engage to repay it in any information you wish for in my power to give.

In a letter to Dr. Stennett, last fall, I gave a pretty full account of the state of religion and some other matters in this new world; it was in answer to his request in a letter by Mr. Mullett. If this letter reached him, it is not improbable that you have seen it, as I requested him to communicate the contents to those of our friends who might wish to hear from us. On the opening again of the communication between both countries, it was pleasing to find our brethren in England, at least a great number of them, so much interested in our welfare. How strong a proof this of the reality of that Christian love and unity in the spirit which is the genuine fruit of a gracious principle ! The same temper is manifested here towards our brethren in England. There is the same joy expressed on hearing that Christ's kingdom is advancing with you which appeared before the war. And why should it not be so, since his kingdom is but one ? Dependence or independence therefore should make no difference amongst his subjects, who consist of the elect out of different people, nations, and languages. The privilege of a correspondence with Mr. Evans I shall highly prize, if not too troublesome to him; and he may depend on punctuality on the part of his unworthy friend and brother,

JAMES MANNING.

To this letter Dr. Evans replies : —

BRISTOL, ENGLAND, Jan. 26, 1785.

DEAR SIR:

As the extensive connections in which my brother is engaged on your wide-extended continent render it advisable for him once more to traverse the mighty waters, and to pay a visit to his American friends, in which number you hold a distinguished place, I gladly embrace the opportunity of accepting your correspondence, and replying to your favor of the 13th of September last, which I received in due course in November. I shall be truly happy to do anything in my power to promote the prosperity of the infant college over which you so worthily preside, and shall omit no opportunity that offers of testifying my regards to it. Charity, you know, the old proverb says, should *begin* at home, but I think it should not *end* there, but flow on without control to the utmost limits of possibility. I had so little time with Dr. Stennett when I was in London that we had no opportunity of entering upon the affairs of your college as I wished to have done, nor could I have a sight of the catalogue of the books lately purchased. I shall nevertheless pursue the design of obtaining for you such of our duplicates as may be worthy your acceptance, without strictly adhering to what you already have, because you may easily exchange, as you observe, such as may prove superfluous. But this cannot be accomplished till August next, as our Society will have no meeting till that time. As to a person's coming over here to solicit benefactions, I rather fear it would not at present be advisable; but should Dr. Stennett think otherwise, and a proper person should come, especially if it were either yourself or Dr. Stillman, I would readily use my utmost efforts to promote his success. Our friends in general are well enough affected to America, but many of them have very little idea of the utility of academical institutions, though it is evident the prejudices are wearing away. I am sorry to see, as well by the account Mr. Mullett gives me as by your letter, that religion is at so low an ebb amongst you, though I doubt not the time will come when it will again run and be glorified. There have been on your continent, in years past, many enemies against revivals, and your set time to favor Zion will, I doubt not, yet come again. Your church is, however, I hear, flourishing, as also Mr. Stillman's and some others. Blessed be God, we have cause for thankfulness here. One of our churches in this city lately baptized twenty, and probably before this letter leaves this place I shall have the pleasure of receiving something more than an equal number to the solemn rite. And yet still we have much cause to complain of lukewarmness and formality. Dr. Stennett's Discourses on Domestic Duties you have probably seen, and probably Mr. Booth's treatise on Baptism, the most elaborate and decisive performance upon that subject that has ever yet been published, or probably ever will be. I enclose you one of our last associational letters, and a sermon lately published by one of our ministers on Walking by Faith, which I beg your acceptance of, as also a fifth volume of Saurin to complete the set which Mr. Mullett tells me he presented to your college, and which he had of me for his own use on the voyage. Amongst the books you may expect in the fall are the Polyglott General Dictionary, 10 vols., including Bayle, Biographical Dictionary, and many others equally valuable. I shall wish your direction how to send them. I will, my dear sir, detain you no longer than to express my warmest wishes for the increasing prosperity of the church and college over which you preside, the revival of the interests of literature and true religion through the American continent and the whole world, and recommend my brother to your continued friendship. I remain,

Yours, affectionately, in the endearing bonds of gospel love,

CALEB EVANS.

In his correspondence with Evans, Dr. Manning, it will be observed, speaks of being "oppressed with cares." The number and variety of his cares may be inferred from the following amusing extract from a letter written by Dr. Waterhouse, which we find quoted in the memoir by Prof. Goddard: "I never shall forget what Dr. Manning, in great good humor, told me were among his 'trying experiences.' He told me that his salary was only eighty pounds per annum, and that for this pittance he performed all the duties of President of the college; heard two classes recite every day; listened to complaints, foreign and domestic, from undergraduates and their parents, of both sexes, and answered them, now and then by letter; waited generally on all transient visitors into college, etc. Nor was this all. 'I made,' said Dr. Manning, 'my own garden, and took care of it; repaired my dilapidated walls; went nearly every day to market; preached twice a week, and sometimes oftener; attended, by solicitation, the funeral of every baby that died in Providence; visited the sick of my own society, and not unfrequently the sick of other societies; made numerous parochial visits, the poorest people exacting the longest, and, in case of any seeming neglect, finding fault the most.'" Amid all these perplexing cares, which allowed him but scanty time for premeditating his sermons, we have the testimony of Dr. Waterhouse for adding that "the honorable and worthy man never complained."

REV. ABRAHAM BOOTH TO MANNING.

LONDON, June 30, 1784.

DEAR SIR:

It is with pleasure that I reflect on a restoration of intercourse between Great Britain and America, after so long an interruption by so destructive a war. May a kind Providence yet render the two countries mutually useful to each other. Having a favorable opportunity, I here present you with a publication or two. Shall be glad to hear of their obtaining your approbation.

You will much oblige me by transmitting the enclosed parcel to Mr. Stillman ; and you will increase the obligation by favoring me with a few lines your first opportunity.

Taking it for granted that Dr. Stennett will give you some account of the state of religion amongst us in the country, I have nothing to add but my ardent prayers that a kind Providence may bless your confederated provinces with peace and prosperity, and that the great Head of the church may cause pure and undefiled religion to flourish in all your academies, your churches, and through all your extensive country. I conclude, and remain,

Your cordial friend and unworthy brother,

A. BOOTH.

P. S.—Mr. Benjamin Wallin died upwards of two years ago.

To the above Manning replies:—

PROVIDENCE, Oct. 3, 1784.

DEAR SIR:

On my return from New York, four days ago, I was so happy as to find a line from Mr. A. Booth, accompanied with the publications mentioned. My present hurry has permitted me to examine but little more than the titlepages, but from my predilection for the author of the Reign of Grace, I am persuaded any publication of his will be highly acceptable. My next shall inform you of my opinion of the publications on perusal. In the mean time I beg you to accept my hearty thanks for the donation. By the ship Hope, belonging to this town, and by the bearer, Dr. Solomon Drowne, who goes as a passenger in her, I embrace the opportunity of acknowledging the receipt of yours. Mr. Drowne is a son of the college, a gentleman of remarkable modesty, who, having passed through the best medical schools in this country, now visits Europe with views of further improvement in the line of his profession. He is a member of the corporation, and of unblemished character, on whose information you may safely rely respecting the college, or any other matters. As such I beg leave to introduce him to your notice, and refer you to him for particulars.

The restoration of public tranquillity and a free intercourse between the two countries, after so long an interruption, is matter of thanksgiving to God. Few, perhaps, in either country, more sincerely regretted this interruption than your unworthy friend; to which no consideration could ever reconcile him except that of making a part of the plan of His administration who is infinite in wisdom. Conciliatory measures, I doubt not, will render both countries reciprocally useful.

I have transmitted the letter and parcel to Mr. Stillman by a safe hand. I have not yet been so happy as to receive a line from Dr. Stennett, which I am daily expecting, with the wished-for information. Enclosed I send you a copy of our last Association minutes. This will give you a general view of the state of a number of our churches. Since that time I have received authentic accounts of a most glorious work of God, in what is called the State of Vermont, formerly the Hampshire grants, on the west side of Connecticut river. It extends over well-neigh half the peopled part of that territory, and appears increasing. The eastern part of Massachusetts continues still to be remarkably visited in the same way, and the prospect brightens at New York and in many parts of the Western States. Some drops have also fallen on Providence, Newport, and Swanzey, with several other places My attention, however, is so much called for at the college, that I cannot visit, as I wish to do, and rejoice together with them. A long letter to Dr. Stennett, last fall, which you have probably seen, gave some general accounts of the state of religion amongst us since the commencement of the war. I shall not therefore repeat what I then wrote, — only observe that two of the leaders in what they called the New Dispensation, but others the Shaking Quakers, have, notwithstanding their boasted immortality, lately died; one of whom was, as they termed her, the elect lady. The adherents, I am told, to that fanatical system, are falling off and renouncing it. Their folly indeed has been made abundantly manifest. It is the general opinion of serious people that these shakings presage something glorious to the church of God. May the Lord grant an accomplishment of their wishes.

The mournful news of Mr. Wallin's death reached us more than a year ago. When he died a truly great man in our Israel tell; but I doubt not it was his gain.

Your ardent wishes for our national prosperity, but more especially for that of the churches of Christ in this new world, are peculiarly acceptable. Permit me to repay them by wishes as ardent for Great Britain and Ireland, those lands of our forefathers' nativity, and for the advancement of the glorious kingdom of our common Lord throughout the same, and indeed throughout the whole world.

A line from Mr. Booth will always be very acceptable to his sincere friend and unworthy brother,

JAMES MANNING.

TO THE REV. JOHN RYLAND, JR.

PROVIDENCE, NOV. 12, 1784.

REVEREND AND DEAR SIR:

I beg leave to embrace this opportunity to confess my fault in not forwarding your diploma before now. By some unaccountable neglect it was mislaid till a few days since.

You will forgive the execution, as the writing is but indifferent, nor could we at that time procure it done otherwise. It is, however, a small testimony of our regard for the merit of Mr. Ryland, and as such we beg you to accept it.

The long and agreeable correspondence I was honored with by your father (to whom I have written since the war) leads me to wish for the continuance of it. But if his advanced age or engagements forbid it, I wish for it from his son, and, as I am told, successor in the school at Northampton. I heartily wish you success in the important employment of educating youth, and in preaching the gospel of our glorious Saviour.

We have seen days of sorrow during the late calamitous war, but blessed be God that I have lived to see a period to it, and a free intercourse again opened between us and Great Britain. Some agreeable letters have already reached me from several friends in England, more of which I hope for soon; also more particular accounts of the state of religion in general and your society in particular. I long to read some of those old-fashioned letters from Rev. John Ryland in this way. They will however be very acceptable from his son.

The college is reviving. Thirty students have already entered, and more are expected. We have in part repaired the damages of the house, which were very great, by the wanton waste of the soldiery. I have the assistance of one tutor. We need more help, but the low state of our funds will not support another, and the scarcity of cash at present in this country forbids our hopes of augmenting our little stock. We were so fortunate, in the wreck of public credit during the war, as to preserve our little fund undiminished. In the eastern part of Massachusetts and in the State of Vermont there is a most glorious work of God, which has continued for some time and still increases. Please to present my best regards to your honored father, and believe me, with every sentiment of esteem, dear sir,

Your unworthy brother,

JAMES MANNING.

TO THE REV. DR. RIPPON.

PROVIDENCE, Nov. 12, 1784.

REVEREND AND DEAR SIR:

This will be handed you by my friend, Dr. Solomon Drowne, of Providence, a son of the college, a gentleman of great modesty, who visits your city with views of further medical improvement. I beg leave to recommend him to you as a man of good character, and a Fellow of the college. Through him you may receive what information you wish respecting the college, etc. Together with this you will receive the diploma I mentioned in my last. We beg you to accept it as a testimony of our respect for the character and merit of Mr. Rippon. I must apologize for the writing. It was done in a hurry, and by a young hand.

The Lord's work still goes on gloriously in the eastern parts of Massachusetts and Vermont. By recent advice from these parts we are assured that whole congregations, almost, of Congregationalists, embrace the Baptist principles; and in one instance their minister was baptized with his people. Several useful ministers are raised up amongst them lately in that wilderness. This looks somewhat like the coming of our Redeemer's kingdom. With me you say amen! Come, Lord Jesus, come quickly. In great haste, I am, dear sir,

Your unworthy brother and fellow-believer in Jesus,

JAMES MANNING.

Mr. Drowne, whom Manning here introduces to Dr. Rippon, graduated from the college in the year 1773. Upon his return from Europe, he practised medicine in Providence for a while, then removed to Ohio, thence to Pennsylvania, and finally settled in the town of Foster, R. I., where he passed the remainder of his days in professional and agricultural pursuits, and in the cultivation of his taste for botany and for elegant letters. In 1811 he was appointed Professor of Materia Medica and Botany in Brown University, and for two or three seasons he delivered lectures to a class of medical students. He also lectured on botany to the undergraduates of the University, and to a private class of citizens. He died in 1834, at the advanced age of eighty-one years. A fine portrait of him is among the collection of portraits in Rhode Island Hall. Mr. Drowne was a Fellow of the University from 1783 until his death, a period of more than fifty-one years.

PROVIDENCE, Dec. 23, 1784.

TO THE HONORABLE DAVID HOWELL,
MEMBER OF CONGRESS IN PHILADELPHIA:

SIR: — Before you receive this, you will doubtless be advised of the melancholy situation of our common friend, Mr. Joseph Brown, who, upwards of four weeks since, received a violent shock of an apoplexy and numb palsy combined, which for some time caused his physicians and friends to despair of his life. But though he is much recovered, as to the use of his limbs and his speech, it forbids, in a great measure, our indulging a hope of his restoration to former usefulness. Joey, daughter of Nicholas Brown, still survives, but is in the last stage of her disorder. Mrs. Thurston, wife of the elder, died of the small pox last Friday. He and his family have it by inoculation, and are in a hopeful way to recover. I left Newport last Monday morning. Your family are in usual health, for aught I have heard to the contrary since my return. Mr. Wilkinson speaks favorably of Jeremiah's proficiency in and attention to Greek.

I have nothing new to advise you respecting the college. Our number is above thirty. We have heard that you very soon adjourned to Philadelphia, after your meeting at Trenton. I suppose you find better living and more diversion in the city; to which, if members of Congress are not entitled, I beg leave to know who are? I hope you will be good natured, unanimous, and attentive to the public business, conducting it to the great honor and advantage of the United States.

What think you of an application to Congress for the rents and damages of the college? Will it do this session or not? I fear it will become an old story, and that we, in the issue, shall lose the whole, if we defer it longer. What we ask is not only just, but greatly wanted at present. I beg you to feel round amongst the members, and form a judgment of the probability of success in case of an application. Should things appear promising, I will forward the papers, and indeed will come myself, *Deo volente*, in the spring, if you think it can be of any use.

You remember I mentioned to you the case of our farm in the Jerseys, and our thoughts of selling it for public securities. What is your opinion? Will Congress, this session, provide for paying the interest on final-settlement notes equally with that of loan-office certificates, or not? From the face of things at present with you, is it your opinion that public securities will appreciate soon? If so, which species of them are the most likely to do so? If Congress takes up this subject, how long do you expect it will be first? I wish a resolution of these queries when your leisure will permit. Are you likely to open a land-office soon, to dispose of any of the Western territory? What concessions have the Indians made to the commissioners sent out to treat with them? Will they sell any part of their lands to the States? or do they oppose our extending our settlements? What will be the terms, if Congress opens an office, on which they will dispose of their lands? It is the ardent wish here that something may speedily be done with our new acquisitions towards raising our public credit, and alleviating the burdens of taxation, under which the people at present groan. And if the way is paved by the commissioners, I see no reason for losing time, as money daily grows scarcer. This must affect the price of them greatly, at a future distant period, unless some expedient can be hit on to replenish the States with that useful article. Will not Congress establish a mint for the Union? I think this measure would be attended with advantage. While we neglect it, do we not, apparently, betray a diffidence or distrust of the continuance of our independence? A national coin would serve to strengthen the sinews of government, in my opinion, and might be managed so as to secure a medium in the country, I should think, which is certainly a great national object. But I shall begin to smile at my scribbling politics, and I shall provoke your risibilities no further; concluding by inquiring how you found friends in the Jerseys, requesting a line from you at your first leisure, and, joined with Mrs. Manning, presenting my best compliments. With sentiments of esteem, I am, respectfully,

Yours, etc.,

JAMES MANNING.

TO THE REV. THOMAS USTICK, PHILADELPHIA.

PROVIDENCE, March 4, 1785.

REVEREND AND DEAR SIR:

Unwilling to saddle you with postage to the amount of three or four shillings, as I had no other medium of conveyance, I have now before me yours of Dec. 24, and January, to which I have given you no answer. I presume, from not mentioning in your last the indisposition of your family, that your children are recovered. This, at least, I hope is the case. In addition to the procedure of the Pedobaptists, mentioned in my last, I now have to inform you that some time in this winter they took three of Mr. Thomas Green's people for minister's rates, and put them into Cambridge jail. You recollect that he lives in that town. Our friends have prosecuted them, and the trial comes on there the 9th inst. Perhaps a degree of this opposition to the truth of the gospel is necessary to engage a suitable attention to its importance. It is no argument in favor of the disposition of those who make it, but it may be a means of great good to those against whom it is made.

Some revivals in various parts of New England are encouraging amidst these trials. Providence in a small degree is blessed with some quickenings amongst Christians, and a few instances of late awakenings. I hope you may yet rejoice on this account in Pennsylvania.

The state of the college is as promising as we could reasonably expect. Our number is thirty-one, and more are expected to enter this spring. Mr. John Brown is about finishing the third story, which we expect to want in the course of this year, if those whom we expect should come. I believe our students are as orderly, industrious, and as good scholars as at any one period of the institution. One tutor is all the assistance which I have at present, Mr. Robbins, from Connecticut, who gives good satisfaction. Probably I shall be able to answer your request relative to Mr. Brown this spring before I visit the Jerseys, which I expect to do in May, without some unforseen cause should prevent it. The corporation at that time had resolved on an application to Congress for reparation of the damage done the college during its appropriation to public uses through the war, and have resolved to send me on that errand. In this I shall want every assistance from the friends of the institution, by letters to the members, etc. If your acquaintance with any of them will enable you to aid me, I know I am sure of that aid.

Mr. Joseph Brown's indisposition is indeed a very heavy stroke to us. The college and the church particularly feel it. There is little probability of his ever being restored to his former usefulness, though he again goes a little abroad. I have attended to your request in respect to the minutes you enclosed. I am sorry to hear of the acrimony among you respecting the officers of government. I think it very imprudent in the Presbyterians, as well as injurious, to wish to engross these to themselves. But that profession has been of old impeached of a propensity this way, and, as St. Paul somewhere says, I partly believe it.

As I am thoroughly conscious of my want of qualifications for the grade you mention, so I do not wish it. It is perhaps, at best, but an empty sound, and rendered, in too many instances, still more so by the characters of those on whom it has been bestowed, for a place in whose catalogue I have no ambition.[1] I thank you, however, for your kind attention. You have my hearty thanks for your expressions of friendship to the college. You reason rightly with the Baptists respecting this matter, who, one would think, have sufficient proofs of the propriety of it, from the struggles amongst themselves. But we are, and ever have been, in these respects, a wrong-headed people. I am happy to have a better opinion of their hearts. I hope Mr. Rogers's lecturing may be of use, and that you may both labor with great success, and, as father Alden says, with good agreement.

I am sensible that your attention to a school must greatly interfere with your discharge of the duty of a pastor, but I hope this may not be without its good effect to counterbalance that loss, since there appears to be a *needs be* for it. In your letter to Mr. Pitman you mentioned Winchester, in possession of his fifth wife and a red coat. Please, in your

[1] President Manning here refers, doubtless, to the honorary degree of Doctor in Divinity, which the University of Pennsylvania, as appears from their triennial catalogue, conferred upon him during the present year. Our readers will not fail to observe, that while Manning seems to have been indifferent in regard to his own honors and emoluments, he was careful in conferring the honors of Rhode Island College upon the worthy who desired them.

next, to give us the particulars of that eccentric genius, his adherents, success, etc., etc.

Mrs. Manning has been restored to her health for some time, except a cold, which at present incommodes her. Joey Brown died in the fore part of winter, — as ripe for heaven, by every evidence which could be wished for, as almost any person I ever saw. Many have dropped off this winter in this town and Newport by chronic complaints, but at present good health is more prevalent.

With best respects to Mrs. Ustick and friends, in which Mrs. Manning joins, and with sentiments of esteem, I am, as ever,

Yours, etc.,

JAMES MANNING.

PROVIDENCE, March 21, 1785.

TO THE HONORABLE DAVID HOWELL,

IN CONGRESS AT NEW YORK:

SIR: — And the snow three and four feet deep! what do you think of that? How do you think Mrs. Howell fares this inclement, protracted winter? — not to mention the cows, old Sorrel, etc., in regard to hay. But I beg pardon for calling your attention from that higher region where you are conversant, in settling the nation, to these sublunary things. To be serious, we have not only had a hard winter, but the spring, thus far, is much of the same tenor. We talk here much of removing to the temperate climate of Kentucky to avoid this snow and frost, which throw us into a torpid state so great a part of the year. I saw your papa and family at meeting yesterday; all well. Your friends in general are well. I have enclosed Mr. Carter's paper of the 12th instant, containing the law made at the last session of the General Assembly in relation to the import, in Mr. Van. Horn's letter, which I authorize you to open that you may see it, provided you have not yet received it. But I beg you to reëndorse it and direct it to Mr. Van Horn, to be left at Mr. Ustick's. The college remains *in statu quo.* item, the church, congregation, politics of the town, etc., for aught I know. I thank you for the newspapers you sent me. I think the address to the York Assembly *labored.* Will it compass their ends? It is diverting enough to hear Doctors Ewing and Rush endeavoring to expose each other for their *latent* zeal for the *Kirk,* and exhibiting to the world the *naked truth.* If, by their quarrel, *an old proverb should be verified,* it might afford matter of rejoicing to many. But they are members of the *militant* church, and so I leave them to box it out. I told you in my last that the corporation had resolved to send me forward in the spring to Congress, as you desired. But as you did not give much encouragement of success from the application, I beg leave to inquire what you think of the probability of our procuring a grant of some part of the Western territory, instead of a grant of money, as I perceive, by your letter to Mr. Brown, you expect a land-office to be opened in the spring? This would not augment the public debt, and would in time be productive for the college. Rather than get nothing, I should be glad to accept of this. This, however, is only a thought of my own, and suggested for your consideration, on which I should be glad of your opinion, in your next, that I may take the sense of the corporation on this subject before I set out.

Pray, how go final-settlement notes and other continental securities in New York at present? You need not have been quite so short in your last, for I make a point of writing whenever I can find anything to say; and would you wish, after reading this, to have me write again and say nothing? If so, I can spill ink and spoil paper as fast as most of my neighbors.

Pray, what is likely to be the result of the wranglings of the Dutch and the Emperor? Will there be a general war, and if so will it reach us? You stand on the watchtower, and can tell us, we presume, what may be depended on. Now there is a claim entered for a very long letter, by next post, by, sir,

Your humble servant,

JAMES MANNING.

To Thomas Mackaness, Esq., of London, to whom, it seems, Dr. Manning had shown kind attentions while a captive at Providence during the war, he thus writes: —

PROVIDENCE, July 10, 1785.

DEAR SIR:

Yours of April 27, 1785, with the box of books, containing five volumes quarto of Witsner's Works, in Latin, came safe by the hand of Mr. Fry. When they arrived I was absent at New York, or I should have embraced an earlier opportunity of presenting my thanks to Mr. Mackaness for the donation, and the kind attention which you have been pleased to pay to me. Your letter last winter, by your son-in-law, came safe to hand, but I had not the pleasure of seeing him. I took the earliest opportunity of forwarding you a letter, by the care of our common friend Deacon Mason, of Boston, in hopes it might have reached Mr. Harvey's hands before he sailed. I am sorry you did not receive it. A visit from you to your Providence friends was greatly wished for, and indeed expected. Messrs. Jos. Rogers and Geo. Benson are well. The former is mourning the loss of a dear and amiable wife. He feels that the hand of God has touched him. He could sympathize with you in calling to remembrance the tender and afflictive scenes through which you have passed. I am glad to find that you think, however stormy the path, that you have been led the right way towards the city of habitation. I sincerely wish your afflictions may be sanctified, so as to work for you "a far more exceeding and eternal weight of glory." I hope you may be so happy as to settle your children to your mind; but I should not think they had fixed upon the most agreeable place. Yet contentment and industry will, anywhere, answer the purposes of this life, which is, at best, but a short passage to a long eternity.

The kind mention which you say you have heard made of me by your honorable friend is pleasingly flattering, as, from his universal character, there are few men on earth of whose approbation I should be more ambitious. The little services, if they may be termed services, in my power to render you when here a captive, gave me, I am confident, a much higher degree of pleasure than they could possibly afford you. That "it is more blessed to give than to receive" I have found to be true as often as God has given me a heart to make the experiment, and I hope he will give me more of that disposition. Whether I shall ever be gratified in my wishes to see the place of your nativity or not, I have yet to learn. At several different times I thought the point nearly decided; but I am yet on the Hill at Providence, overwhelmed with cares. And though I think my services of little importance to the church and college, my brethren and masters, it seems, think my presence here of some importance to both. I have the satisfaction, however, to see my flock, both in the church and college, again collected, beyond what they have been since the war until lately. I have little to say of my success in the ministry. Yesterday I baptized three. The season was solemn. The audience is both large and attentive, and I hope among them are some inquiring souls. One of the members of college has lately, I hope, been brought to know the Lord. Our number of students is about thirty-five, with a prospect of increase. But as we are destitute of an adequate fund, this does but increase my labors, as I am confined to constant teaching.

30*

The Lord is gracious to many parts of this land, in of late pouring out his Spirit upon the people. Mr. Gano has a rich blessing in New York. The eastern part of New Jersey is also visited. In Vermont there is a day of God's power, and so also in several of the interior parts of New England. May that glorious kingdom come over all the earth! I long to hail the approach of the King of Zion, and I *partly believe* I shall live to see the accomplishment of at least *some* of the glorious things spoken of the city of God.

By recent accounts from Kentucky, five hundred miles down the Ohio below Fort Pitt, I learn that God has done and is still doing wonders in that wilderness. Seven or eight Baptist churches are here settled, and a number of faithful but very unlettered ministers are engaged in the harvest. To spread the knowledge of the Redeemer (who came preaching in the wilderness of Judea) in the wilderness, has long been with me a desirable object. And with this view I have conceived a design, if possible, of furnishing their untutored minds with books. My plan is to establish a library for the Baptist Association (to be established there this year) of such books as are best adapted to their situation, to qualify their ministers more thoroughly for their ministerial work, and to assist those young men of promising abilities for the ministry with useful knowledge before they enter on the work. With this view I am about to make collections of books in America, and I recommend the same to my correspondents in England, and request them to send them forward to the Rev. Thomas Ustick, minister of the Baptist church at Philadelphia, with a line to him informing him of the donors and the design. He will take charge of the same, till they can be safely forwarded to Kentucky, for the uses mentioned. Any services you can render in so good a cause will be kindly accepted. They are almost wholly, I am told, destitute of all kinds of books. I propose there shall be a book kept by the association, in which shall be entered the donors' names, and what they contributed. You have my best wishes, in which Mrs. Manning joins.

Your unworthy friend,

JAMES MANNING.

P. S. — Should I not have the pleasure to see you, please to present my Christian salutation to Mr. Thornton when you return.

TO THE REV. DR. EVANS.

PROVIDENCE, July 21, 1785.

DEAR SIR:

Yours of 26th and 31st of January came to hand last month while I was in New York, the perusal of which gave me great pleasure, especially that paragraph which mentions the additions to the churches in Bristol. May you be so happy as to see the good work increase. Things, in reference to religion, remain much as when I wrote last, except a greater attention paid to public worship. Lord's Day before last I baptized three persons. In several parts of New England the Lord is evidently at work. In Vermont there is a glorious shower of divine influence, as also in the city of New York and the eastern part of the Jerseys. My Brother Gano is greatly blessed, upwards of forty having of late been added to his church, among whom are two of his sons and one of his daughters. When I heard last from there the work was increasing. I had the pleasure of a short interview with Mr. Mullett in New York, and he twice or three times gave us the pleasure of his company, though but a short time, as he passed to and from Boston. He was kind enough to engage to transmit my letters safely to England. Your kind proffers of service to myself or Mr. Stillman in soliciting for the college, should either of us be sent, are very acceptable, but we have yet had no advice on that subject from Dr. Stennett. Your account of the ideas of the Baptists with you, respecting literary institutions, are very similar to those of the American Baptists. We shall gladly receive the books you mention, and any others which you can spare, or procure for us. As there is no direct communication between Bristol and Providence, shall wish you to send them *via* New York, to the care of my brother-in-law, John Stites, merchant, at the corner of Queen and Chapel Streets in that city, with a line advising him where to send them. I shall inform him of this advice to you, and request him to forward them immediately to me. Dr. Stennett's Discourses on Domestic Duties I have, and highly esteem them. I wish every family were possessed of the book. Mr. Booth's treatise on Baptism, and his tract on Church Communion, he was kind enough to present to me last year. Upon reading, I recommended it in almost the same words in which you mention it; alleging that I thought it would supersede the necessity of any future publications on the subject. I wish it could be circulated throughout this continent, and am determined to use my endeavors for that purpose. I shall write him on this subject by this opportunity. The Association Letters, the sermon on Walking by Faith, and the fifth volume of Saurin's Sermons, all came safe to hand, for which I beg leave to present to you my hearty thanks, and wish, in my turn, it were in my power to afford you equal pleasure by transmitting some valuable American publications, but this is a barren soil. The embarrassments of trade, especially in the New England States, open before us a gloomy prospect, producing an amazing stagnation of business, which must continue till new channels are opened, or the restrictions on the American trade are taken off in the ports of Britain and France. Our merchants at present sink money by all the trade they drive. This renders it next to impossible to make remittances to Britain, as bills are eight per cent. above par. Were it otherwise I should try to send over for some books on my own account; especially for some of the publications of our ministers, in order to circulate them in this country; and for the *Encyclopædia Britannica,* a book we expected in our catalogue, but it did not come. From the accounts we have had of it I presume it must be a work of the greatest utility.

The college continues to increase gradually in the number of students, which at present is thirty-seven, one of whom, I have reason to believe, has been recently converted. I have long wished for an account of your Education Society, — the foundation, who are admitted and with what qualifications, the course of studies pursued, manner of teaching, time required in completing the course, etc., etc., — but I fear I should be troublesome to ask it of you. Some information on these subjects I received from my dear friend Mr. Mullett, but he referred me to Mr. Evans, and, if I rightly recollect, mentioned a book published from whence I could draw this information. If giving this information should be troublesome, I do not wish it, as from your situation you cannot surely be in want of employment. One thing more I wish to mention, which is, that the new settlement of Kentucky, five hundred miles down the Ohio river below Fort Pitt, was first settled by Baptists. It now contains more than thirty thousand souls. There are seven Baptist churches and eight ministers, who propose forming an association this year. They inform me that they are extremely destitute of books, and the ministers are illiterate, but wish for the means of information. I have proposed to my friends the establishing of a library of some useful books for the benefit of the association, that the ministers and those who are candidates for the ministry may have the use of it; and of it may I say the foundation of a seat of education. To this end I have written to my friends in different parts to collect what books they can, and send them to the care of Rev. Thomas Ustick, minister of the Baptist church in Philadelphia, to be ready to be sent forward by the first good conveyance. Could your ministering brethren in England be induced to send their works, they would compose an excellent library for this purpose. I find by a publication of a Presbyterian, under the title of a History of Kentucky, that his denomination mean to monopolize and gain an establishment there in a literary way. We have in contemplation the putting in for a share. I have paid some attention to this subject, and don't mean to lose sight of it. Your assistance and influence in favor of this design will be the most acceptable. *Charity should not, indeed, end at home.*

With sentiments of esteem, etc.,

JAMES MANNING.

P. S. — It is proposed to have a book in the intended library, containing the names of the donors, and the donations made by them, that posterity may know what attention the present generation paid to the disseminating useful knowledge in the wilderness. Whether the design succeeds or not, I shall have the satisfaction of attempting to do good; and if I am not greatly deceived, a little laid out in this way will turn to good account. I mean to send them, if possible, soon, a person of our denomination to open a seminary amongst them; and, indeed, were I not confined to the college, should spend, God willing, the next winter there myself. Bibles and religious books which are printed to be distributed *gratis* amongst the poor, would be well bestowed there, for the people are religiously disposed. The fullest confidence may be placed in Mr. Ustick, that everything sent to his care will be forwarded to them. He is a man of principle. As the term of human life is so short, and the sphere of our activity so contracted, it behooves us to exert ourselves to fill it up, to the utmost, with acts of public utility, especially in promoting the interests of the Redeemer.

Dr. Manning, as all his writings show, considered piety as the first and indispensable requisite in a minister. No degree of genius or of mental cultivation was allowed by him to compensate for the want of a heart renewed by the Holy Spirit, and moved to undertake the care of souls by the constraining love of Christ. He believed, nevertheless, in an educated ministry. How earnestly he labored to secure this for the churches more especially of his own denomination, the College of Rhode Island and the Warren Association are perpetual witnesses. In these letters to Thomas Mackaness and Dr. Evans we have an illustration of his philanthropic efforts to enlighten the illiterate Baptist ministers of Kentucky, and to provide instruction for the rising generation in that then remote wilderness; and this, too, when "overwhelmed," as he expresses it, with his own cares and duties. For a fuller development of his plans with reference to Kentucky, the reader is referred to a letter addressed to the Rev. Dr. Rippon, and dated July 22. Three years later we find Manning, according to Benedict, corresponding with the Baptists in Virginia, and encouraging them, through their established organizations, to found a seminary of learning for the special benefit of their rapidly-increasing numbers in that section of the country.

During the year 1784 Dr. Manning, it appears, addressed a letter to the Hon. Granville Sharp, LL.D., of London, a zealous member of the Established Church, but liberal to Protestant Dissenters of all classes, and noted for his opposition to the American war. He was also distinguished for his opposition to negro slavery, and for the zeal with which he engaged in various patriotic and philanthropic movements. His publications, which were numerous, he presented to the college library, with a set of the works of his grandfather, Dr. John Sharp, Archbishop of York. He subsequently sent other valuable presents to the library. The following letter was written in reply to Manning: —

OLD JEWRY, LONDON, 21st Feb., 1785.

REVEREND SIR:

On the 22d ult. I received your obliging letter of the 12th October, 1784, by the hands of Mr. Drowne, who seems highly worthy of the excellent character you gave me of him.

My best thanks are due to you for the satisfactory intelligence of the safe arrival of the books which I sent for the library of the college in Providence, and also for your full and explicit account of that very useful institution.

Some additions have been made, I believe, to my tracts on Congregational Courts since I sent the copies of them by Mr. Watson; and therefore I have now sent another copy for the college library, and one for yourself; though indeed the tract is still incomplete by the want of an index; for I have not had leisure to revise and correct the index that has been made for it by a person whom I employed for that purpose some time ago.

Two of the additional tracts relate to the laying out of settlements on uncultivated lands, — a subject of very important consideration to America; for if care is not taken in these early timesi before land becomes scarce, to reserve a due proportion of cottage-land, and common-land around every town, as well as around new settlements, for the accommodation of poor industrious families, and also small portions of land for the maintenance of schools and other public establishments, it will be very difficult, a few years hence, to procure land for such purposes.

A well-regulated agrarian law would also be exceedingly beneficial to America to prevent monopolies of land; for when large tracts of land are engrossed in a few hands, it necessarily occasions not only internal weakness, and an inability to defend a country against foreign invaders, but it also inevitably reduces to slavery the industrious laborers who cultivate the enormous tracts of the haughty overgrown landholders; for this is the very foundation of the detestable aristocratical oppression and monarchial despotism in Russia, Poland, Bohemia, Germany, France, and all other countries under the unmerciful dominion of the two beasts of tyranny, which are now preparing themselves for a speedy retribution of the divine vengeance!

A mediocrity in the proportion of landed possessions in the hands of freeholders, together with an ample provision of cottage-lands for the laboring poor, and common-lands for all other housekeepers, will certainly be most beneficial for every community; and such mediocrity of landed possessions may be gradually obtained, without injury to the rights of the present possessors, by restraining inheritances to an equal distribution in gavel-kind amongst all the sons of landholders; or, if the first-born is to be allowed a preference, it should be only to the amount of a certain limited number of acres (as many as shall be deemed a reasonable competence for an independent gentleman), and the overplus to be divided amongst the nearest of kin, whose possessions are below the said limited competence of landed inheritance, unless the remainder of the land be otherwise legally disposed of, by the will and testament of the late possessor.

The inheritances of heiresses should also be subject to the same limitations; so that if the husband has the legal competence of land already in his own right, the mother's estate should be reserved for the eldest son; but to be held by the latter, when of age, no longer than during his father's life; with an option, however, to give up either his father's or mother's inheritance to the younger children. By this means the overgrown possessions would be soon reduced to reasonable competences, and the number of substantial, independent landholders would be greatly increased, for the general security of the country, wherever such regulations shall take place. This would set bounds to the insatiable thirst of realizing, which prompts some thrifty men to "lay house to house and field to field;" for they would be compelled, by a just agrarian law, to find some more beneficial mode of employing their superfluous wealth, and the most avaricious of them would undoubtedly be induced to employ it in trade, which would greatly promote the extension of commerce, and consequently the welfare of the whole community. I have enclosed a copy of a letter which I wrote to a friend of the Abbé de Mably, to show that the defects which he observed in some of the American constitutions would be effectually remedied by the ancient system of Frank-pledge (as described in my last work), which was manifestly the polity of the commonwealth of Israel whilst under the theocracy; for the same arrangement of the people into exact numerical divisions of tithings, hundreds, and thousands, were then ordained as a part of their political constitutions, though it was even at that time too frequently neglected; whereby the people fell into confusion and anarchy, and "every man did what seemed right in his own eyes." But this was not occasioned by any defect in the constitution itself, but merely by the neglect of it; for I know of no other method but this, if duly maintained by annual renewal, whereby liberty, equal right, and national security can be so effectually supported.

Probably what I have written concerning the popular right of electing bishops (see tract No. 5) may seem superfluous, as well to yourself as to some other learned professors of divinity, who have not been educated in an Episcopal Church; nevertheless, it is a subject worthy your consideration, especially as it will be found that the most important objections that have usually been made by Protestant Dissenters to the order of bishops, would be effectually removed by the restoration of popular right in the election of them; and that all danger of tumults in such elections would be obviated by electing two of the most eminent presbyters, of unimpeachable morality and virtue, whose appointment to the dignity should be decided by lot, after solemn prayer by the whole congregation, according to the apostolic example related in Acts i. 15-26. I remain, with due respect and esteem, reverend sir,

Your most obedient, humble servant,

GRANVILLE SHARP.

To this letter Manning replies: —

PROVIDENCE, STATE OF RHODE ISLAND, July 26, 1785.

DEAR SIR:

In May last, just before I left Providence for New York and Philadelphia, I received by the ship London your most acceptable letters of Feb. 21, 22, as also the copy of your letter to a friend of the Abbé de Mably, dated Dec. 30, 1784, and your letter of March 4, 1785, together with the two copies of your last work on Congregational Courts. As the Hope had a long passage, I received the letters and books by the London first, but the duplicates by the Hope came safe. I have complied and shall comply literally with your desire of making them public. Your letter relating to ecclesiastical matters, after perusal, I communicated to my ministering brethren of the Episcopal Church in my vicinity, who took a copy of it. I then took it to New York and communicated it to some of the members of Congress; lent it to Dr. Provost, the rector, who desired liberty to copy it, which I granted him, withal requesting him to communicate it to his brethren. He proposed doing so, and laying it before the convention of the Episcopal clergy of Virginia and New York inclusive, to meet in September next at the city of Philadelphia. Two weeks since, I received from General Knox, *via* Boston, Archbishop Sharp's Sermons and Works, in seven volumes, with two volumes of Sharp on Congregational Courts. The General informed me that by some accident they had been wet. This had marred the beauty of the binding, but had not injured the print. No letter accompanied them, but I presume they were designed for the library, where I shall place them. The kind attention of Mr. Sharp to this college has laid me and the friends of it under great obligations, which I beg leave most heartily to acknowledge, by returning him, as well in behalf of the college as myself, our united thanks. Shall comply with your wishes respecting Bishop Wilson's works, whenever they may arrive. Your treatise on Frank-pledge, with that on Congregational Courts, I handed to the Hon. Messrs. Howell and Ellery, members of Congress for this State; but they had fixed upon the plan of laying out the back lands before my arrival. As I was pleased with your ideas on that subject, I strongly recommended to them an examination, and an adoption of your plan where it would be an improvement upon theirs. I mean by this opportunity to furnish you with their publication on this subject, if I can procure it. I thank you for the interest you feel in the welfare and future happiness of America, and for your generous and benevolent exertions to promote the same. These exertions I doubt not will meet a due reward from the supreme Judge and Rewarder of merit. Your publications are highly approved by the gentlemen of my acquaintance. To point out an inadequate mode of defending the rights without laying a foundation for subverting the liberties of mankind, is, in my view, the great desideratum of government, and I have yet seen nothing which promises fairer to accomplish this than your scheme, a part of which, at least, I expect will be adopted by the United States.

I concur with you in sentiment exactly concerning the importance of a mediocrity in the proportion of landed possessions in the hands of freeholders. It is the real strength of a nation, and most agreeable to the dictates of reason and the rights of man. In New England a system was adopted when the country was first settled, which remains in full vigor to this day; so that it is hard to find many here in the extremes of poverty or wealth. It was this spirit which, in the last war, captivated British armies, or repelled them from their borders, as it is calculated to disseminate knowledge and the love of liberty throughout the whole community. Many if not most of the States have enacted laws by which the estates of those who die intestate shall be equally divided amongst all the surviving children, both male and female, or at most give the oldest son but two shares. In consequence of this many people make no other will, but appoint executors to execute that which the law has made for them. This is a guard against the danger arising from overgrown estates, as many who devise them by will or otherwise conform, nearly, to what the law points out as equitble. This renders an agrarian law in a measure unnecessary.

For your friendship and assistance afforded Mr. Drowne, I thank you, and shall be happy, in my turn, to testify my readiness to repay the kindness. I have the pleasure to inform you that the college at Providence daily increases in reputation and number of students. Some valuable though small additions have been lately made to our library, which consists now of upwards of two thousand volumes. The prospects from this country of augmenting our funds, so as to establish an adequate number of professors, from the decay of trade and the scarcity of money are at present rather gloomy; but we hope some generous benefactors may yet arise and obviate this difficulty.

I have the pleasure to inform you that there is an evident alteration for the better in the morals of the people throughout this country. Religion too begins again to raise her drooping head; and what affords me peculiar satisfaction is, that a spirit of moderation prevails beyond what has been known since the first settlement of New England. The various denominations of Christians are cultivating a spirit of brotherly love by an unreserved intercourse with each other. Among the many mischievous consequences resulting from the late war, we are happy to find that the prevalence of a spirit of toleration, and a more general knowledge of the doctrine of religious liberty, in some measure counterbalance them.

That you may long live to promote the great interests of mankind by your shining abilities and indefatigable labors, and have the happiness to see the good effects of them on society, and at last be admitted to receive an ample reward of all your labors in the regions of bliss, is the ardent wish of, dear sir,

Your sincere friend and very humble servant,

JAMES MANNING.

TO THE REV. DR. RIPPON.

PROVIDENCE, July 22, 1785.

MY DEAR BROTHER:

Yours of Dec. 24, 1784, came to hand last month, together with the pamphlet occasioned by the death of that eminent man, Dr. Gifford, for which please accept my best thanks. That of Feb. 23, 1785, came by the Hope, together with the acceptable presents of Deacon Shepherd and Rev.

John Ryland, for which, in the name of the college, please to present them my most cordial thanks. This should have been done by the corporation, had a meeting of that body been held since. I am greatly pleased, as well as instructed, by both those valuable works, though my attention has been of late so much taken up in other ways that I can command but little time for reading. With you I regret your want of timely information of the catalogue of books sent for the college; and I make no doubt of your being both able and willing to have made a considerable saving for the college. Had I been then as well acquainted with your character as I have been since, I should have addressed you on that subject. We did then, as we thought, the best we could do; but my expectations were disappointed, I confess, in the price of the books. Should we ever be so fortunate as to have more money to lay out in that way, which I see but little prospect of, we shall take the liberty to solicit Mr. Rippon's assistance. I am pleased to hear that Dr. Gill's Exposition is to be completed. Many of them are now wanted; but the difficulty of making remittances from New England, and the inconceivable scarcity of cash, have almost put an end to business. New channels of trade will probably soon open, but not, I fear, before many of our mercantile people are ruined. I rejoice to hear that the cause of religion is on the advance in your churches, and that our denomination increases in some of the counties. Mr. Evans gives me agreeable information from Bristol of considerable additions to two of our churches in the city.

And though stupidity greatly prevails in general, we still have some agreeable revivals in different parts on this continent. The wilderness of Vermont still continues to blossom as the rose. New York and the eastern part of New Jersey are blessed with a joyful harvest. My Brother Gano appears to be the principal instrument whom God honors in that city, so lately filled with violence. Three of his own children are in the number of converts; and if I augur rightly, one of his sons, a doctor,[1]

[1] The Rev. Stephen Gano, M.D. He was born in the city of New York, Dec. 25, 1762, being the third son of the Rev. John Gano. At the age of thirteen he was placed under the care of his maternal uncle, Dr. Stites, to be educated for the medical profession. Having made honorable proficiency in his studies, he received an appointment as surgeon in the army, and entered the public service. He was at this time nineteen years old. His mother, who had been the principal agent in procuring for him the appointment, having buckled on his regimentals, said to him as they parted, concealing her tears, "My son, may God preserve your life and your patriotism; — the one may be sacrificed in retaking and pre-

must preach Christ to others. Upwards of forty have been lately added, and the work, by late information, is on the increase. Grace reigns also in several places in New England. Some drops have, in mercy, fallen on Providence. Three I baptized Lord's Day sennight. Public worship is better attended than since the war, in our meeting. I should be happy to receive a letter from Mr. Rippon on spiritual things, but business, at proper times, calls for our attention. I thank you for your kind attention to Mr. Drowne, as he is modest to an excess. And since you cannot command, or at least make use of the wings of a dove to visit America, what think you of substituting in their place those of a ship? I would engage that you should have the fervent prayers of many of your American friends for a safe and speedy passage, and a most kindly welcome to these western shores; and *withal I have prepared you a lodging,* which (as a minister once said of his bed), if homely, is a sincere one. I am confident no house in your capital would please me better than Mr. Rippon's, should I ever be permitted to visit your country; nor should any be preferred to it as a home; but I almost give over the expectations of seeing my English

serving the home of your childhood; but let me never hear that you have forfeited the birthright of a freeman." He continued in the service two years, and then retired to settle as a physician in Tappan, now Orangetown, New York. Soon after his conversion he was impressed with the idea that it was his duty to preach the gospel. He was accordingly ordained in the Gold Street Church, New York, his father and President Manning participating in the exercises of the occasion. This was on the 2d of August, 1786. He at once engaged in missionary labors on the Hudson, and wherever he went his preaching awakened a deep interest. He was successively pastor of the Baptist church at Hillsdale and at Hudson. In 1792 he received an invitation to become the pastor of the Baptist church in Providence, which invitation he accepted. Some members of the society, it is understood, at first objected to his being the pastor of a church whose relations with the college were so intimate, on the ground that he had never himself received a collegiate education. These objections, however, were soon removed, and the most cordial and friendly relations were established between himself and his people. Here he continued during the remainder of his useful life. He died on the 18th of August, 1828, in the sixty-seventh year of his age, greatly beloved and respected throughout the entire community. The event was immediately made known by the tolling of the city bells, and the children who were assembled in the several schools were dismissed, out of respect to his memory. His funeral was attended by an immense concourse of people, and a sermon appropriate to the occasion was preached by the Rev. Dr. Sharp, of Boston.

During his pastorate of thirty-eight years Dr. Gano was permitted to witness

brethren till I meet them above, the prospect of which often gives me pleasure. There I hope to see and converse with the whole family at home, without the aid or necessity of pen and ink. In the mean time I feel my obligations to diligence in the business of my holy calling, that I may be found ready.

The college still increases, though gradually. Our number is thirty-seven; one of whom, I hope, has been called by grace. Last week we buried our venerable chancellor, Stephen Hopkins, Esq., LL.D , for many years Governor of the Colony, and one of those distinguished worthies who composed the First Congress. He was one of the greatest men our country has reared. At the first meeting of the corporation he was chosen chancellor, and continued in the office till his death. In him the college has lost a most valuable member and officer, and I myself a particular friend. Mr. Van Horn has obtained something for the college by his solicitations in Pennsylvania and New Jersey, in which business he is still employed. I carried in May last an application to Congress, by a memorial, etc., for compensation for the rents and damages done the college by

many signal manifestations of the divine power and presence. In one year he baptized one hundred and forty-seven converts, swelling the number of church communicants to six hundred and forty-eight. As an evidence of his general usefulness, it may be mentioned, that for nineteen consecutive years he presided as moderator at the meetings of the Warren Association. "He had," says the Rev. Dr. Jackson, "a fine, commanding figure, being more than six feet in stature, and every way well proportioned. His voice was full, sonorous, and altogether agreeable. His manner was perfectly artless and unstudied. He had great command of language, and could speak with fluency and appropriateness, with little or no premeditation. His discourses were eminently experimental."

Dr. Gano was married on the 25th of October, 1782, to Cornelia, daughter of Capt. Josiah Vavasor, of the city of New York. By her he had two sons and two daughters. On the 4th of August, 1789, he was a second time married to Polly, daughter of Col. Tallmadge, of New York. By this marriage there were also four children, three daughters and one son. His third wife was Mary, daughter of Hon. Joseph Brown, by whom he had one daughter, Mrs. Eliza B. Rogers. In 1801 he was married to Mrs. Joanna Latting, of Hillsdale, N. Y., who survived him many years. Of his six daughters, four have married clergymen; namely, the Rev. John Holroyd, the Rev. Peter Ludlow, the Rev. Dr. Benedict, and the Rev. Dr. Jackson. Dr. Gano was an honored and useful member of the Masonic fraternity, having been initiated in Mount Vernon Lodge, Providence, on the 10th of July, 1801. Twenty-five years afterwards (Jan. 5, 1826), he, in company with the late Right Rev. Bishop Griswold, took the Knight Templar's degree in the Providence Encampment.

the troops during the war, but have as yet got nothing done. The papers were read and a committee appointed while I was there, before whom we had a hearing, and their promise of a speedy report; but I fear little is to be expected from that quarter.

In the new settlement of Kentucky, five hundred miles down the Ohio below Fort Pitt, I am credibly informed that there are upwards of thirty thousand inhabitants, amongst whom are seven Baptist churches and eight ministers; that the people incline much to be of our denomination; that the ministers are not only very illiterate, but that there is not a person of our persuasion capable of teaching even the languages amongst them; and that they have a desire to enjoy the means of education, more especially as the Presbyterians, though greatly inferior in numbers, and later on the ground, appear to be manœuvering to avail themselves of advantages from being first in promoting literature in that quarter. I conjectured this from reading a pamphlet, written by one of that society, giving an account of the first settlement of that country. Accordingly I wrote my thoughts on the subject to our Western ministers, withal requesting them to possess themselves of the best information they could get before the next Association at Philadelphia to be held in October, that something might be done to encourage them. Since then I am informed that they propose establishing an association there this year. With a view to assist them, I have proposed the raising of a small library, of such books as may be more immediately serviceable to the ministers, and those who are candidates for the ministry, and am using my endeavors to procure what books I can for that purpose in America. But as I expect the contributions will be small, I greatly wish for the assistance of our English friends. The proposal is to forward the books to the Rev. Thomas Ustick, Baptist minister in Philadelphia, to be forwarded by the first good opportunity; that a book shall be kept in which the names of the contributors shall be enrolled, with an account of their donations, that posterity may know what exertions were made, and by whom, to propagate knowledge and religion in that wilderness. I mean to have this library under such regulations as that it may form the basis of a literary institution there. Those of our ministers who are able, by contributing their works, would greatly assist in laying this foundation; and I doubt not that posterity will rise up and call them blessed. If you think well of this proposal, I doubt not but you will be willing to lend your influence to carry it into effect. I mean not only to propose, but, according to my ability, assist in this matter; and also to promote, as far as possible, an academy amongst them, in which I have some prospect of succeeding. As I shall not write on this subject to any but Mr. Evans and yourself, I would thank you to mention it where and to whom you think proper. Those Bibles and religious books printed by societies to be distributed among the poor, would be well bestowed there at present. I shall be happy on all occasions and by every opportunity to receive a line from Mr. Rippon. With sentiments of esteem,

I am yours, in Jesus,

JAMES MANNING.

Dr. Manning's brief eulogium upon his "particular friend" Governor Hopkins, the first chancellor of the college, was well deserved. This great and good man closed his long, honorable, and useful life on the 13th of July, 1785, in the seventy-ninth year of his age. "From the vigor of his understanding, and the intuitive energy of his mind, he had established," says his biographer, "a character not only prominent in the annals of his country, but in the walks of literature. Possessing a commanding genius, his constant and assiduous application in the pursuit of knowledge eminently distinguished him in the first class of literati. A leading and active promoter of literary and scientific intelligence, he attached himself in early youth to the study of books and men, and continued to be a constant and improving reader, a close and careful observer, until the period of his death. Holding all abridgments and abridgers in very low estimation, it is cited, in exemplification of his habitual deep research, and the indefatigability with which he penetrated the recesses, instead of skimming the surface of things, that instead of depending upon summaries and concentrated authorities, he perseveringly perused the whole of the great collection of ancient and modern history, compiled about half a century ago, by some distinguished scholars in Europe; and that he also read through all of Thurloe's and other ponderous collections of state papers." Governor Hopkins professed the principles of the society of Friends, at whose places of worship he was a regular attendant. He was a firm believer in the Christian religion, but not bigoted in his belief, treating all societies of religious people with respect. As we have before stated, he was a warm friend of the college, and labored zealously to promote its interests.

The following brief letter from the Rev. Dr. Evans, conveys the pleasing intelligence that the books, to which allusion has already been made, had been voted to the college by the Bristol Education Society: —

BRISTOL, Sept. 5, 1785.

DEAR SIR:

I take this opportunity, by my worthy young friend Mr. Waldo, of informing you that at our late annual meeting of the Education Society here, Aug. 24, I obtained a vote in favor of your college, respecting the many valuable books we have to dispose of, and am empowered to send such as I may approve of. I shall take an early opportunity of doing this, and when received shall hope for the favor of a line from you.

I have also to request the favor of a diploma of M. A. for my worthy colleage, the Rev. James Newton, a gentleman whose sound learning and amiable character will do more honor to the title than the title will do to him. He is totally ignorant of this application, nor should I have made it but that it hurt me to think so worthy a man should appear to be neglected, whilst Mr. Hall and myself, who are connected with him in the academy, and esteem it sufficient honor to be his equals, are each of us graduated. And by a late regulation our names will all appear very conspicuously in our Museum.

I write this in haste, and remain, with every wish friendship can dictate for the happiness of you and all your extensive connections, dear sir, your affectionate

Friend and brother,

CALEB EVANS.

This donation — consisting of Walton's Biblio Sacra Polyglotta with Castell's Lexicon, in 8 vols. folio; Bayle's Dictionary, 5 vols. folio; Chambers' Cyclopædia, 2 vols. folio; several Fathers of the church, and standard works in science, history, and literature — was received early the following year. Such evidences of kind feeling on the part of those with whom this country had so recently been at war, must have been highly gratifying at the time, as they most certainly are even at the present day. This society was founded in the year 1780, in aid of the Baptist Academy at Bristol, "to the end that dissenting congregations, especially of the Baptist denomination, in any part of the British dominions, may be more effectually supplied with a succession of able and evangelical ministers." The society has been eminently useful. It is now in the possession of a very valuable library, containing the collection of books, paintings, etc., of the Rev. Dr. Andrew Gifford, for many years sub-librarian of the British Museum, and the library of Thomas Llewelyn, LL.D.

PROVIDENCE, Sept. 9, 1785.

TO THE HONORABLE DAVID HOWELL,

MEMBER OF CONGRESS IN NEW YORK:

SIR: — At the annual meeting of the corporation yesterday, we were appointed a committee to address you, in their name, on the subject of their petition to Congress for an allowance for rents, and for damages done the edifice while occupied by the public, which is so justly due to them; and to request you to exert yourself to bring that business to an issue as speedily and favorably as possible before you leave Congress; more especially as they expect to have no member to succeed you who will have it in his power or in his inclination to serve the interests of the college equal to its secretary.

It is imagined that your intimacy and interest with the committee appointed to report on our petition, will enable you, before the report is made, to discover what will be the tenor of it. Of this advantage we wish you to avail yourself; and, should it wear an unfavorable aspect, prevent its being made. Such a report might preclude us from ever obtaining any allowance from our own Legislature; but if the petition is either pending before Congress, or the prayer of it rejected by them, our prospects of assistance and relief from this quarter will be very unpromising, however they might prove otherwise.

You may rely that this is, by your best friends here, considered as a matter of no small importance; and they believe that your interest in Congress can even obtain the prayer of our petition, if it is in any wise practicable; and they also think that it will be no inconsiderable accession to that rich harvest of honor which, as a delegate of this State, you have already reaped. With sentiments of esteem, we subscribe ourselves,

Your friends and fellow-citizens,

JAMES MANNING,
JOHN BROWN,
ENOS HITCHCOCK, } *Committee.*

On Saturday, Dec. 3, of this year, the Hon. Joseph Brown, LL.D., of whose sickness Manning in his correspondence makes mention, died at his house, in the fifty-second year of his age. "His funeral," says his obituary, "was attended by a numerous train of mourning relatives, and the most respectable inhabitants of the town, and a discourse suitable to the occasion was delivered by Dr. Manning. . . . . The Faculty and students joined the procession as mourners, and felt the loss of a Mæcenas." His character and life we have already given in our sketches of the Brown family.

We close this chapter with a correspondence between Manning and John Gill, a goldsmith of London. It relates principally to the publications of the Rev. Dr. John Gill,[1] and will on this account be found interesting. The

[1] This distinguished Baptist divine died at his house at Camberwell, Oct. 14, 1771, in the seventy-fifth year of his age. He was pastor of the Baptist church

last letter contains a pleasant bibliographical "morceau," which the editor of the forthcoming edition of Backus's Ecclesiastical History will note in his book of references.

LONDON, March 13, 1784.

REVEREND SIR:

I take the liberty to inform you of the death of Mr. George Keith,[1] bookseller in London. He died Dec. 4, 1782, and left me his sole executor.

and congregation at Horselydown Southwark, near London, for fifty-one years. The following is a list of his published writings, all of which are to be found in the library of the University, having been bequeathed to the college by the author (see Chap. IV. p. 199): (1.) Ancient Mode of Baptizing by Immersion maintained. 8vo. London, 1726. (2.) Defense of Ancient Mode of Baptizing by Immersion. 8vo. London, 1727. (3.) Exposition of Solomon's Song. Folio. London, 1728. A fourth edition of this work was published in 1805, in two octavo volumes. (4.) Prophecies respecting the Messiah fulfilled in Jesus. 8vo. London, 1728. (5.) The Cause of God and Truth (in answer to Dr. Whitby on the Five Points). 4 vols. 8vo. London, 1735–8. A fifth edition was published in 1838, in one octavo volume. (6.) Exposition of the New Testament. 3 vols. folio. London, 1746–8. (7.) Exposition of the Old Testament. 6 vols. folio. London, 1748–63. A new edition of both Testaments, with a memoir by Dr. Rippon, and a portrait, was published in 1816, in nine volumes quarto. Vol. I. of another edition was published in 1852, in royal octavo, and the Old Testament was published by Collingridge, of London, in 1854, in six royal octavo volumes. (8.) Anti-Pedobaptism. 8vo. London, 1753. (9.) The Argument from Apostolical Tradition in favor of Infant-Baptism considered. The third edition of this was published in 1765, in octavo. (10.) Dissertation on the Antiquity of the Hebrew Language, Letters, etc. 8vo. London, 1767. (11.) A Body of Doctrinal and Practical Divinity. 3 vols. 4to. London, 1769–70. This has gone through several editions, the latest of which was published in 1839, in two volumes octavo. (12.) Sermons and Tracts, with memoirs of the author. 2 vols. 4to. London. 1773. A new edition of Gill's Sermons, in three volumes octavo, has appeared. In addition to the list here given, Dr. Gill published many occasional sermons and tracts on Baptism, most of which are in the college library.

"If any man," says the Rev. Augustus Toplady, of the Episcopal Church, "can be supposed to have trod the whole circle of human learning, it was Dr. Gill. While true religion and sound learning have a single friend in the British empire, the works and name of Dr. Gill will be precious and revered. . . . . With a solidity of judgment and with an acuteness of discernment peculiar to few, he exhausted, as it were, the very soul and substance of most arguments he undertook."

[1] Mr. Keith was a brother-in-law of the writer, having married his sister Mary, daughter of the Rev. Dr. Gill.

I find by his books that you stand indebted to his estate £2 9s. 9d., which I doubt not you will honorably discharge. At the same time, I beg leave to acquaint you that I have several sets of Dr. Gill's New Testament, five volumes quarto, at £3 15s. each set, in boards. According to the proposals at first delivered out, subscribers for six sets to have a seventh, I am willing to dispose of them on these terms, or, if a less number is wanted, will allow twenty per cent. on delivery, payable by a merchant or trader in London. There is also the Old Testament in quarto, begun by Mr. Keith, but I cannot get any bookseller in London to complete it. It begins with Genesis and ends with the 132d Psalm, in six volumes. These I have to dispose of at £1 16s. The subscription price was £4 10s., or 15s. each volume. Also some few sets of the Doctor's tracts, collected together and printed in three volumes quarto, with memoirs of his life, at £1 16s., or 12s. each volume. Also his Cause of God and Truth, and his Exposition of Solomon's Song, at 12s. each volume, all printed on the same size and paper as the New Testament. As I wish to promote the sale of the Doctor's works in America, on that account I have charged them at a low price, when the discount proposed is considered. A line directed for me to be left at Mr. Ash's, bookseller, No. 15 Little Tower Street, will be conveyed to me. I am, reverend sir, with all due respect,

Your humble servant,

John Gill.

Providence, July 9, 1784.

Sir: — Yours of March 13 reached me the last month. I had before heard of the death of Mr. George Keith, and sympathize with you and the family in the loss. I had no knowledge of a balance due to him till I received your letter, as I had many years ago given orders to a friend of mine, whom I have not since seen, to pay the balance, if any remained due. By this conveyance goes a letter from Mr. Backus to Mr. Henry Kane, executor to Mr. Wallin, to pay you the sum of £2 9s. 9d. on my account, as he had money in Mr. Wallin's hands. If you will please call on him he will doubtless discharge the debt. Of this please to advise me by the first opportunity. I shall be extremely sorry if the edition of Dr. Gill's Bible in quarto cannot be completed, as I had sold my former set, in full confidence that I should soon be able to replace mine from this edition. Others here wish to purchase, but they also wish to have the work complete. They especially wish for his Exposition of the Prophets. Would it not be better for your family to complete the work, than to lose in a great measure the sale of what is already done, and deprive the world of such a valuable treasure? I have on hand some of all the rest of his works you mention; besides, at present it is extremely difficult to make remittances to England, as the mercantile affairs of the country have been so long and so greatly deranged; to which I may add the great inattention, in general, to reading books on religious subjects, — the natural consequence, perhaps, of such a kind of war as that in which we have been involved. This, it is to be hoped, will soon alter for the better, when I shall watch every opportunity of making Dr. Gill's works as much known as possible. This I have hitherto ever had in view, and it was no inconsiderable motive in parting with his Exposition, above mentioned. I was lately desired to inquire whether those editions complete could be obtained in England, by a gentleman who wishes to purchase them. The state of religion amongst our denomination in America appears rather on the gaining hand, as there are revivals in many of the churches. The college, too, although greatly injured by the war, promises soon to regain its former state. The government of it, through the smallness of its funds and the great repairs necessary, find themselves amazingly embarrassed, and consequently wish for every assistance from the friends of the institution, from ever quarter. I am, sir,

Your friend and servant,

JAMES MANNING.

LONDON, Oct. 14, 1784.

SIR: — I received yours in the month of August last. Have applied to Mr. Kane, Mr. Wallin's executor, who informs me that he has no money in hand for Mr. Backus. Mr. Backus sent seventy copies of his History of the Baptists, which never came to the late Mr. Wallin. Mr. Kane intends to acquaint Mr. Backus of his disappointment. I am much obliged to you, sir, for the great regard and kind intentions expressed in your letter of promoting the sale of Dr. Gill's works among your friends. I have now the pleasure to inform you that the quarto edition of the Old Testament will be completed. It is now in the press, and will be finished with all convenient speed. What was contained in my former letter is now set aside, not having any of the Old Testament to sell at the price therein mentioned. What I have will now be wanted to complete sets. I can supply you with a set of the folio edition at ten guineas, and also a set of the Prophets at two guineas. I shall be glad to hear that religion is in a flourishing state among you, that the churches of Christ are increasing, and that you, sir, may again see that seminary of learning over which you have the honor to preside retrieve its former state, and be attended with all the success and usefulness desirable. I am, sir, with great esteem,

Your obliged, humble servant,

JOHN GILL.

PROVIDENCE, July 24, 1785.

DEAR SIR:

Yours of Oct. 14, 1784, came to hand in May, since which I have had no opportunity of sending you an answer. Soon after the reception of it I saw Mr. Backus, who had received the information you mention respecting his books, but informed me that he expected still to obtain them, by getting information of the captain who carried them; but should he be disappointed in his expectations, he had sent a considerable number of the second volume of his History, from the net proceeds of which he had ordered you paid, so that I expect, by or before the arrival of this, your money will be ready for you. He engaged to write you that you might know on whom to call. I am sorry for the disappointment, but hope your money is safe. I am rejoiced to hear that the Doctor's Old Testament is to be completed, and you may be assured that what little influence I possess shall be employed in the sale of his works. But such at present is the scarcity of money, and difficulty of making remittances to Great Britain, by the high price of bills, that business is almost entirely stagnated. We hope, however, for better times. I thank you for your kind expressions of regard for the college with which I am connected. Great indeed have been the damages which it sustained by the war, for which hitherto we have received no compensation; nor are our prospects of it in future very flattering. The institution, under all its disadvantages, begins to flourish, and the number of students increases as fast as might be reasonably expected. Religion too begins amongst us to hold up its head. In several parts there are great revivals, some account of which I have mentioned to Mr. Rippon in a letter of this date. Should my expectations of discharging that balance, through Mr. Backus, be again disappointed, upon advice from you I will take measures which will prove effectual to accomplish it. With sentiments of esteem, I am, sir,

Your humble servant,

JAMES MANNING.

LONDON, March 28, 1786.

REVEREND SIR:

A letter of yours, dated July 24, 1785, was not received by me until about the middle of December. I should be glad when favored with another letter from you, to be informed by whom it was conveyed to me, as no name was mentioned to whom I might apply for the small sum you expected to be paid me by some person in London. I am surprised to find Mr. Backus has not heard what became of the first volume of his History of the Baptists. Last summer a Mr. Thomas saw a sheet of his History brought into a house where he was, wrapped around a pound of cheese or butter. Mr. Thomas went immediately and purchased all the paper relating to that History the cheese-monger had; since which I am informed he has received the second volume, and now makes complete sets. Whether this is done for his own emolument, or whether he intends it for Mr. Backus's advantage, I cannot tell. Honor and justice seem to decide it in favor of Mr. Backus. But as I have no acquaintance with Mr. Thomas, I can say no further about it.

I am sorry to inform you that the printer who had engaged to finish the Exposition has failed and left London. There is now no hope of its being completed. The six volumes of the Old Testament, reaching as far as the 132d Psalm, may now be had at £1 16s., which I think was mentioned to you in a former letter. If your friends choose to have any of them sent, shall allow you twenty per cent. for your trouble. I remain, sir, with all due respect,

Your humble servant,

JOHN GILL.

On the back of this letter Mr. Manning has written "answered." Of the reply, however, no copy has come to our knowledge.

CHAPTER IX.

1786-1788.

Manning as a patriot statesman — Appointed a member of Congress —Account of this event, by Hon. Asher Robbins — Rev. Dr. Perez Fobes appointed to take charge of the College in Manning's absence — Letter to Rev. Dr. Rippon, giving his reasons for entering upon political life — Interests of the College paramount to all others — Manning's description of a minister such as he might wish to succeed him in the pastorate of the Baptist church — Letter from Nicholas Brown to Rev. Dr. Smith, respecting Manning and a proposed vacancy in the pastorate of the church — Letter to Rev. Dr. Evans — Letter to Rev. Abraham Booth — Rev. Dr. William Gordon, of London, author of a history of the American war — Letter to him —Congress passes an act for the relief of the College — Letter to Rev. Dr. Smith, giving an account of his life as a member of Congress — Letter to his colleague, Gen. Nathan Miller, giving an account of his own embarrassed condition from the want of funds, and urging him to take his seat as a delegate — Second letter to Mr. Miller — Letter to Manning from Dr. Gordon — Public exercises of Commencement resumed — Sketch of Hon. Nicholas Brown — Account of the collection of portraits in Rhode Island Hall — Extract from a letter illustrating the difficulties against which the College at this time had to contend — Letter to Rev. Dr. Smith — Severe reflections on the General Assembly of Rhode Island — Trying period in Manning's life — Commencement of 1787 — Sketch of Hon. Samuel Eddy — Biographical sketch of Rev. Dr. Jonathan Maxcy — Confederation — Federalists and Anti-Federalists — Manning's influence in favor of the "New Constitution"— Attends the Convention in Massachusetts for the adoption of the Constitution — Anecdote respecting him — Letter to Rev. Dr. Smith alluding to his attendance upon the debates of the Convention — Letter from Rev. Dr. Rippon — Letter to Rev. Thomas Ustick — Letter to Rev. Dr. Smith — Biographical sketch of Rev. Dr. Asa Messer — Commencement of 1788 — Sketch of Hon. James Burrill — Letter from Rev. Morgan Edwards — Letter from Rev. Dr. Evans — Letter to Rev. Dr. Smith — Early schools of Providence — Manning's efforts in behalf of popular education.

Dr. Manning is now to be exhibited in a new character and in new relations. Hitherto, says Prof. Goddard, we have seen him ministering at the altar, or dispensing the oracles of wisdom amid the shades of the academy. We are now to note his career as a patriot statesman.

The articles of confederation adopted by the United States in 1781, proved, as is well known, utterly inadequate to the purposes of government. Commercial embarrassments multiplied ; the public credit was impaired ; and the great interests of the nation, nay even the whole political fabric, was threatened with destruction. At this crisis of depression and alarm, Dr. Manning was, by a unanimous resolution of the General Assembly, appointed, at its March session in 1786, to represent Rhode Island in the Congress of the Confederation. The story of this interesting event in his life is thus told by the Hon. Asher Robbins, in a letter to Prof. Goddard, which we find in his memoir of Manning.

"Though he had other merits and ample for this appointment of delegate, I have no doubt the dignity and grace for which he was so remarkable smoothed the way to it. It took place in this wise : There was a vacancy in the delegation, and the General Assembly, who were to fill it, were sitting in Providence. No one in particular had been proposed or talked of. One afternoon Dr. Manning went to the State House, to look in upon the Assembly and see what was doing. His motive was curiosity merely. On his appearance there, he was introduced on the floor, and accommodated with a seat. Shortly after, Commodore Hopkins, who was then a member, rose and nominated President Manning as a delegate to Congress, and thereupon he was appointed, and, according to my recollection, unanimously. I recollect to have heard Commodore Hopkins say (it was at the house of his brother, Governor Hopkins, where I shortly after met with him) that the idea never entered his head till he saw the President enter and take his seat on the floor of the Assembly ; and that the thought immediately struck him that he would make a very fit member for that august body, the Continental Congress.

"Congress under the old confederation sat, as you know, in conclave ; no report of their debates was published. How far Mr. Manning mingled in them, therefore, I cannot say. I recollect his speaking of one in which he participated (the subject I have forgotten), on account of a personal controversy to which it gave rise between him and a fiery young man, a delegate from Georgia, by the name, as I think, of Houston. This young man in his speech had reflected upon New England and her people. Mr. Manning repelled the attack, and, by way of offset, drew a picture of Georgia and her people. This so nettled the young man that in his passion he threatened personal violence. The next day he appeared in Congress with a sword by his side. This produced, at once, a sensation in that body, the symptoms of which were so alarming that he thought proper to withdraw, take off his sword, and send it home by his servant. In the course of the day he took an opportunity to meet with Mr. Manning, and to make him an apology.

"He must have given himself much to business then, as he seemed to be master of all the important questions which had been debated, and could give the arguments, *pro* and *con*, offered by the different speakers.

"The famous Dr. Johnson of Connecticut was a member at the same time, with whom Mr. Manning became intimate, and of whom he always spoke with admiration. The Doctor once paid him the compliment of holding the pen of a ready writer, which Mr. Manning very highly valued as coming from such a man. It was upon an occasion of drawing up a report for a committee, of which both were members, and which report the Doctor professed to be much pleased with."

Dr. Manning at first pleaded his connection with the college as a sufficient reason for declining his appointment; but many of the corporation were gentlemen of high political standing, who, regarding the interests of the institution as involved in the character and reputation of the State and the course of public measures, advised him to take his seat, and designate a suitable person to preside in his absence. Accordingly, at a special meeting of the Trustees and Fellows held at his house, March 13, his request for absence was granted, and the Rev. Perez Fobes, LL.D., pastor of the Congregational church and society in Raynham, Mass., was appointed to take charge of the institution from June 1 to Sept. 1, as Vice President. Mr. Fobes was a graduate of Harvard College, in the class of 1762. He accepted the appointment, and discharged the duties of the place with fidelity and good success. Shortly afterwards, it may be added, he was appointed Professor of Natural Philosophy, which position he occupied twelve years, coming in from Raynham once or twice a week, during portions of the year, to deliver lectures. In 1795 he was elected one of the Fellows of the college.

The following letter to his friend the Rev. Dr. Rippon, gives the reasons more especially which induced Dr. Manning to accept this appointment, and also his views in regard to entering the political arena. The interests of the college, it will be observed, in this as in all other matters, were uppermost in his mind.

PROVIDENCE, April 7, 1786.

MY DEAR FRIEND :

Yours of June 22, 1785, came to hand too late to comply with your request relative to Mr. Dunscombe, as it did not reach me till November. He is on my list for the honors of the college next Commencement.

Of Mr. Booth's merit I am fully conscious ; but what apology shall I make to him for not informing him that the degree of Master in the Arts was conferred on him before the late war, and that he stands on our printed catalogue graduated in 1774 ? Some difficulties respecting making out diplomas for him and for a number of gentlemen in England delayed it till the late confusion commenced, which totally deranged the affairs of the college, and effaced the memory of it till of late, especially as our secretary had omitted entering the graduations on the records. This but lately came to my knowledge. The multiplicity of cares which divide my attention and engross all my time, together with the above, is the best excuse I can make. By Dr. Gordon I now send him this feather, as a token of our respect for his great merit. This, with a letter to him, and letters and diplomas to several other gentlemen graduated before the war, I take the liberty to enclose to you, and beg of you to forward them the first good conveyance. During the late war we have been so tremblingly alive, that we have lately started up as from a dream. Of this at least they may be assured, that they were not treated designedly with neglect.

Pray, don't be alarmed should you hear that I am in Congress. The motive of my accepting this most unexpected, unsolicited, but unanimous appointment of the State to that office, was the recovery of a considerable sum due to the college, for the use taken of the edifice, and the damage done to it by the public in the late war. It was thought by those most acquainted with the state of our application to that honorable body, that my presence would facilitate that grant; more especially as none of the persons likely to be elected would greatly interest themselves in that business. My appointment is only from our late session till next November, when I mean to relinquish the office, as in general I always considered politics out of my province. Accordingly I have interdicted my name being mentioned in the next nominating. Both the college and the congregation are, I hope, well provided for during my absence. The latter are now looking out for a minister. I ever declined the pastoral care of the church as quite incompatible with my engagements to the college, though I have preached, administered ordinances, visited the sick, attended funerals, etc., for the last fifteen years, without assistance. Convinced that I cannot hold that place with advantage to them and hold the Presidency of the college, I have strongly recommended to them to obtain if possible a minister, and they are now looking out for one. But there is little probability of their finding the man soon on this continent. A man of letters, politeness, strict piety and orthodoxy, of popular talents, possessed of a good share of human prudence, and no bigot, — in a word, a truly Christian orator is the man they want. Should any of our English brethren of this description incline to visit America, I wish him to take Providence in his way. And should he like the people, and the people him, I believe our congregation would afford him an honorable support, as it is large and composed of some of the most wealthy men and first characters in the State. Pray, have you no Mr. Rippons, Booths, Evanses, etc., to spare from your side of the water? I should for one be very happy to see them on our American shores.

The number of students in college is about fifty, and our prospects would be flattering were it not for the scarcity of money in this country, which embarrasses all kinds of business. A fund to educate pious youth of our denomination is what I have long wished for, but have not yet been able to accomplish. Several hopeful youth for want of this are denied an education, who promised fair to have been ornaments to the ministry. The state of religion, except in Boston, Newport, and in Vermont, is not very flourishing. With sentiments of esteem, I am, sir,

Your assured friend and humble servant,

JAMES MANNING.

P. S. — Some drops of mercy have, I trust, fallen upon Providence. Our common friend Dr. Drowne requested me to mention to you that the gentlemen who appraised the loss he sustained by the bad package of the medicines he received from Mr. Pine, are noted apothecaries, and men to be trusted. Such, indeed, I esteem them; and have every reason to think the Doctor took the utmost pains to render the loss as small as possible. In justice I think myself bound to say this.

The letter herewith enclosed from Mr. Nathaniel Dummer is from one of my particular friends. His wife is a member of our church, and truly an excellent woman. He applied to me to get the information through some of my friends in England. He feared to intrust it to a person in whom I could not place the highest confidence, as he feared he might not get the best information. If it would be compatible with your business to procure the information requested, soon, and transmit it to me directed to New York, and inform me what the expense is, I will engage to see you paid the expense and trouble which it may cost you, over and above thanking you for your kindness. As the information of Gov. Dummer is thought worthy to be relied on, since he came to America after he was grown up, it is thought highly probable that my friend is the next heir to the estate. Should the information coincide with his wishes, he means immediately to embark for England to attend to the business. Pray, let me hear by every good opportunity of your welfare. With every wish which the sincerest friendship can dictate for your temporal and eternal felicity, I subscribe myself,

Your very unworthy fellow-servant in the gospel of Christ,

JAMES MANNING.

"A man of letters, politeness, strict piety and orthodoxy, of popular talents, possessed of a good share of human prudence, and no bigot; in a word, a truly Christian orator,"— such is Dr. Manning's brief and expressive description of a minister to succeed in the pastorate of the Baptist church at Providence. How unconsciously has he here presented his own character as a preacher and pastor!

In reference to Manning's appointment to Congress and the consequent vacancy in the church, Mr. Nicholas Brown thus writes to the Rev. Hezekiah Smith, under date of April 2, 1786: —

"You will perhaps think it strange to hear of Mr. Manning's going to Congress, but I reserve giving a full account of this matter, hoping this may have some influence in inducing you to come at the time proposed, when you will hear all. I will only say here, that as the college increases, Mr. Manning urges, and with reason, that he cannot possibly attend to the duties of both President and pastor, and that the church has suffered for the want of time on his part to visit, etc. He has therefore recommended to the church and society to look up a suitable person as his successor, and as the college funds are not of themselves, in their present state, sufficient for his support, he goes to Congress to get what is due for rents, damages, etc., during the war. . . . . The committee before mentioned are not only to obtain supplies in his absence, but to look up a suitable person to take charge of the church as a pastor. You know he must be a man of learning, and prudently popular. The society will engage such an one a genteel living, etc. Your advice, my dear friend, if nothing more, is absolutely necessary at this juncture. No one, let me add, will be more acceptable, *on all accounts*, than yourself, as a candidate for this important place."

The following letter to the Rev. Dr. Evans is very similar to the one to Dr. Rippon, and bears the same date. We give it, however, as a part of Manning's correspondence, omitting a portion to avoid needless repetition.

PROVIDENCE, April 7, 1786.

DEAR SIR:

Some time in November last I received your most acceptable favor of Sept. 5, forwarded by Mr. Waldo. I am happy to hear that your Education Society, at their meeting in August last, empowered you to send such valuable books as they have to dispose of to our college. As you intended sending them by an early opportunity, and as I have heard nothing on the subject since, I fear they may have fallen into bad hands, or have been lost at sea. This induces me to write now that you may know they have not arrived.

If spared to see another annual meeting of the corporation, at which only we have ever conferred degrees, we shall remember your worthy colleague, the Rev. James Newton, and confer on him the degree of Master in the Arts. Your recommendation of any gentleman for the honors of the college will always meet with particular attention.

The college consists of upwards of fifty members, and would flourish greatly were it not for the scarcity of money in this country, which exceeds description. This scarcity peculiarly affects us. The appropriation of the edifice to public uses during the war was productive of great damage to it, for reparation of which, as well as for the rents, the corporation sent me last year to Congress, with the state of our accounts and claims and sufficient vouchers. We obtained a hearing before a committee appointed to report on the subject of the petition, and obtained a favorable report, but lost it before Congress when the report was acted upon. Our late Professor Howell was then a member, and had great influence; but as he had effectually opposed some continental measures, he thinks the question was lost by that means, together with the small number of the states on the floor. By the articles of the confederation, he is not again eligible for three years; nor could we find any man, probably, to be chosen, who would deeply interest himself for the college. This induced me, at his earnest importunity, together with his giving the greatest encouragement that a grant might be obtained, to accept the unanimous appointment of our Legislature, at their late session, as their first delegate in Congress till next November, — an appointment to me most unexpected, as I had considered politics out of my province, and on that account had declined a former nomination to that office. The interests of the college lay near my heart, and the necessities of it call aloud for the exertions of all its friends. I thought proper to give you these hints, lest upon hearing of my being in Congress you might think I meant to assume the political character; than which, in general, nothing is more remote from my intentions, notwithstanding the great importunity of many of the Legislature for me to continue in the office. I hope the college and congregation will be well provided for during my absence, and I do not doubt it from the arrangements made.

. . . .

The state of religion in this country at present is low; yet our churches in Boston and Newport the last winter and this spring are mercifully visited, and some drops of mercy have, I trust, fallen upon Providence. With every wish for your happiness, I remain, dear sir,

Yours, etc.,

JAMES MANNING.

TO THE REV. ABRAHAM BOOTH.

PROVIDENCE, RHODE ISLAND, April 7, 1786.

REVEREND AND DEAR SIR:

Your most acceptable favor of the 25th of March, 1785, never reached me until November last. I heartily thank you for your translation of Dr. Abadie. I esteem it a masterly performance, and wish it to have a general spread through this country, which, in imitation of the old country, is rejecting the ancient gospel. Dr. Chauncey's book in favor of universal salvation, printed in London, has made many proselytes amongst the New England Congregationalists. Mere nominal Christian ministers now begin to show on whose side they are. I am convinced, however, that these trying times are necessary, and will eventually subserve the interests of the Redeemer. False friends are more dangerous to religion than avowed enemies.

After a cursory reading of your "Pedobaptism Examined" last spring, I loaned it to my Brother Gano at New York, who at that time had great need of it, and I have never been able to get it since. I read it with great pleasure, and shall be happy to see a second edition, without any corrections except such as the judicious author may see fit to make. It is out of my power to comply with your request to criticize it. Some hints when at New York led me to suspect on whom you animadverted in the note you mention. It grieves me that such fine abilities should be prostituted in the support of error. Hope he may return to a better way of thinking. You need not fear any discoveries to your disadvantage.

I thank you for your attention to my friend Dr. Drowne. Having gained his object in France, he returned last summer, and is now well, and retains a high sense of the favors received in your family.

I hope the amiable and worthy Dr. Stennett is recovered, and will yet be spared to do much service to the cause of the Redeemer, in addition to the important service he has already rendered. I rejoice to hear that his son is such a worthy character. I wish he may fill his honored father's place, when he, having served his generation according to the will of God, shall sleep with his fathers.

It is pleasing to hear that the cause of God gains ground in England, and especially in our denomination. Sorry am I to hear of the dissolution of two Baptist churches in London. Dr. Gibbons was an intimate acquaintance of my old President Davies, and through that channel I became acquainted with his character. I esteemed him a worthy, good man. Some more of Mr. Backus's first volume, he tells me, are found in London.

Your letter, accompanying a copy of Dr. Abadie, I forwarded immediately to Mr. Stillman, who received it.

Our Baptist churches in Boston and Newport have through the winter, and still have, a gracious visit. Considerable additions have been made to them, and the good work continues. I have also good tidings of the same kind from Virginia. Some scattering drops I hope have fallen upon Providence, but the number of late conversions is but small.

What apology shall I make for not advising you that the college conferred on you the degree of Master in the Arts in 1774? Directly after Commencement I was called away to the Southern States, and on my return the Lord was pleased to pour out his Spirit on the people of my charge in a glorious manner, which engaged both my time and my attention till that fatal 19th of April following, when hostilities commenced at Lexington, which cut off all intercourse between the two countries, and so deranged the affairs of the college that it is but lately that I recollected that diplomas had never been sent to you and several other gentlemen graduated upon the recommendation of Mr. Riley, of Northampton. If these excuses, with more somewhat similar, are not sufficient, and I seem really to doubt myself, I must take the blame of neglect on myself, and make the best apology I can by complying with my duty at this late hour. As a testimony of our respect for your merit, be pleased to accept the diploma which accompanies this; and if you can, excuse the omission of giving you timely advice. To one not a resident in America it is hard to conceive into what confusion the war threw us, from which it will not be easy to recover soon. The college, however, is in a more prosperous state than ever, and promises fair to hold a rank amongst literary institutions in this new world; but the scarcity of cash greatly embarrasses the college at present, as it is extremely difficult for people of property to raise money to educate their children.

I shall be glad to have a letter from Mr. Booth by every opportunity.

With every wish for your temporal and eternal felicity which the sincerest friendship can dictate, I remain, dear sir,

Yours, in Christ,

JAMES MANNING.

The following letter is addressed to the Rev. Dr. William Gordon, who, it will be remembered, came from England in 1770, with a letter of introduction to Manning from the Rev. Dr. Stennett (page 123). He settled in Massachusetts, and was ordained pastor of a Congregational church in Jamaica Plain, Roxbury, on the 6th of July, 1772. When the Revolution commenced, he took a very active part against his native country, and was appointed chaplain to the Provincial Congress. He preached a Thanksgiving discourse, Dec. 15, 1774, which is published in Thornton's "Pulpit of the American Revolution." In 1786 he returned to England, and two years afterwards published, in four octavo volumes, "The History of the Rise, Progress, and Establishment of the Independence of the United States of America,"— a candid and impartial work, says Alibone, of which there have been several editions. He died at Ipswich, Oct. 19, 1807, aged seventy-seven. Manning it seems cultivated an intimacy with him. In this letter he speaks of a donation of books which Gordon made to the college library. Among them we notice Caryl's Exposition, with Practical Observations upon the book of Job,— a work in two huge folios, published in London, in 1676, of which Charles Lamb playfully says, "What any man can write, surely I may read."

PROVIDENCE, April 13, 1786.

REVEREND AND DEAR SIR:

Yours of the 21st and 27th ult. were long in coming to hand, and the reasons of my delaying to answer them were that I mistook one week in the time set for your sailing, and my having a number of letters to write and several diplomas to get ready to send to some gentlemen in England. All these I have enclosed to Rev. John Rippon, successor to Dr. Gill, who will take care to forward them as directed. I must beg the favor of you to see Mr. Rippon, and deliver them with your own hand.

It was my intention to have seen you myself and brought Mrs. Manning down, who was exceedingly desirous of it, that we might have had the opportunity of a parting kiss ; but, unfortunately, my horse is disordered, and unable to perform the journey. Though denied the pleasure of one more interview with you here, I trust the grace and mercy of God will favor us with one infinitely more agreeable in a better world. You have my unworthy prayers for your own and your family's safety while on the ocean, and my sincere desires for your and their prosperity in your native country, from whence I shall ever rejoice to receive letters from, you and return the favor. I have been informed that you have been greatly abused in the Boston newspapers. You know that is a talent our neighbors there possess. They are ingenious to provoke. I am sorry your success in subscriptions is small here; but such is the scarcity of money that many who wished to be possessors, and amongst the rest your humble servant, were necessitated to forego it. But I hope to see better times. Shall be proud to place Dr. Gordon's History of the American War in the college library at Providence, as a token of his remembrance and friendship for that institution.

Don't imagine that I mean to exchange the sacred for the political character, because until the next November I have accepted an appointment of the State to a seat in Congress. It is purely with a view to obtain, if possible, a grant to compensate the rents and damages for the use of the edifice by the public during the war.[1] However strongly solicited, I have not the least idea of suffering my name to be used in a subsequent election. More than a thousand pounds is our just due from

[1] Dr. Manning did not succeed in his endeavors. Fourteen years afterwards (April 16, 1800), through the exertions mainly of Mr. John Brown, Congress passed an act entitled, "An Act for the Relief of the Corporation of Rhode Island College."

"*Be it enacted*, etc., That the accounting officers of the treasury be, and they are hereby authorized and directed to liquidate and settle the claims of the corporation of Rhode Island College, for compensation for the use and occupation of the edifice of said college, and for injuries done to the same, from the tenth day of December, one thousand seven hundred and seventy-six, to the twentieth day of April, one thousand seven hundred and eighty, by the troops of the United States; and that the sum which may be found due to the said corporation for damages done to and occupation of the said edifice, as aforesaid, be paid them out of any moneys in the treasury not otherwise appropriated."

How much compensation the college finally received, we are unable at present to determine. Dr. Benedict, in his History, states it to have been two thousand dollars.

the public. With our small funds this is too much to lose. I wish with all my heart you may succeed to your wishes in returning to your native country. Mrs. Manning joins in her best regards to you and Mrs. Gordon. We wish you every felicity which the sincerest friendship can dictate, both in time and eternity.

I rest, yours, etc., in gospel bonds,

JAMES MANNING.

P. S. — By Mr. Brown, the wagoner, we received the box of books in good order, and I beg leave in the name and in behalf of the corporation to present you the hearty thanks of the college for the donation. They are delivered to the librarian, and ordered to be set up and your name to be enrolled amongst the benefactors of Rhode Island College.

JAMES MANNING, *President.*

TO THE REV. DR. SMITH.

NEW YORK, 17th May, 1786.

DEAR SIR:

Yours of the 27th ult. came safe to hand, for which I thank you, and should have answered it before had not my hands been full. Mrs. Manning informed me of the application to you to be my successor in the meeting at Providence. I should be happy in your society, and should Providence order your lot there, I shall while there contribute my best endeavors to render your life happy, and useful to the people; but I think it best to interfere as little as may be with their determinations in settling a minister, as I conceive it might lessen my influence in his favor, after his settlement, should they have it in their power to say, when his support might be felt, that I was any means of it. Not that I hereby mean to excuse myself from doing my personal duty in that case, which I hope would be a pleasure. Should you accept of their invitation, your piety, I trust, would more than compensate the defect of politeness, — a high degree of which I cannot deem primarily essential in a gospel preacher, any more than distinguished rusticity. Habits of easiness in access, and gentle, unaffected manners, are most pleasing in that character.

I hope you may have the pleasure to find that your labors at Providence are followed with a blessing. The Lord is doing wonders in this city and its vicinity, but especially in the Jerseys, at the Plains, Mountains, Piscataway, and Cranberry. I attend the June meeting. Mr. Runyan, on Saturday, baptized twelve; the Sabbatarian minister three.

Great power appeared to attend the preaching. Multitudes appeared deeply affected, aud during the meeting several professed to be brought into gospel liberty. Such a meeting I believe was never seen at Piscataway before. I am told the Thursday following twelve were baptized at Quibbletown, and Lord's Day thirteen at the Plains. There appears a considerable turn in the minds of the people throughout that quarter. Mr. Wilson flames out and is remarkably blessed, and goes on preaching, exhorting, and baptizing from place to place with surprising success. The Lord indeed is doing great things in the land.

Of your mother I can give no information, but presume she is living, otherwise Mr. Guthrie or your brother Jeremiah would have told me of her death. My situation here is indeed very awkward, without a colleague, without money, and in doubt what to resolve on. Our public affairs wear a cloudy aspect. I hope it is that the interposition of Heaven may be seen in extricating us from difficulty. His former unmerited favor to this guilty land encourages me to hope for it though it should almost be against hope.

The savages have begun their barbarous depredations on our western frontiers, but probably not without provocation from some of that lawless banditti which forms the van of those settlements. It is expected that, on investigation, this will be found true. Many of the innocent must doubtless be involved in ruin in consequence of it. The wretched, deranged finances of the Federal Government, will allow us, if disposed, to afford these people but feeble aid.

I am treated with respect by Congress and the heads of departments. The present Congress possess great integrity, and a good share of abilities ; but for want of more States on the floor the public and important business is from day to day neglected. We are, however, in daily expectation of a fuller delegation. If personal matters could be so adjusted that I were not disquieted, I should be very happy in my situation here ; for I commonly preach once or twice on Lord's Days, either in town, on Long or Staten Island, or in the Jerseys.

Please to present my best respects to Mrs. Smith and friends, and believe me to be

Your old, unvarying friend,

JAMES MANNING.

Dr. Manning's colleague was Brig.-Gen. Nathan Miller, of Warren. To him he thus writes, giving a graphic description of his own embarrassed condition for want of funds, and urging him in the present crisis of affairs to take his seat as a delegate, and by his presence and influence aid in preventing an impending dissolution of the Federal Government. That Manning fully comprehended the great questions which agitated this Congress of 1786, and which finally led to a more perfect union of the States, is evident from his correspondence, and from the great interest which he felt and the efforts which he made to secure the adoption of the Constitution of the United States.

NEW YORK, 7th of June, 1786.

DEAR SIR:

I think if for a moment you would figure to yourself my situation, alone here for more than a month, reduced to the very last guinea and a trifle of change (which is the case); my lodging, washing, barber's, hatter's, tailor's bills, etc., not paid; without the favor of a single line from you advising me whether you mean to come or not, or sending forward the one hundred dollars on hand, which you proposed doing from the election if you was not likely to follow me soon, — I say if you would but realize my situation, you could not but pity me from your heart. I wrote you long since. I begged an answer from you, one way or another, that I might know what measures to take. But as I am now situated, I can neither stay nor go, except to the new City Hall, if my creditors exact it; and strangers have no more compassion on me than the State that appointed me. I must interest you to forward that sum of one hundred dollars, if no more can be had, by the first opportunity, with a line advising me of your real intentions. Matters highly interesting to this Confederacy, and indeed I think the question whether the Federal Government shall long exist, are now before Congress, and there are not States sufficient to transact the necessary business, as we now have barely nine States on the floor. Our affairs are come very much to a point, and if the States continue to neglect keeping up their delegations in Congress, the Federal Government must *ipse facto* dissolve. I have written the Governor on these subjects, and desired his answer, whether we should keep up our delegation or not. I shall wait till a reasonable time for an answer from you, and quit if I do not receive it. Send me by the post or packets.

Frank your letters by the post. I shall impatiently wait the event, and with sentiments of esteem, I have the honor to be, sir,

Your humble servant,

JAMES MANNING.

TO THE SAME.

NEW YORK, 12th of June, 1786.

SIR: — Yours of 27th ult. came to hand two days ago. Am mortified exceedingly that you have not come forward, nor sent on the money on hand; for I am reduced to but a few shillings, and my bills are not paid. My situation — without a colleague, without money, and without any instructions or favorable prospects from government — is painful. Rhode Island has not many more strides to make to complete her disgrace, and ruin too; but that is not all. She is likely to hold a distinguished rank amongst the contributors to the ruin of the Federal Government. Never probably was a full delegation of the States more necessary than now, for you may rest assured that in the opinion of every member of Congress, and in the several departments, things are come to a crisis with the Federal Government. You say you think the present House do not want a Congress; they may, it is more than probable, very soon see the accomplishment of their wishes; for without a speedy reform in the policy of the States, the Federal Government must be no more. The flagrant violations of the public faith, solemnly plighted, in the late emissions of paper money, on the conditions on which it is emitted, is here considered as the completion of our ruin as a nation: but I wrote you before on this subject; it is too painful to repeat. Pray send me on the money on hand, or come and bring it yourself, without loss of time; at least, write me by every vessel. With sentiments of esteem, I have the honor to be, sir,

Your humble servant,

JAMES MANNING.

The following letter from the Rev. Dr. Gordon will be found especially interesting, in view of the author's position as a defender of America on English soil: —

STOKE NEWINGTON, ENGLAND, Sept. 13, 1786.

MY DEAR SIR:

I have appropriated a few of my busy moments to your friendship, on which I set a high value. You will have heard of our safe arrival. The passage was, blessed be God, good upon the whole, and though longer by a week or two than we could have wished, yet not lengthy. We were in London within six weeks, lacking two days, after leaving Boston, and had a slight sea-sickness only the first day. Many of our friends and acquaintance, and some of our relations, had been removed; but we had the pleasure of finding as many still living as we could reasonably expect. I took care to deliver the parcel for Mr. Rippon safely, of which you will probably have received an account before this arrives. It would have been great pleasure to us to have seen you and Mrs. Manning before our departure; but that having been prevented, I trust with you that the grace and mercy of God will favor us with an interview infinitely more agreeable in a better world. I am exceedingly busy upon my History, and when I have finished it shall not be unmindful of your college library. The abuse in the public papers hindered the subscriptions very much. I hope, however, they will be made up in Britain. The beginning of next month I mean to have the proposals circulating; but am apprehensive that the book will not go to the press so early as I intended. Every one tells me that I must be extremely cautions how I word myself, in speaking of individuals in Britain, lest I should be prosecuted for libelling; and prudence will require my advising with some gentleman learned in the law, that I may avoid falling into the clutches of the malevolent. You would wonder at the coolness with which I have been treated by several, even of my brethren in the ministry, for the part I took while in America; this, however, has not made me repent of engaging on the side of liberty. The Rev. Mr. Martin, of your persuasion, at the Westminster end of the town, was a most bitter enemy to the Americans, as I have heard; and one and another of the Presbyterians and Congregationalists were not less so, and would have rejoiced to have had the promoters and encouragers of the Revolution, whether in civil or sacred orders, hanged as rebels. But Heaven has disappointed and mortified them. They however spit out their venom at times.

We are at present with Mrs. Gordon's brother, who is exceedingly friendly. Where we shall settle is wholly uncertain; but a kind Providence, I hope, will direct in much mercy. Should like to be in the neighborhood of London, for the benefit of corresponding with my American friends, and doing them any particular service. Such a situation would place me also in the midst of my relations and British acquaintance. These matters, however, must all be submitted to infinite wisdom; and I desire not to be at my own disposal and direction.

We have been favored with good health since our arrival. I am concerned that your State should be so overseen as to make paper money, etc. Such policy will never make you prosper, and instead of preserving will drive away property and plenty from you. The Americans must make all kinds of property secure, or confusion will follow. I am most hearty in wishing them virtuous and honorable, and am therefore pained when anything takes place that is prejudicial to their public character. Mrs. Gordon joins in best regards to self and Mrs. Manning. Remember me to Mr. Nicholas Brown, Mr. Benson, and other friends. Let me hear from you by the first opportunity. Direct to Mr. Field's, Apothecary, Newgate Street. I remain,

Your sincere and affectionate friend,

WILLIAM GORDON.

This year the public exercises of Commencement were resumed. Fifteen young men took their Bachelor's degree, and among them Nicholas Brown, Jr., afterwards the distinguished benefactor of the college. He was at this time but seventeen years of age, having entered the Freshman Class in 1782, when the college again began to live. Mr. Brown commenced his benefactions in February, 1792, by presenting to the Trustees and Fellows of the college the sum of five hundred dollars, to be expended in the purchase of law books for the library. This he did, in the language of the letter announcing the donation, "under a deep impression of the generous intentions of my honored father, deceased, towards the college in this town, as well as from my own personal feelings towards the institution, in which I received my education, and from a desire to promote literature in general, and in particular the knowledge of the laws of our country, under the influence whereof not only our property but our lives and dearest privileges are protected." In 1804 he presented to the corporation the sum of five thousand dollars, as a foundation for a professorship of oratory and belles-lettres. It was on this occasion, in consideration of this donation, and of others that had been received from him and his kindred, that the name of the institution was changed, in accordance with a provision in its charter, from Rhode Island College to Brown University. In 1822 he erected at his own expense the second college building, which he presented to the corporation, in a letter bearing date Jan. 13, 1823. At his suggestion it was named "Hope College," in honor of his only surviving sister, Mrs. Hope Ives. In 1835 he erected the third building, which he also presented to the corporation, with a request that it might be named "Manning Hall," in honor of the memory of his own distinguished instructor and revered friend, President Manning. Mr. Brown died Sept. 27, 1841, at the age of seventy-two. A discourse commemorative of his character and life was delivered by President Wayland, in the University chapel, which discourse was afterwards published. The entire sum of his recorded benefactions and bequests to the University amounts to one hundred and sixty thousand dollars, assigning to the donations of land and buildings the valuation which was put upon them at the time they were made.

"Many years," says Prof. Gammell, "have now elapsed since he descended to the tomb, but the monuments of his wise and pious benefactions are all around us, — in the University with which his name is associated; in the Butler Hospital for the Insane, and the Providence Athenæum, to whose founding he so largely contributed; and in the churches, and colleges, and institutions of philanthropy over the whole land, to which he so often lent his liberal and most timely aid. So long as learning and religion shall have a place in the affections of men, these enduring memorials will proclaim his character, and speak his eulogy. *Hi sanctissimi testes, hi maximi laudatores.*"

A few years before his death, at the annual meeting of the corporation in 1835, Mr. Brown was formally requested to sit for his likeness, which was taken, at full length, by Harding, one of the most celebrated American artists. It now graces the collection[1] of portraits in Rhode Island

[1] This collection, to which we have frequently alluded, now comprises twenty-six portraits, many of them painted from life. The following list of them may be of interest, perhaps, to some of our readers: —

COLLEGE OFFICERS, GRADUATES, ETC.

1. JAMES MANNING. Two portraits, one of which is an original, painted by Alexander, of Newport, in the year 1770.
2. WILLIAM ROGERS, the first student of the college. Painted by his daughter, E. J. Rogers, from an original portrait by Rembrandt Peale.
3. FRANCIS WAYLAND, the fourth President. A full-length portrait. A fine marble bust of Wayland, executed by Ball, of Boston, is in the college library.
4. MOSES BROWN, the youngest of the "Four Brothers."
5. NICHOLAS BROWN. A full-length portrait, by Harding.
6. THOMAS POYNTON IVES, a distinguished benefactor of the college. Born in 1769.
7. ASHER ROBBINS, an early tutor, and the first librarian of the college.
8. HENRY WHEATON, Minister Plenipotentiary at Berlin. Graduated in 1802.
9. ADONIRAM JUDSON, missionary to Burmah. Graduated in 1807.
10. TRISTAM BURGESS, the distinguished orator. Graduated in 1796.
11. SOLOMON DROWNE, a Professor twenty-three years. Graduated in 1773.
12. NATHAN B. CROCKER. For nearly sixty years rector of St. John's Church, Providence, and for fifty-five years a Fellow of the University.

SOLDIERS, STATESMEN, ETC., DISTINGUISHED IN RHODE ISLAND HISTORY.

1. WILLIAM CODDINGTON, the first Governor of Rhode Island.
2. CHARLES II., from whom Rhode Island received her charter, in 1663. A fine original picture by Gaspars, an artist contemporary with the King.
3. CATHERINE OF BRAGANZA, his Queen. Also an original, by Gaspars.
4. EZEK HOPKINS, the first commodore in the American navy.
5. WILLIAM BARTON, the captor of Major-General Prescott.
6. ABRAHAM WHIPPLE, the "Daring Commodore."
7. SAMUEL SLATER, the founder of the manufacturing interests of Rhode Island and of America.
8. OLIVER HAZARD PERRY, the hero of Lake Erie.

Nich. Brown

1822

Hall. The visitor will gaze upon it with renewed interest as successive years roll on. It is greatly to be regretted that the portraits of his worthy sire and ancestors cannot be placed by its side.

Returning now to our narrative, we learn from the following extract from a letter addressed by Mr. Nicholas Brown, senior, to the Rev. Dr. Smith, dated Nov. 9, 1786, that Dr. Manning resumed his accustomed duties at the college in the beginning of November of that year. The extract is introduced as an illustration, in part, of the difficulties with which the college had to contend, owing to the scarcity of money and the confused state of the times.

"Mr. Manning arrived here early in this month, so that we have been destitute of a supply for the pulpit only two or three Sabbaths. The corporation were put to the necessity of beginning college exercises with the new tutor, young Mr. Flint, several days after the scholars had arrived, Mr. Robbins having been detained at New London, waiting for a passage, until after Mr. Manning left. The worst of all is that we are still destitute of a steward, several having applied for the place who were not

9. GILBERT STUART, the painter of Washington's portraits. Born in Rhode Island.
10. GEORGE BERKELEY, the distinguished Irish prelate and philosopher. Resided at Newport.
11. WILLIAM ELLERY CHANNING, the distinguished Unitarian divine.
12. CHRISTOPHER GREEN, a lieutenant-colonel in the army of the Revolution.
13. ISAAC P. RODMAN, a Brigadier-General of Rhode Island. Fell at the battle of Antietam.
14. Major-General AMBROSE E. BURNSIDE. A full-length portrait, painted from life, by E. Leutze, of New York.

The collection, as will be observed, includes men of all ranks and professions, and affords a happy illustration of the tie that binds together the varied interests of college and State. Most of the portraits have been obtained within the past five years, through the exertions of the Hon. J. R. Bartlett, Secretary of State, to whom the grateful thanks of the public are justly due for his generous and philanthropic labors. An enterprise so auspiciously commenced will, we trust, be carried on from year to year. Many portraits are still wanting to add completeness to the collection.

judged suitable, and several having been applied to who have declined. The want of some officer of college to attend the place of the institution, will, I fear, be a disadvantage. But the badness of the pay heretofore, and the scarcity of money, the paper currency, and the confused state of law and justice, both in your State and in our own, where the scholars come from, are real difficulties. The fact, too, that the students are obliged to board out, instead of boarding in commons, has greatly increased the expenses. Yet, I believe, if due attention is paid by the officers, we shall have many students in, at least by next Commencement."

TO THE REV. DR. SMITH.

PROVIDENCE, Jan. 18, 1787.

DEAR SIR:

Yours of the 15th ult. came to hand a few days ago. Am happy to hear of your welfare, but am sorry to hear of Mrs. Smith's indisposition. Hope it has proved of short duration. About a month ago I was seized with a violent fit of the bilious colic, which confined me about a fortnight, and threatened my life. Through divine favor I am happily recovered, and we all enjoy usual health. The town is generally healthy. Mr. Nicholas Brown has lost his new-born son. Mr. Jonathan Jenckes is married to the widow Bowers, who lived across the way. No late intelligence from the westward. Trade amongst us is very declining. Brown and Benson, by a seizure at Surinam, have lost about four thousand dollars, and Jenckes, Winsor, and Co. about the same sum by the like means in Virginia. The paper money of this State has run down to six for one, notwithstanding which the Legislature continue it as a tender, and mean to do so, and to pay off all the State debts with it, be it as bad as it may. At the last session I petitioned them to pay my advances, and the remainder of my salary as delegate, amounting to upwards of four hundred dollars. This they offered to do in their paper, but in no other way. Besides, they have ordered all the import orders brought in and exchanged at the treasury for paper at par, so that I must lose five sixths of my salary so paid to me. A more infamous set of men under the character of a legislature, never, I believe, disgraced the annals of the world. And there is no prospect of a change for the better. Of all the arrearages of tuition for the last year, and the quarter advanced in this, I have not received ten pounds. I was taken sick the day after the second great snow, with no provisions in the cellar except one hundred-weight of cheese, two barrels of cider, and some potatoes; with not a load of wood at my door; nor could I command a single dollar to supply these wants. The kindness of my neighbors, however, kept me from suffering. But when a man has hardly earned money, to be reduced to this abject state of dependence requires the exercise of more grace than I can boast of. I feel for you in the situation which you mention, but it is a very trying time, and few of our ministering brethren are exempt from those trials. Nor would it probably be easy for you to better yourself. I have serious thought of removing to the farm at the Jerseys, and undertake *digging* for my support. Should things wear the same unfavorable aspect next year, I believe I shall make the experiment, if my life is spared.

The college consists of about the same number as it did before Commencement, but the delinquency of the students in paying their bills must, if not altered, break up the college, as the affairs cannot be supported, especially as all assistance from our fund is cut off, if indeed it is not totally annihilated, which I greatly fear from the temper of the times.

I completed your business at New York, I believe, agreeably to your wishes, and have your securities and papers all by me ready for your commands, but I did not choose to send them by an uncertain conveyance. You mention an agreeable journey last October, but don't tell me where. I think with you that there is something godlike in preaching to the poor, who cannot recompense us; but it is our misfortune to be so generally of that number that we can only contemplate it. I supply the pulpit when able, but have had no application from the church, as such, to do it. Religion is extremely low with us, and confusion in State matters seems to increase. Please to present my best respects to Mrs. Smith and family, with all friends, in which Mrs. M. joins.

Sir, yours, etc.,

JAMES MANNING.

The language of Dr. Manning, as here applied to the Legislature of Rhode Island, may seem at first unnecessarily severe. A reference, however, to Gov. Arnold's History, and to our biographical sketch of Gen. Varnum, in his forensic effort in the celebrated case of Trevett against Weeden (page 98), will show that it was merited and just. This perhaps was the most trying period of Dr. Manning's life. That he should have had serious thoughts of engaging in agriculture for a support is by no means surprising.

These, however, were but momentary, and soon passed away. Few men, with powers distracted by care, and spirits saddened perhaps by a want of the comforts and conveniences of life, have ever labored more perseveringly, diligently, and cheerfully for the welfare of others, and for the public good, than Manning.

The Commencement for 1787 seems to have been one of unusual interest, "a large, polite, and crowded assembly of gentlemen and ladies attending upon the exercises, and thus doing honor to the day and themselves by encouraging polite literature, and those useful arts which are the glory of civilized countries." Among the orations upon this occasion was one by Nathaniel Lambert, on "The Present Appearance of Public Affairs in the United States of America — portraying the superior advantages to be enjoyed by this country, and the public happiness rationally to be expected, in case the States shall harmoniously agree on the great federal measures necessary for the good of the whole, whereon the convention have been some time deliberating at Philadelphia, and recommending industry, the manufactures of our country, and the disuse of foreign goods; and soliciting the fair daughters of America to set the patriotic example by banishing from their dress the costly gewgaws and articles of foreign production." Doubtless the worthy President had something to do with the selection of this topic, and its happy treatment.

The graduates numbered ten; at the head of whom, on the Triennial, stands the name of Abner Alden, master of the famous school at Raynham, Mass., and author of the "Reader" and "The Spelling-book" which supplied our ancestors in the Old Colony with the "rudiments" half a century ago. Mr. Alden was of the fifth generation in lineal descent from John Alden, of whom and Priscilla Mullins Longfellow sings. Among them too we notice Samuel Eddy,[1] for many years a Fellow and secretary of the corporation, and Jonathan Maxcy, President Manning's successor in office. Mr. Maxcy[2] delivered a poem on the prospects of America, and the valedictory oration.

[1] Hon. Samuel Eddy, LL.D., was born in Johnston, R. I., March 31, 1769. After his graduation he read law, but he never practised it. In 1798 he was elected by the people of Rhode Island Secretary of State, which office he held for twenty-one years in succession. Resigning the secretaryship, he was elected, for three terms, from 1819 to 1825, a Representative in Congress. Subsequently he was appointed Chief Justice of the Supreme Judicial Court of Rhode Island, which position he occupied for eight years, when ill health compelled him to resign. He died February 3, 1839, in the seventieth year of his age. Judge Eddy was justly respected for his uprightness and intelligence, and for the extent and variety of his attainments. He was no debater, says Prof. Goddard, but he wrote with uncommon purity, accuracy, and force. The volumes of the Massachusetts Historical Society are enriched with several contributions from his pen. He was thrice married. His last wife was Mrs. Sarah Dwight, widow of Gamaliel Lyman Dwight, and daughter of the Hon. David Howell. She survived him many years, dying recently at an advanced age.

[2] Rev. Jonathan Maxcy, D.D., was born in Attleboro, Mass., Sept. 2, 1768. Immediately upon graduating, at the early age of nineteen, he was appointed tutor in the college, which position he filled with great acceptance four years, or until 1791, when he was chosen pastor of the Baptist church. In 1792 he assumed the duties of the presidency of the college, having been elected President *pro tempore.* In 1797 he was formally elected President, as appears from the records of the corporation. "The splendor of his genius, and his brilliant talents as an orator and divine," says Dr. Blake, "had become widely known; and under his administration the college acquired a reputation for belles-letters and eloquence inferior to no seminary of learning in the United States." "His voice," says the Hon. Tristam Burgess, one of his most devoted and admiring pupils, "seemed not to have reached the deep tone of full age; but most of all to resemble that of those concerning whom the Saviour of the world said, 'of such is the kingdom of heaven.' The eloquence of Maxcy was mental. You seemed to hear the soul of the man; and each one of the largest assembly, in the most extended place of worship, received the slightest impulse of his silver voice as if he stood at his very ear. So intensely would he enchain attention, that in the most thronged audience you heard nothing but him and the pulsations of your own heart. His utterance was not more perfect than his whole discourse was instructive and enchanting."

In the year 1802, Dr. Maxcy, having resigned his office, was appointed Presi-

34*

The fears and forebodings of Dr. Manning in regard to the Confederation proved but too well founded. Notwithstanding the efforts of the wisest statesmen, it was found inefficient to promote social order, and all those paramount interests which it is the design of government to foster and protect. Accordingly, in 1787, a national convention met at Philadelphia, and proposed a union of the States upon a more substantial and popular basis, in order that the blessings of freedom might be preserved. A small number of the States adopted the New Constitu-

dent of Union College, Schenectady, N. Y., as successor of the Rev. Dr. Jonathan Edwards, deceased. In reference to this appointment, we find in Forsyth's Memoir of the Rev. Dr. Alexander Proudfit (pp. 55-59) a curious and interesting letter from the Rev. J. B. Johnson, then of Albany, and a Trustee of the college, objecting to Maxcy on the ground of his being a Baptist, and hence that his influence as such would be unpropitious to the prosperity of the institution, the support of the college being derived chiefly from those who were opposed to the Baptist persuasion, and perhaps had no inconsiderable prejudice against them. Another objection was that he appeared to the writer to be a violent politician, judging from a Fourth-of-July oration delivered by him, which had been praised as containing some very brilliant expressions and keen sarcasms against the Anti-Federalists. A third and more serious objection, however, was the unsoundness of his theological opinions, of which the following extract from the preface to his sermon on the death of Manning, republished in June, 1796, was quoted as an illustration: "The only thing essential to Christian union is love, or benevolent affection. It is, therefore, with me, a fixed principle to censure no man except for immorality. A diversity of religious opinions, in a state so imperfect, obscure, and sinful as the present, is to be expected. An entire coincidence in sentiment, even in important doctrines, is by no means essential to Christian society, or the attainment of eternal felicity. How many are there, who appear to have been subjects of regeneration, who have scarcely an entire comprehensive view of one doctrine of the Bible? Will the gates of paradise be barred against these because they did not possess the penetrating sagacity of an Edwards or a Hopkins? Or shall these great theological champions engross heaven, and shout hallelujahs from its walls, while a Priestley, a Price, and a Winchester, merely for difference in opinion, though preëminent in virtue, must sink into the regions of darkness and pain?"

Notwithstanding these objections, Dr. Maxcy, as we have already stated, was chosen President of the college. Previous to this event, when only thirty-three years of age, Harvard University had conferred on him the honorary degree of Doctor in Divinity, such was his celebrity as a scholar and divine. Here

tion, so called, without hesitation, but in most of them it met with great opposition. Especially was this the case in Massachusetts, where the Federalists and Anti-Federalists, as the friends and enemies of the Constitution were pleased to style themselves, were nearly equal in number. The convention for the adoption or rejection of this important instrument met at Boston, on Wednesday, the 9th of January, 1788. It was composed of nearly four hundred delegates, representing the talent and patriotism of the ancient commonwealth, as well as the conflicting interests of opposing parties. The debates were continued for a month, and attracted the most profound attention throughout the country. Upon the fate of the Federal Constitution here, it was supposed, depended the fate of the National Government; or, as Manning expresses it,

at Schenectady he officiated with increasing reputation until 1804, when he accepted the unsolicited appointment of President of South Carolina College, with the fond anticipation of finding a warmer climate more congenial to his physical constitution. Over this latter institution he presided, with almost unprecedented popularity, during the remainder of his life. He died at Columbia, S. C., June 4, 1820, aged fifty-two years.

In his person Dr. Maxcy was small of stature, but of a fine and well-proportioned figure. His features, says his biographer, were regular and manly, indicating intelligence and benevolence, and, especially in conversation and public speaking they were strongly expressive. Grace and dignity were also combined in all his movements. His writings, or "Literary Remains," edited by the Rev. Dr. Romeo Elton, were published in 1844, in a handsome octavo volume. Eight years later a selection from his "Remains," consisting of collegiate addresses, was published in London, making a pleasant little duodecimo volume of one hundred and ninety-one pages. This was also edited by Dr. Elton. Dr. Maxcy was married to Susan, daughter of Commodore Ezek Hopkins, of Providence, a name intimately associated with the history of the Revolution. Besides several daughters, they had four sons, all liberally educated; one of whom, the Hon. Virgil Maxcy, was killed by the explosion of a gun on board the United States steamship Princeton.

No painted canvas or sculptured marble perpetuates the likeness of President Maxcy; but so long, says Elton, "as genius, hallowed and sublimed by piety, shall command veneration, he will be remembered in his country as a star of the first magnitude."

Massachusetts was considered "the hinge on which the whole must turn." As an evidence of the deep interest which he felt in this momentous question, we quote from Mr. Howland's Memoir the following passage : —

"Dr. Manning was extremely solicitous for ratification. He viewed the situation of the country with all the light of a statesman and a philosopher, and as a prudent and well-informed citizen he took his measures accordingly. He had saved the college funds through the fluctuations and storms of one revolution, and he now saw them dissipated and lost forever, unless the new form of government should be established. He knew that several clergymen with whom he was connected in the bonds of religious union were members of the convention, and that they were generally opposed to the ratification. He therefore repaired to Boston, and attended the debates and proceedings of the convention. His most valued and intimate friend, the Rev. Dr. Stillman, was one of the twelve representatives of the town of Boston in the convention, and zealous for the adoption ; and in their frequent intercourse with their friends who were members, they endeavored to remove the objections of such as were in the opposition. . . . . With the Rev. Isaac Backus, who was a delegate from the town of Middleborough, and considered one of the most powerful men of the Anti-Federal party, they were not able to succeed. The question of ratification was finally carried, by a majority of nineteen (one hundred and eighty-seven yeas, and one hundred and sixty-eight nays), after a full and able discussion. The writer of these sketches well recollects the cordial congratulations with which Dr. Manning greeted his friends on the decision of this convention, after his return from Boston."

In connection with the facts stated by Howland, we cannot forbear to add an incident mentioned by Dr. Waterhouse, which we find quoted by Prof. Goddard. On the last day of the session of the convention, and before the final question was taken, the President, Gov. Hancock, invited Dr. Manning to "close the solemn convocation with thanksgiving and prayer." Dr. Manning, though taken by surprise, immediately dropped on his knees, and poured out his heart in a strain of exalted patriotism and fervid devotion, which awakened in the assembly a mingled sentiment of admiration and awe. The impression which he made must have been extraordinary; for, says Dr. Waterhouse, who dined in a large company, after the adjournment, "the praise of the Rev. Dr. Manning was in every mouth. Nothing but the popularity of Dr. Stillman prevented the rich men of Boston from building a church for Dr. Manning's acceptance."

In the following letter Manning alludes to his attendance upon the debates of the Massachusetts Convention: —

TO THE REV. DR. SMITH.

PROVIDENCE, Feb. 11, 1788.

TO THE REV. DR. SMITH:

MY DEAR SIR: — This morning was handed me your agreeable favor of the 30th ult. I am happy to hear that you and yours enjoy health; but sorry that with me you have cause to complain of the low state of religion. To be useful, is and must be the wish of every good man; but perhaps we may not always be the most competent judges of our usefulness. God may be doing that by us, which we little think of, that may redound to his glory. One or two, I hope, have lately met with a change amongst us, and there appears a greater degree of attention than for some time past. I continue still to preach to the people as a supply, till Mr. Stanford, from New York, arrives, whom the church and congregation have unanimously chosen their pastor. He is expected as soon as winter breaks. He paid us a visit at the invitation of the committee last Christmas, and spent two Lord's Days with us to great acceptance. He was to have been with us by the middle of this month, but had a three weeks' passage back. Elder Asa Hunt called on me last week on his way from Virginia, where he has been for several months, having travelled seven hundred miles in that State, and preached, I think, seventy times. He brings refreshing tidings of the work of the Lord there, and of the great increase of our churches. Two most agreeable letters I received from respectable ministers there, of whom I had not before heard. One of them mentions that there are about one hundred Baptist churches in that State, averaging each at least one hundred members. Great additions are daily making to them, and they call aloud for ministers of education. I never wanted to visit that country so much as now.

The college continues gradually to increase. The expense of boarding in commons, tuition, room-rent, and library and apparatus privileges, granting one fourth of the year for vacations, amounts to just £20 5s. 9d. lawful money (about sixty-eight dollars) at present, but I expect the commons will be lowered as soon as stability in government takes place, — a period I now hope not far distant. Wood is about twelve shillings per cord; and other incidental expenses as moderate here, or more so, than at Dartmouth. Two of our young men the Commencement before were at Dartmouth, Gov. Bowen's son and Mr. Nicholas Brown's son, who made particular inquiry, and they assure me that the expense of living equally well was greater there than here. I make not a doubt but he would find his account in coming to Providence, and we should be happy to receive him and do well by him. I hoped to have more particulars of your last fall tour. The reason of Brother Gano's leaving New York, is want of an adequate support, which fails through the opposition of a certain Mr. Robbins and his adherents in that church, who wish to govern it in their own way.

I felt so deeply interested in the adoption of the new Federal Constitution by your State, that I attended the debates in convention more than a fortnight, and expected to have seen you at Boston on that occasion. I considered Massachusetts the hinge on which the whole must turn, and am happy in congratulating you on the favorable issue of their deliberations. I am mortified to find Father Alden among the *nays*. The good work at New London and its vicinity, I am told, increases, and has spread to Norwich; and there is a great awakening where Grow used to preach, and in Canada Parish. Please to present my best respects to Mrs. Smith and family and other friends, in which Mrs. Manning joins with, dear sir,

Yours,

JAMES MANNING.

From this time Dr. Manning held no political office, although he always took a prominent part in public affairs, and was thoroughly familiar with the discussions and controversies of the day. The final adoption of the Federal

Constitution by the people of Rhode Island, notwithstanding the persistent and bitter hostility of its opponents, was a result due in no small measure, doubtless, to his wise counsels and superior influence. We present his correspondence for the remainder of the year, commencing with a letter from the Rev. Dr. Rippon of London.

LONDON, Feb. 14, 1788.

REVEREND AND DEAR SIR :

I have but a few minutes to spare this forenoon, which should have been devoted to your service, having passed in company, which unexpectedly has detained me. However, I most sincerely thank you for the short but comprehensive sketch of religious affairs communicated in your last of September, 1787, and also for your respectful introduction of the Selections[1] at the Chelmsford Association. The first edition of three thousand is gone, except about fifty books, and the second edition, I hope, will be quite printed off in April next. In case it meets with the approbation of our American brethren, and there is any probability of its spread, would it be against any rule of your Association to advertise the second edition? I have mentioned this to one or two brethren on your side of the water. No book printed in any time has had so rapid a sale among the Baptists as this.

With this please to accept a pamphlet or two, by which you will see in some measure what we are about in this country. The three denominations of Presbyterians, Independents, and Anti-Pedobaptists in this city are united together by a *political* bond. We met about a week since, and drew up a petition to Parliament for the abolition of the slave trade. The meeting was perfectly unanimous. We fear that there will be great opposition to the petition, but we hope to prevent the importation of any more slaves, from Africa at least. The petitions to be presented by clerical and political bodies are likely to be numerous and very general. While so many thousands are nobly engaged in this, the cause of humanity, may you succeed in your own peculiar career, distinguished from every other by a "glory that excelleth."

[1] "A Selection of Hymns from the best authors, intended to be an Appendix to Dr. Watts's Psalms and Hymns. By John Rippon, A.M." 12mo. London. Printed by Thos. Wilkins; and sold on weekdays at the vestry of Mr. Rippon's meeting-house. 1787.

You mention the number of sixty students. Of what advantage may the wise and good among these be, not only to the present but future generations! *Long* may you live, and under your auspices may the college enjoy your felicity; and in a *remote* period, when the public prints announce that Dr. Manning was, may it be said, "He shone through a *long-lengthened* day, the ornament and boast of all his connections, and then set, like the sun, to rise and shine forever."

Indeed, dear sir, I do feel a great union of heart to you, and to many of our brethren on your side of the Atlantic. It would be an unutterable joy were it in my power to do them any service, but if I can show my love to them no other way,

> "My soul shall pray for Zion still,
> While life or breath remains;
> *There* my best friends, my kindred dwell,
> *There* God my Saviour reigns."

Mr. Stillman's account of Miss Stillman's death was very affecting and edifying. How plain it is that true religion is produced in the heart of good men by "the self-same spirit"!

I shall rejoice to have a long letter from you, as you would have had from me but for the reason mentioned before. I have not time to read this scrawl, but I should suppress some of the first emotions of my mind, were I not to subscribe myself ever, ever *very affectionately*,

Your obliged brother in Christ,

JOHN RIPPON.

P. S. — Please to remember me to Doctor Drowne. I hope to write him, and shall be very glad to receive a line from him.

TO THE REV. THOMAS USTICK, PHILADELPHIA.

PROVIDENCE, Aug. 21, 1788.

MY DEAR BROTHER:

Yours of June 10th was long in coming, but is now before me. I am glad to hear that you are so happily restored as to be able to preach to the people, but sorry that you have reason to complain of the low state of religion amongst you. I hope you may see better days in Philadelphia. It is a complaining time, in general, among ministers. Perhaps they themselves, if properly engaged, might in part prevent the cause of it. My own difficulties, I know, call for the exercise of Christian fortitude, but I find it easier to talk of than to exercise it. I thank you, however, for the just remarks contained in your letter. I agree with you that the gospel is an estimable jewel, which we cannot too highly prize. May we be properly anointed by the glorious hopes which it is calculated to inspire.

Brother Caleb Blood, of Newtown, is the person whom I mentioned to have removed to Vermont. Our Brother Joseph Grafton, of this town and church, is ordained and settled in his place, whose labors appear to be owned amongst that people. He was here last week. Elders Backus, Hunt, and Williams have lately visited us, who are well. I am told that there is a happy revival at Bridgewater, under the ministry of Brother Robinson. Nothing new respecting the college has occurred since our last. Possibly I may see you this fall at Philadelphia, as I have thoughts of visiting New York. Please to make my best respects to Mrs. Ustick and the family, in which Mrs. Manning unites, with, dear sir,

Your unworthy brother,

JAMES MANNING.

TO THE REV. DR. SMITH.

PROVIDENCE, June 10, 1788.

DEAR SIR:

Yours of the 6th inst. came to hand a few hours since, by Mr. Messer.[1] We have examined and entered the young gentleman into the Sophomore class, though he had not read quite so much as the class. His abilities

[1] Rev. Asa Messer, D.D., LL.D. He was born in Methuen, Mass., in the year 1769. His father was a farmer on the banks of the Merrimac. At the age of thirteen he left the town school in his native place, and went to live in Haverhill, where for nearly a year he was clerk in a wholesale grocery store. Having given up his clerkship, he studied for a short time under the instruction of the Rev. Dr. Hezekiah Smith, and then finished his preparation for college at Windham, New Hampshire. He graduated in 1790. Soon afterwards he became interested in religious truth, was baptized, and received into the fellowship of the church in Providence, of which Dr. Maxcy was then pastor. By this church he was, in 1792, licensed to preach, and in 1801 he received ordination. He was elected a tutor of the college in 1791, and remained in this office till he was elected, in 1796, Professor of the Learned Languages. In 1799 he was appointed Professor of Mathematics and Natural Philosophy; and this station he continued to hold until the resignation of Dr. Maxcy, in 1802, when he was chosen President. For twenty-four years he presided over the affairs of the college; diligently and efficiently participating in the duties of instruction, and supervising, with no common practical sagacity, its disordered finances. In 1826 he resigned the office of President. Possessing, says his biographer,

and proficiency appear very good; and from your commendation of him we hope the will do well. Am obliged to you for your interest in forwarding him.

I rejoice to hear of the Lord's work at Byfield and Rowley. Hope it may become universal. Then Haverhill and Providence will receive a

a handsome competence, the fruit in part of his habitual frugality, he was enabled to pass the remainder of his life in the enjoyment of independent leisure. After his retirement from collegiate toils, his fellow-citizens of Providence elected him, for several years, to responsible municipal trusts; and these trusts he discharged with his characteristic punctuality and uprightness. He died October 11, 1836, in the sixty-eighth year of his age.

Dr. Messer was married to Deborah Angell, by whom he had four children, a son that died in infancy, and three daughters. The youngest daughter was married to the late Hon. Horace Mann, and the second to Sidney Williams, Esq., of Taunton, Mass. Mr. Williams now resides on the paternal estate. The eldest daughter was never married.

Dr. Messer's "religious opinions," says Prof. Goddard, "especially for the last twenty years of his life, corresponded nearly to those of the General Baptists of England. He was a strenuous advocate for the supremacy of the Scriptures, and for their entire sufficiency in matters of faith and practice. As a preacher, he wanted the attractive graces of elocution; but he never failed to address to the understanding and the conscience the most clear and cogent exhibitions of the great practical truths of the Bible. For what is termed polite literature he had no particular fondness, but he was a good classical scholar, and was well versed in the mathematics and the several branches of natural philosophy. In moral science, also, we have known few better reasoners or more successful teachers. In fine, Dr. Messer was remarkable rather for the vigor than the versatility of his powers; rather for solid acquirement than for captivating embellishments; rather for wisdom than for wit; rather for grave processes of ratiocination than for the airy frolics of fancy. In 1824 he received from Harvard University the honorary degree of Doctor of Divinity, having previously received the same degree from his ALMA MATER, and that of Doctor of Laws from the University of Vermont."

"I cannot remember," says the Rev. Dr. E. A. Park, in a recent letter which he furnished for Sprague's Annals of the American Pulpit, "the time when I was not familiar with the countenance of President Messer. Before I entered college I saw him every week, and while I was a member of college I saw him every day; and no one who has ever seen him can ever forget him. His individuality was made unmistakable by his physical frame. This, while it was above the average height, was also in breadth an emblem of the expansiveness of his mental capacity. A 'long head' was vulgarly ascribed to him, but it was breadth that marked his forehead; there was an expressive breadth in his maxillary bones; his broad shoulders were a sign of the weight which he was able to bear; his manner of walking was a noticeable symbol of the reach of

blessing. Am surprised that mine in answer to yours of March 17, and every other I have received, has not reached you. I have been punctual in writing, and giving you all the information I could. Our wicked State has rejected the Constitution by the town meetings to which the Legislature sent it, instead of complying with the recommendation of the General Convention. Our rulers are deliberately wicked, but the people of some of the towns begin to wake up since South Carolina has adopted the new Constitution, and Massachusetts has so effectually crushed Shayism. My visit to New York was very short and full of business, so that I did not go to visit one of my brothers or sister, though I was at the Plains. My object was to assist Brother Gano off for Kentucky, which took up all my time. I heard from none of your friends. Indeed, I had no opportunity. Mr. Gano with his family left the Plains the first Wednesday in May. Many families of his people, Mr. Van Horn's and Mr. Hart's, are gone also, and more are proposing. A surprising spirit of emigration prevails there. The church at New York are without a supply, and probably will be for a time. Mr. Stanford is still very acceptable to all evangelical hearers. The house is pretty full, but he meets with some trials. Two weeks ago Mr. Alison of Bordentown paid us a visit, and entered a young gentleman in the Junior Class.

The college has more students than ever it had; consequently my services are greater than ever. Our oldest tutor, Robbins, has been unable to do any duty since last December, and is gone to Connecticut, five weeks since, from whom we have had no certain accounts. I doubt his ever being well again, or taking his place in college. So you see I must deny myself the pleasure of attending the New Hampshire Association. The state of religion in York is not as promising as in times past. Near

his mind; he swung his cane far and wide as he walked, and no observer would doubt that he was an independent man; he gesticulated broadly as he preached; his enunciation was forcible, now and then overwhelming, sometimes shrill, but was characterized by a breadth of tone and a prolonged emphasis which added to its momentum, and made an indelible impress on the memory. His pupils, when they had been unfaithful, trembled before his expansive frown, as it portended a rebuke which would well-nigh devour them; and they felt a dilating of the whole soul when they were greeted with his good and honest and broad smile. . . . . As a son, brother, husband, father, he was the central object of attraction, and the beams of joy and love uniformly radiated from him over all the inmates of his happy home."

It is exceedingly to be regretted that no portrait or engraving exists to perpetuate the likeness of this remarkable man.

Peekskill and higher up it flourishes, and so it does in the Jerseys under the ministry of Brother Wilson. The York church has sent out a flaming young preacher, Tommy Montague, who outshines us all they say. I think the church at York have some thoughts of Brother Foster at Newport, and he of them. He visits them by request in July. My spring letters from London bring nothing of importance now, except the completion of the second edition of Mr. Booth's treatise on Baptism, which is much enlarged. I have not perused it. My best love to Mrs. Smith and family, in which, as well as to yourself and all friends, Mrs. Manning cordially unites with, dear sir,

Yours, etc.,

JAMES MANNING.

The Commencement for this year occurred on Wednesday, Sept. 3. As the day, says the passing record, was fine, so the concourse of people was prodigious. The procession — composed of the corporation and the officers, of the graduates and the students, of the clergy and other literati, from abroad in greater numbers than ever attended here before — began in the usual order at college, about eleven o'clock in the morning, and was escorted by the gallant company of artillery commanded by Col. Tillinghast to the Baptist meeting-house. In looking over the order of exercises on this occasion, we notice, besides the salutatory oration in Latin, an oration in Hebrew on the eloquence of the Scriptures, an oration in French on letters in general, an oration in Greek on the importance of encouraging genius, a dialogue in blank verse on the situation and prospects of America, and a comic dialogue to ridicule false learning. As was the custom at all the earlier Commencements of the college, the exercises were continued through the day, with a recess at noon. The valedictory oration was pronounced by Amos Maine Atwell, of Providence. Among those who graduated on this occasion, was James Burrill,[1] who for sixteen years was successively elected, amid all the vicissitudes and competitions of party, to the responsible office of Attorney General of Rhode Island, and who was afterwards a member of the United States Senate.

FROM THE REV. MORGAN EDWARDS.

PHILADELPHIA, Aug. 18, 1788.

MY OLD ACQUAINTANCE:

I am now thinking how long it is since you and I have seen each other's face or perused each other's letters; and what the reason is, and whose fault (if a fault) it is. But as the inquiry hardly deserves a decision, I let all pass in silence, that I may proceed to inquire after your present state of health. I hope this will find you in a comfortable situation; at least I wish it may. I feel as well and as strong as an old man of sixty-seven years can expect to be.

Some years ago I sent you a manuscript; whether you received it or not I cannot say. It was a collection of some historical facts relative to the Baptists. If you have the book, please return it to me as soon as conveniency offers. Herewith I send you a small piece newly published. Your remarks upon it will be interesting to me as an editor, especially if it should pass through another edition.

My love and good wishes attend you and yours.

M. EDWARDS.

[1] Hon. James Burrill, LL.D., was born in Providence, in 1772. He was prepared for college by William Wilkinson, Esq., then an eminent classical and mathematical teacher in that town. He graduated at the early age of sixteen, and after completing his professional studies commenced, at the age of nineteen, the practice of the law in his native town. So rapid was his rise at the bar, that, at the age of twenty-five, he was elected by the people to the office of Attorney General, and this office he continued to hold for about sixteen years, until bodily infirmity compelled him to retire from the bar. In 1816 he was elected Chief Justice of the Supreme Court of Rhode Island, and a few months afterwards a Senator in Congress. He attended only four sessions of that body, — his valuable life having been prematurely terminated by a pulmonary disease, Dec. 25, 1820, in the forty-ninth year of his age. "During his short career in Congress," says Prof. Goddard, "Mr. Burrill won for himself a very high rank. To the Senate of the United States there perhaps never had belonged a more useful legislator or a more practical statesman. All who knew Mr. Burrill marvelled

FROM THE REV. DR. EVANS.

DOWN END, NEAR BRISTOL, Sept. 20, 1788.

DEAR SIR:

As a memorial of my friendship, and some slight atonement for former neglects, I write you this billet by my dear Brother and Sister Mullett, to thank you for your former attentions to the first, and to commend them both to your further notice. Our anxieties and emotions at parting with those we have so much reason to love, and especially with a sister endeared to us from her earliest infancy by every quality that can render any character truly respectable and truly amiable, are not to be described. But we cast all our care on that God who careth for all those who trust in him, and has promised not to leave nor forsake them.

I enclose you a few Association letters, etc., which may give you more information than I have leisure to communicate. Dr. Stennett's Sermons on the Parable of the Sower you have doubtless seen. They are truly excellent, as giving the best instructions to preachers as well as hearers. I would also recommend to your notice Dr. Priestley's Lectures on History, as the best book on that interesting subject I ever met with. If I can I will herewith send it, and beg your acceptance of it for the library of your college. I wish also to acquaint you with the reasons we have to expect soon a capital history of the Baptists, by William Robinson of Cambridge, and if possible, will get some of his letters to me on that subject transcribed for that purpose.

It gives me no small concern to find your government making so disgraceful a figure amongst the other sister States. Surely, if they knew how foreigners look upon them, they would blush. I should, however, have scarcely ventured to say this, if I could not have added that I am happy to find the town of New Providence shines forth as a luminous spot upon this dark mass, and appears the brighter for the darkness which surrounds it.

What shall I say to tempt you to renew a correspondence you have

at the opulence of his resources, and at his power to command them at pleasure. In the operations of his mind there was no indication of excess, of feebleness, or of confusion. On the contrary, he was always judicious, luminous, and forcible — master of an infinite variety of facts and principles, and ever ready in applying them. He seldom wrote, although he was capable of writing well; and it is sad to think that his fame, as a lawyer and as a statesman, must soon become only a matter of dim traditionary recollection."

hitherto found so fruitless? May I not remind you that it is more blessed to give than to receive? And you have much to give which will be thankfully received, though you may receive little or nothing in return. I shall also be glad to hear of the general state of religion in America, of the progress of civilization, etc., etc., in Kentucky, the prosperity of the Baptist college, the health and usefulness of its worthy President, etc. And you may possibly, now my connections with America are so tender, find me a more punctual, if not a more intelligent correspondent than I have hitherto been. Dr. Priestley's writings in the theological line you are probably no stranger to, and surely he has gone to the *ne plus ultra* of heresy. Further he cannot go and retain the *name* of Christian, for the substance of Christianity he has long since discarded. I am preaching a few sermons on the atonement, in opposition to his strange, unsupported notions. Such doctrines cannot long prevail. They have no internal energy.

I have heard an excellent character of the son of the late Jonathan Edwards. Can you give me any anecdotes respecting him?

I remain, dear sir, with every wish the sincerest friendship can dictate for you and your family and extensive connections,

Your affectionate friend and brother,

CALEB EVANS.

P. S. — I write this in haste, at a country retreat four miles from town, and have not my papers with me, or I would make a regular acknowledgment of your repeated favors before and since the safe arrival of the books.

I had like to have forgot to say, do you want a good linguist to assist in the college or grammar school with you, or to send to Kentucky? A young man of this description left our academy last vacation, who, having few friends here, and a very slender voice, which is a bar to his popularity, seems willing to go abroad could he have any encouragement. He is a good young man, has very tolerable talents as a preacher, and is an excellent mechanical scholar in Latin, Greek, Hebrew, Syriac, and has some knowledge of the first rudiments of the mathematics. He is deficient in a general course of knowledge and reading, but habituated to diligence, and very capable of improvement. I should have kept him here another year, had not some particular circumstances prevented it. I really think he might be an important acquisition in such a department as I have mentioned, and I am persuaded he would come over upon very moderate encouragement.

TO THE REV. DR. SMITH.

PROVIDENCE, Dec. 17, 1788.

DEAR SIR:

Yours of the 25th ult. came safe to hand. Am sorry for and sympathize with you in your trials, but God means them for good to you; though we are impatient, oftentimes, under the salutary discipline of a heavenly parent. I cannot bear to think of your leaving Haverhill. I hope God has work for you to do there yet, and is now preparing you for it. I should be sorry should you come to a resolution of taking your son from college. I hope you may yet see a brighter sky, which will encourage you to proceed. The conduct of the people I doubt not is trying. You did well in not being precipitate. We must let our moderation be known, and indeed we need much of it. I hope you meet with success in the petition to the House of New Hampshire, but fear, as their session was so short, they did not take that up; if not, I hope they will when they meet next. Am glad to hear that things were agreeable at Mr. Wood's settlement at Ware. I hope he will prove a blessing to them. I think him a valuable man.

The abridgment of Dr. Gill, through the scarcity of money, is stopped for the present, as very little encouragement has yet been given for the work. Dr. Jones himself does not expect it will go on, and the money which was put into my hands for that purpose I have returned long since. *Thus endeth that lesson.*

Your son, I think, wants a little more stability; he seems to fluctuate too much. Upon giving him your letter to me to read, he seemed to conclude he is not likely to come to college any more. Instability is natural to young minds, but it may be checked in some degree by proper culture; and a parent greatly beloved can accomplish this the best. Mr. Stanford has hinted to the people that they are not to expect his stay after the expiration of the term agreed on; but the committee have within a few days past had two meetings, the last of which was with him, and are determined to use their influence to prevent it. With sentiments of esteem, and love to Mrs. Smith, in which Mrs. Manning joins, I am, etc.,

JAMES MANNING.

It seems proper in this chapter, which illustrates more particularly Dr. Manning's political character and life, to give some account of his efforts in behalf of popular education.

The late Samuel Thurber, in a letter addressed to Judge Staples, which we find in his Annals of Providence, says of schools, that, "previous to about the year 1770, they were but little thought of. There were," he says, "in my neighborhood, three small schools, with perhaps a dozen scholars in each. Their books were the Bible, spelling-book, and primer. One kept by John Foster, Esq., in his office; one by Dr. Benjamin West. Their fees were seven shillings and sixpence per quarter. One kept by George Taylor, Esq., for the church scholars. He, it was said, received a small compensation from England. Besides these there were two or three women schools. When one had learned to read, write, and do a sum in the rule of three, he was fit for business." "The Rev. James Manning," Mr. Thurber remarks in another place, "did great things in the way of enlightening and informing the people. Schools revived by means of his advice and assistance. Previous to him it was not uncommon to meet with those who could not write their names."

The leading facts pertaining to the history of popular education in Providence are given by Judge Staples. That Manning was prominent in all efforts made in his day for the improvement of society and the public good, is evident from the tenor of his life and correspondence thus far. He was a member of the school committee of the town, and for many years the chairman. One of the last acts of his life was to draw up a report in favor of the establishment of free public schools, which report was presented at an adjourned town meeting held in the State House, Monday, Aug. 1, 1791, only two days after the author had been followed to the tomb. We shall be pardoned if we give an extract from this valuable report, which, although not carried into immediate execution, was cordially received and adopted at the time, and which, doubtless, paved the way for the introduction, a few years later, of the present free-school system of Providence.

It seems that, at the annual town meeting in June, a petition had been presented, praying that a sufficient number of schoolmasters be appointed to instruct all the children in town at the public expense; which petition was referred to the school committee, of which Manning was chairman, with instructions to report thereon at an adjourned meeting. The report thus begins: —

"To the freemen of the town of Providence, to be convened next by adjournment, the underwritten members of your school committee, in pursuance of your resolution at your last meeting, report: —

After the most deliberate and mature consideration of the subject, we are clearly of opinion that the measure proposed by the petitioners is eligible, for many reasons.

1. Useful knowledge, generally diffused among the people, is the surest means of securing the rights of man, of promoting the public prosperity, and perpetuating the liberties of a country.

2. As civil community is a kind of joint tenancy in respect to the gifts and abilities of individual members thereof, it seems not improper that the disbursements necessary to qualify those individuals for usefulness should be made from common funds.

3. Our lives and properties, in a free state, are so much in the power of our fellow-citizens, and the reciprocal advantages of daily intercourse are so much dependent on the information and integrity of our neighbors, that no wise man can feel himself indifferent to the progress of useful learning, civilization, and the preservation of morals in the community where he resides.

4. The most reasonable object of getting wealth, after our own wants are supplied, is to benefit those who need it; and it may with great propriety be demanded, in what way can those whose wealth is redundant benefit their neighbors more certainly and permanently than by furnishing to their children the means of qualifying them to become good and useful citizens, and of acquiring an honest livelihood?

5. In schools established by public authority, and whose teachers are

paid by the public, there will be reason to hope for a more faithful and impartial discharge of the duties of instruction, as well as of discipline among the scholars, than can be expected when the masters are dependent on individuals for their support."

The report goes on to recommend that the "Brick Schoolhouse" and "Whipple Hall" be purchased of the proprietors, and that two additional houses be erected, one on the west side of the river. It also recommends that the four schools thus established be under the care and supervision of the school committee, who shall appoint the necessary instructors. It is signed by James Manning, Enos Hitchcock, Moses Brown, Joseph Snow, Moses Badger, Jabez Bowen, David Howell, Benjamin Bourn, John Dorrance, Theodore Foster, and Welcome Arnold. Providence, July (seventh month), 1791. Although, as we have already stated, this report was adopted, its provisions were not carried into effect until the year 1800, when the General Assembly passed their first act in relation to free schools, in accordance with a petition to this effect from the Providence Association of Mechanics and Manufacturers, drawn up and presented by John Howland. On the last Monday in October, 1800, four schools were opened in Providence, under the most favorable auspices.

CHAPTER X.

1789-1791.

Letter from Rev. Dr. Gordon, illustrating his political views, and his position in England as the historian of the American war — Manning appointed to draft and present to Congress a petition in behalf of Rhode Island — Address to the Graduating Class of 1789 — Jeremiah B. Howell — James Fenner — Manning's customary charge to candidates for the ministry — Letter to Rev. Abraham Booth — Booth's reply — Letter from Rev. Dr. Evans — Letter to Rev. Dr. Smith — Religious interest in Providence — Tutor Flint — Final adoption of the Federal Constitution in Rhode Island — George Washington's visit to Providence — Reception at the College — Address of President Manning in behalf of the Corporation — Washington's reply — Commencement for 1790 — Moses Brown — Degree of LL.D. conferred on Washington — Anecdote respecting him — Letter to Rev. Dr. Smith respecting Asa Messer, Tutor Flint, etc. — Ordination of Mr. Flint — Letter from Rev. Abraham Booth — Letter from Rev. Dr. Rippon — Letter from Rev. Dr. William Richards, of Lynn, England — Announces his intention of bequeathing his library to Rhode Island College — Account of Mr. Richards — Corresponds with President Messer — Bequeaths his library to the University — Last letter from Manning, addressed to Rev. Dr. Smith — Manning preaches his farewell sermon to the people of his charge — Notifies the Corporation of the College to look out for a successor to fill his place — Singular presentiment of his approaching mortality — His death — Universal sorrow and regret — Proceedings of the Corporation — Funeral — Extracts from Maxcy's Funeral Sermon — Letter on the occasion of Manning's death from Rev. Dr. Stillman, addressed to Rev. Dr. Smith — Letter from Hon. David Howell, in behalf of members of the Corporation, announcing Manning's death to Rev. Dr. Samuel Jones, and in an informal manner designating him as his successor in the Presidency — Letter from Rev. Isaac Backus to Rev. Dr. Rippon — Extracts from Simeon Doggett's Commencement "Oration on the Death of Rev. President Manning" — Extracts from the circular letters of the Warren and Philadelphia Associations — Manning's personal appearance, habits, character, and influence, as given by Hon. David Howell — Original portrait of Manning, by Cosmo Alexander — Manning's corpulency — Conclusion — The College founded by Baptists to secure for the churches an educated ministry — The improvement and elevation of the Baptist denomination through the College the object and aim of Manning's entire professional life.

From this date Dr. Manning, it appears, did not preserve copies of his letters abroad, as had heretofore been his custom. We can only therefore present, besides one or two additional letters of his own, a few replies from his friends, which will doubtless be regarded as an interesting part of his correspondence. The following, from the Rev. Dr. Gordon, will serve to illustrate the author's position and views as the historian of the American war.

RINGWOOD, ENGLAND, Feb. 27, 1789.

MY GOOD FRIEND:

I am mistaken or you are indebted to me for an answer to my last letter. You might delay sending it till you heard where I was settled; and this you will not do by the present means, but the reverse. You will inquire after the situation of Ringwood, and the reason of my being here. You know I have a pleasure in gratifying you; and therefore turn to your map of England, look for Hampshire, find out Pool, next the church, which is twelve miles off, then Christ's Church, which is ten in the contrary direction, then Southampton, which is twenty, and so calculate the proper distance between Southampton and Pool, and from Christ Church, then make your dot, and you will either hit or be not far from Ringwood in imagination. I should be glad to see you in reality, though I should be astonished at the sight, and wonder what drove you from the land of the whereases, whether the inhabitants are suddenly going from one extreme to another and becoming *all* honest, so that they no longer wanted your instruction or example, or are being so confirmed in their malpractices as that you had forsaken them, from a conviction that they were a set of incurables. Now for the other part of the question, What brought me hither? Freedom among friends is best, you know; and therefore, to be plain with you, when I had seen to the delivery and sending off my History to the subscribers in London and the country, I pushed off to this retirement for a few months, that I might at the distance of ninety-seven miles be out of the way of the conversation that my publication would produce. I was sufficiently tired with composing, transcribing, and publishing; and did not wish to have my spirits fatigued more with the queries and observations that either malevolence or curiosity might excite. I judged it as needful to give myself a few months' relaxation, as to turn out to grass for a season an old horse worn down by a long, tedious journey, that so he might recruit and be fit for a little more service. Here we shall remain, if spared, at the country house of Mrs. Gordon's younger brother, till April or May, when I propose giving a look at London for a few days, on our way to Ipswich in Suffolk, seventy miles from the metropolis, eighteen miles from Colchester, and twelve from Harwich. Here we were first settled and lived thirteen years. Our former people and their successors, like their quondam pastor, were the friends of America, so that we shall agree in politics as well as religion. They have a great affection for us; and had there been a vacancy in the pastorate, they would, I have reason to believe, have urged my renewing our former relations. Here and in the neighborhood I shall be likely to preach occasionally, while abilities admit; but though I have great reason to adore the goodness of God that I am so well in body and mind, now that I am within nine days of sixty, yet I perceive that they are upon the decline. You will think my eyesight good when you read that I write, as you see, whether by day or candlelight. I was in hope that some ministerial settlement with a small congregation, and a salary that might have made our circumstances more easy, would have offered. But the great Head of the chuch has ordered otherwise, — not only with wisdom for the general good, but with mercy for our particular benefit. I do not intend to lie by in a state of lazy indolence, but to apply myself to some kind of service that may be useful to the church and the public, and yield me, with the blessing of God, some advantage to supply present deficiencies. What that should be I have not yet determined, and delay till I get into a habitation of my own, if an earthly one remains designed for me. But I mean it to be of that nature that will not disgrace a D.D., the creature of Princeton College Trustees. Much will depend upon the voice of the public, on both sides of the Atlantic. If the numerous part of impartialists will exclaim *well done*, and call for a second edition of my History, the way will be plain. The profits arising from it will suffice, especially if the heads of American colleges will let me have their orders and their cash for the various books that may be wanted in their seminaries and libraries, which I might be able to supply them with on lower terms than they now have them, by exchanging copies of my work with the booksellers having the copyright of such as are to be furnished. Your friendship will lead you to improve upon this hint; and methinks I am entitled to the countenance and aid of the American States, for my past and present attachment to their freedom and independence, and for the disadvantages the same has subjected me to in my native country.

I had finished writing thus far, and taken a breathing-walk into the garden, when yours of September, 1788, was brought to Mrs. Gordon in a parcel. Upon opening the last, I had the pleasure of reading that and another from the same continent. To what it has been owing that so much time has elapsed since that day to the present, before the parcel reached me, I know not; *but better late than never*, and *long-looked-for is come at last.* And now for answers to, and comments upon it. Through divine goodness Mrs. Gordon's hand has been so far restored as to be very serviceable, though not as formerly. The labors I had been called to while printing, and which had near exhausted me by the time I had finished, led one of my intimate friends to say he was astonished at observing how my spirits had kept up. Relaxation, country air, the severe cold of last winter, and the pleasures of the present spring, have given to them a fresh start; and I promise myself they will recover their former tone. The produce of America just received from New York and Massachusetts has raised them some degrees above par. When you read the History, I flatter myself you will pronounce me the friend of the American cause, and that I have pointed out the faults of the United States in divers instances without basting them *severely*. I can go beyond most of the members of the old superannuated Congress, or even of the new Federal Constitution, and say, I pray daily that the United States of America may be a holy, free, and happy people, which is the way to be lasting. It used to be one of my petitions that good government might be established among them; but that being answered, I have only to be thankful for it. You will not charge me with having spared Great Britain, when you are convinced how faithfully their cruelties in America are related. Your account of Massachusetts merits confirmation, and I hope will obtain it. The infinitely wise Governor of the universe often makes great evils the parents of lasting and great benefits. But where did you leave your orthodox divinity, when you went from Providence to New York, that you should venture to declare, that if my native country does not smart in your lifetime for her conduct to the East Indians and Africans, not to say Americans, that so you might see it, you should alter your opinions respecting the divine dispensations toward communities of men in this world? Methinks, Brother Doctor, I have caught you napping. Besides, had the Americans smarted equal to their crimes toward their public and private creditors, the Africans, etc., when you was provoked to leave off glorying in being an American?

Our common friend Mr. Rippon will give you fuller and better intelligence concerning Winchester than I can do. I wish his most influential days may be at an end, unless he goes *right about* as he was, to allude to a military phrase. May the college at Providence, and all other colleges where learning, good morals, and Christian piety are encouraged, flourish more and more. And may my friends there continue to enjoy good health. I have desired Mr. Mason to accompany this letter with six sets of my History to you. One is a present to the college ; the other five are for Jabez Bowen, Esq., Messrs. John Brown and Francis Benson, Mr. Nicholas Brown, Mr. Caleb Greene, and Mr. John Jenckes. I pray you to present my best respects to these gentlemen, to receive the remaining five pounds from them, and to forward the same to Jonathan Mason, Jr., Esq., Boston. If no other way that is more agreeable offers, either of those careful and obliging postriders, Messrs. Mumfords, to whom my respects, I am certain will take a pleasure in serving me by conveying it. It might not perhaps be amiss to hint to them, that if by their peregrinations they could dispose of twenty-five or fifty sets, I might likely supply them at twenty-five shillings sterling per set, delivered at Boston or Providence. . . . . I remain, dear sir,

Your very affectionate friend though unworthy brother,

WILLIAM GORDON.

The services of Dr. Manning were still, it would seem, in popular demand at this trying period in the history of Rhode Island as a State. From the records of the day, we learn that —

"At an adjourned meeting of the town on Thursday (Aug. 27, 1789), a committee, that had been appointed on Tuesday for the purpose, reported a draft of a petition to be presented to the Congress of the United States, setting forth the distressed situation of this State, the probability of our soon joining the Union, and praying that vessels belonging to our citizens may be exempted from foreign tonnage, and goods shipped from this State from foreign duties, for such time and under such regulations and restrictions as Congress in their wisdom shall think proper.

"The petition was unanimously voted ; and after having been signed by the moderator and town clerk, the Rev. Dr. Manning and Benjamin Bourn, Esq., were appointed to proceed to New York and present the same."

The committee appointed to draft the petition consisted of Dr. Manning, Benjamin Bourn, Thomas Arnold, Nicholas Brown, Theodore Foster, Welcome Arnold, and John Brown. The petition itself, which was probably drafted by Manning, as chairman of the committee, may be found in Staples's Annals of Providence.

Dr. Manning, as we have before observed, presided on all Commencement occasions with remarkable dignity and grace. His addresses to the graduating class were especially noted for excellent good sense, and were pervaded by a tone of piety and delivered with an eloquence which could hardly fail to produce happy and lasting impressions upon the young men, as they stood before him to receive final words of counsel and love. The only production of this kind that has come down to us, was copied from the original, by the Rev. Isaac Backus, several years after the author's death. It was delivered at the Commencement held Sept. 2, 1789. Among those to whom it was especially addressed, we notice the names of Jeremiah Brown Howell, afterwards a member of the United States Senate, and the late James Fenner, for many years the popular and efficient Governor of Rhode Island. Mr. Fenner, it may be added, was the valedictorian of his class.

PRESIDENT MANNING'S CHARGE.

Having completed your academical course, you now commence members of the great community of the world. Here, while your country offers you a fairer opportunity to display your abilities, and improve to advantage that knowledge which you have acquired, than any age or country ever before presented, it becomes my duty to point you to that line of conduct which will most probably insure your success.

The narrow limits prescribed by the occasion will allow me to hint at only a few general observations.

The first attention of a youth stepping forward into life should be to acquire and preserve a good character. A destitution of this places him beyond the possibility of ever becoming eminent. For, bad as the world is, it has always paid a voluntary tribute to virtue; and though some vicious men have arisen to a degree of respectability, it will be found, on a nearer view, that they are indebted for that respectability to some virtuous traits in their character.

To avail yourselves of this supreme advantage, I cannot recommend to you a subject more important and interesting than the Christian religion; of whose divine Founder it was a favorite maxim, *Seek first the kingdom of God and his righteousness, and all other things shall be added unto you.*

This divine religion creates principles in the heart of its subjects the most operative, and the best adapted to regulate the life and conduct that can possibly be conceived. This at once portrays in the strongest colors, the state, connections, and claims of man; and disrobes the world of all its imaginary glory, and presents it in its own fugitive, fading colors, *the fashion of which passeth away,* while it inspires that unassuming humility which renders a man less vulnerable by the envenomed shafts of malevolence; it moulds the heart into a divine benevolence, and is the purest of that exquisite sensibility which deeply interests itself in the fortunes of others, so that it *weeps with those who weep, and rejoices with those who rejoice.*

This divine religion carries forward our thoughts to futurity, contemplates as a reality our dissolution, and that awful approaching judgment in which we must all become a party. It places us in that new eternal world, reaping the fruits of what we have sown in this. In a word, it places us immediately under the eye of God, now the witness of our actions, and soon to be our Judge.

How operative this divine principle to check the irregularity of the passions, and guard against the force of temptations! How divine a prompter to the discharge of every obligation we are under to God or man!

Next to this attention to religion, let me earnestly recommend the forming betimes the habits of industry. Man was made for employment. All his internal as well as external powers testify to this great truth. To comply with this great dictate of nature is of the utmost importance; and youth, of all seasons of life, is the fittest for this culture. That is the period to form and give a proper direction to the habits, on the right constitution of which depends, almost entirely, the happiness of man.

In selecting a profession, consult the strong bias of natural inclination;

for against this current few if any have made a figure; and be sure that the object lies within reach of your talents.

Should the Christian ministry with any of you become an object, reflect on the absurdity of intruding into it while strangers to experimental religion. See that yourselves have been taught of God before you attempt to teach godliness to others. To place in the professional chairs of our universities the most illiterate of mankind, would be an absurdity by far less glaring than to call an unconverted man to exercise the ministerial function. This is to expose our holy religion to the scoffs of infidels, and to furnish to their hands the most deadly weapons. I omit to insist on the account such must render in the great, tremendous day!

May that wisdom which is from above direct your steps in your journey through life; and may you, after the discharge of the duties of good citizens, men of science and religion, meet the approbation of the Supreme Judge, and reap the harvest of immortal glory in the world above.

With this devout wish, I bid you farewell.

The reader will observe how earnestly and forcibly President Manning urges candidates for the ministry to seek first of all the "kingdom of God and his righteousness." This was in accordance with his usual custom on all Commencement occasions. On this point we may be allowed to quote from Backus, who, in the Abridgment of his Church History, thus writes: "Dr. Manning was a good instructor in human learning, but at every Commencement he gave a solemn charge to his scholars never to presume to enter into the work of the ministry until they were taught of God, and had reason to conclude that they had experienced a saving change of heart."

TO THE REV. ABRAHAM BOOTH.

PROVIDENCE, Dec. 25, 1789.

DEAR SIR:

Your most acceptable favor of July 11, with the package, met me at the Association at Philadelphia the 5th of last month. I thank you for your expressions of kindness towards me, and your wishes for my usefulness. Indeed, I cannot but consider myself as a very barren tree in my Lord's vineyard.

The paragraph respecting Dobson's republishing your Pedobaptism I showed to the Association, and queried with them whether your painful labors and extensive services to the Baptist cause, in that publication, did not entitle you to our assistance on this side of the Atlantic, by aiding in the sale of the book. They agreed they did; but as Mr. Dobson had circulated proposals, they doubted the propriety of taking the matter up till Dobson had given up the design. Thus it remains.

It seems Mr. Williams has rallied his forces and attacked you. I am glad, however, to find that you are not panic-struck at the onset. Indeed, I think you have taken a ground too strong to be easily dislodged. We should be gratified with a sight of his piece. If the Pedobaptists, in general, think it masterly, we doubtless shall soon see it in America. The strength of the advocates of that tenet is *to sit still.* It is too late in the day for them to avail themselves, in this age of inquiry, of those plausible colorings which formerly passed very well for solid arguments. At best, if observation has not deceived me, this is the fact with respect to America.

Your Essay on the Kingdom of Christ met a most hearty welcome, and its author has my warmest thanks. It was a subject which had employed my thoughts at intervals for several years, and I was almost determined to have committed them to paper, with a design to publish them. I am happy that I had *only thought* of doing it, as the subject has fallen into much abler hands. I am most heartily pleased with it, and think it lays the axe to the root of that wide-spreading tree, *infant-baptism* and *infant church membership.*

. . . .

Your portrait of Winchester is so exactly to the life that all his acquaintance must see the man in it. The Baptist society still increases in the Southern States, especially in Virginia, and I may add the Middle States also, especially New York. Mr. Jonathan Maxcy, our youngest tutor in the college, a youth of genius and no small degree of literature for his age, about twenty-one years old, has lately found Christ, and followed his Lord into the watery grave. There is another youth under serious impressions, and more appearance of attention to divine things in the college than for some years past. Our second tutor, Mr. Abel Flint, a young Congregationalist preacher, has turned his attention to the subject of baptism for some weeks past, and your Pedobaptism Examined has been his almost constant companion. He told me, some days since, that if that tenet could not be supported from Abraham's covenant, it must fall. If I was as well satisfied of his being a subject of divine grace as I am that Maxcy is, I should think him no small acquisition. May God grant him grace and guide him into all truth! Our number of students lacks but two of seventy.

Yours, etc.
JAMES MANNING.

FROM THE REV. DR. EVANS.

BRISTOL, Feb. 22, 1790.

DEAR SIR:

The literary degree with which the respectable Society over which you preside have thought proper to honor me, I duly received, accompanied with your truly friendly letter, for which I beg you to accept my best thanks. I rely upon you, sir, to make known my acknowledgments to the other members of the college for this mark of distinction and favor, and to assure them that it will always give me peculiar pleasure to promote the prosperity of so useful and honorable an institution.

I received from King's College, Aberdeen, the same honor, before the degree from America was announced here, so that I consider myself under double obligations to take care that I do nothing to discredit the title which has been so honorably conferred upon me by two such respectable bodies. I not only did not seek this honor, but I ought to decline it; but as it has been so generously decreed me, I think it my duty to receive and improve it as a motive to activity and zeal in the sphere in which Providence has placed me.

We are clogged here with test laws, and in vain struggling to get rid of them. You know no such shackles. And yet you know what it is to have bad men disappoint the desires of the good, and outnumber them in their best-intentioned projects.

Does not the French Revolution astonish you? It astonishes and delights me beyond measure. But our great folks here dislike it exceedingly. The counsel of the Lord, however, shall stand, and he will do all his pleasure.

I am astonished at the resolve of your Association about rebaptizing, but refer you to a letter of Mr. Booth's upon the subject, I believe to you. Surely you are more narrow than the Papists upon this subject.

I congratulate you upon the increase of your college and church, and the rising state of the Baptist interest. We go on as usual, are well attended, but have few additions. The love of many waxeth cold. We have great reason to cry mightily to Him with whom is the residue of the Spirit.

The young man I wrote to you about is in too bad a state of health to think of a voyage to America. I rejoice you have rooted out ———, that pest of society, a truly filthy, infamous fellow; but I know not how to refrain asking, How came you ever to admit him, without the least testimonial to his character?

But I am obliged abruptly to break off, only begging to be favored with a line whenever opportunity offers, and that you would believe I truly am

Your affectionate and obliged friend and brother,

CALEB EVANS.

FROM THE REV. ABRAHAM BOOTH.

LONDON, Feb. 25, 1790.

DEAR SIR:

Your letter by favor of Mr. Mullet came safe to hand about a fortnight ago. So far from being wearied by your circumstantial account of the conduct of ———, I think myself much obliged to you for it. Unhappy man! I fear he is *hardened through the deceitfulness of sin*. May the Lord have mercy on him, and give him repentance.

I am very much obliged to you for your generous concern on my behalf respecting the sale of the second edition of my Pedobaptism Examined. That the composing of it required much labor, that I laid out no small sum of money in purchasing books, especially on the popish controversy, with a view to the new impression, and that I am much more likely to lose by it than to gain anything, are facts; but I am of opinion that, after Dr. Dobson had received encouragement to publish proposals for the reprinting of it, my brethren in America could not with honor desert him, while he continues his design in reference to that affair.

It gives me pleasure to find that my Essay on the Kingdom of Christ meets with your approbation. The subject is undoubtedly of great importance, and I sincerely pray that the Lord may bless the pamphlet to the promoting of that spiritual kingdom. The first volume of Mr. Robinson's History of the Baptists has been in the press for these five or six months, but it is not yet published. That volume, indeed, is to contain a history of *baptism*, and three more volumes that are to follow, a history of the *Baptists*. A great extent of reading, much wit, and many curious anecdotes, may be expected to appear in the work whenever it comes out; but I have my fears that it will, on the whole, be of no great utility to the real cause of Jesus Christ. The author is now known to have adopted Dr. Priestley's system in general; but he is justly considered as far inferior to the Doctor in respect of candor and of integrity. Dr. Priestley *speaks out;* you know what he means. Not so the other gentleman. I have often thought that if it had not been for his *uncommon share of wit,* he would before now have sunk into universal contempt among serious people; and he is, indeed, much sunk of late in the estimation of numbers. I have been lately well informed that Dr. Priestley considers him as doing no honor to any cause. This you will observe, however, is *inter nos.*

The beginning of January last I received a letter from Dr. Samuel Jones, of Lower Dublin, respecting the *validity of baptism administered by immersion and on a profession of faith,* by an *unbaptized* — that is, Pedobaptist — *minister;* on which question he desired my opinion. I have given it, in a very long letter enclosed in one to Dr. Stillman of Boston. I have sent it unsealed, that Dr. Stillman might have an opportunity of perusing it before he sent it off to Dr. Jones. I am very sorry that I was obliged, in opposition to the determination of the Association at Philadelphia, to take the affirmative of the question; that is, I think such baptism, though irregular, valid. If you should by any means have a sight of that letter, I should be glad to know your thoughts on the argument contained in it. I have expressed my views of the subject with the utmost freedom, and I trust without giving any cause of offence to the Doctor.

My respects, if you have opportunity, to Dr. Drowne. I earnestly pray that the Lord may cause his truth to prosper all around you, as I am glad to hear it does in Virginia. Winchester seems to be losing ground pretty fast; for some of his principal admirers have turned their backs upon him, and have renounced his notion of universal restitution, of which they were once extremely fond. Shall be glad to hear from you at any time when an opportunity presents. The Lord be with you in all your departments of labor and in all your connections. I remain, dear sir,

Your unworthy brother,

A. Booth.

TO THE REV. DR. SMITH.

PROVIDENCE, 20th April, 1790.

DEAR BROTHER:

I snatch a moment to inform you that the good work still continues, and I think has been gradually increasing amongst us since you left. Last Lord's Day I baptized two, and a third was prevented by indisposition of body. Two profess to have met with a change the last of last week. Several profess to have received comfort, but are not fully satisfied. I believe that there are from fifty to one hundred under serious impressions; and they crowd the evening meetings whenever and wherever they are appointed. Numbers come to my house to converse with me about their souls. Many of Dr. H——k's people attend the evening meetings, of whom several appear seriously impressed. Some people, you will naturally guess, do not like this, and look rather shy. Poor Mr. Flint has come to a point, and must be a Baptist, notwithstanding the reproaches he has to endure; but he has not full satisfaction about his own state. He is amazingly engaged for the persons under awakening, and attends meetings whenever he can. He has been sick, but is recovered. Mr. Maxcy has been called and licensed, but has been at home some time, much indisposed. He is now very ill with the measles. He preaches to admiration. Several of the students are also down with the measles, and others have had them. Not a few of the students are under serious impressions. Many of the people here are often wishing to see Mr. Smith again; and, for your encouragement, I can inform you that many profess to have been first awakened by your labors amongst us. No account has yet been received from Dr. Gano, and I expect to go for Jersey the beginning of May. The people really lament and mourn at the thought of being left destitute. What think you of coming and making another visit to Providence the beginning of next month? I believe this would diffuse a general joy through both church and society. You will find work enough to employ you day and night. I heartily wish you could come, but I have not had an opportunity of speaking to the committee on the subject. I expect they would embrace this opportunity of writing you if they knew of this opportunity to send to Boston, — more especially if they had not sanguine hopes that Dr. Gano would soon be here; but I really fear some disaster has happened to him. If my wishes could bring you to Providence, you would soon be here. Attleboro is visited, and several other places. Mrs. Manning joins in love to you and lady, with, dear sir, yours, etc.,

JAMES MANNING.

On Monday, May 24, of this year, the final State convention on the Federal Constitution was held at Newport. On Thursday the body adjourned, for more ample accommodations, from the State House to the Second Baptist Church, where for three days the great debate between the contending parties was continued. At five o'clock on Saturday afternoon the final vote was taken. Thirty-four members voted to adopt the Constitution, and thirty-two voted in the negative. Thus a majority of two votes saved the people of Rhode Island from anarchy, and the State from dismemberment.

The news reached Providence before midnight, and was announced by the ringing of bells and the booming of cannon. The next day the returning delegates were received with a national salute of thirteen guns. Again, says Staples in his Annals, "patriotism encroached on piety, as when the vote for calling the convention passed in the preceding January, and the stillness of the Sabbath morning was broken by the joyful roar of artillery."

In about two months after this event, on Tuesday, August 17, President Washington with his suite, accompanied by Gov. Clinton of New York, Thomas Jefferson, Esq., Secretary of State, and several members of Congress, made his first visit to Providence. A large procession was formed to escort them from the packet in which they arrived, and the occasion was made a gala-day throughout the town. In the evening, says the *Gazette*, "the President and many others took a walk on the college green, to view the illumination of the building by the students, which made a most splendid appearance."

On Thursday, the 19th, the President and his suite were escorted to the college by the students, and by Dr. Manning introduced to the Library and Museum, where in behalf of the corporation he thus addressed him : —

SIR : — Though among the last to congratulate you on your advancement to that dignified and important station to which the unanimous voice of a grateful country has called you, the corporation of Rhode Island College claim to be among the first in warmth of affection for your person, and in esteem for your public character. In placing you at the head of the United States, regard was had no less to the influence of your example over the morals of the people than to your talents in the administration of government. Happy are we to observe, that similar motives have influenced your conduct in filling the lower offices in the executive department. We must devoutly venerate that superintending Providence which, in the course of events propitious to this country, has called you forth to establish, after having defended, our rights and liberties.

Agitated in the hour of doubtful conflict, exulting in your victories, we watched your footsteps with the most anxious solicitude. Our fervent supplications to Heaven, that you might be furnished with that wisdom and prudence necessary to guide us to freedom and independence, have been heard and most graciously answered.

For the preservation of this freedom, one great object still demands our peculiar attention, — the education of our youth. Your sentiments, sir, on this subject, "that knowledge is in every country the surest public basis of happiness," and the strongest barrier against the intruding hand of despotism, as they most perfectly accord with those of the most celebrated characters that ever adorned human nature, so they leave no room to apprehend you will refuse the wreath with which the guardians of literature here would entwine your brow.

By restoring your health, and protracting your life so dear to this country, Divine Providence has, in a late instance, furnished to millions matter of thanksgiving and praise.

That you may long remain on earth, a blessing to mankind, and the support of your country, — that you may afterwards receive the rewards of virtue, by having the approbation of God, — is our most sincere desire and fervent supplication.

This address, which had been formally adopted by the corporation, at a special meeting held in the State House, August 17, was duly presented to the President, signed by Jabez Bowen, Chancellor; James Manning, President; and David Howell, Secretary. To Manning's address in behalf of the corporation, President Washington thus replied: —

To the Corporation of Rhode Island College:

Gentlemen: — The circumstances which have until this time prevented you from offering your congratulations on my advancement to the station I hold in the government of the United States, do not diminish the pleasure I feel in receiving this flattering proof of your affection and esteem, for which I request you will accept my thanks.

In repeating thus publicly my sense of the zeal you displayed for the success of the cause of your country, I only add a single suffrage to the general testimony which all, who were acquainted with you in the most adverse and doubtful moments of our struggle for liberty and independence, have constantly borne in your favor.

While I cannot remain insensible to the indulgence with which you regard the influence of my example and the tenor of my conduct, I rejoice in having so favorable an opportunity of felicitating the State of Rhode Island on the coöperation I am sure to find in the measures adopted by the guardians of literature in this place, for improving the morals of the rising generation, and inculcating upon their minds principles peculiarly calculated for the preservation of our rights and liberties. You may rely on whatever protection I may be able to afford in so important an object as the education of our youth.

I will now conclude, gentlemen, by expressing my acknowledgments for the tender manner in which you mention the restoration of my health in a late occasion, and with ardent wishes that Heaven may prosper the literary institution under your care, in giving you the best of its blessings in this world, as well as in the world to come.

At the Commencement this year twenty-two young gentlemen took their first degree, being the largest number that had ever graduated at one time since the college was founded. Among them was Moses Brown, youngest son of Nicholas Brown, a bright and promising youth, who a few months later, just as he had entered upon his sixteenth year, was seized with a disorder which suddenly put an end to his life. In this class also graduated the third President of Brown University, Asa Messer, of whom we have given a sketch in the preceding chapter. At the close of the exercises, the degree of Doctor of Laws was conferred on George Washington,[1] President of the United States of America. This was the last Commencement at which Dr. Manning presided.

TO THE REV. DR. SMITH.

PROVIDENCE, 18th Nov., 1790.

DEAR BROTHER:

Yours of the 25th ult. is before me. The tide of business which, on my return home, flowed in upon me, prevented my recollecting the case of Mr. Messer. But in my journey to the West I had him constantly in view, but found no opening which I thought worthy his attention. Mr. Read, from Virginia, has not returned, nor have I had any intelligence from him respecting a chance for teaching; so that I cannot at present give any encouragement from this quarter, as it was the general opinion that it would be imprudent for him, all things considered, to take a place

[1] In reference to this we find the following pleasant anecdote in Rippon's Baptist Register: —

"In a conversation between several friendly gentlemen (in London) some time since, which turned chiefly on the confinement of Lewis the *Little*, who, like an absolute sovereign, had said to five and twenty millions of people, *I will be obeyed*, — contrasted with the popularity of Washington the *Great*, — it was mentioned that the Baptist College in Rhode Island had conferred the degree of Doctor of Laws on the President of the United States. While it seemed to be the general mind that this distinguished character in the history of man would prefer the laurels of a college to a crown of despotism, one of the company, it is said, quite impromptu, gave vent to the feelings of his heart in the following effusion: —

'When kings are *mere* sovereigns, or tyrants, or tools,
No wonder the people should treat them as fools;
But *Washington*, therefore, presides with applause,
Because he well merits the Doctor of Laws.
I'll ne'er be a ruler till I'm LL. D.,
Nor England nor Scotland shall send it to me;
I'll have my diploma from *Providence Hall*, —
For Washington had, — or I'll have none at all.'"

in college, till the present Senior Class are out of the way. We have appointed a Mr. Lyndon Arnold to that office for the present, who has no thoughts of continuing more than a year. If Mr. Messer should not fall into better business by that time, it would be very agreeable to me to have him for an assistant; and sooner, should Tutor Maxcy leave us, which he talks of, though I shall reluctantly agree to it. He has with great persuasion consented to supply the pulpit for six months, and does it to great acceptance. He has many hearers, and his labors appear to be owned. He improves amazingly. The good work still prevails, and the prospect is as promising at present as at any period past. Our dear friend Mr. Jenckes appears almost gone. It is not likely that he will stay with us many weeks. Nicholas Brown is in a very poor way, but yet goes out. I fear his disorder is radical and will prove fatal.

Your son's standing shall remain as it has done. The instances of Catholicism amongst the Presbyterians are, their opening their houses of worship to the Baptists, and flocking to hear them, at Brunswick, Woodbridge, Elizabethtown, Newark, etc. The Association of Danbury consists of thirteen churches, and there are, probably as many more in that quarter which will join them. There has been a great increase of the Baptists in the western part of Connecticut and in the lower part of York State of late. I suppose Mr. Flint has concluded to commence a preacher among the Congregationalists, and I conclude is about to accept a call to the South Parish in Hartford. Either the cross was too heavy to commence a Baptist, or he had little reason to expect that he should be called to the work among us, unless he could give better evidence of a change of heart; or probably something of both had weight in his determination. I have said nothing to him on the subject lately, as I was convinced of the strong bias he had for preaching at all events. I suppose he has been borne down with a torrent of influence from Pedobaptist connections.

. . . .

By a letter from Mr. E. Robbins I hear that the two churches in York are very happy together. I wish this feeling may continue and increase. The day appointed for Mr. Baldwin's instalment I attended the ordination of Mr. Ebenezer ——. The letter from the Boston church did not reach me until late in the evening of the preceding Lord's Day, so that it was out of my power either to come or send them word. I hope you had a comfortable season. Our friend Mr. Sutton is settled nearly in the centre of Kentucky, and, I believe, in regard to worldly prospects, is more happy than ever he was, though he has not the charge of a church, as there are four ordained elders in that to which he belongs. He has purchased two hundred acres of good land, has enough cleared to raise his bread, which his sons manage, together with carrying on a considerable share of the hatter's business. This leaves him at leisure to travel, as he has lost his wife; and among other journeys, he contemplates one to New England, to visit once more all his friends in this quarter. With best respects to you, lady, and family, with all friends, in which Mrs. Manning joins,

I remain, as ever,

JAMES MANNING.

Mr. Flint, to whom Manning here refers, was ordained as a pastor of the Second Congregational Church in Hartford, on Wednesday, April 20, 1791. The Rev. Dr. Strong of Hartford made the introductory prayer, the Rev. Dr. Hitchcock of Providence preached the sermon, the Rev. Dr. Goodrich of Durham gave the charge, the Rev. Nathan Perkins of Hartford gave the right hand of fellowship, and the Rev. David Macclure of East Windsor made the concluding prayer.

FROM THE REV. ABRAHAM BOOTH.

LONDON, April 1, 1791.

DEAR SIR:

It being more than twelve months since I wrote you a letter, I have been much disappointed in not having had the pleasure of hearing from you. At the same time I sent a very long letter to Dr. Samuel Jones, in answer to one I received from him, relative to the propriety of baptizing such persons as had been solemnly immersed on a profession of faith by a Pedobaptist minister, — both of which I enclosed in a packet to Dr. Stillman at Boston; but, to my great surprise, I have not received a line from America since. The name of the captain (nor yet of his ship) by whom the little packet was sent, I do not now recollect, but should be very sorry to learn that the letter never came to hand.

It is probable that you have heard, ere now, of the death of Mr. R. Robinson, of Cambridge. He died the last summer, a little before his History of Baptism was finished at the press; by which book it appears he was a thorough-faced Socinian at the time of his decease. He died in the neighborhood of Birmingham, at the house of a gentleman belonging to Dr. Priestley's community, after having preached at the Doctor's meeting-house the Lord's Day before; was buried at the Doctor's burying-ground (he at least spoke at the grave) at the expense of the Doctor's people, and the Doctor preached and published a funeral sermon for him; a sermon contemptible as to its composition, and detestable as to the sentiments contained in it. Some of the sentiments, in my view, are an insult, not only on the Scriptures but on common sense, except the latter be debauched by vain philosophy. Mr. Robinson's History of Baptism you may probably have seen before now. It seems to me to be a work of both labor and learning. It contains various particulars, in opposition to infant-sprinkling, that are both new and pertinent; but there is much extraneous matter; there are many indications of rank Socinianism; various detestably fanciful interpretations of passages in the Old Testament; and such marks of enmity against the character of Augustinus as I did not expect. We have very lately lost by death that worthy Baptist minister, Mr. Robert Hall, of Amsby, in Leicestershire. He is, I doubt not, now with God, and his memory is much respected.

Socinianism is, I fear, still gaining ground in England, especially in the national Establishment; and several of our young Baptist ministers have, within these two or three years, adopted that pernicious system of error and of blasphemy. But our divine Jesus lives and reigns, to govern the world and to take care of his own cause.

I hear but little of Mr. Winchester of late, and have never seen him. I am inclined to think, however, that his corrupt principles lose rather than gain ground in this metropolis.

Hope you will indulge me with a letter as soon as you can after you receive this; and that, among other things, you will inform me whether my Pedobaptism Examined be yet republished. I have been informed that proposals for publishing by subscription my Essay on the Kingdom of Christ, have appeared at Philadelphia. I was a little surprised to hear of republishing, by subscription, so small a piece, nothing of that kind being issued here.

It has been and now is a sickly time among my people. Three of the members of the church under my imperfect pastoral care have departed out of life since the present year came in, and another of them is on the verge of the grave, by the envenomed tooth of a devouring cancer. The Lord grant that we may be prepared for his whole will concerning us. Oh for more genuine spiritual-mindedness!

And now, sir, I most affectionately commend you to God, and to the word of his grace, earnestly praying that peace and prosperity may attend you and yours and all the churches of Christ. I remain, dear sir,

Your unworthy brother in the gospel of Jesus Christ,

A. BOOTH.

FROM THE REV. DR. RIPPON, OF LONDON.

REVEREND AND DEAR SIR:

Last evening Capt. Mesnard delivered me his letters from New York, and to-morrow the Eagle sails, so that I have but a few minutes for each letter.

The Register is taking a prodigious spread through almost all our churches, the country friends themselves ordering from fifteen to one hundred copies for each church. I feel myself honored in seeing your name among the brethren who encourage the design. I refer now to the advertisement in the Philadelphia Association letter. I had hoped that I might have received your painting by Capt. Mesnard, but I must now beseech you to forward it by the very *first* safe conveyance, informing me at what age it was done. Dr. Evans is beautifully engraved, and so is Providence meeting-house, from a copy in the *Massachusetts Magazine* for August, 1789. No part of the *Magazine* have I seen besides. The account of the Providence church cannot, I suspect, be brought into the First Part of the Register, though, on account of its early date, it should be one of the first societies under Article the 8th, where it stands. I would not so soon have advertised its insertion, had I not known it would have afforded great pleasure to *many* of our English brethren; though, by the way, some of them are *astonished* at the STEEPLE! I was the more unwilling to bring this article forward so early, because I was unacquainted with your opinion of the narrative. It came here to a friend of John Stanford, said to have been written by him and approved by the church. Of course you have seen it. No one in the city but myself and the family to whom it was sent know that Stanford had any hand in it; and his name *must* be *entirely* kept out of sight in this country. If I introduce the account of the church in the Second Part of the Register, with your corrections, I *dare* not go any further than 1787, unless you will give the narrative such a finish that the close may introduce your *present* condition. Mr. Foster informs me that Mr. Maxcy (named in your former letter) has engaged to supply Providence one year. I beg to be affectionately remembered to him. I never had any correspondence with Mr. ——; am sorry to find he did not behave well at Providence.

The happiness of the American churches lies near my heart. I see my brethren have too much neglected them. There is not public spirit enough in this country; but I have *hinted* by this conveyance to two friends, that the Register is intended to serve the *American* brethren particularly. I am *sure* when we have larger accounts of Kentucky, well authenticated, the design you proposed a few months since can naturally be brought forward; and I have laid some foundation already for its success. This I have mentioned to no American but yourself.

I find Mr. Wesley's people are aiming to have a new college in America (*vide* Dr. Coke's Missions). I wish I had a good drawing or engraving of your college edifice, and a history of the college. I have the printed charter; wish for a proof of the old seal, with the explanations thereof. Would you favor me with the history? Dr. Evans has offered an account of the Bristol Academy. If you are too busy, could not Dr. Drowne draw it up? I wish I could see Mr. Maxcy's handwriting. I have a copy of Robinson's History of Baptism for your acceptance. Hope to send it next month, with an article ordered by Dr. Drowne. My respects to him. My Christian love to your good lady.

I remain, affectionately and truly, yours,

JOHN RIPPON.

P. S. — I dare not dictate, but if the Register meets the approbation of the American brethren, perhaps each Association would say what number they would certainly take, and appoint the clerk, or some other brother, to convey materials for me to Boston, Philadelphia, or New York, from time to time.

In December of this year, Dr. Manning addressed a letter to the Rev. William Richards, LL. D., of Lynn, England, to which Mr. Richards thus replies. The letter, it may be added, did not reach Providence until nearly four months after Manning had passed from the scenes of his earthly labors.

LYNN, IN NORFOLK, OLD ENGLAND, June 6, 1791.

MY DEAR SIR:

Embracing an opportunity which has suddenly and unexpectedly presented itself, of sending to America a packet by a private hand, I can do little more than just to acknowledge the receipt of your kind letter of the fifteenth of December, which made its way here about the middle of last month, *via* Liverpool and Birmingham. I sincerely thank you, sir, for this favor; and I rejoice exceedingly in the prospect which your letter exhibits of the growing greatness and the increasing felicity and prosperity of America. I have long been partial to that country, and at a very early period of my life (sixteen or seventeen years ago) was on the point of removing from Britain thither. The war deterred me then, and for some years after, from accomplishing my purpose; and having been settled in this place some years when the peace took place, I found it rather inconvenient then to quit the country. Should I live a few years longer, it is still probable that I shall remove, but it is most likely that that removal will be to Wales and not to America. I am and have always been very much attached to my dear native country; but I should like it much better were it connected with the United States, than as it is, a branch of the corrupt British empire.

As to the issue of my late controversy with Mr. Carter, my last piece, The History of Antichrist, brought it to its conclusion. I have never seen my opponent since, but he has repeatedly sent me his friendly compliments, and invited me to call upon him whenever I should pass through his neighborhood, but it has not suited me to pay him a visit yet. Our Independent brethren have treated their poor Baptist neighbors somewhat more civilly since this controversy took place than they were wont to do. In these counties of Norfolk and Suffolk they are a very powerful body. That party, sir, as I suppose you know, originated here, and have continued here ever since, as numerous and respectable as in any part of Britain. Their ministers are in general men of considerable abilities and learning, while the Baptist ministers, on the contrary, are possessed of but a moderate share of either. The former seemed conscious of their superiority, and in general affected to treat the latter with the most manifest contempt. In short, sir, I am the first of the Particular Baptists, and even of the Baptist denomination, who has had the temerity to accept a challenge from or to enter the lists with a Norfolk or Suffolk Independent. I hope the adventure was not altogether useless to the Baptist cause. The Independents have never since discovered the least disposition to oppose us again in print; and it is the general opinion that it will be long before they will attempt to provoke the Baptists into another paper war. Many of them were convinced, during the debate, that the Pedobaptist scheme was not tenable, and they of course joined us; and not one was known to be confirmed, in the mean time, in that scheme.

Since the conclusion of this dispute, I have been called, by the unanimous voice of the Welsh Baptists, to engage in another of a similar nature with the Presbyterians and Independents of the Principality, who had just then broken the peace by violently attacking their principles, and who were likewise strongly supported by the Whitefieldites, a very numerous body in that country. The person intrusted by them with the direction of this war is a Mr. Benjamin Evans, a very popular minister in Cardiganshire, very dexterous and very obstinate in debate, and a perfect adept in the sophist and the quibbler's trade. He has already published *three* pieces, and I am now about beginning my *third* piece in reply. What will be the issue of this war must be left for time to determine. My opponent, by the vigor and violence of his exertions, and frequent rallyings and renewals of the combat, seems to think that he has a great deal at stake. He, too, and his brethren, took it for granted that he was greatly superior to any that the Baptists could call out to oppose them in the Welsh language. God grant that the truth may not, in this hard struggle, be anywise dishonored by its very unworthy advocate.

Report says that this controversy has already been productive of some very pleasing and happy effects, and that the Baptist interest is likely to be considerably benefited by it. I sent a copy of my first Welsh tract to your good Brother Dr. Samuel Jones, and had you known the language I should have been very happy to have presented you with another, and submitted it to your examination. I deem these much superior to my English pieces. They cost me much more thought, and I bestowed much more pains upon them every way.

Some suppose that the piece I have now on hand will be the last of this controversy, but that seems to me rather doubtful. I almost think that some things I shall advance this time will provoke some kind of a reply. Nor am I at all anxious about that matter, so long as our countrymen continue to give us a patient and attentive hearing. I am willing to give my labor, and my Welsh brethren seem at present as willing to be at the expense of printing what I write.

The Baptists are very numerous and greatly on the increase in Wales. Some churches there are the largest we have in Britain. That of Lanjloffan, in Pembrokeshire, which is the largest of all, consists of between eight hundred and nine hundred members. The great increase of the Welsh Baptists is seemingly what provoked their Pedobaptist brethren to commence this quarrel with them. I hope they will not in the end have any cause to triumph over us.

I have had some thoughts of writing the Life of Roger Williams. Could you, sir, tell me where he was born, or add any materials towards his history, over and above what Mr. Backus's history contains? I have some of his works which Mr. Backus never saw. He is with me, in several respects, a favorite character.

I am sorry to hear of the smallness of your fund, and of your pecuniary difficulties at the college. I wish the British Baptists would take your case under consideration, and afford you some effectual aid. They ought to do so, I think; and yet I am afraid it will not be an easy matter to persuade them to it, unless some of the Londoners, and other opulent Baptists, were to take it up.

I thought your library was more considerable, and am sorry to find it is not. The Bristol Library is now a very capital one by the addition of the collections of Drs. Gifford and Llewelyn, and especially the latter, which was a very excellent one. I wish some others in this country would bequeath their collections to your college. I have myself near fifteen hundred volumes, some of them of value. But a man in my situation, in very moderate circumstances, and with a very small salary from the congregation, and having withal an aged mother to provide for, — a man in such a situation, I say, must make no resolution in matters of this kind. Perhaps my circumstances when I die may not admit of my disposing of my books as I might have wished. Therefore please to keep this hint to yourself. Now, my dear sir, I must take my leave. May every blessing attend you, is the earnest wish and prayer of

Your sincere, affectionate, and faithful friend, brother and servant,

W. RICHARDS.

P. S. — Is there any truth, sir, in the reports, which our public papers daily circulate in this country, of very dreadful ravages committed by the natives among your people about Kentucky and other back-settlements? I suspect it is only a contrivance of our Government for the purpose of checking the progress of emigration, and to persuade the good people of Britain that there is not so blessed a country anywhere as their own. Our papers are in like manner stuffed with falsehoods relating to the state of things in France, and the proceedings of the National Assembly. These tricks will not always serve their purpose.

I received a letter lately from Mr. Curtis, son-in-law to the late Mr. Robinson. The second volume of Mr. Robinson's long-expected work is now in the press. It is not intended to print any more than seven hundred and fifty copies of it, so that I suppose it will soon become scarce. It was the author's design to have called it the First Volume of the History of the Baptists; but as he did not live to complete his plan, or to finish any more than this volume of it, it is, by the advice of Dr. Abraham Rees, to be entitled Ecclesiastical Researches. I am sorry to learn that there are still near four hundred copies of the History of Baptism unsold.

Dear sir, pray pardon the intolerable length and blunders of this scrawl. When I began, I little thought I should scribble half so much, nor indeed did I expect that the opportunity would permit me to do so, as I thought the messenger could not stay. Excuse me this time.

Mr. Richards[1] was a native of South Wales. At the age of twelve he had been at school only one year. From this time till the twenty-fourth year of his age, when he entered the academy at Bristol, he received no instruction. But his application to study was vigorous and persevering. He remained at the academy in Bristol two years. After preaching for a short time as an assistant to Dr. John Ash, of Pershore, he accepted an invitation from the Baptist Church at Lynn to become their pastor, and entered upon his public ministry in that town July 7, 1776, where he continued to reside — more than half of the time as pastor of the church — till his death, which occurred in 1818, in the sixty-ninth year of his age.

Mr. Richards seems to have been a man of considerable learning, particularly in English and Welsh history, and in the Welsh language and literature. His writings are historical, political, and controversial.[2] His most important work is The History of Lynn, in 2 vols. 8vo. Dr. Evans says of it: "It is not only well written, the style perspic-

1 See Memoirs of the Life and Writings of Rev. William Richards, LL.D., by John Evans, LL.D., of Islington. 12mo. Chiswick, 1819.

2 For a list of his writings, — comprising nearly the whole, — see under his name in the catalogue of the college library.

uous and manly, but it is replete with information as well as entertainment." His review of Noble's Memoirs of the Protectoral House of Cromwell is characterized by Lowndes[1] as "severe, but at the same time just."

"His Dictionary of Welsh and English," says Dr. Evans, "a work of minute and wearisome labor, is in high repute." Mr. Richards was of the General Baptist denomination, and a strong advocate of religious liberty. It was his love of the liberal character of the college which induced him to bestow upon it his library, as appears from the following passage in his Memoirs: —

"Mr. Richards had corresponded with Dr. James Manning, once President of the Baptist college in Rhode Island. From this gentleman he learned the liberal constitution of that respectable seminary, and for some years previous to his death meant to bequeath to it his library. He accordingly made inquiry of Dr. Rogers [of Philadelphia], whether it was still conducted on the same liberal footing, in which case he should cherish the same generous intentions towards it."

This inquiry was answered by Dr. Messer, then President of the college, in a letter from which we extract a single passage: —

"Though the charter requires that the President shall forever be a Baptist, it allows neither him, in his official character, nor any other officer of instruction, to inculcate any sectarian doctrine. It forbids all religious tests; and it requires that all denominations of Christians, behaving alike, shall be treated alike. This charter is congenial with the whole of the civil government established here by the venerable Roger Williams, who allowed no religious tests, and no preëminence of one denomination over another; and none has ever been allowed unto this day. This charter is also congenial with the present spirit of this State and of this town."

[1] Bibliographer's Manual.

Gratified with this letter, Mr. Richards, in accordance with the purpose which he cherished twenty-seven years previous to his death, and which he hints in his letter to Dr. Manning, bequeathed his books, consisting of about thirteen hundred volumes, to Brown University. This was the most important donation that the library had as yet received. It is a singular fact, that his will was made on the very day on which the honorary degree of Doctor of Laws was conferred upon him by the college. Mr. Richards had received no intimation that the honor was intended for him, nor did he live to hear that it had been bestowed.

The library which he thus bequeathed is in many respects valuable. It contains a considerable number of Welsh books, a large collection of works illustrating the history and antiquities of England and Wales, besides two or three hundred bound volumes of pamphlets, some of them very ancient, rare, and curious. The collection is particularly valuable for its treatises on civil and religious liberty. The original manuscript catalogue of Mr. Richards's library has recently come into our possession. It is now among the archives of the University.

Dr. Evans, in his account of Brown University, appended to his Life of Richards, says: "Whilst the library of my friend Richards remains amongst them, to perpetuate the name and character of its donor, may it urge its worthy President, as well as the members of this truly respectable institution, to the continued exercise of that spirit of liberality which induced *an honest* Cambro-Briton, at the distance of three thousand miles, to mark and reward it."

The last letter from Manning of which we have any

account, is addressed to his college classmate and life-long friend, the Rev. Dr. Smith: —

PROVIDENCE, 4th June, 1791.

DEAR SIR:

Yours of Feb. 15th ult. came to hand three months to a day after it was written, so that we now stand on even ground. As you say of mine, it met a welcome reception. I am sorry it has not been in my power to provide for Mr. Messer agreeably to my wishes and ideas of his merit. There will be an opening at Providence for a tutor in the fall; but Mr. Alden, of senior standing, appears to incline to fill the place. If so, there will be an opening at Taunton in the academy which he will leave. I hope that Mr. Messer may be accommodated at one or other of these berths. Please to present my best respects to him, and tell him he shall have my interest. Ere this comes to hand, the news of the departure of our two good friends Messrs. John Jenckes and Nicholas Brown must have reached you. Providence, church, and society are bereaved indeed! But *Jesus lives*, and lives to support his cause when earthly supporters fail.

The affairs of the college do not prosper as I could wish. With the twenty-two who graduated last fall, we have lost twenty-nine this year, which is a great defalcation from our small number. More are about to come soon, but I think it will be some time before we shall make the number of last year good. Our number is about fifty-five. The last intelligence from Brother Gano is, that early this spring his kitchen caught fire by accident, and consumed with it all their kitchen furniture, smoked meat, etc. Poor ill-fated man! He is not to have his portion here. Well, I believe he is secure of it above. I am glad to hear that you found my friends the Newbolds agreeable. I saw Caleb at York a few days since, and he mentioned you with great affection, as also all the eastern people to whom he was introduced. I saw none of your relations to the westward, as my journey was hasty and attended with business. Nothing remarkable in the Middle States in a religious way, save that Brother Foster and people are very happy and prosperous. The Second Church rent again, and in a miserable situation. Our old friends generally well. My brother Enoch died in February last, and John Manning, Esq., my cousin; also Aunt Randolph, wife of Uncle Ephraim. The people of Providence have chosen Mr. Maxcy for their minister, and he has resigned his tutorship and accepted. He gives very general satisfaction, and promises usefulness. Religious impressions are not all erased from the minds of the people here. With best respects to you and lady, in which Mrs. Manning joins,

Your old friend,

JAMES MANNING.

Dr. Manning, as his correspondence shows, had repeatedly and earnestly requested his people to seek for a proper person to succeed him in the ministry. This he did, not because his interest in preaching had diminished, but rather on account of his multiplied duties as President of the college, which would not permit him to do justice to his flock. "At length, in a most honorable way, he resigned his pastoral office." On the last Sabbath in April, 1791, a few months only before his death, he preached to the people of his charge his farewell sermon. The occasion was one of unusual solemnity. For twenty years he had been to them their spiritual guide. Under his teachings and influence the church had been greatly improved in its discipline and worship, and the society had become large and flourishing. Revivals had attended upon his ministry, so that again and again he had come to them "in the fulness of the blessing of the gospel of Christ," announcing to not a few "glad tidings of great joy." Scores of his hearers he had led down into the baptismal waters. And now, as he uttered from the pulpit his last affectionate address, and, as if in prophetic anticipation of his approaching end, expressed the improbability of his ever preaching to them again, sorrow filled their hearts, and their emotions found utterance in sobs and tears.

At a meeting of the corporation held on the 13th of April, Dr. Manning had notified them to look out for a successor to fill his place; and shortly after preaching his farewell sermon, he had made a request in writing for a meeting of the Baptist society, to make arrangements for finishing the meeting-house and lot, stating in this request that it would probably be his last. What gave him this singular presentiment of his approaching mortality, can never, perhaps, be ascertained. It proved, alas! to be but too well founded. On Saturday, July 23d, he dined at the hospitable table of his friend Mr. John Brown. On Sabbath morning following, while uttering the voice of prayer around the domestic altar, he was seized with a fit of apoplexy, in which he remained, but with imperfect consciousness, till the ensuing Friday, when, about four o'clock in the morning, he expired, in the fifty-fourth year of his age.

The sudden death of a man who was universally esteemed and loved, and who had filled, for so many years, such various and commanding stations of usefulness and trust, produced throughout the entire community the most profound sorrow, reaching to every part of the city in which he lived. When, a month previous, his intimate friend and associate Nicholas Brown, whose munificence had flowed in a thousand channels, and whose example had given a new impulse to the public mind, quitted the scene which he had so long adorned with his presence and enriched with his bounty, it was to be expected that there should be, as there was, a general expression of sorrow and regret. But that the removal of a Christian minister, and a teacher of science and letters, who possessed none of the advantages of wealth, but whose later years, on the contrary, had been oppressed by economic solicitude and care, should produce a regret so universal and so deep, "is a pleasing homage" — adopting the language of Robert Hall on a similar occasion — "to the majesty of moral power and intellectual greatness."

The corporation immediately assembled in the college hall, when the death of the President was announced by the Hon. Jabez Bowen, LL.D., Chancellor. Among other demonstrations of respect and affection for the deceased, a committee, consisting of the Rev. Dr. Hitchcock and Messrs. John Brown and George Benson, was appointed to wait on Mrs. Manning, and express to her their sincere condolence on the death of her "late worthy husband." Messrs. Joseph Russell, Welcome Arnold, and George Benson were also appointed a committee to superintend the funeral, the expenses thereof to be defrayed by the corporation.

On Saturday, July 30, the next day after his death, the remains of Dr. Manning were conveyed from his residence to the college hall, where the funeral solemnities were performed by the Rev. Dr. Hitchcock, at that time the pastor of the Congregational church in Providence, and one of the most active Fellows of the college. "The funeral," says Prof. Goddard, "though a public one, was no empty pageant. Multitudes flocked to the college, to look for the last time upon a face which had so often beamed upon them in kindness; and multitudes followed him to the grave which was so soon to hide him forever from their sight." Indeed, the funeral, in the language of the *Providence Gazette*, was thought to "have been the most numerous and respectable ever attended in town."

The corpse, placed upon a hearse,[1] was borne to the north burying-ground, where it now rests by the side of Nicholas Brown, in the family lot. "United in life, in

[1] We have it upon the authority of the late Mr. John B. Chace, that at Dr. Manning's funeral a hearse was used for the first time in Providence. It was imported from England.

death they are not separated." The following was the order of the funeral procession : —

STUDENTS.
STEWARD.
GRADUATES OF THE COLLEGE.
TUTORS.
PROFESSORS FOBES AND WEST.
THE CORPSE.
MOURNERS IN A COACH.
CHANCELLOR OF THE COLLEGE.
MEMBERS OF THE CORPORATION.
CLERGY.
PHYSICIANS.
MEMBERS OF THE BAPTIST CHURCH.
CITIZENS IN GENERAL.

On the ensuing Sabbath, an eloquent and impressive funeral sermon was preached in the Baptist meeting-house, by the Rev. Perez Fobes, LL.D., pastor of the Congregational church in Raynham, Mass., and also Professor of Natural and Experimental Philosophy in the college. A sermon was also preached on the same day by the Rev. Dr. Maxcy, Manning's successor. Both these sermons were afterwards published. From the former we cannot forbear making brief extracts : —

"The amiable Manning has given up the ghost; and where is he? Not in the college, where lately we saw him presiding with mild dignity and parental affection, greatly beloved by every member of that collected family; not in the house of God, where he often met you; nor in the pulpit, where you have so frequently heard him preach the glad tidings of great joy; — not at the communion-table, breaking to you the bread of life, and praying for the health of languishing souls; not in his own house, with his family and friends around him, where he was ever known as the revered head and illustrious example of religion, of government, and of every domestic and social virtue. No, he is not here."

"The corporation of the college, with the instructors and students, all feel and recognize the loss. Their hearts echo to the voice of mourning, to the deep-toned bell, and to all the badges of sorrow. With multitudes around us, we have dropped the involuntary tear. We have felt the sigh unbidden heave, and followed the *hearse*, solemn and slow, with a numerous train of mourners, all united in the attestation of high esteem and affection for the lamented man of God. We are witnesses, and God also, how piously, and justly, and unblamably he lived among us, — we are witnesses to the amiableness of his natural temper. How pleasing his condescension and affability! How conspicuous his candor and impartiality, even in circumstances of peculiar trial! These, added to a strong mind, well furnished with useful learning, and with ample resources for eloquence, popularity, and pleasing address, rendered him highly esteemed through the large circle of his acquaintance. But, alas! all these amiable and useful qualities could not exempt him from the fate of mortals."

To the foregoing, we add several letters by Dr. Manning's intimate friends, announcing his death, together with extracts from a Commencement oration, and the circular letters of the Warren and Philadelphia Associations. The following letter is addressed to the Rev. Dr. Hezekiah Smith: —

BOSTON, July 30, 1791.

DEAR SIR:

I am sorry to be the messenger of news that will give you pain, but you must know it. Dr. Manning was taken with a fainting fit last Lord's Day morning, at family prayer, and expired yesterday morning, at half-past four o'clock. The complaint was of the apoplectic kind. He had no senses from the time he was taken. Great the loss to his amiable wife, great to the college and Baptist interest in general. But the Lord reigns; submission to him is our certain duty. We must immediately look around for a person to fill his place; but where to find him I know not. What think you of Mr. Allison, or Dr. Jones? Has the former had a public education? Or has the latter the various qualifications for a President? You and I must exert ourselves on this occasion. Friends at Providence and elsewhere will expect it. Write freely to me on this subject. I suppose it will be best that Mr. Howell be desired to preside at the next Commencement, as the oldest Fellow. Peace be with you Adieu.

Yours,

SAMUEL STILLMAN

The following letter to the Rev. Dr. Samuel Jones gives particulars of Manning's death and funeral. It was written, it will be observed, in behalf of the members of the corporation of the college, and in an informal manner, designates Mr. Jones as Manning's successor in the presidency.

PROVIDENCE, Aug. 3, 1791.

DEAR SIR:

Before these lines will come to your hands you will doubtless have heard the melancholy tidings of the death of our late worthy President Manning. He departed this life about four o'clock on Friday morning, the 29th ult., after an illness of only five days, during which time he discovered little or no signs of reason. His funeral was attended last Saturday. It was the largest and most solemn that I have seen in this place. I need not tell you that his death is universally lamented by all ranks of people, but the loss is more severely felt by the corporation of the college, and by the students under his care. As he was the founder of the college, and celebrated for many shining abilities which peculiarly qualified him to preside in it, we are apprehensive that the institution may suffer a temporary relapse, unless some known and established character can be induced to supply the vacancy soon.

At a meeting of as many of the corporation in this town as could be readily convened to take into consideration measures relative to the ensuing Commencement, some conversation passed about the election of a President, when it was the voice of all present that I should write to you on the subject, and call on you for assistance on this occasion, so critical to the interests of the college. It is our unanimous and very earnest request, dear sir, that you will come to our help. The eyes of the corporation seem fixed on you for a successor to President Manning.

From my long acquaintance with you, I have not the least doubt of your disposition to serve the best interests of mankind. A door seems now opened in divine Providence to call forth to public usefulness those great and very useful talents I know you possess. Let me entreat you to consider the application weightily. I am sure you will do it sensibly. I am to request a line from you in answer, by the first post after the receipt of this letter, or as soon as you find it convenient to give us an answer to the subject of it, and I have it in charge in particular and very urgently to request your attendance with us at the ensuing Commencement.

Pray give my respects to Mrs. Jones, by whom I trust I am still remembered, and to any others in your good family to whom I may be known, and to inquiring friends. With very great esteem, I remain, dear sir,

Your affectionate friend and very humble servant,

DAVID HOWELL.

To the Rev. Dr. Rippon, of London, the Rev. Isaac Backus, under date of Aug. 19, 1791, writes: —

"I was with President Manning two days in June past, and when I parted with him, the 8th of that month, I had as little thought of its being the last parting for time, as at any parting we ever had. But near night, on July 29, I received a line from Providence, informing me of his decease at four o'clock that morning. I went there the first instant, and met the college corporation the next day, who have thought of Dr. Jones for his successor, if he can be obtained; but we have no idea of obtaining any man who will equal President Manning in all respects, at least soon. His extensive knowledge, fervent piety, constant study to be serviceable to mankind, — his easy access to every class of people, with his gift of governing so as to be feared and loved by all, where keen envy did not prevail, — rendered him the most accomplished man for that station of any one I ever saw. Yet, in the midst of his usefulness, he is gone, as universally lamented as any man that I have known."

At the Commencement in 1791, an "Oration on the Death of Rev. President Manning" was delivered by Simeon Doggett, of the class of 1788, then a candidate for the Master's degree. Mr. Doggett was a tutor in the college from 1791 to 1796. He afterwards had the charge of an academy in Taunton, Mass. He was pastor of the Congregational church in Mendon, Mass., from 1815 to 1831, and from the latter year to 1846 was the pastor of the

Congregational church in Raynham. He died March 20, 1852, in the eighty-seventh year of his age. From his oration on Manning, which is preserved in manuscript among the college archives, we present extracts: —

"He is gone, alas! never to return. No more, O Manning! must thou grace that sacred desk with thy majestic presence. No more shall the temple of the Lord seem like the gates of heaven from the sweet droppings of thy lips. No more shall Christian assemblies be moved, be pleased, be instructed, be enraptured by thy inspired tongue. No more shalt thou lead the devout heart up to the throne of God. No more shall thy conciliating tongue and precious counsels be heard in church and state. Thy placid countenance, thy pleasing converse, thy soft and graceful manners shall no more delight the friendly circle. No more shall you, respected patrons of yonder seat of learning, boast of the shining character of your President and friend. No more shall we, my dear elder brothers, sit in council with our wise, our mild, our beloved President...... O, relentless Death! — not even the worth of a Manning could elude thy stroke. But in the midst of his usefulness, when that nursery of science, planted and reared by his fostering hand, extending its branches, began to require all those abilities to inspect and preserve it which were exerted to rear it; when it was under his watchful eye and industrious hand flourishing in all the beauties of knowledge, and moulding human nature into her most pleasing forms; when he began to see and rejoice in the fruit of his labors, in the midst of all his glory, cruel Death! thou hast suddenly snatched him away, and hurried him to the grave...... Though these his exertions to increase knowledge were almost unparalleled, yet merely to increase knowledge was not his end, but the means, the end of which was to regenerate the heart and to advance the Redeemer's kingdom. Hence, while engaged to promote learning, he was still more engaged to promote religion. Of this all his pupils are witnesses who have seen his devotion and enjoyed his instructions. How naturally at our college exercises would a very slight connection lead his discourse to moral and religious subjects! Upon these subjects, with what additional ardor would he discourse! These occasions seemed to add new life to his faculties. They would add warmth to his heart, brightness to his understanding, and eloquence to his tongue. And still more did his devotion ever show that his heart's desire and constant prayer to God was that true religion might flourish. And of this his pupils are not the only witnesses. All Christian societies within his extensive acquaintance, especially those of this town, are also witnesses. It was this which led him to the study of divinity, and finally made him so eminent in the ministry. It was this which caused him, like the primitive apostles, to travel through all parts of the country to instruct, to purify, to organize, and to confirm the church..... Perhaps no one of his age had a greater influence in the Redeemer's kingdom; and his usefulness was parallel with his influence. And was it not also this ardent desire for the triumph of religion that inspired him with such distinguished eloquence? Few preachers of his age spoke like him. He moved, he pleased, he instructed all who heard him. Notwithstanding the diversity of dispositions, and the indifference of hearts in Christian assemblies, his eloquence made its way to all. Sometimes clothing himself with the threatenings of the law, he seemed to thunder forth all the terrors of Mount Sinai, causing the most hardened and stubborn sinners to tremble before him. At other times, putting on the garment of mildness, the peace of the gospel, his eloquence breathed naught but benevolence, diffusing tenderness, and melting all hearts into grief and love. Thus following this great man from his first appearance upon the stage of active life to his disappearance, we invariably find him holding in his left hand the classics, in his right the word of God, with his eye fixed on the good of mankind, widely diffusing, as he passed along, knowledge, and religion, and happiness. Here we might add his more particular character. We might amplify the majestic but mild beauties of his person and appearance; the vast resources of his mind; the uncommon greatness of his acquirements, considering the activity of his life; his remarkably amiable disposition; his astonishingly popular talents, and his distinguished and inflexible virtue and piety...... Time not affording me the pleasure of further addressing the particular connections of this great man, I proceed to ask whether a character so distinguished, so useful, so amiable, could possibly be the object of detraction? Alas! the depravity of human nature, it could, it was. But mark the issue. Where now is detraction? Confounded with shame and remorse, she has forever hidden her head. The universal lamentation at his death, the surprising throng of mourners at his funeral, and the universal approbation of his character, have eternally stopped her mouth, and reflected her deadly shafts back upon herself, where they will continue to sting like serpents, and to caution her to be careful how she deals with real merit."

The circular letter of the Warren Association alludes to the death of Manning as a great loss in Zion: —

"Should we close this letter without taking notice of the providence of God in the removal of two of our ministers by death the year past, we should betray a criminal inattention. The one is Brother Nathaniel Green, of Charlton, who hath long sustained a good character in our churches. The other was our much esteemed Brother JAMES MANNING, D. D., President of Rhode Island College, whose abilities and usefulness were well known to us all, and whose attention to the interests of learning and religion justly claim our esteem. Oh that the great Head of the Church, in whom are all gifts and grace, would favor us with other persons of equal accomplishments, that thereby the breaches in the walls of Zion may be built up."

From the circular letter of the Philadelphia Association we also make an extract: —

"But our joys abate, while we reflect on the heavy tidings, so generally mentioned in your letters, of the death of our highly esteemed and dearly beloved brother, DR. MANNING; who, engaged in the dearest interests of religion, of science, and the prosperity of his country, fell from the zenith of glory and usefulness. In the general loss we sustain an important part. No longer shall we enjoy his able counsels, his divine and persuasive eloquence, nor his personal friendship. But while we trust he fell to rise to higher, to celestial glories, and joys unspeakable, resignation becomes us. May the Lord sanctify to the churches and ministers of Christ the awful stroke, enable us to feel and faithfully discharge the duties devolving on us, and imitate his amiable example."

A review of Dr. Manning's life, as presented in the several chapters of our work, affords a pleasing illustration of the truth which Cowper has so well expressed, —

"God gives to every man
The virtue, temper, understanding, taste
That lifts him into life, and lets him fall
Just in the niche he was ordained to fill."

It only remains to add a few particulars relating to Manning's personal appearance, habits, character, and influence. This we shall do in the language of his intimate friend, and early associate in the instruction of the college, the Hon. David Howell, who wrote his obituary notice, and who also penned the inscription upon the stone erected by the Trustees and Fellows of the college to his memory. The following extracts from his obituary notice were originally published in the *Providence Gazette* for Saturday, Aug. 6, 1791:—

"In his youth he was remarkable for his dexterity in athletic exercises, for the symmetry of his body, and gracefulness of his person. His countenance was stately and majestic, full of dignity, goodness, and gravity;[1] and the temper of his mind was a counterpart to it. He was formed for enterprise. His address was pleasing, his manner enchanting, his voice harmonious, and his eloquence almost irresistible.

"Having deeply imbibed the spirit of truth himself, as a preacher of the gospel, he was faithful in declaring the whole counsel of God. He studied plainness of speech and to be useful more than to be celebrated. The good order, learning, and respectability of the Baptist churches in the Eastern States are much owing to his assiduous attention to their welfare. The credit of his name, and his personal influence among them, have never, perhaps, been exceeded by any other character.

"Of the college he must be considered, in one sense, as the founder. He presided with the singular advantage of a superior personal appearance, added to all his shining talents for governing and instructing youth. From the first beginning of his Latin school at Warren, through many discouragements, he has, by constant care and labor, raised this seat of

[1] The likeness of Dr. Manning accompanying the present work was engraved from an original portrait, which has long been in the possession of Brown University. It was painted in the year 1770, by Cosmo Alexander, a Scotch gentleman, who came from Edinburgh to Newport about this time, and who is said to have patronized Gilbert Stuart, and to have given to him his first lessons in drawing. He returned to Scotland in the winter of 1772, taking young Stuart with him. An account of Alexander may be found in "Dunlap's History of the Arts of Design in the United States."

learning to notice, to credit, and to respectability in the United States. Perhaps the history of no other college will disclose a more rapid progress or greater maturity, in the course of about twenty-five years.

"Although he seemed to be consigned to a sedentary life, yet he was capable of more active scenes. He had paid much attention to the government of his country, and had been honored by this State with a seat in the Old Congress. In state affairs he discovered an uncommon degree of sagacity, and might have made a figure as a politician.

"In classical learning he was fully competent to the business of teaching, although he devoted less time than some others in his station to the study of the more abstruse sciences. In short, nature seemed to have furnished him so completely, that little remained for art to accomplish. The resources of his genius were great. In conversation he was at all times pleasant and entertaining. He had as many friends as acquaintances, and took no less pains to serve his friends than to acquire them.

"His death is a loss, not to the college or church only, but to the world. He is lamented by the youth under his care, by the churches, by his fellow-citizens; and wherever his name has been heard, in whatever quarter of the civilized earth, the friends of science, of virtue and humanity will drop a tender tear on the news of his death.

"His amiable lady, the wife of his youth, and the boast of her sex, with all her fortitude of mind, which is great, must have sunk under the distressing loss were she not sustained by divine grace. May Heaven continue to support her, for earth must have lost its charms. Few persons ever enjoyed a more excellent constitution, or better health. Increasing corpulence,[1] occasioned chiefly by his confinement to the labors of his station (for he was temperate in his diet), gave him some complaints of ill-health of late years; but what in particular furnished him with a singular presentiment of his mortality, is unknown."

[1] Concerning Dr. Manning's "bulk," the Hon. William Hunter, one of his pupils, thus writes: "His motions and gestures were so easy and graceful that ordinary observers thought not of his immense volume of flesh, and those who criticized, admired the manner by which it was spontaneously wielded. I do not know that he had ever read Hogarth's Analysis of Beauty, but he moved in *his* line of grace."

Our task is done. We have endeavored to trace the origin, and to exhibit the early progress, of Rhode Island College, or, as it is now called, Brown University. So far as possible, we have allowed the writers, the actors, and the records of the past, to tell their own story in their own way, having no theories to advance, and no interests save those of truth and justice to subserve. That members of the Philadelphia Baptist Association planned the college in the outset, admits not even the shadow of a doubt. It was designed, in the language of the preface to Morgan Edwards's subscription book, "to adorn human nature, and promote the true interests and happiness of mankind," by disseminating sound knowledge and useful literature. Its main design, however, was to secure for the churches an educated ministry. For this its friends toiled and prayed, amidst difficulties and discouragements, growing out of indifference on the one hand, and opposition on the other. Under the auspices of its devoted President it became a centre of influence, and a rallying point for the denomination, "greatly promoting," says Manning, "Baptist principles, and the spread of civil and religious liberty throughout New England, ... and adding respectability to the Baptist profession."

We have traced the career of Dr. Manning from its commencement to its close, and, so far as our materials would admit, have made him his own biographer. Our readers have thus obtained a more correct idea of his character and life than could have been obtained by any formal delineation of his virtues as a man, or of his genius as an educator, a statesman, and a preacher. Devotion to the interests of the college appears to have been the animating motive of his conduct, and the improvement and elevation of the Baptist denomination through the college, the object and aim of his entire professional life. The sentiment, so beautifully expressed by Dr. South, that "the Spirit always guides and instructs before he saves; and as he brings to happiness only by the ways of holiness, so he never leads to true holiness but by the paths of knowledge," was by no means an universal sentiment, it will be observed, in the days of Manning. The Baptists as a denomination were not specially friendly to learning, and the provision for the education of their clergy was exceedingly limited. To the work of removing existing prejudices against collegiate institutions, and of securing for the denomination to which he was attached the benefits of an educated ministry, he devoted his best energies. His mental acquisitions, his distinguished piety, his great ministerial excellence, which, combined with his natural gifts and endowments, gave him so rare and so extensive an influence over the minds of men, were all alike consecrated to this one cherished object. For this he declined, at the beginning of his public life, the call of the church at Charleston, having already committed himself to the interests of the college. For this he resigned his pastoral charge at Warren, greatly to the surprise and the regret of his people. For this he perseveringly labored amidst the discouragements of poverty, the opposition of enemies, the indifference of friends, and the conflicts of war. To benefit the college he left its quiet shades, and the pulpit where his labors had been honored and blest, and entered the arena of political strife; and when his object was attained, so far as it could be through his own personal exertions, he returned from the halls of Congress to his accustomed duties, resisting all the allurements of political life and the public distinctions to which his talents would naturally have entitled him. And toward the close of his career, although in the midst of gracious manifestations of the Divine presence, and enjoying the emoluments of a large and flourishing church and society, which had been built up mainly through his exertions, he again and again requested his people to provide a successor in the pastorate, in order that he might give himself more exclusively to the care of the college, and to the great work of laying broad and deep the foundations for an educated Baptist ministry. In all this "he labored," says Prof. Goddard, "not for himself, but for others, and, in language breathing a holier inspiration than that of poetry, may be conveyed the grand moral of his life: —

> 'Love thyself last;
> Let all the ends thou aim'st at be thy country's,
> Thy God's, and truth's.'"

The narrative has, in several instances, presented illustrations of sectarian bitterness, of which Manning and his associates were sometimes the objects, and also of the unfair dealings to which the college in its infancy was subjected, but it is only as a part of the history of the times, and, we trust, only in the spirit of candor and of historical fidelity. The animosities and strifes of a hundred years ago have long since been buried, and both the college and its self-sacrificing founders are enshrined in the reverence and affection of all, of every ecclesiastical name, who have shared in the manifold benefits they have conferred upon mankind. May the record here made of the consecrated benevolence and the persevering efforts of our fathers stimulate the patrons and friends of Brown University, which now enters upon the second century of its existence, to renewed exertions on its behalf; and may all its scattered sons, and the religious denomination especially whose present prosperity is so largely due to his intelligent devoted labors, hold in grateful remembrance the virtues, the talents, and the piety of JAMES MANNING.

> "Peace to the just man's memory, — let it grow
> Greener with years, and blossom through the flight
> Of ages; let the mimic canvas show
> His calm benevolent features; let the light
> Stream on his deeds of love, that shun'd the sight
> Of all but heaven; and, in the book of fame,
> The glorious record of his virtues write,
> And hold it up to men, and bid them claim
> A palm like his, and catch from him the hallow'd flame."

APPENDIX.

CHARTER drafted by the Rev. Dr. Stiles, and presented to the General Assembly of Rhode Island in the month of August, 1763.[1]

The Governor and Company of his Majesty's English Colony of Rhode Island and Providence Plantations, in America, in their General Assembly held at Newport, within aforesaid Colony, on the first Monday of August, Anno Domini One Thousand Seven Hundred and Sixty-Three, and in the third year of the reign of his Majesty George the Third of Great Britain, France, and Ireland, King: To all to whom these presents shall come, Greeting:

WHEREAS, institutions for liberal education are highly beneficial to society, by forming the rising generation to virtue, knowledge, and useful literature, and thus preserving in the community a succession of men duly qualified for discharging the offices of life with usefulness and reputation; they have therefore justly merited and received the attention and encouragment of every wise, polite and well-regulated State:

CHARTER granted by the General Assembly of Rhode Island, in the month of February, 1764.[2]

At the GENERAL ASSEMBLY of the Governor and Company of the English Colony of Rhode Island and Providence Plantations, in New England, in America, begun and holden by adjournment at East Greenwich, within and for the Colony aforesaid, on the last Monday in February, in the year of our Lord One Thousand Seven Hundred and Sixty-four, and fourth of the reign of his most sacred Majesty George the Third, by the grace of God King of Great Britain, and so forth.

AN ACT FOR THE ESTABLISHMENT OF A COLLEGE OR UNIVERSITY, WITHIN THIS COLONY.

"polite"-omitted.

[1] From the original copy in Dr. Stiles's own handwriting.

[2] Only the changes and additions made by the Committee are here given. See Chap. I. p. 50.

And whereas a public school or seminary, erected for this purpose within this Colony, to which the youth may freely resort for education in the vernacular and learned languages, and in the liberal arts and sciences, would be for the advantage and honor of this government: And whereas the Hon. Stephen Hopkins Esq., the Hon. John Gardner Esq., the Hon. Samuel Ward Esq., the Hon. William Ellery Esq., James Honyman, Francis Willett, Simon Peas, Daniel Jenckes, Jno. Tillinghast, Nicholas Tillinghast, Joseph Russel, Edw. Scott, Joseph Clark, James Helme, Esquires, Col. Elisha Reynolds, Col. Josias Lyndon, Col. Benj. Hall, Col. Job Bennet, Messieurs David Cheesebrough, Joseph Jacob, Nath. Coggeshall, Ephraim Bowen, William Ellery Jun., Gideon Wanton, Rev. Messrs. Othniel Cambell, Edw. Upham, Jno. Burt, William Vinal, John Maxson, Gardner Thurston, Ezra Stiles, Marmaduke Brown, Samuel Aldborough, Thos. Moffat M.D., George Hazard, Joshua Clark Esq., Samuel Nightingale, Sherjashub Bourn Esq., Messrs. Nicholas Brown, Thomas Eyres, Elnathan Hammond, William Rogers, Jno. Tanner, Ezekiel Burroughs, Henry Peckam, etc., etc., appear as undertakers in this valuable design: And thereupon a petition hath been preferred to this Assembly praying that full liberty and power may be granted unto them to found, endow, order, and govern a College or University within this Colony; and for the more effectual execution of this design to incorporate them into one body politic, to be known in the law with the powers, privileges, and franchises necessary to the purposes aforesaid:

erected for that purpose

for the general advantage and honor of the government: And whereas Daniel Jenckes Esq., Nicholas Tillinghast Esq., Nicholas Gardner Esq., Col. Josias Lyndon, Col. Elisha Reynolds, Peleg Thurston Esq., Simon Pease Esq., John Tillinghast Esq., George Hazard Esq., Col. Job Bennet, Nicholas Easton Esq., Arthur Fenner Esq., Mr. Ezekiel Gardner, Mr. John Waterman, Mr. James Barker Jr., Mr. John Holmes, Solomon Drown Esq., Mr. Samuel Winsor, Mr. Joseph Sheldon, Charles Rhodes Esq., Mr. Nicholas Brown, Col. Barzillai Richmond, Mr. John Brown, Mr. Gideon Hoxsey, Mr. Thomas Eyres, Mr. Thomas Potter Jr., Mr. Peleg Barker, Mr. Edward Thurston, Mr. William Redwood, Joseph Clarke Esq., Mr. John G. Wanton, and Mr. Thomas Robinson, with many other persons, appear as undertakers in the valuable design: And thereupon a petition hath been preferred to this Assembly, praying that full liberty and power may be granted unto such of them, with others, as are hereafter mentioned, to found, endow, order, and govern a College or University within this Colony; and that, for the more effectual execution of this design, they may be incorporated into one body politic, to be known in the law, with the powers, privileges, and franchizes necessary for the purposes aforesaid:

NOW, THEREFORE, KNOW YE, that being willing to encourage and patronize such an advantageous and useful institution,	honorable and useful
we, the said Governor and Company, in General Assembly convened, do, for ourselves and our successors, in and by virtue of the power and authority, within the jurisdiction of this Colony, to us by the Royal Charter committed,	granted and committed,
enact, grant, ordain, constitute, and declare, and *it is* hereby enacted, granted, ordained, constituted, and declared	
that the said Stephen Hopkins, John Gardner, etc., etc., or such and so many of them as shall within six months from the date hereof accept of this trust and qualify themselves as hereinafter directed, and their successors, shall forever hereafter be one body corporate and politic, in fact and name, to be known in law by the name of the TRUSTEES AND FELLOWS OF —— COLLEGE OR UNIVERSITY IN THE COLONY OF RHODE ISLAND AND PROVIDENCE PLANTATIONS, IN AMERICA; the Trustees and Fellows at any time hereafter giving such	that the Hon. Stephen Hopkins Esq., the Hon. Joseph Wanton Jr. Esq., the Hon. Samuel Ward Esq., the Hon. William Ellery Esq., John Tillinghast Esq., Simon Pease Esq., James Honyman Esq., Nicholas Easton Esq., Nicholas Tillinghast Esq., Darius Sessions Esq., Joseph Harris Esq., Francis Willett Esq., William Logan Esq., Daniel Jenckes Esq., George Hazard Esq., Nicholas Brown Esq., Jeremiah Niles Esq., Joshua Babcock Esq., Mr. John G. Wanton, the Rev. Edward Upham, the Rev. Jeremiah Condy, the Rev. Marmaduke Brown, the Rev. Gardner Thurston, the Rev. Ezra Stiles, the Rev. John Graves, the Rev. John Maxson, the Rev. Samuel Winsor, the Rev. John Gano, the Rev. Morgan Edwards, the Rev. Isaac Eaton, the Rev. Samuel Stillman, the Rev. Samuel Jones, the Rev. James Manning, the Rev. Russel Mason, Col. Elisha Reynolds, Col. Josias Lyndon, Col. Job Bennet, Mr. Ephraim Bowen, Joshua Clarke Esq., Capt. Jonathan Slade, John Taylor Esq., Mr. Robert Strettell Jones, Azariah Dunham Esq., Mr. Edward Thurston Jr., Mr. Thomas Eyres, Mr. Thomas Hazard, and Mr. Peleg Barker, or such or so many of them as shall, with-

	in twelve months from the date hereof, accept of this trust, and qualify themselves as hereinafter directed, and their successors, shall be forever hereafter one body corporate and politic, in fact and name, to be known in law by the name of TRUSTEES AND FELLOWS OF THE COLLEGE OR UNIVERSITY IN THE ENGLISH COLONY OF RHODE ISLAND AND PROVIDENCE PLANTATIONS, IN NEW ENGLAND, IN AMERICA;
more particular name to said College, in honor of the greatest and most distinguished benefactor, or otherwise, as they shall think proper; which name, so given, shall, in all acts, instruments, and doings of the said body politic, be superadded to their corporate name aforesaid, and become a part of their legal appellation, by which it shall be forever after known and distinguished: And that, by the same name, they and their successors, chosen by themselves, as hereinafter prescribed, shall and may have perpetual succession; and shall and may be persons able and capable, in the law, to sue and to be sued, to plead and to be impleaded, to answer and to be answered unto, to defend and to be defended, in all and singular suits, causes, matters, actions, and doings, of what kind soever: And also to have, take, possess, acquire, purchase, or otherwise receive and hold lands, tenements, hereditaments, goods, chattels, or other estates; of all which they may, and shall, stand and be seized, notwithstanding any misnomer of this College, or the Corporation thereof; and by whatever name, or however imperfectly the same shall be described in gifts, bequests, and assignments, provided	the, instead of "said." forever known and distinguished: as hereafter prescribed, and to be defended against, of the College, gift, bequest, and assignment,

the true intent of the assigner or benefactor shall be evident: Also the same to grant, demise, aliene, lease, use, manage, and improve, according to the tenor of the donations, and to the purposes, trusts, and uses to which they shall be seized thereof: And full liberty, power, and authority is hereby granted unto the said Trustees and Fellows, and their successors, to found a College or University within this Colony, for promoting the liberal arts and universal literature; and with the moneys, estates, and revenues, of which they shall from time to time become legally seized as aforesaid, to endow the same; and erect the necessary edifices and buildings thereof in such place within this Colony as they shall think convenient; and generally to regulate, order, and govern the same, appoint officers, and make laws, as hereinafter prescribed; and hold, use, and enjoy all the liberties, privileges, exemptions, dignities, and immunities enjoyed by any college or university whatever.

And furthermore, that the said Trustees and Fellows, and their successors, shall, and may, forever hereafter have a public seal, to use for all causes, matters, and affairs whatsoever, of them and their successors, and the same seal to alter, break, and make anew, from time to time, at their will and pleasure; which seal shall always be deposited with the President, or senior Fellow.

And furthermore, by the authority aforesaid, it is hereby enacted, ordained, and declared, that it is now, and at all times hereafter shall continue to be, the unalterable constitution of this College or University,

or benefactor be evident:

buildings and edifices thereof, on such place

matters, and affairs whatever,

same to alter

that the Corporation thereof shall consist of two branches; that of the Trustees, and that of the Fellowship, with distinct, separate, and respective powers: And that the number of the Trustees shall and may be thirty-five; of which nineteen shall forever be elected of the denomination called Baptists, seven shall forever be elected of the denomination called Congregationalists or Presbyterians, five shall forever be elected of the denomination called Friends or Quakers, and four shall forever be elected of the denomination called Episcopalians: And that the succession in this branch shall be forever chosen and filled up from the respective denominations in this proportion, and according to these numbers, which are hereby fixed and shall remain in perpetuity immutably the same: And that the Hon. Stephen Hopkins Esq., the Hon. John Gardner Esq., the Hon. Samuel Ward Esq., the Hon. William Ellery Esq., James Honeyman, Francis Willet, Simon Peas, Nicholas Easton, Daniel Jenckes, Jno. Tillinghast, Nicholas Tillinghast, Joseph Russel, Edward Scott, Joseph Clark, James Helme, Esqrs., Colonels Elisha Reynolds, Josias Lyndon, Benj. Hall, Job Bennet, Messieurs David Cheesebrough, Joseph Jacob, Nathl. Coggeshall, George Hazard, John Wanton, the Rev. Messrs. John Maxson, Samuel Aldborough, and Gardner Thurston, and Joshua Clark Esq., Messrs. Nicholas Brown, Elnathan Hammond, Jno. Tanner, William Rogers, Ezekiel Burroughs, Henry Peckam, etc., or such and so many of them as shall qualify themselves as aforesaid, shall be and they are hereby declared and established the

branches; to wit'

And that the number of the Trustees shall and may be thirty-six; of which twenty-two shall forever be elected of the denomination called Baptists or Anti-Pedobaptists, five shall forever be elected of the denomination called Friends or Quakers, four shall forever be elected of the denomination called Congregationalists, and five shall forever be elected of the denomination called Episcopalians; and that the succession in this branch shall be forever chosen and filled up from the respective denominations in this proportion, and according to these numbers, which are hereby fixed, and shall remain to perpetuity immutably the same. And that the said Stephen Hopkins, Joseph Wanton, Samuel Ward, William Ellery, John Tillinghast, Simon Pease, James Honyman, Nicholas Easton, Nicholas Tillinghast, Darius Sessions, Joseph Harris, Francis Willett, Daniel Jenckes, George Hazard, Nicholas Brown, Jeremiah Niles, John G. Wanton, Joshua Clarke, Gardner Thurston, John Graves, John Maxson, John Gano, Samuel Winsor, Isaac Eaton, Samuel Stillman, Russel Mason, Elisha Reynolds, Josias Lyndon, Job Bennet, Ephraim Bowen, John Taylor, Jonathan Slade, Robert Strettell Jones, Azariah Dunham, Edward Thurston Jr., and Peleg Barker, or such or so many of them as shall qualify themselves as aforesaid, shall be and they are hereby declared and established the first and present Trustees. And that the number of the Fellows, inclusive of the President (who shall always be a Fel-

first and present Trustees. And that the number of the Fellows (inclusive of the President, who shall always be a Fellow), shall and may be twelve; of which eight shall forever be elected of the denomination called Congregationalists, and the rest indifferently of any and all denominations: And that the Rev. Messrs. Edward Upham, Othniel Campbell, John Burt, William Vinal, Ezra Stiles, and Marmaduke Brown, Samuel Nightingale Esq., Thos. Moffat M. D., Sherjashub Brown, and William Ellery Jr., Esqrs., and Dr. Thomas Eyres, or such and so many as shall qualify themselves as aforesaid, shall be and they are hereby declared and established the first and present Fellows and Fellowship, to whom the President, when hereafter elected, shall be joined to complete the number.

And furthermore, it is declared and ordained, that the succession in both branches shall at all times hereafter be filled up and supplied according to these numbers, and this established and invariable proportion, from the respective denominations, by the election and concurrence of both branches of this Corporation, which shall at all times sit and act by separate and distinct powers, the concurrence of which to become and produce the joint act of the Corporation: And in general, that in order to the validity and confirmation of all acts, there shall be, in the exercise of their respective separate and distinct powers, the joint concurrence of the Trustees and Fellows by their respective majorities, except in adjudging and conferring the academical degrees, which shall forever belong exclusively to the Fellow)shall and maybe twelve; of which eight shall be forever elected of the denomination called Baptists, or Anti-Pedobaptists, and the rest indifferently of any or all denominations: And that the Rev. Edward Upham, the Rev. Jeremiah Condy, the Rev. Marmaduke Brown, the Rev. Morgan Edwards, the Rev. Ezra Stiles, the Rev. Samuel Jones, the Rev. James Manning, William Logan Esq., Joshua Babcock Esq., Mr. Thomas Eyres, and Mr. Thomas Hazard, or such or so many of them as shall qualify themselves as aforesaid, shall be, and they are hereby declared the first and present Fellows and Fellowship, to whom the President, when hereafter elected (who shall forever be of the denomination called Baptists or Anti-Pedobaptists), shall be joined to complete the number.

And furthermore, it is declared and ordained, that the succession in both branches shall at all times hereafter be filled up and supplied according to these numbers, and this established and invariable proportion, from the respective donominations, by the separate election of both branches of this Corporation, which shall at all times sit and act by separate and distinct powers; and in general, in order to the validity and consummation of all acts, there shall be in the exercise of their respective, separate, and distinct powers, the joint concurrence of the Trustees and Fellows, by their respective majorities, except in adjudging and conferring the academical degrees, which shall forever belong, exclusively, to the Fellowship, as a learned Faculty.

lowship as a learned Faculty; and the election of a President, which shall forever belong exclusively to the Trustees, they the said Trustees consulting, advising with and taking the opinion of the learned Faculty previous to their choice and appointment of such a learned and important officer.	This clause, "and the election of a President," etc., omitted.
And furthermore, it is constituted that the instruction, immediate government of the College, nomination of all officers, except the President, together with the origination, preparing and enacting all laws, shall forever be and rest in the President	And furthermore, it is constituted, that the instruction and immediate government of the College shall forever be and rest in the President and Fellows or Fellowship.
and Fellows or Fellowship; and that the election of the President, and confirmation of all officers and laws, shall forever be and rest in the Trustees.	This clause, "and that the election of a President," etc., omitted.
And furthermore, it is ordained, that there shall be a general meeting	
of this Corporation on the first Wednesday of September annually, within the College edifice, and until the same be built, at such place as they shall appoint, to consult, advise, and	of the Corporation on the first Wednesday in September
transact the affairs of said College or University; at which, or at any other time, the public Commencement may be held and celebrated.	of the college;
And that, on any special emergency,	special emergencies,
the President, and any two of the	with any two
Fellows, or any three of the Fellows, may convoke, and they are hereby empowered to convoke, an assembly	Fellows, exclusive of the President,
of the Corporation on six days' notice: And that, in all meetings, the	twenty days' notice:
major votes of those present of the two branches respectively shall be deemed their respective majorities aforesaid: Provided, that not less than twelve of the Trustees, and	major vote
eight of the Fellows, be the quorum of their respective branches. That the President, or, in his absence, the	and five of the Fellows, be a quorum

senior Fellow present, shall always be Moderator of the Fellows. That this Corporation, at their annual meeting, once in three years, or oftener in case of death or removal, shall and may choose a Chancellor of the University and Treasurer from among the Trustees, and a Secretary from among the Fellows. That the nomination of the Chancellor shall be alternately in the Trustees and Fellows, whose office shall be only to preside as Moderator of the Trustees; and that, in his absence, the Trustees shall choose a Moderator for the time being, by the name of Vice-Chancellor. And at any of the meetings, duly formed as aforesaid, shall and may be elected a Trustee or Fellow, or Trustees and Fellows, in the room of those nominated in this charter, who may refuse to accept, or in the room of those who may die, resign, or remove out of this Colony, or be otherwise removed. And in case the Corporation shall omit above one year to fill up any vacancy or vacancies in their body, the respective branches shall and may supply the succession in their own separate elections, which elections shall in such cases be complete and valid.

shall be in the Trustees "and Fellows," omitted.

of their meetings,

Trustees or Fellows,

resign, or be removed.

This last clause, "And in case the Corporation," etc., omitted.

And furthermore, it is enacted, ordained, and declared, that this Corporation, at any of their meetings, regularly convened as aforesaid, shall and may elect and appoint the President and Professors of languages, and the several parts of literature (the President being always chosen by the Trustees as aforesaid): And upon the demise of him or them, or either of them, their resignation or removal from his or their office, for misdemeanor, incapacity,

"the President being always chosen by the Trustees as aforesaid," omitted.

or unfaithfulness (for which he or they are hereby declared removable by this Corporation), others to elect and appoint in their room and stead: And at such meeting, upon the nomination of the Fellows (who shall also have the nomination of the Professors), to elect and appoint tutors, stewards, butlers, and all such other officers usually appointed in colleges or universities, as they shall find necessary, and think fit to appoint, for promoting of liberal education, and the well ordering the affairs of this College; and them, or any of them, at their discretion, to remove, and substitute others in their places. And in case any President, Trustee, or Fellow shall see cause to change his religious denomination, or remove out of this Colony, this Corporation are hereby empowered to declare his or their place or places vacant, and may proceed to fill it up accordingly; which upon the request of either branch being omitted by the body, either branch may proceed to declare and fill up their vacancy separately as aforesaid; otherwise each Trustee and Fellow, not an officer of instruction, shall continue in his office during life, or until resignation. And further, in case either of the religious denominations should decline taking a part in this catholic, comprehensive, and liberal institution, the Trustees and Fellows shall and may complete their number, by electing from their respective denominations indifferently, always preserving their respective proportions herein before prescribed and determined: And all elections shall be by ballot, or written suffrage: And that a quorum of four Trustees and three Fellows may

"who shall also have the nomination of the Professors," omitted.

"or remove out of this Colony," omitted.

accordingly, as before directed; "which upon the request," etc., to the word "otherwise," omitted.

"indifferently" omitted.

transact any business, excepting placing the college edifice, election	
of Trustees, President, Fellows or	Fellows and Professors,
Professors, that is to say, so that their act shall be of force and validity until the next annual meeting, and no longer.	
And it is further enacted and ordained by the authority aforesaid, that each Trustee and Fellow, as well those nominated in this Charter as all that shall hereafter be duly elected, shall, previous to their acting in a corporate capacity, take the engagement of allegiance prescribed	
by law of this Government to his	of this Colony
Majesty King George the Third, his heirs and rightful successors to the crown of Great Britain, which engagement shall be administered to the present Trustees and Fellows by the Governor or Deputy-Governor of this Colony, and to those from time to time hereafter elected by their respective Moderators, who are hereby empowered to administer the same.	
And still more clearly to define and ascertain the respective powers of the two branches, on making and enacting laws, it is further ordained and declared, that the Fellowship shall have power, and they are hereby empowered from time to time, and at all times hereafter, to make, enact, and publish all such laws, statutes, regulations, and ordinances, with penalties, as to them shall seem meet, for the successful instruction and government of said College or University, not contrary to the spirit, extent, true meaning, and intention of the acts of the British Parliament or the laws of this Colony; and the same laws, statutes, and ordinances to repeal: Which laws, and the re-	

peals thereof, shall be laid before the Trustees, and with their approbation shall be of force and validity, but not otherwise. And further, the Trustees and Fellows, at their meetings aforesaid, shall ascertain the salaries of the respective officers, and order the moneys assessed on the students for tuition, fines, and incidental expenses, to be collected by the Steward, or such other officer as they shall appoint to collect the same; and the same with their revenues, and other College estates in the hands of the Treasurer, to appropriate in discharging salaries and other College debts: And the College accounts shall be annually audited in the meeting of the Corporation.	audited and adjusted
And furthermore, it is hereby enacted and declared, that into this liberal and catholic institution shall never be admitted any religious tests; but, on the contrary, all the members hereof shall forever enjoy full, free, unmolested, and absolute liberty of conscience: And that the places of Presidents, Professors, Tutors, and all other officers, shall be free and open for all denominations of Protestants:	full, free, absolute, and uninterrupted liberty of conscience: And that the places of Professors, Tutors, and all other officers, the President alone excepted,
And that youth of all religious denominations shall and may be freely admitted to the equal advantages, emoluments, and honors of this College or University; and shall receive a like fair, generous, and equal treatment during their residence therein, they conducting themselves peaceably, and conforming to the laws and statutes thereof:	the, instead of "this."
And that to all the purposes of this Corporation persons of different sects shall be sufficiently distinguished and known by their free profession or declaration, and by their general attendance on the public worship of	The rest of this section, beginning "And that to all the purposes," and ending with "morals of the College" (p. 478), omitted. In place thereof, the following: And that the public teaching shall, in general, respect the sciences; and that the sectarian differ-

their respective denominations: And it is hereby ordained and declared, that in this College shall no undue methods or arts be practised to allure and proselyte one another, or to insinuate the peculiar principles of any one or other of the denominations into the youth in general; which, as well as the monopoly of offices, might discourage the sending of students to this College, involve unhappy controversies among the instructors, and defeat this good design: And it is thereupon agreed, declared, constituted and established, that everything of this nature shall be accounted a misdemeanor, mutually avoided as much as possible, and by all the denominations, generously disdained and discountenanced as beneath the dignity, and foreign from the true intention, of this Confederacy: That accordingly the public teaching shall in general respect the sciences, and that the sectarian differences of opinion, and controversies on the peculiarities of principle, shall not make any part of the public and classical instruction: Although all religious controversies may be studied freely, examined, and explained by the President, Professors, and Tutors, in a personal, separate, and distinct manner to the youth of any and each denomination, *they or their parents requesting the same.* And that in this the President, Professors, and Tutors shall treat the religion of each denomination with peculiar tenderness, charity, and respect; so that neither denomination shall be alarmed with jealousies or apprehensions of any illiberal and disingenuous attempts upon one another, but on the contrary an open, free, undesigning, and generous harmony ... ences of opinion shall not make any part of the public and classical instruction: Although all religious controversies may be studied freely, examined, and explained by the President, Professors, and Tutors, in a personal, separate, and distinct manner, to the youth of any or each denomination: And above all, a constant regard be paid to, and effectual care taken of, the morals of the College.

mony; and a mutual honorable respect shall be recommended and endeavored, in order to exhibit an example in which literature may be advanced on Protestant harmony, and the most perfect religious liberty: Yet, nevertheless, shall be publicly taught and explained to all the youth, the existence, character, and dominion of the Supreme Being, the general evidences of natural and revealed religion, and the principles of moral philosophy, and a constant regard be paid to, and effectual care taken of the morals of the College.

And furthermore, for the honor and encouragement of literature, we constitute and declare the Fellowship aforesaid a learned Faculty; and do hereby give, grant unto, and invest them and their successors with full power and authority, and they are hereby authorized and empowered by their President, and in his absence by the senior Fellow, or one of the Fellows appointed by themselves, at the anniversary Commencements, or at any other times, and at all times hereafter, to admit to and confer any and all the learned degrees, given and conferred in any of the colleges or universities in Europe, and particularly in the Universities of Cambridge and Edinburgh in Great Britain, or any such other degrees of literary honor as they shall devise, upon any and all such candidates and persons as the President and Fellows, or Fellowship, shall judge worthy of the academical honors: Which power of conferring degrees is hereby restricted to the learned Faculty alone, who shall or may issue diplomas or certificates of such degrees, or confer degrees by diplomas, and authenticate them with the public seal of the

which can or ought to be given

"in Europe, and particularly in the Universities of Cambridge and Edinburgh in Great Britain," omitted. In place thereof, the words, "in America," substituted.

Corporation, and the hands of the President and Fellows, and in this case with the hands of all the Professors as witnesses, and deliver them to the graduates as honorable and perpetual testimonies thereof.	President and Secretary, and of all the Professors "thereof" omitted.
And furthermore, for the greater encouragement of this seminary of learning, and that the same may be amply endowed and enfranchised with the same privileges, dignities, and immunities enjoyed by the American Colleges and European Universities, We do grant, enact, ordain, and declare, and it is hereby granted, enacted, ordained, and declared, that the College estate, the estates, persons, and families of the President and Professors, for the time being, lying and being within this Colony, with the persons of the	[This clause on exemption from taxation was changed by the General Assembly, at its February session, in 1863, the Corporation of Brown University consenting, as follows: "The estates, persons, and families of the President and Professors for the time being, and of their successors in office, shall not hereafter be freed and exempted from taxes for more than the amount of ten thousand dollars for each of such officers; his estates, person, and family included."]
tutors, graduates, and students, during their residence, shall be freed and exempted from all taxes, serving on juries, and menial services: And that the persons aforesaid, together with those that shall have received the degree of Bachelor of Arts, or any of the higher degrees, and the diploma thereof, shall be exempted from bearing arms, impress, and military service.	"graduates" omitted. residence at the College, And that the persons aforesaid shall be exempted from bearing arms, impresses, and military services, except in case of an invasion.
And furthermore, for establishing the perpetuity of this Corporation, and in case that at any time hereafter, through oversight, or otherwise through misapprehensions and mistaken constructions of the pow-	

ers, liberties, and franchises herein contained, any laws should be enacted, or any matters done and transacted by this Corporation contrary to the tenor of this charter, it is hereby enacted, ordained, and declared, that all such laws, acts, and doings shall be in themselves null and void: Yet, nevertheless, the same shall not, in any courts of law, or by the General Assembly, be deemed, taken, interpreted, or ajudged into an avoidance, defeasance, or forfeiture of this Charter; but that the same shall be and remain unhurt, inviolate, and entire, unto the said Corporation, in perpetual succession; which Corporation may, at all times and forever hereafter, proceed and continue to act: And all their acts, conformable to the powers, tenor, true intent and meaning of the charter, shall be and remain in full force and validity; the nullity and avoidance of any such illegal acts to the contrary in any wise notwithstanding.

And lastly, We, the Governor and Company aforesaid, do, for ourselves and for our successors, forever hereby enact, grant, and confirm unto the said Trustees and Fellows, and to their successors, that this Charter of incorporation, and every part thereof, shall be good and available in all things in the law, according to our true intent and meaning: And shall be constructed, reputed, and adjudged, in all cases, most favorably on the behalf and for the best benefit and behoof of the said Trustees and Fellows, and their successors, so as most effectually to answer the valuable ends of this useful institution.

In full testimony of which grant,

and of all the articles and matters therein contained, the said Governor and Company do hereby order, that this act shall be signed by the Governor and Secretary, and sealed with the public seal of this Colony, and registered in the Colony Records: And that the same, or an exemplification thereof, shall be a sufficient warrant to the said Corporation to hold, use, and exercise all the powers, franchises, and immunities herein contained.

STEPHEN HOPKINS, *Governor.*
HENRY WARD, *Secretary.*[1]

Signed and sealed at Newport, the twenty-fourth day of October, in the year of our Lord One Thousand [L.S.] Seven Hundred and Sixty-five, and in the fifth year of His Majesty's Reign, George the Third, by the grace of God, of Great Britain, etc., King.

SAMUEL WARD, *Governor.*
EDWARD THURSTON, Jr.,
Deputy Secretary.

On the back of the original draft of the Charter, from which the foregoing has been copied, is written, " For the Rev. Dr. Cha. Chauncy, Boston," in Dr. Stiles's handwriting, and also the following remarks, intended evidently for Mr. Chauncy's benefit: —

"This Charter was presented to the Assembly Aug. 1763; recopied, with some alterations by the Baptists, in October; and passed the Assembly February 1764. Principal alterations were: —

1. By omitting 'To all people, etc., Greeting,' in the initiatory address, the subsequent insertion in the body of the Charter, " Now, therefore, know ye," is an impropriety in clerkship.

2. The Baptists have shown a greater affection for all other denominations than for the Congregationalists.

3. Instead of eight or a majority of Congregationalists in the branch of the Fellowship, according to the original agreement, they have inserted eight Baptists; thus assuming a majority of about two thirds in both branches, hereby absorbing the whole power and government of the College, and thus, by the immutability of the numbers, establishing it a party college more explicitly and effectually than any college upon the continent. This is the most material alteration.

4. Most of what is contained between the marginal crotchets in page 6 is omitted; and the whole paragraph for securing the freedom of education with respect to religion, so mutilated as effectually to enable and empower

[1] These signatures were added to the document by the author. Not having passed the General Assembly, it could not, of course, be signed and sealed.

the Baptists to practise the arts of insinuation, and proselyting upon the youth by private instruction, without the request of the parents."

These remarks are by the author of the original draft of the Charter of Brown University. What "original agreement" was violated by the adoption of the present Charter, in what respects Brown University is established "a party college more explicitly and effectually than any college upon the continent," referring of course to the six colleges in existence in the year 1764 (see page 38), and how the paragraph pertaining to religious freedom and sectarian differences of opinion "enables and empowers the Baptists to practise the arts of insinuation and proselyting," we leave to the judgment and candor of our readers to decide.

INDEX.

The End.

www.ingramcontent.com/pod-product-compliance
Lightning Source LLC
LaVergne TN
LVHW021307110826
845150LV00003B/508

* 9 7 8 1 4 2 5 5 5 9 2 6 7 *